SCHERBATSKOY
PO BOX 136
HANCOCK BROOK RD.
WORCESTER, VERMONT 05682

Sexually Abused Children and their Families

WITHDRAWN

Other Pergamon Titles of Interest

K. S. CALHOUN & B. M. ATKESON
Treatment of Victims of Sexual Assault

G. CARTLEDGE & J. F. MILBURN
Teaching Social Skills to Children

R. F. DANGEL & R. A. POLSTER
Teaching Child Management Skills

J. JACOBS
In the Best Interest of the Child

H. C. MASSON & P. O'BRYNE
Applying Family Therapy

C. E. WALKER, B. L. BONNER & K. L. KAUFMAN
The Physically and Sexually Abused Child

A Related Journal

CHILD ABUSE & NEGLECT
THE INTERNATIONAL JOURNAL

The Official Journal of The International Society for Prevention of Child Abuse and Neglect

Editor-in-Chief: RAY E. HELFER

Founding Editor: C. Henry Kempe

Child Abuse & Neglect provides an international, multi-disciplinary forum on the prevention and treatment of child abuse and neglect, including sexual abuse. The scope also extends further to all those aspects of life which either favour or hinder optimal family bonding

Contributors are from the fields of social work, nursing, medicine, psychology and psychiatry, and law, including police, legislators, educators and anthropologists as well as concerned lay individuals and child oriented organizations.

Free specimen copy supplied on request

UC gift

Sexually Abused Children and their Families

Edited by

PATRICIA BEEZLEY MRAZEK

Instructor of Pediatrics, University of Colorado Health Sciences Center,
Denver, Colorado, U.S.A.

and

C. HENRY KEMPE

Professor of Pediatrics,
University of Colorado Health Sciences Center,
Denver, Colorado, U.S.A.

PERGAMON PRESS

OXFORD · NEW YORK · BEIJING · FRANKFURT
SÃO PAULO · SYDNEY · TOKYO · TORONTO

U.K.	Pergamon Press, Headington Hill Hall, Oxford OX3 0BW, England
U.S.A.	Pergamon Press, Maxwell House, Fairview Park, Elmsford, New York 10523, U.S.A.
PEOPLE'S REPUBLIC OF CHINA	Pergamon Press, Room 4037, Qianmen Hotel, Beijing, People's Republic of China
FEDERAL REPUBLIC OF GERMANY	Pergamon Press, Hammerweg 6, D-6242 Kronberg, Federal Republic of Germany
BRAZIL	Pergamon Editora, Rua Eça de Queiros, 346, CEP 04011, Paraiso, São Paulo, Brazil
AUSTRALIA	Pergamon Press Australia, P.O. Box 544, Potts Point, N.S.W. 2011, Australia
JAPAN	Pergamon Press, 8th Floor, Matsuoka Central Building, 1-7-1 Nishishinjuku, Shinjuku-ku, Tokyo 160, Japan
CANADA	Pergamon Press Canada, Suite No. 271, 253 College Street, Toronto, Ontario, Canada M5T 1R5

Copyright © 1987 Pergamon Press Ltd.

All Rights Reserved. No part of this publication may be reproduced, stored in a retrieval system or transmitted in any form or by any means: electronic, electrostatic, magnetic tape, mechanical, photocopying, recording or otherwise, without permission in writing from the publishers.

First edition 1981
Reprinted 1982, 1984, 1985, 1987

British Library Cataloguing in Publication Data

Sexually abused children and their families.
1. Child molesting
I. Mrazek, Patricia Beezley
II. Kempe, C. Henry
362.7'04 HV6626 80–42146

ISBN 0-08-030194-0 (Flexicover)

Printed in Great Britain by A. Wheaton & Co. Ltd., Exeter

Contents

Contributors

David J. Aldridge, M.A.
Lecturer, Faculty of the National College of District Attorneys
Child Protective Services
El Paso Department of Social Services
Colorado Springs, Colorado

Helen Alexander, M.S.W.
Clinical Social Worker
The National Center for the Prevention and Treatment of Child Abuse and Neglect
University of Colorado Health Sciences Center
Denver, Colorado

Arnon Bentovim, F.R.C. Psych., D.P.M.
Consultant Psychiatrist, Department of Psychological Medicine, Hospital for Sick Children
Great Ormond Street and Tavistock Clinic
London, England

Janet Dean
Research Associate
The National Center for the Prevention and Treatment of Child Abuse and Neglect
University of Colorado Health Sciences Center
Denver, Colorado

Gay Deitrich
Information Specialist
The National Center for the Prevention and Treatment of Child Abuse and Neglect
University of Colorado Health Sciences Center
Denver, Colorado

Jack E. Doek, J.D.
Professor of Juvenile Law
Vrije Universiteit, Amsterdam
Juvenile Judge, Al Kmaar, the Netherlands

Brian G. Fraser, J.D.
Executive Director
National Committee for the Prevention of Child Abuse
Chicago, Illinois

Anna Freud
Director
Hampstead Child Therapy Clinic
London, England

Henry Giarretto, Ph.D.
Executive Director
Parents United, Inc.
San Jose, California

Bruce Gottlieb, M.S.W.
Director, Sexual Abuse Program
The National Center for the Prevention and Treatment of Child Abuse and Neglect
University of Colorado Health Sciences Center
Denver, Colorado

C. Henry Kempe, M.D.
Director
The National Center for the Prevention and Treatment of Child Abuse and Neglect
Professor of Pediatrics
University of Colorado Health Sciences Center
Denver, Colorado

David L. Kerns, M.D.
Medical Director for Ambulatory Services
Children's Hospital Medical Center
Oakland, California
Formerly, Associate Director
The National Center for the Prevention and Treatment of Child Abuse and Neglect
University of Colorado Health Sciences Center
Denver, Colorado

Margaret A. Lynch, D.C.H., M.R.C.P.
Senior Lecturer in Community Paediatrics
Department of Paediatrics
Guys Hospital Medical School
London, England

John M. Macdonald, M.D.
Professor of Psychiatry and Director of Forensic Psychiatry
University of Colorado Health Sciences Center
Denver, Colorado

David A. Mrazek, M.D., M.R.C. Psych.
Assistant Professor of Psychiatry
University of Colorado Health Sciences Center
Director of Pediatric Behavioral Sciences
National Jewish Hospital and Research Center
Denver, Colorado

Patricia Beezley Mrazek, M.S.W., Ph.D.
Instructor of Pediatrics
University of Colorado Health Sciences Center
Formerly, Sheldon Fellow, Tavistock Clinic
London, England
Formerly, Assistant Director
The National Center for the Prevention and Treatment of Child Abuse and Neglect
University of Colorado Health Sciences Center
Denver, Colorado

Brandt F. Steele, M.D.
Professor of Psychiatry
University of Colorado Health Sciences Center
Acting Director
The National Center for the Prevention and Treatment of Child Abuse and Neglect
Training Analyst
Denver Institute of Psychoanalysis
Denver, Colorado

Anne B. Topper, M.S.W.
Administrator, Family and Children's Services
El Paso County Department of Social Services
Colorado Springs, Colorado
Adjunct Professor, Graduate School of Social Work
University of Denver
Consultant and Trainer on Incest
Colorado State Department of Social Services
Denver, Colorado

Acknowledgments

The editors are grateful to the contributing authors and to the many others who have helped with the preparation of this manuscript. We owe special thanks to our spouses, David Mrazek and Ruth Kempe, for their support and their willingness to read and reread the entire material. We also want to acknowledge the unique help provided by Arnon Bentovim, Donald C. Bross, Roy Fairfield, Rhona Rapoport, and especially Marion Rex, whose patience and excellent secretarial skills helped us through many drafts of this volume. Finally, we want to thank the William T. Grant Foundation, the Henry J. Kaiser Family Foundation, and the Friends of the National Center for their support of the National Center for the Prevention and Treatment of Child Abuse and Neglect of the Department of Pediatrics, University of Colorado Health Sciences Center.

PATRICIA BEEZLEY MRAZEK
C. HENRY KEMPE

Introduction

This book on child sexual abuse has been written to provide information on the current "state of the art" in this developing field of study. It is directed primarily toward professionals who will aid in the recognition, evaluation, and treatment of sexually abused children and their families. However, the authors are well aware of the wide interest in this social problem, and we hope this volume will be of use to other persons as well.

As in any edited volume, the topics which are selected for inclusion and the experts who are asked for contributions in their fields of specialty reflect, to some degree, the editors' own biases. From the outset we were clear that to us the best interests of the children were paramount although we also believe that entire families should be helped whenever possible. From our clinical experiences we know that sexual abuse in childhood can have deleterious consequences. Therefore, while there may be some who disagree with us, we see sexual abuse as part of the child abuse spectrum, requiring intervention by external authorities including social services and the court.

The views expressed by the individual authors of the chapters will occasionally conflict, but we regard this as an asset, showing, as it does, that there is still much more to be understood and that there may be different points of view which may be equally valid in the light of each writer's own experience. From the outset the editors had a working format for the division of the contents of the book, planning for contributions from both sides of the Atlantic, for there is still much to be learned among us all.

Sexually Abused Children and Their Families is divided into five sections which correspond with the major areas of study in the field.

I. DEFINITION AND RECOGNITION
II. SEXUAL CHILD ABUSE AND THE LAW
III. PSYCHODYNAMICS AND EVALUATION
IV. TREATMENT
V. PROGNOSIS AND OUTCOME

Each section is introduced briefly, and some of the primary issues relating to that topic are raised.

Throughout the chapters there is variation in the use of pronouns referring to the child; some contributors have chosen to use "he/she" and "his/her" while others have used the feminine gender pronoun exclusively because their clinical work is primarily with female children. All of the authors though are well aware that male children are sexually abused, probably to a much larger extent than is known at this time.

The referencing in the chapters is not exhaustive, but it does represent important conceptual ideas which directly relate to child sexual abuse. The extensive bibliography with selected annotation at the end of the book and the list of audiovisual materials will give the readers a more comprehensive overview of the publications in the field and lead them to source material which is rapidly growing.

The editors are keenly aware that not only each section but each chapter of this volume could, itself, be the title of a book, and some day there will be enough known to provide for more detailed understanding of each of the fields covered in this collection. It is our hope that readers will write us about their own experiences and any suggestions they have in improving this contribution in its future editions. We are particularly interested in learning about the very young child under the age of four or five who is sexually abused and through bribery with presents of candy becomes trained to be what others regard as a professional prostitute. Such children, who seem to lack all sense of modesty, are difficult for teachers or foster parents to tolerate, and much more needs to be understood before we can help them.

Clearly, all forms of sexual abuse, including incest, are being discussed more openly, and both victims and perpetrators can now look for help. Public acceptance of this social problem as a reality, requiring care and attention, is rapidly developing in many countries. This book hopes to contribute to such progress.

PATRICIA BEEZLEY MRAZEK
C. HENRY KEMPE

Part I.
DEFINITION AND RECOGNITION

Introduction

The definition and recognition of child sexual abuse present many problems. Personal and professional values and ideologies of those who are concerned about this social problem often makes consensual agreement regarding its nature difficult. Chapters One and Two by the Mrazeks help to establish a frame of reference and a shared theoretical basis for the readers. Chapter One points to the attitudinal changes regarding adult–child sexual relations throughout time and across cultures. A diversity of definitions is offered to the reader and current problems in recognizing sexual abuse cases are explored. In Chapter Two the psychosexual development of the individual and the life cycle of the family system are reviewed. Using this framework, a conceptualization of the psychosexual development of the family is put forward which emphasizes the critical nature of the "mesh" between the child's and parents' personal psychosexual issues. Sexual abuse of a child can then be seen as an extreme dysfunction, representing the pathological end of a continuum of sexual experience. Anna Freud, in Chapter Three, discusses the complex relationship between the sexual abuse and a child's own secret wishes which normally remain in the realm of fantasy. Using the United Kingdom as an example of how difficult the recognition process can be, Mrazek, Lynch, and Bentovim in Chapter Four present the results of a large survey they conducted while all three authors were living in England. The United Kingdom is not unique in its reluctance to acknowledge that sexual abuse of children is a serious problem; rather, social denial and avoidance appear to be the usual case and represent early stages in the national recognition process.

This section raises many specific questions. Is sexual abuse part of the child abuse syndrome? How should child sexual abuse be defined? Should cases of "borderline" abuse be included? What function does a definition serve? How can reliable and valid information be gathered on incidence? What organization(s) should assume primary responsibility for professional and public education about child sexual abuse? How are attitudes about family sexuality likely to change over the next decade?

PATRICIA BEEZLEY MRAZEK
C. HENRY KEMPE

Chapter One

Definition and Recognition of Sexual Child Abuse: Historical and Cultural Perspectives*

PATRICIA BEEZLEY MRAZEK

Variations in values, beliefs, and practices pertaining to all aspects of sexuality have occurred throughout time. Attitudes about the existence of childhood sexuality and about the occurrence of sexual practices between adults and children are no exception; there have been considerable changes in thought in these areas as well. While sexual abuse of children has existed throughout history and across cultures, whether such behavior was conceived of and defined as abuse has been dependent on the societal values of the particular period.

This chapter discusses the issues of definition and recognition of child sexual abuse from historical and cultural perspectives. The range of definitions used by the various contributors to this book are presented here as a way of helping the reader determine his or her own criteria for making judgments about this issue. Most of the contributors share the fundamental principle that, despite a family focus and concern for each family member, the child's best interests are paramount in any decision regarding identification, investigation, and intervention with sexual abuse cases.

An Historical View

Changes in thought about particular sexual practices have sometimes occurred in a continuous cycle rather than in a linear progression. Particular behaviors may be defined as normal at one period in history; later, these same behaviors are defined as immoral and still later as criminal and then as psychopathological. If the cycle is to come full circle, the behaviors once again become defined, at least by subgroups of the population, as normal. Of course the boundaries are not clearcut, and alternative viewpoints do co-exist. However, there is usually a predominant attitude in a particular society at a specific point in history. Figure 1 diagrams this general attitudinal change.

---

* Portions of this chapter were presented as a paper at the Second International Congress on Child Abuse and Neglect, London, England, September 13, 1978.

Figure 1
ATTITUDINAL CHANGE REGARDING SEXUAL PRACTICES

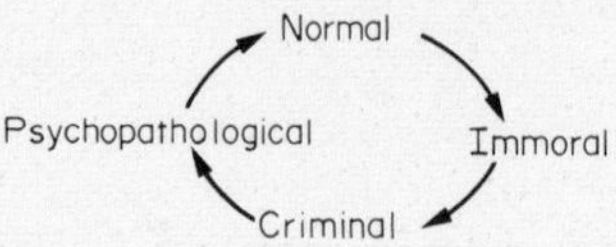

Considering homosexuality between consenting adults as an example, the evolution of thought can be demonstrated. The ancient Roman civilization accepted homosexuality as just another sexual practice, but the Greeks tended to idealize it as a superior form of sexuality.[16] Some religious movements had a different view, however. The Jews and Christians tried to eradicate what they considered to be immoral by imposing severe sanctions. Later, harsh criminal sanctions were brought to bear by the legal branches of many societies; some of these punishments have existed to modern times. More recently, with the development of psychodynamic thinking, homosexuality has been seen as a psychiatric disorder. This currently may be the most prevalent public viewpoint in Western societies about homosexuality. However, the Gay Liberation movement has been attempting to persuade society at large to accept homosexuality as a normal alternative to heterosexuality. Indeed, to some extent, these efforts have been successful in that the American Psychiatric Association no longer classifies homosexuality as a psychiatric disorder. As values and beliefs have changed over time, practices have changed as well. Attitudes toward homosexuality have undergone considerable changes and are likely to continue doing so.

Whether other sexual behaviors have undergone similar attitudinal changes is the question. While the cycle may not necessarily be in these same steps for all sexual behavior, it does appear to apply to sexual practices between adults and children.

Adult–Child Sexual Practices Perceived As Normal

The child in antiquity lived his/her early years in an atmosphere of acceptance of sexual practices between adults and children.[7] In Greece and Rome there was child prostitution with boy brothels in almost every city. Castration of young boys was common as was anal intercourse between teachers and pupils. Free-born children were somewhat protected by law, but slave children, particularly boys, were used for sexual gratification by adult men with the approval of the community. In other ancient civilizations, such as the Incan of pre-Spanish Peru, the Ptolemaic Egyptian, and old Hawaiian, certain types of incest were permitted in isolated, privileged classes.[6,18]

Adult–Child Sexual Practices Perceived as Immoral

Many religious viewpoints of adult–child sexual relations were considerably different. The ancient Jews had an inconsistent attitude about sexual practices with children despite Moses' injunction against corrupting children. For example, the penalty for sodomy with children over nine years of age was death by stoning, but copulation with younger children was not considered a sexual act and was punishable only by a whipping.[7,10] With the advent of Christianity, the notion of childhood innocence came into being. Children were thought to be entirely without any sexual thoughts, feelings, or capacities. This attitude hindered the protection of children until the 17th century when the Catholic Church took a harsh stand against any sexual relations between adults and children, including parent–child and sibling incest. In some countries, such as England, the Ecclesiastical courts have continued to have significant power in these matters well into the 20th century.

Adult–Child Sexual Practices Perceived as Criminal

With the decline of the Church as the prevailing authoritarian body and with the passage of time, the sanctions against sexual involvement with children have become matters for the judicial systems in most Western countries. The actual charges against adults who involve children in sexual acts have varied, but many countries currently have criminal charges such as "Contributing to the Delinquency of a Minor", "Indecent Assault", "Indecent Act", "Gross Indecency", "Sodomy", "Statutory Rape" and "Incest". What charge is used with a particular offender often depends on the evidence available and the likelihood of obtaining a conviction. In many countries a charge similar to "Contributing to the Delinquency of a Minor" is the easiest to prove even though it might not accurately indicate the extent of the sexual involvement that has occurred. "Statutory Rape" usually is defined as sexual intercourse (heterosexual or homosexual) with a child below the legal age of consent. Even though the child may have agreed to participate in this sexual act, the "Statutory Rape" charge can be filed. The age of consent varies considerably among various countries and American states. Thus, sexual intercourse with a 16-year-old girl may be legal in one state and illegal in an adjoining state with a maximum penalty of life imprisonment. An adult female who entices a youth to have sexual relations with her can be charged with "Statutory Rape" in some of the American states. In many countries the rape offender may be sued in civil court as well as charged and sentenced in criminal court.

Incest is defined as sexual intercourse between relatives within the prohibited degrees of relationship defined by the law. Most countries have specific laws on incest. These include the United States of America states, the Australian states, England, Scotland, Germany, Sweden, New Zealand, South Africa, and Canada. France and the Netherlands have not had specific laws on incest but punish such behavior under other criminal prohibitions.[17] Incest was not a criminal offense in England until 1908, except for a short period from 1650 to 1660. Prior to 1909, incest was punishable by the Ecclesiastical courts.[17]

The incest laws vary cross-culturally regarding *what* relationships are to be regarded as incestuous. Some include only relationships between close blood relatives, that is, the nuclear family. Most also include some secondary and tertiary relatives, and some also include adoptive and ceremonial relatives with whom no biological kinship can be traced.

Anthropologists[18] have documented that all societies have some type of incest taboo whether or not they have formalized the sanctions into criminal punishments. In some so-called "primitive" societies, people who are incestuous also practice witchcraft and are regarded as a menace to the entire tribe.[9]

With such cross-cultural variability in the laws regulating sexual practices between adults and children and the variability in the application of the laws, any international comparison of criminal statistics is of questionable value. Most of the American States have included sexual abuse in their child abuse legislation. (See Chapter Five.) This means that children can be brought under the jurisdiction of the juvenile court whether or not criminal charges have been filed against the adult. Despite under-reporting, these figures more accurately reflect the actual incidence of sexual activity between adults and children than do the criminal statistics.

Adult–Child Sexual Practices Perceived as Psychopathological

Following a predominantly legal perspective on adult–child sexual relations, increasing numbers of people in the last 50 years have begun to view such behavior as psychopathological in nature. Freud's formulation of the theory of infantile sexuality, with the parent being the primary love object during the Oedipal years, was directly contrary to the Christian notion of childhood innocence. Freud also postulated that adult sexual psychopathology was based on early childhood experiences and traumas.[12] This concept of sexual deviance and sexual perversion as a type of psychopathology focused on the adult perpetrator rather than on the child victim. (See Figure 2.)

Figure 2

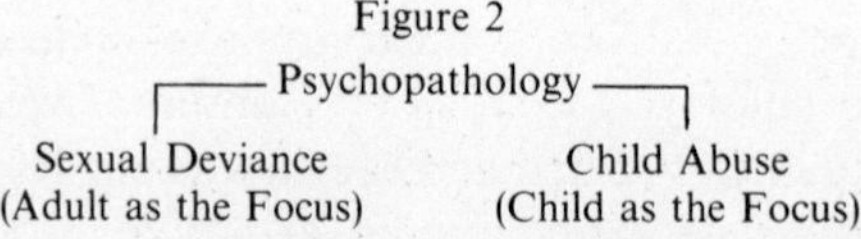

Sexual Deviance:

Adult sexual perversion involving children includes exhibitionism, child rape, and pedophilia, all of which can be either heterosexual or homosexual. Exhibitionism is the expressed desire for sexual pleasure through the display of genital organs to another person, not necessarily a child. Child rape is intercourse with a person under legal age. Pedophilia, the expressed desire for immature sexual gratification with prepubertal children, is also referred to as child molestation and covers a wide range of offenses. Sometimes pedophilia is defined as excluding attempted or actual intercourse, whereas child rape and incest include intercourse. In some instances there is an overlap between these perversions with one offender committing various acts. (These various types of sexual deviance are more thoroughly discussed in Chapters Seven and Eight.)

Child Abuse:

Because the psychopathological view of adult–child sexual practices has tended to focus on the adult's social deviance, rehabilitation and treatment efforts have been directed toward the adult while little attention has been paid to the children who have been involved unless they have had substantial physical injuries or psychiatric symptoms. The exception to this has been the child who has been thought to be the provoker or initiator of the sexual act. Viewing overt sexual behavior between an adult and a child as sexual abuse as well as sexual deviance is a very recent development in medical and child protective services. Such an orientation implies a primary focus on the child with attention paid to the adult and to the interaction which occurred between them.

The denial and avoidance by professionals of all disciplines to the issue of child sexual abuse is similar to attitudes about physical abuse 20 years ago. In the United States, many of the people, particularly pediatricians, who led the way for the recognition, treatment, and prevention of physical abuse to children have been slow to respond to the problems of sexual abuse. In part, this is due to the fact that most sexually abused children have no physical injuries or evidence of sexual assault at the time of examination. (See Chapter Ten.)

Much of the early recognition of child sexual abuse came from clinicians working in victim-oriented programs for adult women who had been raped or assaulted. The professional literature from rape crisis centers[4,23] and feminist literature[27,29] continue to reflect an awareness of child sexual abuse. One of the pioneers in the comprehensive treatment of child sexual abuse has been Dr. Hank Giarretto, a psychologist from California, whose work was originally viewed with some skepticism by the leaders in the protection of physically abused children. (See Chapter Fourteen.) Gradually, most of the state legislatures across the United States have included sexual abuse in their definition of child abuse and have begun to consider specialized treatment programs for these families. Many European countries, while having laws prohibiting sexual exploitation of children, including incest, are just beginning to acknowledge on a practical clinical basis that sexual abuse is a part of the child abuse syndrome. (As an example, see Chapter Four.)

Future Perceptions of Adult–Child Sexual Practices

If adult–child sexual relations are seen within their historical and cultural framework, then the final question which remains is whether or not these attitudinal changes will go full circle and such behavior become an accepted part of Western society. There are organizations in both the United States and in England which advocate the acceptance of adult–child sexual relations. In 1977 the International Paedophiliac Information Exchange in England advocated that adults and "consenting" children be allowed to engage in sexual practices.[8] The Rene Giuon Society in California has claimed to have 2,500 members who have filed an affidavit that they have each had intercourse with a female or male child under 8 years of age.[8] It is also a well-known fact that child pornography is a multi-million dollar business in the United States and Europe. However, the public outrage and legislation which have followed the recognition that these groups and practices do exist is some indication that sexual abuse of children will not be further tolerated in Western civilization. Only by the inclusion of sexual abuse in the child abuse field can there be any assurance that efforts will be made to protect the children's rights.

A Cross-Cultural View

At approximately the same time that adult–child sexual relationships came to be seen as psychopathological, anthropologists and sociologists, as well as psychiatrists, began to be interested in the origins and functions of the incest taboo and the consequences of any disregard for these values. Although the incest taboo in some form occurs in every known society, there is considerable variation among societies with regard to the extensiveness of its application, the range of intensity of associated emotions, and the frequency of specific types of infraction.[18]

The predominant thinking about the origins of the incest taboo and the function it serves for the individual, family, and society can be summarized in six points.

1. *Prohibition = Instinct*
   In the 1920s the incest prohibition was thought to be an instinct, but this is no longer an accepted view.
2. *Biological Survival: Prevention of Inbreeding*
   For almost 90 years theorists[1,18,30] have written about the biological dangers of inbreeding, that is, genetic defects and racial degeneration. It is unlikely, however, that this theory could have been the basis of the origin of the taboo in tribes of "simple" people around the world for many of them did not even understand the concept of biological paternity.
3. *Societal Survival: Prevention of Overly Intense Family Dyads*
   The incest taboo has also been seen as providing boundaries for the continuation of specific types of social ties. Some groups of people, such as the Mohave Indians,[9] have not tolerated incest because such intense dyads would prevent "dispersal of libido" over the whole group and survival of the culture would be threatened. However, the Mohaves have disapproved of intense romantic love between two non-related persons for the same reason; that is, such love would lead to a lack of societal cohesion among the larger group.
4. *Prolonged Childhood Association → Sexual Disinterest*
   The prohibitions against incest have also been seen as habits or attitudes of "positive aversion" formed during childhood and resulting from the dulling of sexual appetite through prolonged association.[13] One supposedly feels no erotic attraction for a person of the opposite sex with whom one has grown up in the same household from childhood. Evidence to support this hypothesis has been provided by studies of children who have been reared as "an age set in a fictive setting", as, for example, in an Israeli kibbutz.[11,18,26] However, this may result from an informal taboo as much as from any positive aversion.
5. *Strong Impulse → Psychoanalytic Defense*
   Psychoanalytic theory explains the emotional intensity of incest taboos as reaction formations to repressed impulses and genuine temptation.[13,14]
6. *Family Survival: Prevention of Sexual Rivalry*
   Incest prohibitions have been thought to prevent sexual rivalry within the family and promote social unity and authority patterns within the nuclear unit. Thus, the integrity of the family is protected.[21]

The controversy as to the origin and function of the incest taboos will probably continue, but it is most likely that the taboos have multiple functions and are related to specific cultures and periods of history.

Today's cross-cultural differences regarding the wide range of adult–child sexual experiences, including incest, have not been thoroughly examined. It is known that in societies that encourage premarital intercourse, it is common for boys and girls to be active participants in full sexual relations by age 10 or 11.[6] It is also known that cultural practices exist throughout the world which condone the mutilation of genitals in childhood. For example, there are an estimated 30 million women in the world who suffer the results of some degree of clitoridectomy. The age at which the entire clitoris or a portion of it is removed varies with the type of procedure and the local tradition. Researchers[19] have cited the existence of such practices in areas as diverse as Australia, Brazil, Malaya, Pakistan, El Salvador, Egypt, Nigeria, and the Soviet Union. Quite obviously, child sexual abuse takes on an entirely different meaning in such cultures. Any evaluation of whether such practices should be redefined as sexual abuse must be done by the people of those particular countries.

Of more relevance is the question of values and accepted sexual practices of subcultures in Western society. There is a danger of making unproven assumptions about minority groups of certain geographic areas. The incidence of incest may indeed be higher in certain areas, just as physical abuse is. However, this may be related to other social and psychological problems and not to cultural approval of the behavior.

Mead[18] has cautioned that the "widespread failure to observe incest regulations is an index of the disruption of a sociocultural system that may be even more significant than the more usual indexes of crime, suicide, and homicide".

Problems of Definition

Any attempt to define "sexual abuse of children" is fraught with difficulties, for all definitions are culture- and time-bound. They are not based on rigorous scientific inquiry but on values and beliefs of individuals, professional organizations, and societies at large. Indeed, the term "child sexual abuse" is not universally accepted and is frequently interchanged with "sexual exploitation", "sexual misuse" and "sexual assault". Rather than referring to any specific type of sexual behavior, the term "sexual abuse" may mean anything from exhibitionism to genital manipulation to intercourse to child pornography. Within a legal frame of reference, sexual abuse is classified by criminal act, such as rape, incest, unlawful sexual intercourse, buggery, and indecent assault. The incest laws have often failed to take into consideration the changing nature of the family, particularly step-parenthood and adoption. Medically, the definition may become confused with consequences such as genital injuries, venereal disease, or pregnancy. Clearly, legal and medical frameworks fail to consider the psychological and interactive aspects of the sexual experience.

One of the most widely referenced definitions, given by Schechter and Roberge[22] in 1976, refers to the sexual exploitation of children as "the involvement of dependent, developmentally immature children and adolescents in sexual activities that they do not fully comprehend, are unable to give informed consent to, and that violate the social taboos of family roles".

A useful conceptualization of the entire spectrum of parent–child sexuality has been made by Summit and Kryso.[28] They define a progression of categories of sexual involvement with an ascendency of apparent individual and social harmfulness: incidental sexual contact, ideological sexual contact, psychotic intrusion, rustic environment, true endogamous incest, misogynous incest, imperious incest, pedophilic incest, child rape, and perverse incest.

There are a range of definitions used by the contributors to this book. In Chapter Two, the Mrazeks discuss child sexual abuse as being the sexual use of a child by an adult for his or her own sexual gratification without consideration of the child's psychosexual development. In Chapter Four, Mrazek, Lynch, and Bentovim define three types of child sexual abuse:

1. Battered child whose injuries are primarily in the genital area.
2. Child who has experienced attempted or actual intercourse or other inappropriate genital contact with an adult.
3. Child who has been inappropriately involved with an adult in sexual activities not covered by 1 or 2.

"Child" was defined as being under 16 years of age, which is the age of legal consent in England. Chapter Five by Fraser discusses in detail the problems of formulating workable legal definitions. Sexual abuse is classified into three types: non-touching, touching, and violent touching, and each of these is, in turn, defined. For the purposes of the chapter, he uses an operational definition: "Child sexual abuse is the exploitation of a child for the sexual gratification of an adult". As he points out, the definition problems are exemplified by the fact that although 45 states specifically require that cases of sexual abuse be reported, only 13 states make any attempt to define it. Döek, in Chapter Six, reviews the criminal definitions of child sexual abuse which have been formulated in the European countries. He goes on to define "sexual child abuse", in a broad sense, as "including all kinds of sexual activities committed by an adult with or in the presence of minors; these are activities which are detrimental to normal development of the sexuality of the child or which curtail or inhibit his/her sexual self-determination". Macdonald uses the definitions of the sexual perversions of exhibitionism, child rape, and child molestation in Chapter Seven. Half of the remaining chapters focus on incest while the others include extra-familial sexual molestation as well as incest.

While any definition raises as many questions as it answers, one of the more important governing principles of the editors has been the avoidance of an overly inclusive description. All parents at some time have erotic feelings toward their children, just as they have aggressive feelings. (See Chapter Two.) Also, there is a wide range of "acceptable" family values. If one aim of those involved in clinical and legal services is to maximize family functioning, efforts should be made so that parental anxiety is not unduly raised. With so many serious cases of sexual exploitation being reported, the "grey" areas might best be left as they are. There is always the danger that a worker in this field can become too narrowly focused and not cautious enough in his or her approach to identification.

Legal and medical definitions are usually too narrow for the mental health professional. A working clinical definition of sexual abuse of children must include consideration of:

1. An explicit description of what occurred: nature of the sexual act(s), frequency (single incident or continuum of acts over time), occurrence of violence or threats of bodily harm.
2. Information about the age and development of the people involved: age differences, intelligence, mental status.

3. An understanding of the nature of the relationship between the people involved: whether or not they know each other and in what context, the quality of other aspects of their relationship, their perceptions and feelings regarding what occurred and why.
4. A description of the attitudes and involvements of other family members and of the prevailing cultural attitudes about sexuality in the community.[20]

The clinician whose primary interest is in helping the child will focus on the process that has occurred between the child and the perpetrator rather than on criminal charges, psychiatric diagnoses, or violation of taboos. The primary question is who did what to whom, in what kind of a relationship, and with what consequences. Figure 3 reflects the complexity of this interaction.

Figure 3
INTERACTION BETWEEN THE PERPETRATOR AND THE CHILD VICTIM

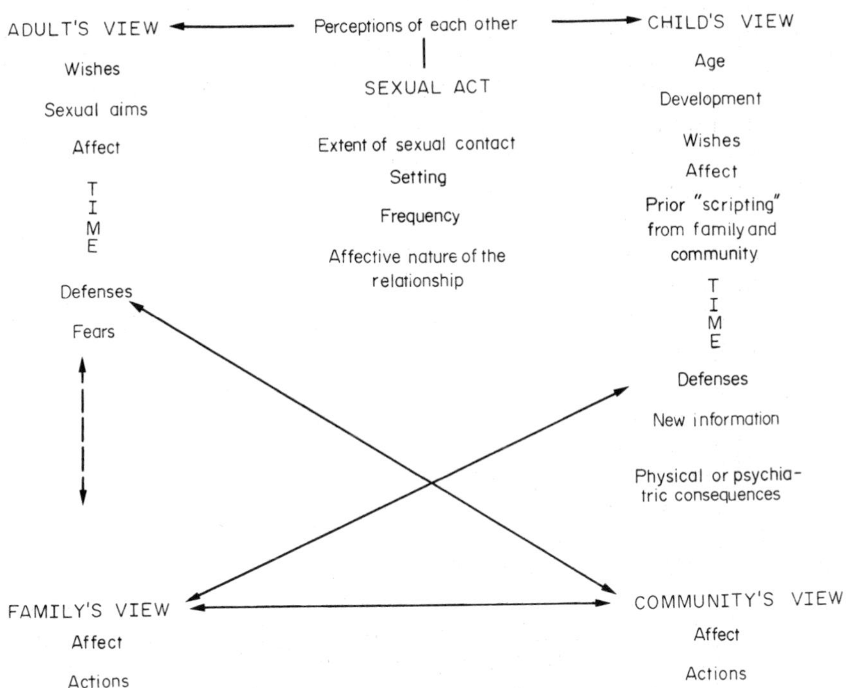

The interaction between the adult and the child must be considered from each of their perspectives at the time the incident occurred and from their perspectives later when the passage of time and the attitudes and actions by the family and society have had their impact. The adult's conscious and unconscious wishes, aims, affects, and behaviors have meaning for the child based on the child's available intellectual and emotional resources for organizing experiences. It is important to understand that the incidents which occurred between the adult and the child may not have been perceived by either of them as a sexual act. The behavior may take on this connotation only after the intervention by other members of the child's family or child protection authorities. For example, an adult may have sought physical affection and nurturance from a young child who perceived the adult's sexual excitement as anger or unusual, frightening behavior. Later, as the child received new information from his or her family or caretakers and as the child was interviewed and interrogated by social workers and police, the adult and child may have changed their perceptions of each other and viewed the sexual act more in terms of its sexuality and its violence.

Problems of Recognition

Recognition is, of course, intrinsically connected with definition, but even those professionals who have a clinical definition with which they are comfortable will still have problems in identifying sexually abused children. As Sgroi[24] has written, "Recognition of sexual molestation in a child is entirely dependent on the individual's inherent willingness to entertain the possibility that the condition may exist."

Frequently, there is no physical evidence that a sexual assault has occurred. Vaginal, anal, or oral penetration may not have happened, and even if it did, any signs of abrasion or sperm may have disappeared. The battered child with injuries to the genitals is the easiest type of sexual child abuse to recognize. Painful manipulation of the child's genitals may be a parent's method of disciplining a child. For example, one infant boy who urinated on his mother had a string tied around his penis to "teach him a lesson". A five-year-old girl had cigarette burns on her genitals to prevent her from further masturbation. Such acts are clearly sadistic and may not be related to any attempt to obtain sexual gratification on the parent's part. On the other hand, some physically abused children whose injuries are not in the genital area may still have been sexually abused by their parent or caretaker. For example, a six-year-old girl was sexually assaulted but without penetration by her father on the same day he broke her jaw for her refusal to dress quickly for school. Physical abuse and sexual abuse are not mutually exclusive. Whenever one diagnosis is made, careful exploration is necessary to determine whether the other has occurred as well.

The child who has experienced attempted or actual intercourse or other inappropriate genital contact with an adult is much more difficult to diagnose than the battered child with genital injuries. The sexual activity may have included sexual intercourse, anal intercourse, oral-genital contact, and molestation such as fondling, masturbation, and digital manipulation. The common stereotype that sexual abuse by a family member or caretaker, as opposed to a stranger, is a non-violent act must be seriously questioned in relation to each child for physical and emotional threats often occur.[24] Children who have had genital contact with an adult may first be detected by bruises and abrasions where they have been held down forceably, by gonorrhea,[25] and by behavioral symptoms such as sleep disturbance, enuresis and encopresis, excessive masturbation, phobic states, depression, running away from home, and psychosomatic complaints. Occasionally, an adolescent may develop a homicidal rage toward the parent with whom he or she is involved in incest. Sometimes children try to tell an adult what has happened, but it often takes a great deal of sensitivity to understand the child's words and expressions. Too often the adolescent who tells is dismissed as being "hysterical" and out to cause trouble.

Recognition of child sexual abuse, in turn, causes its own problems. When large numbers of children are identified, it is essential that psychotherapeutic intervention follow. To diagnose and not provide service raises serious ethical questions. On the other hand, caseloads of social service departments are increasing at dramatic rates while federal and state fiscal tightening prevents the addition of workers and new programs. The National Center on Child Abuse and Neglect in Washington, D.C.[25] estimated that in 1976, 12% of the over one million reported child abuse cases were cases of sexual abuse. The Kempes[15] have reported that incest cases now reach 150 per million population per year. While the criteria for such estimates are variable, it is generally acknowledged that underreporting of child sexual abuse is a massive problem. It is conceivable that sexual abuse is as large a social problem as physical abuse.

Conclusion

As the level of awareness of child sexual abuse rises, questions regarding definition, etiology, prevalence, treatment, and outcome also increase. Viewing sexual abuse from historical and cultural perspectives may aid in assuring that a cautious approach is taken to the study of this issue. Because problems, such as overly inclusive or vague definitions and inadequate assessment of treatment outcome, have plagued the field of physical child abuse, those involved in the research and treatment of sexual child abuse perhaps can learn from their predecessors and take an even more careful and thorough approach in their work.

References

1. Aberle, D. F., *et al.* (1963) The incest taboo and the mating patterns of animals. *Am. Anthropologist*, New Series, **65:** 253.
2. Armstrong, L. (1978) *Kiss Daddy Goodnight: A Speakout on Incest.* Hawthorn, New York.
3. Branch, G. and Paxton, R. (1965) A study of gynococcal infections among infants and children. *Public Health Reports* **80:** 347.
4. Burgess, A. W. and Holmstrom, L. L. (1975) *Rape: Victims of Crisis.* R. J. Brady, Bowie, Md.
5. Cohen, Y. A. (1964) *The Transition from Childhood to Adolescence: Cross-Cultural Studies of Initiation Ceremonies, Legal Systems, and Incest Taboos.* Aldine, Chicago.
6. Davenport, W. H. (1977) Sex in cross-cultural perspective. In *Human Sexuality in Four Perspectives.* (Edited by Beach, F. A.) Johns Hopkins Univ., Boston.
7. de Mause, L. (1974) The evolution of childhood. In *The History of Childhood: The Evolution of Parent-Child Relationships as a Factor in History.* (Edited by de Mause, L.) Souvenir Press, London.
8. Densen-Gerber, J. and Hutchinson, F. F. (1978) Medical-legal and societal problems involving children—child prostitution, child pornography and drug-related abuse; recommended legislation. In *The Maltreatment of Children.* (Edited by Smith, S. M.) MTP Press, Lancaster, England.
9. Devereaux, G. (1939) The social and cultural implications of incest among the Mohave Indians. *Psychoanal. Q.* **8:** 510.
10. Epstein, L. M. (1948) *Sex Laws and Customs in Judaism.* New York.
11. Fox, J. R. (1962) Sibling incest. *Br. J. Sociology* **13:** 128.
12. Freud, S. (1905) Three essays on the theory of sexuality. In *Standard Edition of the Complete Psychological Works of Sigmund Freud.* (Edited by Strachey, J.) Hogarth, London.
13. Freud, S. (1913) Totem and taboo. In *The Standard Edition of the Complete Psychological Works of Sigmund Freud.* (Edited by Strachey, J.) Hogarth, London.
14. Freud, S. (1919) The "uncanny". In *The Standard Edition of the Complete Psychological Works of Sigmund Freud.* (Edited by Strachey, J.) Hogarth, London.
15. Kempe, R. S. and Kempe, C. H. (1978) *Child Abuse.* Fontana/Open Books, London.
16. Kosovich, D. R. (1978) Sexuality throughout the centuries. *Psychiatric Opinion* **15:** 15.
17. Manchester, A. H. (1979) The law of incest in England and Wales. *Child Abuse and Neglect* **3:** 679.
18. Mead, M. (1968) Incest. *International Encyclopedia of Social Sciences.* **7:** 115. MacMillan and Free Press, New York.
19. Morgan, R. and Steinem, G. (1980) The international crime of genital mutilation. *Ms.* March: 65.
20. Mrazek, P. B. (1980) Annotation: sexual abuse of children. *J. Child Psychol. Psychiatry* **21:** 91.
21. Parsons, T. (1954) The incest taboo in relation to social structure and the socialization of the child. *Br. J. Sociol.* **5:** 101.
22. Schechter, M. D. and Roberge, L. (1976) Sexual exploitation. In *Child Abuse and Neglect: The Family and the Community.* (Edited by Helfer, R. E. and Kempe, C. H.) Ballinger, Cambridge, Mass.
23. Schultz, L. G. (1975) *Rape Victimology.* C. C. Thomas, Springfield, Ill.
24. Sgroi, S. M. (1975) Sexual molestation of children: the last frontier in child abuse. *Children Today*, May–June: **19**.
25. Special Report (1978) Child sexual abuse: incest, assault, and sexual exploitation. National Center on Child Abuse and Neglect, U.S. DHEW Pub. No. (OHDS) 79–30166.
26. Spiro, M. E. (1958) *Children of the Kibbutz.* Howard University, Cambridge, Mass.
27. Strucker, J. (1977) I tried to fantasize that all fathers had intercourse with their daughters. *Ms.* April: **66**.
28. Summit, R. and Kryso, J. (1978) Sexual abuse of children: a clinical spectrum. *Am. J. Orthopsychiatry* **48:** 237.
29. Weber, E. (1977) Sexual abuse begins at home. *Ms.* April: **64**.
30. Westermarck, E. A. (1889) *The History of Human Marriage.* Allerton, New York.

Chapter Two

Psychosexual Development Within the Family

DAVID A. MRAZEK AND PATRICIA BEEZLEY MRAZEK

Understanding psychosexual development within the family requires an appreciation of how multiple dyadic interactions make up a more complex interpersonal system. Knowledge of individual psychosexual development from biological, ethological, psychodynamic, and behavioral perspectives is a necessary beginning. However, integration of the progression of individual development with what is known about family life cycles, including stages, transitions, and tasks, is an important next step. Together these two primary areas of study lead to a conceptualization of sexuality within a family based on reciprocity and accommodation between parents and children. This chapter will establish such a framework.

Before beginning, it is necessary to make some of our biases and values explicit. These include the belief that the family is a primary social institution which provides rewards and varying levels of intimacy based on the individuals' capacities. Despite the inevitability of tensions and conflicts, an individual's development can be enhanced by his or her family experience. Early experience affects later adaptation, but since development continues throughout life, the possibility for change always exists. While sexuality is an inevitable and necessary part of development with a clear biologic basis, its final expression is heavily influenced by the family.

The concept of normality is inevitably broad as it pertains to parent/child sexuality for we live in a pluralistic society with a diversity of family styles, values, and changing mores. Sexual expression requires adaptation, but when defense mechanisms such as denial and repression are used excessively, normal expression of sexuality can be inhibited as well as personal growth and enjoyment. However, exploitation of children for the sexual gratification of adults, which is the focus of the following chapters, is generally felt to be harmful to the child's later psychosexual development although many of its effects may be reversible.

The Psychosexual Development of the Individual

The study of psychosexual development has primarily focused on biological and psychological phenomenon within the individual. In this chapter, sexual development will refer to biologic changes as the child matures into adulthood and to the concomitant evolution of sexual behavior. Psychosexual development will refer to the emotional and attitudinal changes of the individual related to his or her evolving sexual maturity.

This approach acknowledges the fact that a child is not initially "sexual" in the way the word is usually used. It is true that the child's gender does have an important influence on how others relate to him or her from the first days of life. However, the child's perception of sexuality requires time for development. It is perhaps more appropriate to describe the young infant as being sensuous rather than sexual. An infant is clearly able to experience pleasure and contentment from the first weeks of life, but the association of these pleasurable affects with erogenous stimulation is relatively slow to develop. This view has some empirical support in that most of the pleasurable affect expressed by young infants takes place within the context of close contact with attachment figures. The young infant's expression of pleasure is usually related to satiation of hunger, relief from physical distress, or exploration of novel circumstances, rather than being linked to the relatively less common experience of infantile masturbation.

Before focusing on the reciprocal nature of the development of sexuality within the family, we will briefly review the basic theoretical concepts related to *intrapersonal* development, that is, the biological and concurrent psychological changes *within* the individual. *Integration* of several diverse theoretical perspectives provides a better appreciation of the conditions and experiences required for normal sexual functioning.[43] This knowledge of individual development permits analysis of the more complex interactions within the family system.

Biological Perspective on Individual Sexual Development

The innate biologic nature of sexuality may be considered the foundation on which sexual development is built. Endocrinological differences are responsible for sexual differentiation during fetal development. Specifically, exposure to androgen is required for male genital development to take place. Without androgenic stimulation, female genital development occurs regardless of the nature of the chromosomal karyotype of the fetus.[7] In addition to the obvious genital consequences of the presence of androgen, considerable speculation exists related to probable central nervous system differences which result from early hormonal exposure.[48]

Androgen production in boys gradually diminishes shortly after birth. From this point until puberty, there are no major differences between boys and girls in sex hormone production. Specifically, androgen production gradually increases in both sexes until the child is about eight to ten at which point it stabilizes. It is then at puberty that androgen levels greatly increase in boys. Girls in contrast show a marked increase in estrogen levels at the onset of puberty.[43]

These hormonal changes occur with considerable regularity in normal children. As a consequence of some biological abnormalities, such as the genetic absence of one of the sex chromosomes, the usual progression of growth and development of secondary sexual characteristics can be markedly altered. Concomitantly, major psychological repercussions occur both in the child's emotional development and for other family members. Nevertheless, normal sexual maturation is the rule for the vast majority of children, and the arrival of puberty is inevitable and anticipated. In fact, the timing of puberty has long been an important signal for a variety of changes in family organization. Whether the child or family is psychologically ready for puberty has little effect on delaying it. The most notable exception to this general rule is anorexia nervosa. In this condition, girls can successfully prevent normal menstruation and obliterate any secondary sexual physical development through self-starvation.[5,32]

Puberty is a period during which rapid biological changes occur in both sexes. Menstruation and ejaculation are events which reflect physiological maturation. With fertility, child-bearing becomes a possibility along with a complex concurrent series of biological changes. The hormonal variations of the normal menstrual cycle have been correlated with shifts in psychological states.[33] Early work examined differences in perceptions and attitudes during the first and second half of the menstrual cycle and associated these observations with the relative influence of estrogen and progesterone. A specific physiological effect of estrogen as a central nervous system stimulant and progesterone as a corresponding sedative has been postulated.[36,47]

Biological changes are also prominent in pregnancy and delivery. It is particularly interesting to note the relative infrequency of psychological disorders during pregnancy and the increased risk of emotional problems within the first ten days following delivery. Dramatic decreases in the levels of a variety of hormones occur during this period as well as major changes in fluid balance related to decrease in the secretion of aldosterone. While attempts have been made to correlate changes in hormonal level to psychological states in the post partum period,[46] specific associations have not yet been established.

In considering sexual development later in the life cycle, there is a paradoxical reversal in direction of effect with greater maturation usually being related to decreased function. However, there is wide variability in the decline of sexual interest and performance among individuals. In some cross-cultural studies sexual functioning past the age of 100 has been documented[6] with menopause extending well beyond the 45–49 age range typical of Western cultures. An interesting physiological observation is that in both sexes there is a decline in the enzymatic activity of monoamine oxidase at about 45.[41] This change has been suggested to have a central nervous system effect which could be related to decreased function or changes in affective state. In women, this is followed by a gradual decrease in estrogen secretion and subsequent increase in gonadotrophin production. It is now thought that low estrogen levels are primarily responsible for the physiological symptoms during this period as replacement therapy with estrogen can result in considerable improvement. Marked variation in sexual activity and pleasure following menopause suggest that, while hormonal changes play a role in subjective experience, a decrease in estrogen clearly need not be associated with the cessation of sexual functioning or orgastic capability.

Despite attempts to establish a male menopausal syndrome, there is no dramatic physiological change in men such as the cessation of the menses in women. Instead, a gradual decline in sexual performance and interest is typical of the end of the male life cycle and is associated with hormonal changes and decreasing potency. However, variation as to the rate of these changes is great, and research is needed before behavioral or psychological correlations will be possible.

Ethological Perspective on Individual Psychosexual Development

Since the work of Darwin, sexuality has been conceptualized as an innate evolutionary survival factor. Adequate sexual development is essential for a given species or population to survive. The study of ethology combines an interest in animal behavior, including its evolutionary significance, with the study of the psychological consequences of these patterns of behavior.

Bowlby[4] reviewed the sexual behavior of animals and infants, acknowledging the instinctual nature of sexual behavior. He suggests that the development of sexual behavior occurs in component segments with gradual integration of these isolated behaviors into a "set goal" activity. Mason,[31] studying rhesus monkeys, and Lewis,[29] focusing on the direct observation of the human infant, describe the emergence of a series of these sexual components.

The concept of mate selection has also been studied from an ethological perspective in a variety of species. Perhaps one of the clearest examples of the concept of sensitive periods for species mating preference is demonstrated by Schutz[44] with his work with mallard ducks. While no parallel sensitive period has been established in human development, the work of Green,[19] documenting the development of a sense of gender identity, highlights predictability of establishing a sexual orientation at a specific point in development.

Bowlby,[4] using three arguments, stresses that the development of attachment and sexual behavior are different processes. First, they are activated independently. Second, the class of objects towards which they are directed vary. Third, the sensitive periods during which they develop in non-human species occur at different ages. However, the interrelationships between attachment and sexual behavior are multiple. A classic example is Harlow's[22] study of aberrant sexual development arising in rhesus monkeys reared without maternal contact. While some improvement in sexual competency can occur if peers are introduced as "surrogate attachment objects", sexual behavior is still aberrant. In humans, the similarity of some of the components of attachment, sexual, and parental behavior (such as kissing and cuddling) suggest some linkage in the developmental origins of these functions.

Naturalistic observations have led to a better understanding of the emergence of *early* sexual behavior. This is less true of sexuality occurring during the later stages of the life cycle. While, for example, several ethologists[3,4,24] have studied basic elements of parenting, little progress has been made in defining mechanisms by which mastery of the decline of sexuality is attained. This is not to say that issues of mate selection, mate fidelity, and struggles for dominance related to sexual choice do not have animal models. Rather, the problem is in extrapolating directly from them to humans. Some broad conceptual issues do lend themselves to this process. An example is Lorenz's[30] discussion of the role of instinct in a wide variety of "drive-related" human sexual behaviors. Nevertheless, the elucidation of specific mechanisms related to the evolution of *human* sexual behavior will probably require direct study within an interpersonal system which integrates the influence of subjective attitudes and desires as well as overt naturalistic behavior.

Psychodynamic Perspective on Individual Psychosexual Development

The central organizing principle of Freud's[14] early theories of psychosexual development was that "libido" (a sexual energy) existed within the individual and acted as a motivating force. The intrapsychic accommodation to this force shaped personality and psychosexual development. In some ways, this concept is similar to the notion of sexual instinct as an evolutionary characteristic which provides motivation for human development and behavior. Freud hypothesized that the direction and expression of this energy during the first years of life explained the behavior of children and later problems of adults. As genital preoccupation was not common in young children, the focus of this "libidinal energy" was directed to other sensory or motor components of the child's body. This sequential shifting of focus led to the early labeling of psychosexual stages as oral, anal, phallic, or genital, depending upon the sensory channels being utilized.

Freud made a major contribution in his demonstration of the early sexual activities and interests of young children. This is all the more impressive as most of his clinical work was with adults, thus limiting his access to direct observation of children's development. However, this lack of direct observation may partially account for some of the difficulty in fitting Freud's theoretical thoughts about the first years of psychosexual development with current empirical observation.

Extensive reviews of Freudian psychoanalytic theory are available,[37] and there has been much ongoing theoretical development.[17,26,27,28] This chapter will consider only some of the psychodynamic concepts which apply to psychosexual development within the family. One of these is the "Oedipal Complex" which has been considered to be of particular importance and controversy.[15,25] The associated overt interest in sexuality on the part of the child during this period provides a new challenge to which the family must accommodate. The preschool child often exhibits a fascination with sexuality which can become associated with an intense attachment to a parent. How a family subsequently handles this phase of sexual interest can have considerable impact on later sexual expression.

Another focus will be on the psychological consequences of puberty. The mechanisms by which adolescents cope with their increasing sexuality has been the source of considerable psychodynamic conceptualization.[2,16,21] During this phase, issues of family cohesiveness and the sexual competency of both the adolescents and their parents become relevant and may challenge the basic integrity of the family. Empirical evidence that such forces exist can be found in the increased rate of marital discord and subsequent divorce which occurs at this stage of family development.

Another important contribution to psychodynamic theory has been the work of Erikson.[11,12,13] He has described human experience throughout the life cycle, highlighting the interface of the individual with social systems. Specifically, his developmental tasks of adulthood have helped to clarify the ever-changing nature of personal growth. There are some problems with his epigenetic model; for example, new "tasks" continue to arise without clear resolution of earlier "tasks". Nevertheless, it is a useful schema for organizing a chronological series of developmental challenges. Additionally, it provides a conceptual basis for the development of a systems-oriented model which still accommodates intrapersonal influences.

Environmental Influences on Individual Sexual Behavior

It is becoming increasingly less common that explanations for the development of sexuality are put forward without recognition of the importance of the social and cultural contexts within which these changes occur. Social learning theorists see imitation and identification with same-sexed models and differential reinforcement of sex-typed behavior as constituting the basis for psychosexual development. Societal variations and individual differences are explained in terms of variations in the models available and in the patterns of reinforcement.[43]

To focus exclusively on imitation, identification, and social reinforcement fails to take into consideration the complexity of the interaction between society, the family, and the child. Gender-role learning is a *process* with age-specific acquisition of information and new behavior. Certain events and behaviors acquire particular meaning to a child because of the connotations parents, siblings, peers, teachers, and others ascribe to them. The social scripts, symbols, and rules are unique to each culture and to each family.[18] Thus, in one subculture nudity may be common and the focus of little attention, while in another subculture it may be associated with secrecy, shame, and intense preoccupation. Similarly, in one family sexual behavior may be accepted while in another it may not be tolerated.

The Family Life Cycle and the Family System

The developmental approach has been applied to families as well as to individuals since the early 1950s.[8,9,11,23] The family has stages of development with key tasks and goals. Typically, these stages have been formulated as a progression: marriage, birth of the first child, child entering school, child's adolescence and leaving home, the adult's middle years, and old age. The transition from one stage to the next tends to have a "critical" character,[39] upsetting people's ways of doing things and stimulating anxieties about whether the new challenges can be handled.[40]

Theories of family development often have been too static. They have failed to account for the diversity of modern families and cultural contexts and have focused on the needs of children without fully appreciating the needs of parents. Primarily, weaknesses and vulnerabilities of families have been described rather than strengths and capacities for change. More recent work has stressed the reciprocity in family relations throughout the life cycle and alternatives to the idealized nuclear family model.[20,40,45]

From a clinical viewpoint, there has been a shift from a focus on the *issues* of the family life cycle, such as a child's entering school, to the inclusion of multiple feedback mechanisms and system effects within the family. This model of the family as a social system in transformation has been conceptualized by family therapists such as Minuchin.[35]

> "Family structure is the invisible set of functional demands that organizes the ways in which family members interact. A family is a system that operates through transactional patterns. Repeated transactions establish patterns of how, when, and to whom to relate, and these patterns underpin the system.... They are maintained by two systems of constraint. The first is generic, involving the universal rules governing family organization.... The second... is idiosyncratic, involving the mutual expectation of particular family members..... Thus, the system maintains itself. It offers resistance to change beyond a certain range, and maintains preferred patterns as long as possible.... But the family structure must be able to adapt when circumstances change."[34]

From an even more inclusive perspective, Engel[10] uses systems theory to examine the multiple consequences of a crisis. These extend beyond the family to include the impact in the community. This biopsychosocial model, which is an expansion of the family systems model, provides a means of examining the impact of cultural variables on personal adaptation.

Sexuality Within the Family

From the theories which have been reviewed, it is possible to delineate two fundamental premises which pertain to psychosexual development within the family:

1. Sexuality is a basic aspect of life which has a predictable biological development.
2. The basic biological sexual characteristics of the child are from the very earliest period of life influenced in a reciprocal manner by the child's family. Both the parents' and child's perceptions of sexuality will be mutually influenced by each other's reactions throughout the life cycle. Because of the reciprocal nature of this process, the clarification of the parallel psychosexual development of all family members is necessary to fully appreciate the child's progress.

Four general aspects of the psychosexual equilibrium within the family can be conceptualized:

1. *The current sexual adjustment of the parents.* Consideration of sexual satisfaction of the marital couple as well as appreciation of the impact of sexual gratification outside the family structure is important in evaluating this component.
2. *The child's developing sensuality and later overt sexual development.* While biological forces provide the origin of the child's sexual expression, the parental response to and tolerance of the child's sexual development clearly plays a critical role in its manifestation.
3. *The psychological impact of the child's sexual development upon the parents' current sexual adjustment and their subsequent response to the child.*
4. *The interactional effect which results in the parents reexperiencing their own early childhood memories and feelings related to their own sexual development* in response to their child's increasing sexual curiosity and behavior.

Even though every family deals with the developmental stages of sexuality in its own unique manner, the interrelationship of these four aspects of psychosexual development can be demonstrated by a family with an adolescent daughter. The stage is set when the daughter enters puberty. The obvious changes in physical appearance often become a focus of both pride and embarrassment for the young adolescent. If this event should occur during a period when the parental sexual adjustment is satisfactory, the family may negotiate this stage with relatively little difficulty. However, consider the circumstance when the parental sexual relationship is either stressed or dysfunctional. If the father is experiencing considerable lack of sexual gratification, alternative sources of sexual pleasure in either fantasy or reality are likely. These may be stimulated by his daughter's emerging sexuality, resulting in frank incestuous impulses. Usually, these incestuous impulses are intolerable and are subsequently repressed, but the increased awareness of sexual dissatisfaction can lead to increased stresses in the marriage or result in the direct expression of sexual impulses outside the family setting.

The mother in this situation might have a heightening of feelings of sexual inadequacy and an increase of fantasies and impulses to achieve direct sexual satisfaction and seek confirmation of her own sexual desirability. The blossoming sexuality of her daughter and the concomitant increased male attention paid to the daughter can be an intolerable stress. Intense jealousy of her daughter's attractiveness and youth as well as a strong sense of guilt based on her conscious awareness of this envy might result. A particularly negative response to these feelings occurs when the mother becomes an active competitor with her daughter. This is made more likely if her husband's incestuous impulses are acknowledged.

Other interactional aspects of this family might include the daughter's finding her father's attention extremely stimulating but at the same time finding her own incestuous response intolerable. Despite considerable guilt, the potential victory over her mother for her father's affection may prove to be an overwhelmingly exciting possibility.

While a variety of consequences may occur as a result of this constellation of events, they all have a direct impact on the daughter's emerging sexuality. It may be necessary for her to deny her sexual development as a defense against the intense feelings which are aroused in her and her parents. Alternatively, her sexuality may become a central preoccupation but be divorced from her more total sense of self to the point that she begins to feel that she can only be valued as a sexual object rather than as an integrated individual. The intensity of her impulses in this situation may lead to an incestuous liaison with her father and fragmentation of the family. Even if an incestuous solution is intolerable, the intensity of her feelings may result in impulsive or self-destructive sexual relationships outside the family.

Clearly, it is a mistake to focus exclusively on the impact of family members on psychosexual development. Other important influences, such as job satisfaction, community support, and health, may modify the course of sexual expression and satisfaction. Considering the struggles of the family with an adolescent daughter, a totally different outcome could result even in the presence of considerable sexual dissatisfaction on the part of the parents. For example, if the father or mother were able to compensate for a lack of sexual gratification in their relationship by finding fulfillment in other areas, they would both be buffered from the impact of their daughter's increased sexuality. A common mechanism is for energy to be directed towards occupational goals or creative expression. If the mother can find alternative ways of sustaining her sense of self as an adequate adult, she will be more able to accept the emergence of her daughter's sexuality and experience it in part as a confirmation of her own parenting ability.

The mother's remembering her own conflicts and pleasures during adolescence may be a critical factor in the family's outcome. If the mother had a relatively positive adolescent experience, it may be easier for her to identify with her daughter and support her struggles of separating and individuating from the family. However, if the mother's own adolescence was one of considerable disappointment, this re-kindling of earlier memories may add an element of bitterness and foster a sense of envy about her daughter's potentially successful adolescent experience. Clearly, a mother's unhappy adolescence does not necessarily have to result in this negative outcome. The remembering of these unhappy times can help a mother to marshal her energies in order to insure that her daughter does not repeat her own less satisfying experience. Ideally, a balance is needed. A mother runs considerable risk of inhibiting the development of her daughter's own individuality if she persists in trying to relive her own adolescence through her child. However, the lessons of life which she has learned can be extremely important for her daughter if they can be shared in a less self-oriented manner.

An Example of a Developmental Interactional Perspective

Maintaining a developmental interactional perspective requires a continual re-evaluation of the impact of changing variables upon the subsequent equilibrium of the entire system. While this approach is vastly more complicated than a linear model of development, it begins to approach more accurately the influences which actually shape behavior. The interlocking developmental changes within the family are dependent upon the adaptive capacities of the individuals within the family system. For example, *three entirely different sequences of events result from the consequences of the parents beginning the child-rearing phase of family development in adolescence, young adulthood, or middle life.* (See Figure 1.) While this may appear self-evident, it is an aspect of family development which is sometimes ignored, especially in the clinical literature, when discussing parameters of parenting. The various permutations of outcome are quite complex. Actually, parental age is only one of a number of important influences. This life chart, for example, holds the variable of an intact nuclear family constant even though this traditional configuration is becoming an increasingly less common system. However, analysis of the impact of parental age can serve as a model which subsequently can be applied to the analysis of any developmental variable.

Psychosexual Developmental Issues When Parenthood is Begun in Adolescence

When child-bearing begins in adolescence, the most striking consequence is the relatively abrupt shift which takes place in the orientation of a young couple. After only a brief opportunity to establish their own identities and to begin to develop an intimate and trusting relationship with each other, they must shoulder the responsibilities of looking after their own child. In addition to having only recently begun to be independent of their own families of origin, they are often quite unprepared for the specific tasks of parenting. The arrival of their first child often interferes with educational and career objectives and can be experienced as a loss of desired opportunities for themselves.

A variety of issues are raised related to the parents' identity formation. A particularly important stress is the change in the young mother's physical appearance during pregnancy. While coping with this change is a challenge for women of any age, the adolescent mother must accommodate to it at a point in her own development when she is trying to establish a sense of herself as an adult woman. The "loss" of her sexual attractiveness, increased tiredness, and the demands of nursing and early child care

Figure 1
Life Chart of Normal Family Psychosexual Developmental Issues (Assumes Minimal Parental Psychopathology)

Major Developmental Milestones	Adolescent Parents	Parents in Early Adulthood	Midlife Parents
Birth of First Child	(Parental age 15–20) 1. Abrupt closure on aspects of identity formation (potential problems in developing intimacy) 2. Societal pressure may exist to delay commitment to marriage and child 3. Relatively early curtailment of sexual exploration	(Parental age 21–30) 1. Identity issues likely to have resolved 2. Societal norms support familial relationships 3. Previous opportunity for sexual development prior to responsibilities of parenthood	(Parental age 31–40) 1. Long standing identity consolidation including sexual identity 2. Societal pressure may exist to conform to nuclear family pattern 3. Extended prior opportunity for sexual exploration (although not necessarily actualized)
Child's Sexual Interest Increases (3–5 yrs)	(Parental age 18–23) 1. Potential major problem if intimacy has not developed within the marriage 2. Re-evaluation of marital sexual relationship	(Parental age 24–33) 1. Greater likelihood of the establishment of intimacy within the marriage 2. Re-evaluation of marital sexual relationship	(Parental age 34–43) 1. Extended prior opportunity for the establishment of intimacy within the marriage 2. Re-evaluation of marital sexual relationship
Child Enters Adolescence (12–15 yrs)	(Parental age 27–32) 1. Re-experience of sexuality of adolescence likely to be intense 2. Completion of parenting role in early mid-life provides developmental re-emergence of identity conflicts including sexual issues	(Parental age 33–42) 1. Re-experience of sexuality of adolescence more variable 2. Societal supports for post-parenting role shifts may ease identity conflicts	(Parental age 43–52) 1. Re-experience of sexuality of adolescence may be less intense 2. Identity conflicts of mid-life may be delayed and coincides with declining sexual potency and menopause
Birth of First Grandchild	(Grandparental age 30–37) 1. May resist role redefinition effecting attachment to grandchild	(Grandparental age 34–48) 1. Some potential resistance related to mid-life re-evaluation	(Grandparental age 49–) 1. Minimal resistance to role shift due to developmental congruence with issues of generativity

can be resented and have considerable negative consequence for her capacity to relate to the child.

The issue of the child's sex may have particular psychological significance for the adolescent mother. It is not unusual for the close intimate caregiving relationship with an infant boy to be experienced as stimulating. The mother's defensive psychological structure may then determine her response to him. While some mothers may give in to impulse and sexually stimulate the child, others may avoid any contact with his genitals. Either of these extreme responses may have implications for the boy's later sexual development and behavior.

In addition, there may be community influences which affect the family's functioning. These can include a disapproval of an early commitment on the basis that the couple has had inadequate opportunity to make a wise decision. Alternatively, there may be direct pressure to prematurely formalize the couple's relationship in order to provide a socially acceptable family unit in which to raise the child.

The couple's sexual development may be at risk in two quite different ways. First, adolescent parents may feel that they had a premature curtailment of their opportunity to explore a variety of sexual experiences. This feeling of being trapped or of having missed out on some of the pleasurable experiences of youth may become a persistent theme in their later sexual adjustment. Second, the birth of their child can affect the sexual gratification within their relationship. The necessary changes in sexual practices during and immediately following pregnancy may be particularly difficult to adapt to if a previous extended period of satisfying sexual compatibility has not existed.

Given these potential stresses on psychosexual adjustment, the emergence of a child's sexual interest can have a variety of repercussions. When the child becomes four or five years of age, he or she may begin to focus his/her sexual feelings toward the parent of the opposite sex. This is classically referred to as the Oedipal or Electra Complex and is a normal aspect of the child's development. The resolution of this phenomena is partially dependent on the parents' ability to respond to the child in a positive and loving manner.[38] In a family where sexual issues are not in conflict, the parents can welcome the child's affectionate desire with a reciprocal warm and loving response. Within this mutually positive matrix, the child will gradually come to understand that, despite the returned warmth of the parent in response to his/her affection, sexual gratification is both inappropriate and impossible. Young, adolescent parents may find the child's overt sexuality too threatening to their own somewhat tenuous sexual adjustment and may act harshly to prohibit the child from any expression of sexuality. Another maladaptive response is the fostering of the child's sexual attention in an attempt to seek compensation by the parents for inadequacies within the marital relationship. Although neither of these responses are unique to adolescent parents, they may be more at risk as a result of their lack of opportunity to have stabilized their own sexual relationship. Clearly, this emergence of the child's sexual interest results in a re-evaluation within the marital relationship of sexual adequacy regardless of the developmental level of the parents.

When a couple who began parenthood in their adolescence faces the increased sexuality of their child as he or she enters adolescence, specific family issues emerge. The parents are still young adults and usually feel strongly identified with their adolescent child. These parents' closeness to their own adolescence often results in an intense re-experiencing of the sexuality of their early years. This may be coupled with a strong sense of having "missed out" on a variety of sexual experiences as a result of a premature commitment. Thus, the stage may be set for considerable stress within the marriage. This will be particularly true if there is only one child, for as the adolescent begins to separate from his young parents and becomes more independent, the parents are less able to structure their own identity around the tasks of child-rearing. This may result in a second identity crisis for the parents which is likely to have strong sexual components.

Psychosexual Development Issues When Parenthood is Begun in Early Adulthood

Much of the literature describing child and family development refers to this particular constellation. Erikson[11] describes early adulthood as having the developmental tasks of intimacy and child-rearing. Current societal norms support the formation of commitments at this time, and for a majority of parents there has been an adequate resolution of the identity conflicts of adolescence. Additionally, most parents of this age have experienced some sexual experimentation, and their own sexual gratification may be a less central issue. Often, an eager anticipation of parenthood is prominent.

In this constellation, the emergence of the child's sexual interest and the vicissitudes of the Oedipal or Electra Complex are often more easily managed by the family. Success is related to the degree of parental sexual satisfaction, and re-evaluation of the parental sexual relationship is inevitable. If both parents have made a good adjustment to the added responsibilities of parenthood, it is unlikely that this developmental challenge will be traumatic.

When the children of these familes enter adolescence, the parents have reached mid-adult life. This is usually accompanied by considerable development in career and community activities. While it is usual for these parents to re-experience their own adolescent sexuality and be stimulated by this developmental stage in their children, it is unlikely to be disorganizing for the family unless specific marital or individual tensions are already pre-existing. In addition, numerous societal supports exist for these parents which facilitate the parents' allowing their children to separate as well as helping them to cope with a mid-life re-evaluation.

Psychosocial Development Issues When Parenthood is Begun in Mid-Life

In families in which the parents have entered their thirties prior to the beginning of child-rearing, considerable opportunity has existed for the consolidation of their respective identities both as individuals and as a couple. The arrival of a child at this point in a couple's life may have considerable impact as it confirms their continued sexuality and their capacity to be productive. The pregnancy is less likely to be unplanned and often is a particularly valued and anticipated event. Additionally, societal pressures may support this couple's wish to be productive and experience child-rearing. However, with the emphasis on career development for women as well as men, interruption in career momentum presents a major intrapersonal conflict for some women. One important factor in the resolution of this stress is that the couple usually has had an adequate opportunity to weigh priorities and therefore has some control regarding the decision to have a family. If the decision is a mutual one and both partners plan to share the anticipated child-rearing responsibilities, this stress can be greatly diminished. Another characteristic of these couples is that they have often had an extended period of sexual exploration and sexual experience within an intimate and committed relationship. This more secure commitment can provide a solid foundation for the continuation of their sexual development during their child-rearing years.

When a child from this family constellation begins to show sexual interests within the family, there is again a re-evaluation of the marital sexual relationship. As with younger parents, the successful adaptation to this developmental challenge will be dependent, in large part, on the parents' maturity and their satisfaction with their marriage. Parents at this age do have the advantage of having had more opportunity to have dealt with their own sexual issues. However, when the child in a family with older parents reaches adolescence, a new set of stresses may emerge. At this time the parents' greater maturity may actually be a stress in itself. While these parents are often less in touch with their own adolescent sexual experiences, they may be struggling with the gradual decline of their sexual potency or the onset of menopause. Consequently, the emergence of their child's new sexuality may be particularly difficult for them to accept as they struggle with their own anxieties about sexual adequacy. If this dimension of a family's adjustment begins to assume central importance, the adolescent's separation from the family may lead to a variety of attempts on the part of both parents to reconfirm their own sexuality.

Normality: Successful Resolution of Conflicts

In society today, there is a wide range of what can be considered "normal" sexual expression. Consequently, there is an acceptance of a considerable variety of family responses to this increased range of sexual behavior. As was discussed in Chapter One, the period of history and the culture of a society influence the concept of "normality". What is acceptable to a given society changes from generation to generation. Even within a given culture at a given time, the range of accepted sexual expression varies considerably from family to family.

It is not the goal of this chapter to narrowly define the boundaries of normal sexual expression.* One approach to the definition of normality is to consider the prevalence of a given behavior and establish the behavior's acceptability on the basis of its frequency. Alternatively, the concept of normality can refer to a congruency with a set of societal values. In this case, if a frequent behavior is contradictory to a societal ideal, it can still be considered to be "deviant".

Psychosocial development within the family can be conceptualized as a series of developmental accommodations. The child's increasing sexual activity must be acknowledged and accommodated to by the parents. Reciprocally, the parents' response to the child as well as their own sexual expression will have an impact on the child

* Research regarding the sexual practices of families without identified psychosexual problems is currently being carried out at Stanford University.[42]

and result in his accommodation to them. In this sense, sexual development can be seen as a series of conflicts and resolutions. These developmental conflicts are predictable in both nature and sequence as they are linked to the child's biologic development. All families experience these conflicts to some degree, and thus, by definition, they are a part of normal development. Most families find some accommodation which allows them to adapt to these developmental challenges. In those families who do not accommodate, a variety of maladaptive responses can be seen. Sexual abuse can be conceptualized as an extreme lack of accommodation, representing a maladaptive response to normal sexual development. In this pathological circumstance, the child's psychosexual development is not considered by the parent or adult who uses the child sexually for his or her own sexual gratification. Sexual abuse represents a breakdown in the normal developmental progression of the formation of intimacy within the marital relationship. It dramatically distorts the emerging sexuality of the child who is exploited to satisfy the impulses of the parent.

Conclusion

Normal psychosexual development is a dynamic process which can best be understood from a developmental interactional approach. The schematic representation of the multiple influences on psychosexual development is presented to provide a model for understanding the interactive impact of environmental experiences. The single variable of parental age is used to illustrate the reciprocal nature of family influence. Sequential family accommodations to the sexual maturation of the child provide an organizing framework in which to understand the wide diversity of sexual adaptation.

References

1. Benedek, T. and Rubinstein, B. (1939) The correlations between ovarian activity and psychodynamic process: the ovulative phase. The menstrual phase. *Psychosom. Med.* **1**: 245 and **1**: 461.
2. Blos, P. (1962) *On Adolescence: A Psychoanalytic Interpretation.* Free Press, New York.
3. Blurton-Jones, N. G. (Ed.) (1974) Biological perspectives on parenthood. In *The Family in Society: Dimensions of Parenthood.* DHSS, HMSO, London.
4. Bowlby, J. (1969) *Attachment.* Hogarth, London.
5. Bruch, H. (1973) *Eating Disorders.* Basic Books, New York.
6. Davenport, W. H. (1977) Sex in cross-cultural perspective. In *Human Sexuality in Four Perspectives.* (Edited by Beach, F. A.) Johns Hopkins Univ., Baltimore, Md.
7. Diamond, M. (1977) Human sexual development: biological foundation for social development. In *Human Sexuality in Four Perspectives.* (Edited by Beach, F. A.) Johns Hopkins Univ., Baltimore, Md.
8. Duvall, E. M. and Hill, R. (Eds.) (1948) *Dynamics of Family Interaction.* National Conference on Family Life, New York.
9. Duvall, E. M. (1957) *Family Development.* Lippincott, Philadelphia. (Rev. 1962).
10. Engel, G. L. (1980) The clinical application of the biopsychosocial model. *Am. J. Psychiatry* **137**: 535.
11. Erikson, E. H. (1950) *Childhood and Society.* W. W. Norton, New York.
12. Erikson, E. H. (1959) Identity and the life cycle. *Psychological Issues* **1**: 1.
13. Erikson, E. H. (1969) *Identity, Youth and Crisis.* W. W. Norton, New York.
14. Freud, S. (1905) Three essays on the theory of sexuality. In *Standard Edition of the Complete Psychological Works of Sigmund Freud.* (Edited by Strachey, J.) Vol. VIII. Hogarth, London.
15. Freud, S. (1913) Totem and taboo. In *Standard Edition of the Complete Psychological Works of Sigmund Freud.* (Edited by Strachey, J.) Vol. III. Hogarth, London.
16. Freud, A. (1958) Adolescence. In *Psychoanalytic Study of the Child.* XIII: 255.
17. Freud, A. (1965) *Normality and Pathology in Childhood: Assessments of Development.* International Univ., New York.
18. Gagnon, J. H. and Simon, W. (1973) *Sexual Conduct: The Social Sources of Human Sexuality.* Aldine, Chicago.
19. Green, R. (1974) *Sexual Identity Conflict in Children and Adults.* Basic Books, New York.
20. Group for the Advancement of Psychiatry (1973) *The Joys and Sorrows of Parenthood.* Scribner, New York.
21. Group for the Advancement of Psychiatry (1968) *Normal Adolescence: Its Dynamics and Impact.* Scribner, New York.
22. Harlow, H. F. (1961) The Development of Affectional Patterns in Infant Monkeys. In *Determinants of Infant Behavior,* Vol. 1 (Edited by Foss, B. M.) Wiley, New York.
23. Hill, R. and Rodgers, R. H. (1964) The developmental approach. In *Handbook of Marriage and the Family.* (Edited by Christensen, H. T.) Rand McNally, Chicago.
24. Hinde, R. A. (1974) *Biological Bases of Human Social Behavior.* McGraw-Hill, New York.
25. Klein, M. (1928) Early stages of the Oedipus Complex. *Int. J. Psychoanal.* **9**.
26. Klein, M. (1932) *The Psychoanalysis of Children.* Hogarth, London.
27. Kernberg, O. (1975) *Borderline Condition and Pathological Narcissism.* John Aronson, New York.
28. Kohut, H. (1971) *The Analysis of the Self.* International Univ., New York.
29. Lewis, W. C. (1965) Coital movements in the first year of life. *Int. J. Psychoanal.* **46**: 372.
30. Lorenz, K. (1966) *On Aggression.* Harcourt, Brace, and World, New York.
31. Mason, W. A. (1965) The social development of monkeys and apes. In *Primate Behavior* (Edited by DeVore, I.) Holt, Rinehart, and Winston, New York.
32. Masterson, J. F. (1977) Primary anorexia nervosa in the borderline adolescent—an object relations view. In *Borderline Personality Disorders* (Edited by Hartocollis, P.) International Univ., New York.

33. Melges, F. T. and Homburg, D. A. (1977) Psychological effects of hormonal changes in women. In *Human Sexuality in Four Perspectives.* (Edited by Beach, F. A.) Johns Hopkins Univ., Baltimore.
34. Minuchin, S. (1974) *Families and Family Therapy.* Tavistock, London, p. 51.
35. Minuchin, S., Rosman, B. N., and Baker, L. (1978) *Psychosomatic Families.* Harvard Univ., Cambridge, Mass.
36. Moos, R. H. (1968) Psychological aspects of oral contraceptives. *Arch. Gen. Psychiatry* **19:** 87.
37. Nagera, H. (Ed.) (1969) *Basic Psychoanalytic Concepts on the Libido Theory.* Basic Books, New York.
38. Pincus, L. and Dare, C. (1978) *Secrets in the Family.* Faber & Faber, London.
39. Rapoport, R. (1963) Normal crisis, family structure and mental health. *Fam. Process* **2:** 1.
40. Rapoport, R., Rapoport, R. N., and Strelitz, Z. (1977) *Fathers, Mothers, and Others.* Routledge & Kegan Paul, London.
41. Robinson, D. S., Davis, J. M., Nies, A., Raviris, C. L., and Sylvester, D. (1971) Relation of sex and aging in monamine oxidase activity of human brain, plasma, and platelets. *Arch. Gen. Psychiatry* **24:** 536.
42. Rosenfeld, Alvin (1980) Stanford Univ., Palo Alto, California. Personal communication.
43. Rutter, M. L. (1980) Psychosexual development. In *Scientific Foundations of Developmental Psychiatry.* (Edited by Rutter, M. L.) Heinemann, London.
44. Schutz, F. (1965) Sexuelle pragung bei anatiden. *Z. Tierpsychol.* **22:** 50.
45. Skolnick, A., and Skolnick, J. H. (1974) *Intimacy, Family and Society.* Little, Brown, Boston.
46. Treadway, C. R., Kane, F. J., Janahi-Zadeh, A., and Lipton, M. A. (1969) A psychoendocrine study of pregnancy and puerperium. *Am. J. Psychiatry* **125:** 1380.
47. Vogel, W., Braverman, D. M., and Klaibel, E. L. (1971) EEG responses in regularly menstruating women and in amonorrheic women treated with ovarian hormones. *Sciences* **172:** 388.
48. Whalen, R. E. (1977) Brain mechanisms controlling sexual behavior. In *Human Sexuality in Four Perspectives.* (Edited by Beach, F. A.) Johns Hopkins Univ., Boston.

Chapter Three

A Psychoanalyst's View of Sexual Abuse by Parents

ANNA FREUD

It is the psychoanalyst's task to examine external events from the aspect of their impact on internal life and to trace their past, present and, possibly, future significance. Seen in this light, sexual abuse of children by their own parents seems to belong in a category of its own, different in some respects from other forms of maltreatment.

That children do not necessarily hate or shun parents who treat them harshly, punitively or even sadistically, is a well-known fact. When rescued from their own unsuitable environment, there are some who object to the separation, secretly or openly longing to return. What has happened to them is that fear of the parent, coupled with natural dependency, has given rise to a passive-submissive attitude which makes suffering exciting and which ties the victim as firmly to his aggressor as do positive, loving bonds. However, it is important to note in this respect that masochistic trends are not inevitable manifest ingredients in a child's mental equipment and behavior; they are potentialities which can be aroused and perpetuated in response to parental behavior.

The situation is different in the case of sexual seduction. Infantile sexuality, as it proceeds in stages, characterized by the erotic excitability of body zones, is inevitably tied up with the child's emotional life and with the persons of his parents who are the first objects of the sexual libido. The mother is bitten and clung to during the oral stage, dominated and tortured during the anal-sadistic one. Father and mother are exhibited to, voyeuristically inspected, sexually desired in the phallic oedipal phase. Normal progress towards adult forms of sexuality depends on careful handling of these very vulnerable processes, on the one hand not to interfere with their sequential order, on the other hand neither totally to frustrate nor excessively give licence to them. However, it is exactly in these two respects that the sexual seducer sins.

Infantile and adult sexuality are not on the same wavelength. An adult who uses (or misuses) a young child to satisfy his own exhibitionistic, phallic or genital needs, may have for his partner an individual with erotic wishes and impulses on an earlier level, in the case of a young child, for example, the anal-sadistic one. The abused young child therefore is not merely exposed to an unfortunate and unsuitable sexual encounter, he is also experiencing a type of stimulation for which, developmentally, he is wholly unprepared. Nevertheless, he cannot avoid being physically aroused and this experience disastrously disrupts the normal sequence in his sex organization. He is forced into premature phallic or genital development while his legitimate developmental needs and their accompanying mental expressions are by-passed and short-circuited. Even though some of the psychological repercussions of such experiences may be open to modification in therapy, the harmful effect on later sexual behavior may be lasting.

What is, obviously, of even greater pathogenic significance, is the actual consummation of a sexual relationship between child and parent. Different from the situation of the masochistic children, mentioned above, whose masochism is called forth by parental action, here the phantasy of being father's or mother's sexual partner is a normal and ubiquitous one, rudimentally in existence in the pre-phallic phases and in full bloom during the oedipal period. It exists regardless of the presence or absence of parental inclinations. However, normal development presupposes that these oedipal phantasies remain just what they are, namely irrealities. It is their frustration which leads to the overcoming of the Oedipus complex; which initiates entrance into the latency period with its inestimable benefits for ego advancement, superego formation and personality development; which allows for its transitory upsurge in pre-adolescence; and which, finally, allows the adolescent after reaching genitality, to replace the original parental objects by sexual partners outside the family.

Few, if any, of these developmental achievements are open to children whose oedipal phantasy has been replaced by reality, their age-adequate frustration by fulfilment; where sexual union with a partner, normally reserved for adolescence or post-adolescence, has prematurely become an immediate event; and where the growing young person, instead of being allowed to shed his dependent involvement with the parents for the sake of new objects, is bound all the tighter to them on the basis of shared excitement and experience.

Due to the underlying oedipal phantasies, children may be more or less willing victims of the assault, which explains why incestuous abuse often continues undetected for long periods, usually until a sudden revulsion against the situation or fear of accompanying violence causes the victim to run for protection and betray the secret. However, even then such accusations against the parent are frequently withdrawn again by the child, with the true facts exceedingly difficult to substantiate.

After-effects of an incestuous experience, as known to psychiatrists and psychoanalysts, are of two contrasting kinds. In some cases an insatiable longing for repetition persists, with the individual concerned either in the role of seducer or seduced. In others there is massive defence activity, denial, repression, inhibition, etc. directed against sexuality as such, leading in adult life to frigidity and impotence.

Far from existing only as a phantasy, incest is thus also a fact, more widespread among the population in certain periods than in others. Where the chances of harming a child's normal developmental growth are concerned, it ranks higher than abandonment, neglect, physical maltreatment or any other form of abuse. It would be a fatal mistake to underrate either the importance or the frequency of its actual occurrence.

Chapter Four

Recognition of Child Sexual Abuse in the United Kingdom

PATRICIA BEEZLEY MRAZEK, MARGARET LYNCH AND ARNON BENTOVIM

In the United States in 1978 sexual abuse of children was a growing national concern. The number of reported cases was increasing considerably, and many communities were developing treatment programmes for victims and their families. In the United Kingdom, however, this was not happening. There was not as yet any widespread recognition of child sexual abuse as a major social problem. Even though there is no mandatory reporting of child abuse in Britain, identification and intervention are heavily influenced by government guidelines. Up until 1980 circulars from the Department of Health and Social Security had not included sexual abuse within the definition of child abuse. The only figures available in the United Kingdom on the incidence of child sexual abuse were criminal statistics, particularly those on incest.

The authors initiated an investigation to ascertain the extent to which various professional groups in the United Kingdom recognized or were referred cases of sexual abuse of children by adults, the nature of the cases seen, and the events which followed the identification of these cases.

This chapter presents the survey data as an example of the process of recognition of child sexual abuse. The authors' intent is not to make a comparative analysis among nations but to highlight the obstacles and patterns which are likely to exist in any country as consideration is given to the inclusion of sexual abuse within the child abuse syndrome.

Method

Questionnaires were mailed to 1,619 family doctors*, police surgeons†, paediatricians, forensic psychiatrists, child psychiatrists, and chairmen of Area Review Committees‡. All of the family doctors in one London Area Health Authority and one

* Every family in the United Kingdom has a Family Doctor who provides primary medical care to them. A family does not go directly to a paediatrician or child psychiatrist for specialized treatment but is referred by the Family Doctor.

† A Police Surgeon is a Medical Practitioner with an appointment to the Police Department who is called in at their request to gather medical evidence.

‡ Area Review Committees were established in England in 1973 and 1974 on the recommendation of the Department of Health and Social Security of the National Government for the purpose of overseeing the management of cases of non-accidental injury to children. Multi-disciplinary teams review policy on child abuse and make recommendations in guidelines to their local authorities.

rural county were circulated. The paediatricians and child psychiatrists who were asked to participate were selected from the membership lists of their professional organizations. The entire membership of the Association of Police Surgeons of Great Britain and all of the Area Review Committees in England were circulated. The forensic psychiatrists were selected by the Chairman of the Forensic Section of the Royal College of Psychiatrists as those who would most likely see child-related cases.

The questionnaires were in two sections. Part I was concerned with the frequency of sexually abused children seen during a target year, designated as June 1, 1977 through May 31, 1978. Enquiries were made as to the age and sex of those children and the type of abuse they experienced. Part II of the questionnaire was concerned with the date and details of the most recently identified or referred case of child sexual abuse. Enquiries were made as to who referred the child to the respondent, the age and sex of the child, the type of abuse which was experienced, the extent of violence or injury associated with the sexual abuse, the relationship of the perpetrator to the child, the degree of family disturbance, and the nature of actions taken following identification of the sexual abuse. The questionnaires to the forensic psychiatrists referred to perpetrators of child sexual abuse rather than to the child victim. The Area Review Committee questionnaires did not refer to specific cases but rather to policies and procedures regarding child sexual abuse.

In the questionnaires, three types of sexual abuse were defined:

Type I: Battered child whose injuries are primarily in the genital area.

Type II: Child who has experienced attempted or actual intercourse or other inappropriate genital contact with an adult.

Type III: Child who has been inappropriately involved with an adult in sexual activities not covered by I or II.

Child was defined as a person 15 years of age or younger. In England, 16 is the legal age of consent for marriage and leaving school. Only sexual abuse by adults was included in the study. Therefore, the cases which respondents included in their returned questionnaires regarding sexual abuse by adolescents to each other or to younger children and cases of sibling incest (unless one of the siblings was an adult) were excluded.

Results: Direct Care Providers

Return Rate and Recognition Rate

Of the 1,619 questionnaires which were mailed out, 685 (42%) were returned. Table 1 gives the number of professionals who were circulated in the groups who had direct contact with the children, the response rates, and the percentage of the respondents who remembered ever having seen a case of child sexual abuse during their professional careers.

Five hundred and four family doctors from two different areas in England were circulated. One group consisted of all of the family doctors (260) in an entirely urban area. This was done in cooperation with the Area Health Authority. The total number of children under the age of 16 in this district is approximately 46,000. Additionally, all the family doctors (244) in an area which is both urban and rural were circulated in

Table 1
Circulation of Direct Care Providers

	Number circulated	Number responding	Number who have seen case at some time
Family Doctors	504	122 (24%)	20 (16%)
Police Surgeons	563	250* (44%)	121 (56% of 217)
Paediatricians	282	143 (51%)	40 (28%)
Child Psychiatrists	250	107 (43%)	58 (54%)
Total	1,599	622 (39%)	239 (41%)

* Thirty-three could not provide information because they had retired from police surgeon duties.

cooperation with the local Family Practitioner Committee. The total number of children under the age of 16 in this area was approximately 100,000.

One hundred and twenty-two (24%) of the family doctors returned their questionnaires. Of these, 20 (16% of those responding) had ever seen a case of child sexual abuse. The percentage of family doctors who returned their questionnaires was quite similar in the two districts. Likewise, the percentage of those who had at some time seen a case was quite comparable based on population size. Ten percent of the doctors in the area with 46,000 children had seen a case compared to 23% of the doctors who had seen a case in the area with 100,000 children.

Five hundred and sixty-three police surgeons were circulated, and 250 (44%) of the questionnaires were returned. However, 33 of those could not provide any information, primarily because these physicians had retired from police surgeon duty. Of the remaining 217, 121 (56%) recalled seeing a case of sexual abuse.

Two hundred and eighty-two questionnaires were circulated to paediatricians whose names and addresses were obtained from the *British Paediatric Association Handbook*; approximately a quarter of the membership was randomly selected to participate in the survey. One hundred and forty-three (51%) returned their questionnaires. Of these, 40 (28% of those responding) had seen a case of child sexual abuse. Three cases were reported but excluded from the tabulations: a 12-year-old girl whose partner was a 15-year-old boy, a patient who was the offspring of a 14-year-old girl and her 19-year-old uncle, and a baby who was brought in dead to the hospital but was not seen by the respondent personally.

The names and addresses of 250 child psychiatrists were obtained from the membership list of the Association of Child Psychology and Psychiatry. One hundred and seven (43%) returned their questionnaires. Of these, 58 (54%) had at some time seen at least one case of child sexual abuse. Five reported cases were excluded from the tabulations: two adolescents who assaulted younger children, a nine-year-old boy who assaulted a six-year-old boy (anal penetration), a child whose paranoid schizophrenic mother falsely accused the father of sexual abuse, and a 12-year-old girl who was impregnated by her boyfriend.

Combining these four groups of physicians, 39% had seen a case of child sexual abuse at some time. Of course, there is no way of knowing if those who did not respond to the questionnaire had ever seen a case. Following the survey, there have been many physicians who have told the authors of cases of child sexual abuse which they have recently seen. This may reflect either an increase in the incidence of this type of abuse or, more likely, an increase in awareness of the problem and willingness to discuss such cases.

A similar survey conducted in America, in which 300 general practitioners and paediatricians were circulated, yielded a similar return rate, that is, 32%.[7] Fifty-three percent of those respondents reported seeing at least one identifiable sexually abused child *annually*. They reported seeing an average of two and as many as five cases in the last year. In addition, each of these physicians also saw annually at least one case and as many as seven cases that were thought to have involved sexual abuse but were not reported to the physician as such. Compared to the circulation of the British family doctors and paediatricians, the Americans saw twice as many cases in just a year as the British had ever seen. As recognition has increased in the United States, the rate of referral has also gone up dramatically.[8] The authors anticipate that the same thing will happen in the United Kingdom.

Cases Seen in Target Year

During the target year the professionals who provided direct care to children, that is, family doctors, police surgeons, paediatricians, and child psychiatrists, saw a total of 1,072 cases of child sexual abuse. The police surgeons saw by far the largest number of cases, seeing 874 of the total. Child psychiatrists saw the next most frequent number, that is, 158. Family doctors and paediatricians saw relatively few, 11 and 29 respectively. Most of these professionals reported seeing either one or just a few cases of sexual abuse, but there were exceptions to this, such as one child psychiatrist who reported seeing 56 cases in the target year.

Table 2 gives the sex, type of abuse, and age of the children who were seen during the target year by direct care providers. The majority of the cases seen were girls in the older age groups with Type II abuse.

Based on these referral rates and projecting this for the child population in the United Kingdom as a whole, this would imply that at an absolute minimum three per 1,000 children could be recognized at some point in their childhood by a professional as having been sexually abused. These figures differ remarkably from the criminal statistics available from the Home Office. For example, in 1977 the Home Office reported 295 cases of incest and 243 cases of unlawful sexual intercourse with children

Table 2
Cases Seen in Target Year by Direct Care Providers

			Total Cases		
	Family Doctors		11		
	Police Surgeons		874		
	Paediatricians		29		
	Child Psychiatrists		158		
	Total		1,072		
Girls	450 (42%)	Type I	29 (3%)	0–5 years	29 (3%)
Boys	77 (7%)	Type II	800 (75%)	6–10 years	66 (6%)
Not given	545	Type III	203 (19%)	11–15 years	175 (16%)
		Not given	40	Not given	802
Total	1,072		1,072		1,072

Table 3
Last Case Seen by Direct Care Providers

	Prior to June 1, 1977	Between June 1, 1977 and May 31, 1978	Following May 31, 1978
Family Doctors	(n = 20) 11	8	1
Police Surgeons	(n = 112) 14	25	73
Paediatricians	(n = 37) 13	17	7
Child Psychiatrists	(n = 51) 11	27	13
Total	(n = 220) 49 (22%)	77 (35%)	94 (43%)

under 13 years in England and Wales. The National Center on Child Abuse and Neglect in Washington, D.C. estimates that the current annual incidence of child sexual abuse is between 60,000 and 100,000 cases per year in the United States.[11] Because the cases reported in this survey are only those which are recognized by or referred to professionals as being cases of child sexual abuse, they do not reflect the actual incidence rate. It is likely that child sexual abuse is even more common than these figures indicate.

Last Case Seen by Direct Care Providers

The questionnaire asked the respondents to indicate the date on which they had seen their most recent case of child sexual abuse and to give details of that case. For some of the professionals this was during the target year, but others had not seen a case for quite some time. (See Table 3.)

The date of the most recent case of the family doctors ranged from two months to 14 years prior to June 1977. Five of them had not seen a case for at least nine years. The majority (65%) of the police surgeons had seen at least one case since May 31, 1978, usually within a matter of weeks prior to completing the questionnaire. The majority (55%) of the paediatricians and the majority (78%) of the child psychiatrists had seen at least one case since June 1, 1977.

Referrals to Direct Care Providers

Table 4 gives the primary referral source to each of these groups of direct care providers. The referral source was given for 16 cases seen by family doctors. The majority of these (56%) were referrals directly from the family. Thirty-one percent came from police and 13% came from the hospital. It is interesting to note that no referrals came to family doctors from social workers or health visitors.

Table 4
Primary Referral Sources to Direct Care Providers

Family Doctors received 56% of their referrals from *Family Members*
Police Surgeons received 97% of their referrals from *Police Departments*
Paediatricians received 50% of their referrals from *Family Doctors*
Child Psychiatrists received 48% of their referrals from *Social Workers*

The referral source was given for 111 cases seen by police surgeons. Almost all of these (97%) came directly from the police department. There were no referrals from the court or social services. Seven referrals came from other sources including one from a family doctor and five directly from the family. In 96 cases it was known who had made the initial complaint to the police. Seventy-three (76%) of the complaints were made by parents, primarily the mother. Eleven were made by the child, and four were from other relatives, including a sibling, an aunt, and grandparents. One complaint came from a friend, and seven came from professionals, including police officers, teachers, the courts, and a social worker.

The referral source was noted for 32 of the cases seen by paediatricians. Half of these were referrals from family doctors. Nine (28%) came from Accident and Emergency Departments, and seven came from a variety of other sources. Social Services had initiated several referrals, but only one child had been referred directly by a police surgeon. Not all the referrals, whatever their source, were initially for sexual abuse. A number of children had been known to the paediatrician before sexual abuse occurred or was recognized. One family did not give the history of sexual assault for several years after the incident despite police involvement at the time. The child was being followed up in the paediatric out-patient department for enuresis. Other initial reasons for paediatric involvement included recurrent abdominal pains, chest pain, vaginal discharge proving to be gonococcal, self-poisoning, and hysterical reactions. The sexual abuse was subsequently recognized during out-patient care or hospitalization.

The child psychiatrists gave the referral source for 50 cases. Almost half (24) were referrals from social workers. Ten (20%) were referred by family doctors, five (10%) by paediatricians, three by the family, and nine by other sources including four from schools.

It is interesting to note that certain groups of professionals do not seem to refer on to other professional groups. For example, because the police surgeon's role is to collect medical evidence, he may not see the child's needs as paramount and may not consider referral to either a paediatrician or a child psychiatrist. Likewise, even though family doctors seem to refer on to paediatricians, one wonders how often they make a child psychiatry referral. Paediatricians do not seem to be referring on to child psychiatrists; this may be because of their lack of recognition of family disturbance.

Case Characteristics: Age, Sex, and Type of Abuse

Two hundred and eighteen respondents went on to give further details of the child most recently identified as sexually abused. However, not all the respondents had full information on each case. Table 5 gives the relationship between the age, sex, and type of abuse by each professional group and by the combined groups. Totally, 158 girls and 25 boys were abused. Of these, 23 were under five years of age; 49 were between six and ten, and 111 were between 11 and 15. (There were 25 children for whom age and sex were not known.) The girls in the 11 to 15 age group were the ones most likely to be sexually abused. This was most commonly attempted or actual intercourse or other inappropriate genital contact with an adult. The next largest group of vulnerable children were girls between the ages of six and ten who were also most frequently subjected to Type II abuse. It is noteworthy that there were 23 girls below the age of five who were identified as sexually abused, some in each of the three types of abuse.

Table 5
*Type of Abuse, Age and Sex of Last Case Seen by Each Professional Group**

Type of Abuse		0–5 years		6–10 years		11–15 years		Not given	
		Girls	Boys	Girls	Boys	Girls	Boys	Girls	Boys
						Family Doctors			
I	(0)	—	—	—	—	—	—	—	—
II	(11)	2	—	—	1	5	1	1	1
III	(3)	1	—	1	—	1	—	—	—
Total	(14)	3	—	1	1	6	1	1	1
						Police Surgeons			
I	(1)	—	—	—	—	1	—	—	—
II	(90)	6	—	17	2	56	4	3	2
III	(13)	3	—	3	3	3	1	—	—
Total	(104)	9	—	20	5	60	5	3	2
						Paediatricians			
I	(6)	4	—	—	—	1	—	—	1
II	(15)	2	—	7	1	4	1	—	—
III	(9)	4	—	2	—	3	—	—	—
Total	(30)	10	—	9	1	8	1	—	1
						Child Psychiatrists			
I	(1)	—	—	—	—	—	—	—	1
II	(35)	—	—	7	4	19	5	—	—
III	(9)	1	—	1	—	4	2	1	—
Total	(45)	1	—	8	4	23	7	1	1
						Combined Totals of 4 Groups			
I	(8)	4	—	—	—	2	—	—	2
II	(151)	10	—	31	8	84	11	4	3
III	(34)	9	—	7	3	11	3	1	—
Total	(193)	23 (12%)	—	38 (19%)	11 (6%)	97 (50%)	14 (7%)	5 (3%)	5 (3%)

* Information was incomplete for 25 cases; therefore, total is 193 rather than 218.

There were no boys identified in this age group, but older boys were more vulnerable. It is possible that as boys and girls become more sexually developed as they approach adolescence their chances of being sexually abused increase. Another possibility is that it is easier for professionals to identify sexual abuse in this age group because these children talk about their experiences. Younger children may not communicate what is happening to them, and if they do perhaps they are not believed as often as older children are. It is also noteworthy that of the cases seen by police surgeons more than half (34 of 60) of the girls in the 11 to 15 age group were 14 and 15 years of age. Of the girls under five years of age who were seen by police surgeons, all were three, four and five, except for one child who was nine months old and had Type II sexual abuse.

Violence or Injury

Because the question of overlap between physical and sexual abuse is an important one, the respondents were asked which of the cases they had seen were associated with violence or injury. Ten (4%) of the 218 cases were Type I abuse, that is, battered children whose injuries were primarily in the genital area. Additionally, 23 (11%) of Types II and III sexual abuse also involved violence or injury. Therefore, *15% of the reported cases were associated in some way with violence.* This figure is much higher than what one might expect. The injuries included cigarette burns and other minor burns, bruises, injuries to the genitals, being pulled into a car by the hair, and buggery (anal intercourse). In 15 (7%) of the 218 cases, physical abuse had occurred or had been suspected previously. One of these children was subsequently reported as having Type I sexual abuse, 11 as having Type II, and three as having Type III. Two of the children who experienced Type I sexual abuse were not previously reported for any physical abuse.

Perpetrator and Type of Abuse

The relationship between the perpetrator and the type of abuse as reported by each of the professional groups is shown in Table 6 and as a combined group in Table 7. In 57% of the cases the perpetrator was from outside the child's family, that is, either a family acquaintance (31%) or a stranger (26%). The natural father was the perpetrator in 20% of the cases, whereas step-parents were involved in 12%. Sexual abuse by natural mothers comprised only 2% of the total. Other relatives were perpetrators in 8.5% of the cases. Therefore, *in most of the reported cases of sexual abuse (73.5%) the child knew who the perpetrator was.* Sexual abuse by perpetrators outside of the child's family were most frequently reported by police surgeons.

Family Disturbance

In 56% of the families some type of family disturbance was noted. This included parental mental illness, unemployment, alcoholism, poor marital relationships, criminality, previous physical abuse of index child, sexual abuse of other siblings, and emotional problems in the index child. A poor marital relationship between the parents was the most common type of family disturbance (34%); the second most common was emotional problems in the child (25%). Many of the families had a number of the above factors identified. (See Chapter Eight for a review of the literature in this area.)

Table 8 gives the type and distribution of disturbance in the families which were seen by each of the professional groups and by the combined group. The low reported incidence of family difficulty as noted by family doctors is likely to reflect the latter's lack of knowledge of the family circumstances. Many of the family doctors stated they

Table 6
Perpetrator and Type of Abuse

		Type I	Type II	Type III
		Family Doctors		
Natural Father	(2)	—	1	1
Natural Mother	(0)	—	—	—
Step-parent	(3)	1	1	1
Other Relative	(1)	—	1	—
Family Acquaintance	(7)	—	6	1
Stranger	(3)	—	2	1
Total	(16)	1	11	4
		Police Surgeons		
Natural Father	(20)	1	19*	—
Natural Mother	(0)	—	—	—
Step-parent	(4)	—	3	1
Other Relative	(8)	—	8	—
Family Acquaintance	(36)	—	30	6
Stranger	(35)	—	29	6
Total	(103)	1	89	13
		Paediatricians		
Natural Father	(7)	—	6	1
Natural Mother	(3)	1	—	2†
Step-parent	(4)	1	—	3‡
Other Relative	(5)	1	3	1
Family Acquaintance	(9)	2	5	2
Stranger	(6)	1	3	2
Total	(34)	6	17	11
		Child Psychiatrists		
Natural Father	(12)	1	9	2
Natural Mother	(1)	—	—	1
Step-parent	(13)	—	9	4
Other Relative	(3)	—	3	—
Family Acquaintance	(10)	—	9	1
Stranger	(9)	—	7	2
Other	(1)	—	—	1
Total	(49)	1	37	11

* In one case a brother also may have been a perpetrator.
† Mother and step-father involved together; coded as mother as perpetrator.
‡ One case also may have involved other family members.

simply did not have this information. The paediatricians noted that there was a trend for more disturbance to be recorded the closer the relationship of the perpetrator to the child. Thus, none of the types of disturbance were recorded for five of the six cases where the child was abused by a stranger. This may have been because no disturbance existed in these families or, alternatively, no disturbance was expected and therefore not sought. Families in which the child was abused by a stranger were the least likely to have seen a social worker who may have been the one responsible for the recognition of family problems in the other cases. However, unlike this trend which was noted by paediatricians, child psychiatrists found family disturbance regardless of who the perpetrator was. Perhaps this is because they are more likely to expect emotional difficulties even in those families whose child has been assaulted by a stranger.

Table 7
*Perpetrators**

	Frequency	Percentage of total group
Natural Father	41	(20%)
Natural Mother	4	(2%)
Step-parent	24	(12%)
Other Relative	17	(8.5%)
Family Acquaintance	62	(31%)
Stranger	53	(26%)
Other	1	(0.5%)
Total	202	(100%)

* Data is combined information from the four professional groups. Information was incomplete for 16 cases; therefore, total is 202 rather than 218.

In general, the *actual* frequency of disturbance is likely to have been even higher in all of the families seen by all types of professionals simply because the latter did not always have access to all the information.

Events Following Identification

Following recognition of the child's sexual abuse, there were a variety of possible actions which could be taken. Some of these resulted from direct referral and/or recommendation from the professional who had been involved. Other actions may

Table 8
Frequency of Family Disturbance

Type	Frequency noted by 16 Family Doctors	113 Police Surgeons	35 Paedia- tricians	54 Child Psychiatrists	Combined Group of 218
Parental Mental Illness	3 (19%)	3 (3%)	7 (20%)	17 (31%)	30 (14%)
Unemployment	3 (19%)	8 (7%)	6 (17%)	12 (22%)	29 (13%)
Alcoholism*	1 (6%)	8 (7%)	6 (17%)	7 (13%)	22 (10%)
Poor Marital Relationship†	4 (25%)	27 (24%)	11 (31%)	32 (59%)	74 (34%)
Previous Parental Criminality	1 (6%)	6 (5%)	4 (11%)	10 (19%)	21 (10%)
Emotional Problems in the Child	2 (13%)	11 (10%)	10 (29%)	32 (59%)	55 (25%)
Previously Suspected Abuse of Child	—	8 (7%)	4 (11%)	2 (2%)	14 (6%)
Current or Previous Sexual Abuse of Child's Sibling(s)‡	1 (6%)	7 (6%)	2 (6%)	9 (16%)	19 (9%)
Total Number of Families Seen Having Family Disturbance	8 (50%)	48 (42%)	20 (57%)	46 (85%)	122 (56%)

* Additionally, two families with a drug problem.
† Many others were single-parent families.
‡ Suspected sexual abuse of siblings in two additional cases.

Table 9
Actions Taken Following Recognition of Sexual Abuse

	16 Family Doctors	113 Police Surgeons	35 Paediatricians	54 Child Psychiatrists	Combined Group of 218
Criminal Prosecution of Adult Perpetrator	6 (38%)	54 (48%)	15 (43%)	19 (35%)	94 (43%)
Referral to Family Doctor	—	32 (28%)	—	—	32 (15%)
Referral to Social Worker (or SW already involved)	4 (25%)	21 (19%)	20 (57%)	14 (26%)‡	59 (27%)
Referral to Child Psychiatry Clinic	2 (13%)	1 (1%)	4 (11%)	28 (52%) offered therapy	35 (16%)
Child Taken into Care	2 (13%)	1 (1%)	8 (23%)	18 (33%)§	29 (13%)
Child's Name Placed on At-Risk Register	1 (6%)	4 (4%)	†	6 (11%)	11 (5%)
Parent Removed from Home	3 (19%)	2 (2%)	—	—	5 (2%)
Perpetrator Referred to Adult Psychiatrist	1 (6%)	6 (5%)	2 (6%)	4 (7%)	13 (6%)
Referral to Paediatrician	—	1 (1%)	—	—	1 (0.5%)
Referral to Gynaecologist	—	5 (4%)	—	—	5 (2%)

* Another child was made the subject of a supervision order.
† Two children were already on at-risk registers because of previous physical abuse.
‡ Additionally, many of the referrals to child psychiatry came from social workers, so it is likely that there was some form of social work involved with the majority of the families.
§ Three additional children were already in care at the time the second abuse was discovered.

have been taken by other agencies who knew of the case. *Criminal prosecution was by far the most common consequence* (43%). The concepts of deferred prosecution and deferred sentencing which are used with sexual abuse cases in the United States are not applied in the United Kingdom. Table 9 gives the frequency of other actions taken following identification. Only in a minority of cases was action taken to remove the child from the home or to draw attention to the abuse by placing the child's name on the at-risk register.*

Results: Forensic Psychiatrists

Thirty forensic psychiatrists were circulated in an effort to determine what other professionals might know of child sexual abuse cases. Of course, the forensic psychiatrists are perpetrator-oriented in that they often do evaluations for the court and prison system of adults who have assaulted young children. Of the 30 questionnaires sent, 12 (40%) were returned.

Eight of the 12 respondents knew of the at least 75 children who had been sexually abused during the target year. This was a minimum number, and the actual number is likely to be much higher. The number of victims of some perpetrators was unknown,

* At-risk registers in England are similar to child abuse registries in the United States.

but for the purposes of this survey the tabulated number was counted at the minimum. The 75 reported cases involved 55 different perpetrators. Two cases (3%) were Type I; 31 (41%) were Type II, and 42 (56%) were Type III.

All eight forensic psychiatrists had seen their most recent case following the target date. Six of these were Type II, and two were Type III. Six were girls, and no sex was given for two of the children. One of the children was under five years; two were between six and ten; three were between 11–15; the age was not given for two. No violence or injury was associated with any of the eight cases. As far as the forensic psychiatrists knew, none of the eight children had previously been suspected as having been physically abused. Half of the perpetrators (three natural fathers and one other relative) were from within the child's family; two were family acquaintances, and two were strangers. Six were Type II abuse, and two were Type III. The perpetrators in these two cases were a family acquaintance and a stranger.

More than half of the referrals to the forensic psychiatrists came from the prison system and the court, but there were no referrals directly from the police department.

Five of the perpetrators were recorded as showing some evidence of family disturbance, primarily poor marital relationship, previous parental criminality, and recurrent or previous sexual abuse of a child.

Following recognition of the sexual abuse, the most frequent action taken was criminal prosecution of the perpetrator. This occurred in seven of the eight cases. Three of the perpetrators were offered therapy by an adult psychiatrist, and in three families one of the child's parents was removed from the home. Two families were referred for social work help. None of the families were referred to a child psychiatry clinic nor were any of the children taken into care or their names placed on the at-risk registers as far as the forensic psychiatrists knew.

In many ways the relationship between the forensic psychiatrist and the perpetrator resembles the relationship between the adult psychiatrist who sees a parent who has physically abused his child. That is, the psychiatrist primarily is concerned with the adult's problems and may not know or be involved in any treatment for the child's emotional or physical difficulties. (For more on the role of the forensic psychiatrist see Chapter Seven.)

Area Review Committees

The chairman of 103 Area Review Committees were circulated. (See earlier footnote for definition.) Fifty-one (50%) responded, but two of these did not contain adequate information. Therefore, the following data is based on 49 returns.

The primary purpose of the enquiry was to determine whether the Area Review Committee considered sexual abuse to be within the rubric of their definition of child abuse. They were specifically asked whether they included Types I, II, and III within the definition. Forty-two (86%) of the 49 Committees included Type I within their definition of child abuse, whereas only 18 (37%) included Type II, and another 18 (37%) included Type III. Of course, there was some overlap, and there were some Committees which included all three types of sexual abuse within their definition of child abuse.

The Committees were asked whether they would only include children who had been sexually abused by a family member within their definition. Thirty-four (69%) of the Committees would use a broader definition, including other members of the household. However, some specifically excluded sexual abuse by a stranger.

Forty-two (86%) of the Committees indicated that they did not have a recommended procedure for dealing with sexual abuse of Types II and III which was different from the non-accidental injury procedure. It was unclear whether the Area Review Committees thought it appropriate to apply the same policies to sexual abuse as they did to physical abuse. Three Committees indicated that they utilized procedures other than those for non-accidental injury. These included procedures in the Children's and Young Person's Acts and departmental policies for dealing with children in moral danger. One Committee thought it was more appropriate to leave such decisions to casework decision than to formulate a policy.

None of the Area Review Committees had any written guidelines for the management of sexual abuse. Although not directly asked on the questionnaire, 18 (37%) of the Committees indicated they were discussing the issue of child sexual abuse and considering some revision of their definitions of non-accidental injury or child abuse and some change in their policies. One other Committee indicated that it was willing to undertake such a review if the survey results indicated that sexual abuse was being widely missed as a problem.

The Committees were asked which types of sexual abuse were placed on their at-risk register. Twenty-five Committees placed Type I on the register; 13 included Type II; 11 included Type III. Very few of the Committees directly stated that they would not place sexually abused children on the register. Many gave qualifying or vague answers; for example, some Committees would only place cases on the register if the case involved physical injury or was serious in nature.

In summary, there is much discrepancy in whether or not sexual abuse is included within the definition of child abuse in the various areas of England. Some Committees are anxious about overloading the present system for identification and treatment of abusive families. "Our Committee is worried about overloading the special child abuse procedures... and thus possibly missing a serious case involving a small baby." These Committees are holding firm to a strict definition of non-accidental injury, excluding sexual abuse unless it involves physical injuries. Other Committees, while sharing some of these same worries about not having enough staff or facilities to cope with an increased number of referrals and the necessity of reviewing cases every six months, are trying to understand the extent of the problem and what can be done by the Review Committee. In some areas sexual abuse was considered to be primarily a criminal matter and, therefore, dealt with almost exclusively by the police and police surgeons.

Only six (12%) of the 49 Area Review Committees were able to provide any statistics regarding the incidence of sexual abuse in their area.

1. Zero of 36 children on register
2. One since 1974
3. One Type I case in 1978; no statistics for Types II and III
4. Seven case conferences in 1978 because of sexual assault; four led to court action
5. 12 unregistered because they were at-risk for sexual abuse
6. Two on register in last three years.

A seventh Committee indicated there was a "fairly high incidence of incest" in their county, but they did not have any statistics.

An attempt was made to directly circulate social service departments in England, but the Association of Directors of Social Services recommended that the Area Review Committees be approached. Therefore, it was not possible to explore procedures within social service departments which were not initiated by Area Review Committees. From the number of cases referred between field social workers and health professionals, it is clear that the sexual abuse cases are being dealt with by social workers without invoking child abuse procedures from the Area Review Committees.

Discussion

The recognition of sexual relations between adults and children as a social problem is a lengthy, difficult process in any country. Avoidance and denial are widespread not only among the public but also among professionals who are concerned about families. Despite publication of research studies, case reports, and editorials on incest and other types of child sexual abuse, it is not until the social and political climate is right that the issue will take hold, generating public and professional interest, increasing the willingness to report such cases, and leading toward improved clinical and legal interventions. The dynamics involved in such an attitudinal change within a country or within certain sub-groups are usually most difficult to determine.

Considering the United Kingdom as an example, it is possible to see how slowly the change has come. In 1958 Greenland[6] and Wells[12] published material on child sexual abuse, and five years later this was followed by the well-known study by Gibbens and Prince[5] of 82 child victims of sex offences which included recommendations for legal reforms. In 1964, McGeorge[9] reported on 400 children who had been sexually assaulted and made specific recommendations regarding interventions. In 1968, Burton[1] published her widely quoted study of 41 children who had been sexually assaulted. (See Chapter Eighteen for an evaluation of this research investigation.) Farn,[4] in 1975, wrote a detailed article for police surgeons in which he reviewed the laws on sexual assaults of children and outlined procedures for medical examination. Editorials and brief commentaries[2,3,13] have also been published. Yet, despite these attempts to enlighten the professional community, no further efforts were made to determine the incidence of child sexual abuse or provide specialized treatment services for the children and families.

Some speculations regarding the factors which have interfered with change are possible. In England, the privacy and sanctity of the home are highly valued, so investigation into a family's personal life is made with extreme caution. Also, the women's movement and rape crisis centers for adult females have played a major role in the recognition of child sexual abuse in the United States, but these social forces are not as well developed in England. The National Society for the Prevention of Cruelty to Children (NSPCC), which has carried a primary responsibility in the area of physical child abuse, initially was reluctant to include sexual abuse cases within its auspices. This organization, like many others, felt that the severe criminal sanctions which could follow recognition would negate any therapeutic efforts with the families. Until the law became less punitive, many social agencies and clinicians did not want to become involved.

In 1980 the climate was changing. Influenced by the work done in the United States, there was more open discussion of the issue, a review on the subject was published,[10] and the government and NSPCC were becoming more involved. The survey reported in this chapter helped to focus some attention on child sexual abuse and generate dialogue among various professional groups.

As recognition of child sexual abuse increases in any country, there are many issues which must be considered. The criteria for making the necessary judgments often will not be explicit but may be intertwined with broader values, beliefs, and practices of the country and/or subcultures of that society. Regardless of the outcome, the questions are very similar. Should child sexual abuse be included within the child abuse spectrum? How should it be defined for legal and therapeutic purposes? How can the law be balanced so the child and family, the perpetrator, and society as a whole can be protected? What services can be provided with client-receptiveness, cost effectiveness, and outcome taken into consideration? How can reliable and valid information be obtained on incidence, individual and family prognosis, availability of treatment resources, treatment effectiveness, and long-term outcome? What professional organization(s) should assume primary responsibility for investigation of suspected cases, treatment, professional and public education, and long-term case coordination? These are the issues to be addressed in this book; their resolution will vary among various countries, local areas, agencies, and professional groups.

References

1. Burton, L. (1968) *Vulnerable Children.* Routledge & Kegan Paul, London.
2. Editorial (1961) Sexual assaults on children. *Br. Med. J.* **2:** 1623.
3. Editorial (1972) Incest and family disorder. *Br. Med. J.* **5810:** 364.
4. Farn, K. T. (1975) Sexual and other assaults on children. *Police Surgeon* **8:** 37.
5. Gibbens, T. C. N. and Prince, J. (1963) *Child Victims of Sex Offences.* Institute for the Study and Treatment of Delinquency, London.
6. Greenland, C. (1958) Incest. *Br. J. Delinquency* **9:** 62.
7. James, J., Womack, W. M., and Stauss, F. (1978) Commentary: physician reporting of sexual abuse of children. *J. Am. Med. Assoc.* **240:** 1145.
8. Kempe, R. S. and Kempe, C. H. (1978) *Child Abuse.* Fontana/Open Books, London.
9. McGeorge, J. (1964) Sexual assaults on children. *Med. Sci. & Law* **4:** 245.
10. Mrazek, P. B. (1980) Annotation: sexual abuse of children. *J. Child Psychol. Psychiatry* **21:** 91.
11. Special Report (1978) *Child sexual abuse: incest, assault and sexual exploitation.* National Center on Child Abuse and Neglect, U.S. DHEW Pub. No. (OHDS) 79–30166.
12. Wells, N. H. (1958) Sexual offences as seen by a woman police surgeon. *Br. Med. J.* Dec. **6:** 1404.
13. Williams, N. H. (1978) Some thoughts on sexual assault. *Police Surgeon Suppl.* **5:** 42.

Acknowledgments

We wish to thank the International Society for the Prevention of Child Abuse and Neglect under whose auspices this study was carried out. We are grateful to the two Family Practitioner Committees who circulated the questionnaire on our behalf.

Part II.

SEXUAL CHILD ABUSE AND THE LAW

Introduction

The laws on sexual child abuse are complicated and diverse, regardless of the country. In this section Fraser reviews the child protection and criminal statutes in the United States and Doek compares the criminal laws of Western and Eastern European countries. While both chapters are theoretical rather than practice-oriented, they raise important issues regarding intervention, some of which are addressed in later chapters by Topper and Aldridge and by Giarretto. Do criminal proceedings give the best solution to child sexual abuse, or do they at least contribute toward that goal? How successful are alternatives such as deferred prosecution, deferred sentencing, and the Israeli system of youth examiners for investigation and court testimony? Is it possible to balance the legal rights of the perpetrator and the psychological needs of the child victim? What are the implications of recent changes in legislation on sexual child abuse?

PATRICIA BEEZLEY MRAZEK
C. HENRY KEMPE

Chapter Five

Sexual Child Abuse: The Legislation and the Law in the United States

BRIAN G. FRASER

Legislation and the law are often viewed as a panacea for all social problems. What they are, however, is simply a framework within which a particular problem may be addressed. If legislation is drafted with some common sense, insight, and a deft hand, it can provide a standardized, efficient, and coordinated system for dealing with that problem. Legislation is never, however, a solution to the problem itself. Similarly, the courts do not provide a solution for they are utilized when everything else fails; they react to a social problem after it has occurred.

This chapter will discuss sexual abuse in the context of the legislation and the law in the United States. It will look at definitions, responsibilities, and shortcomings within the child protection and criminal systems. Finally, it will describe the Israeli system of Youth Examiners, which is an alternative investigatory process for sexual abuse cases.

State and Federal Responsibility for the Sexually Abused Child

Primary responsibility for dealing with sexual abuse rests with each individual state. Each state through a doctrine known as "police powers" has the ultimate authority and right to enact laws which deal with the health, safety, and welfare of its citizens. The federal government does not have the right nor the authority to enact laws which mandate how individual sovereign states will deal with the problems of sexual abuse. Responsibility of debating, drafting, enacting, reviewing, and revising these statutes is with the state legislatures throughout the country.

Each state may enact two different types of laws to deal with the problems of sexual abuse. The first type of law is a *criminal statute.* Deeming some sexual acts between adults and children as abhorrent and reprehensible, the state then classifies these acts as crimes against the state. The purpose of the criminal statute is to punish and deter the perpetrator, and the scope of the criminal statute and the jurisdiction of the criminal court extend only to the perpetrator of the crime. The criminal statute and the criminal court do not provide services or treatment to the abused child or his family. The penalty for conviction of a violation of a criminal statute can be a fine, a jail sentence, or both, even though agreement to undergo treatment can occur, for example, under plea-bargaining arrangements. (See Chapter Nine for a description of how deferred criminal procedures can be utilized.)

The second type of law is a *child protection statute.*[1] The state may deem some sexual acts between children and caretakers so potentially injurious to the child's health, safety, and welfare that certain courts are granted the right to intervene within the family unit.[2] The purpose of the child protection statute is to protect the child's short- and long-range interests and provide treatment where appropriate. While there is no criminal penalty, such as a fine or jail sentence, for violating a child protection statute, there can be responses such as placement of children in foster care and even termination of parental rights if treatment plans are not followed. Also, criminal prosecution may begin in cases which are initially known through the child protection system.

Each of the 50 states has at least two statutes which deal with the problems of sexual abuse: a criminal statute and a child protection statute. The definitions of sexual abuse vary among the states, and even within a particular state there is often no correlation between the definitions of sexual abuse in the two types of statutes.

It is possible that one case of child sexual abuse would work its way through the criminal system and the child protection system. The purpose of the criminal court proceeding would be to punish the perpetrator. The purpose of the child protective proceeding would be to protect the child victim and to provide treatment. The involvement of the child in both the criminal system and the child protective system can prove to be extremely traumatic for the child.

Although the United States Congress is not empowered to enact laws which mandate how the states will deal with sexual abuse, it has had an impact in this area. Through a federal act, which conditions a substantial appropriation to each state upon compliance with federal standards, the Congress can *suggest* how a state should respond.

In 1974, the President of the United States signed into law the Child Abuse Prevention and Treatment Act.[3] The Act defined child abuse to include the element of sexual abuse, but sexual abuse was not defined. Eighty-five million dollars was appropriated to prevent and treat child abuse. The Act also contained ten "suggestions" that were, in effect, ten conditions precedent to a state's receiving federal funds. The Act "requires" a state:

1. To provide a mechanism for the *reporting* of suspected child abuse.
2. To provide a mechanism for the prompt *investigation* of a report of suspected child abuse.
3. To provide appropriate and *trained personnel* to receive and investigate reports of suspected child abuse.
4. To provide *immunity* for civil and criminal liability for persons making good faith reports of suspected child abuse.
5. To provide for the *confidentiality* of child abuse records.
6. To provide for the *cooperation* between agencies involved in child abuse.
7. To provide a *guardian ad litem* to represent the interests of an abused child if the case goes to court.
8. To insure that *state support* for child abuse does not decrease once federal support is provided.
9. To insure that there is a *dissemination of information* about child abuse throughout the state.

10. To provide *preferential treatment* to "parental organizations" dealing with child abuse.

Today, 46 states have fulfilled the above ten conditions and are eligible to receive federal funds under the Child Abuse Prevention and Treatment Act. Therefore, through the Act, the federal government has had a substantial impact on the manner in which individual states deal with the problems of sexual abuse in the child protective system.

The federal government has also had an effect on child sexual abuse through its regulation of interstate commerce. The right to control and regulate interstate commerce was utilized by the federal government in 1948 to enact the *Mann Act*,[4] which made it a federal crime to transport females across state lines for the purpose of prostitution. In 1977, in recognition of the fact that children were increasingly being used in the prostitution trade, the Mann Act was amended.[5] The Mann Act now makes it a federal crime to transport any minor (male or female) across state lines for the purpose of engaging in prostitution or any other prohibited sexual contact.

Developing Legislation and a Legal Definition for Sexual Abuse

The problems of forging prudent legislation, including a definition, to deal with child sexual abuse are sixfold:

1. The range of possible sexual activity between children and adults seems limitless.[6]
2. As a factual matter, it is quite often difficult to distinguish between appropriate displays of affection and the less damaging forms of sexual abuse.
3. In many instances of sexual abuse it is the intent of the perpetrator which is the central issue. Intent can be very difficult to determine.
4. There is some debate concerning the amount of trauma, if any, to children who have been involved in certain types of sexual activity with adults.
5. Minors today are much more sexually active than they were a decade ago, and there no longer seems to be a clear line of demarcation between acceptable and non-acceptable sexual behavior. This is especially true if the child is between 16 and 18 and consents to the act or if there is a small age differential between the two participants and the child consents or initiates the activity.
6. Sex remains an embarrassing subject for many adults. Rather than being specific about terminology and sexual activity, there is a proclivity to ignore it or define it in vague language.

Two primary issues must be resolved before any concise legislation can be drafted. What specific sexual activity is to be prohibited? Can this sexual activity be defined? Both issues may be resolved affirmatively and have been in several states. Failure to forge a workable legal definition for sexual abuse will contribute to underreporting and inability to determine the scope of the problem. It is difficult to expect professionals to report suspected sexual abuse if they are not given guidance in determining what sexual abuse is.

Types of Sexual Abuse Which Could be Included Within a Legal Definition of Sexual Abuse

Sexual abuse of children may be classified into three different types: non-touching, touching, and violent touching. (For other definitions see Chapter One.) The type of sexual abuse is likely to make a considerable difference in the impact that it has on the child victim. Since criminal statutes are often interwoven with the concept of damage or trauma to the victim, it is not unusual to see different criminal definitions of sexual abuse within the same state, each with a different penalty.

Non-touching acts include verbal sexual abuse (continual, ongoing discussions, referrals, or solicitations concerning sexual activity), obscene telephone calls, exhibitionism (a difficult issue if the perpetrator is a member of the child's household), voyeurism (again, a difficult issue if the perpetrator is a member of the child's household), and visual or auditory exposure to adults engaged in sexual activity.

The *touching acts* include fondling (once again, a difficult issue if the perpetrator is a member of the child's household), masturbation, fellatio, cunnilingus, anilingus, anal intercourse, and sexual intercourse.

Violent touching acts include fondling, masturbation, fellatio, cunnilingus, anilingus, anal intercourse, or sexual intercourse coupled with serious bodily injury or the threat of serious bodily injury (rape).

With a few limited exceptions in the touching category (primarily having to do with the age of the participants and consent of the child) most legal definitions, that is, child protection statutes and criminal statutes, include the touching and violent touching activities. While each of the touching and violent touching acts can be specifically defined, a surprising number of states do not do so. Instead, they attempt to include such activity within the legislation by utilizing such vague and broad terms as "lewd and lascivious behavior".

Additional Factors to Consider

Although the type of sexual abuse may make a considerable difference in the impact that it has on a child (and consequently, it is closely tied to the severity of the penalty), there are some additional factors which should be considered in the drafting of sexual abuse legislation. The majority of sexual abuse cases involve a family member or friend of the family, are not violent in nature, and in all likelihood have been occurring over a period of time. Therefore, the length of the abusive behavior, the child's familiarity with perpetrator, and the amount of violence involved in the sexual activity need to be considered when determining the severity of the penalty and the need to intervene within the family unit.

An Operational or Working Definition of Sexual Abuse

For the purposes of this chapter, child sexual abuse will be given an operational definition as follows: "the *exploitation* of a child for *the sexual gratification* of an adult".

The word "exploitation" conveys a meaning of an unjust and improper use of another person for one's own profit or advantage. In our society children are frequently exploited. In part, this is because they have diminished knowledge and experience, a desire to please, and innate curiosity. They are easily enticed, entrapped, and intimidated by fears of being blamed, not being believed, and of being punished or abandoned by their parents. They have been brought up in an environment which rewards obedience to adults. Many children because of their age do not have the ability to articulate their fears, concerns, and problems. The developmental needs of children must be considered when determining what constitutes exploitation. The intent of the perpetrator and the effects of the sexual abuse on the child are separate matters.

The word "child" is neutral. The child victim can be male or female. Child is not defined in terms of age.* What is clearly not permissible for a 10-year-old child may not be so neatly resolved for a 17-year-old adolescent. In many of the legal definitions which follow in the next section, there are two or more age categories of children within a single statute. For example, many states believe that a child under 14 years of age is emotionally immature and incapable of making reasonable judgments about sexual relationships with adults. In these states, any sexual activity between a child under 14 and an adult is prohibited. The same is not true of children above the age of 14 but under the age of 18 (age of emancipation). In this age bracket, some sexual activity with adults is permitted. The limiting conditions are that the child consent to the sexual activity or initiate it, the sexual activity be short of sexual intercourse, and the age differential between the child and the adult be less than four years.

The term "sexual gratification" means that the act was done for the purpose of deriving some sexual arousal or sexual pleasure. For example, the purpose of the fondling was not to demonstrate affection for a close family member or friend but to derive sexual satisfaction.

The word "adult" is neutral. The perpetrator can be male or female. A specific age is not indicated although it usually means that the individual is above the age of emancipation.

Comprehensive and Specific Definitions

The problem of sexual abuse is so complex that a short, simple definition will not suffice. The fact that a legal definition cannot be short does not mean that it cannot be specific, for it can. In order to address appropriately the issues of different types of sexual activity, sexual activity with a minor's consent, sexual activity of an older minor, and sexual abuse coupled with violence, a comprehensive act is a necessity. There are no comprehensive sexual abuse codifications in child protection legislation, but there are in some state criminal laws. The development of these comprehensive acts was a recent and welcome change. They clearly delineate what sexual activity is permissible at which age and what sexual activity is not permissible, and each form of sexual abuse is clearly and specifically defined.

---

* *Editors' note:* Power, as well as age, must be taken into consideration. Having superior physical strength and/or intelligence as well as an aura of authority may differentiate the perpetrator and the victim when they are close in age or one is handicapped.

The Child Protection System

In America, a parent is given the rights of care, custody, and control of his or her children. When a parent unreasonably or grossly abuses these rights, the state may intervene under the doctrine of *parens patriae* to insure that the child's health, safety, and welfare will be protected. This process of intervention into the family is through the child protection system. When a child is sexually abused by a parent or caretaker, the state may intervene under the doctrine of *parens patriae.* The steps involved in resolving a case of sexual abuse are identification, investigation, and intervention.

Identification

Every state has a mandatory child abuse reporting statute which requires that a report be made when an individual believes or suspects that a child has been abused. A majority of states define child abuse to include sexual molestation. Additionally, each reporting statute identifies at least one statewide agency to receive and investigate such reported cases.

Identification is complicated when child sexual abuse is not clearly defined. Although 45 states[7] specifically require that suspected cases of sexual abuse be reported, only 13 states[8] make any attempt to define sexual abuse. Twelve of the states do this by referring to another section of the state statutes, usually the criminal code. Indiana, for example, defines child sexual abuse to mean,

> "... circumstances where the child is a victim of a sex offense as defined by I.C. 35-42-4, I.C. 35-45-4.1 or I.C. 35-46-1.3 ..."[9]

Only one state, Maryland, has attempted to define sexual abuse within the mandatory reporting statute itself. In Maryland, sexual abuse is defined as,

> "Any act or acts involving sexual molestation or exploitation, including but not limited to incest or rape, or any sexual offense in any degree, sodomy, or unnatural or perverted sexual practice on a child by any parent, adoptive parent, or any other person who has permanent or temporary custody or responsibility for supervising a minor child".[10]

The remaining 32 states which require that sexual abuse be reported do not define it. These statutes simply say that sexual abuse must be reported to the appropriate state agency. Alabama, for example, mandates that certain professionals report suspected cases of child abuse. Child abuse is defined as,

> "... harm or threatened harm to a child's health or welfare. Harm or threatened harm to a child's welfare can occur through non-accidental physical or mental injury, sexual abuse or attempted sexual abuse".[11]

It is fair to say that the states which require that sexual abuse be reported but do not define it would require, at a minimum, that sexual intercourse between children and adults be reported. Beyond this point, the lines of demarcation separating acceptable from non-acceptable behavior are not clear.[12] Activities which fall within the non-touching component of sexual abuse are particularly problematic for reporting purposes.

In an effort to meet the requirements of the federal Child Abuse and Prevention Act, some states simply met the minimum standards which included expanding the definition of child abuse to include sexual abuse. The legislators may have done this with the intent of coming back at a later date and sharpening up the language, that is, defining sexual abuse more specifically.

Investigation

In most states the mandatory reporting statute requires that reports of sexual abuse be made to the local department of social services.* Since each reporting statute requires that reports be made when a person believes or suspects that a child has been sexually abused, it is the department's responsibility to conduct a thorough investigation to determine, if indeed, the child has been sexually abused. That is, the investigating agency must determine if a child's injuries or the parents' behavior can be classified as sexual abuse under state law. Once abuse has been established, the prognosis must be determined and a treatment program established.

Social service departments can only make thorough investigations if they have an adequate number of well-trained social workers who are given standards to guide them in making appropriate decisions and have the support of multidisciplinary teams. (The role of social services and the option of conjoint investigations with caseworkers and juvenile court officers is discussed in Chapter Nine.)

Intervention

The term "intervention" means that the treatment plan developed at the conclusion of the investigation is made operational. There are two types of intervention in the child protection system: voluntary and involuntary.

In a situation involving intervention, the social worker and the child's family agree that a problem does exist, and the family voluntarily agrees to undergo treatment. The social worker will continue to work with the family and monitor progress. When the home environment is stabilized, the child is safe, and the treatment plan seems to be working, the social worker will withdraw.

Involuntary intervention means that the juvenile court or district court with juvenile jurisdiction mandates the treatment plan. This is done when the parents will not cooperate with the social worker, there is a long history of abuse, or there is continual concern for the child's safety. Involuntary intervention, which is a much more formalized procedure than voluntary intervention, requires many additional steps.

Juvenile Court

The majority of sexual abuse cases that are identified and reported eventually find their way into the juvenile court. The purpose of the juvenile court is to protect the

---

* *Editors' note:* Police departments may also be informed in accordance with state law. The district attorney usually has an obligation to investigate all cases of sexual abuse including rape and incest, but he may elect not to proceed with prosecution.

health, safety, and welfare of the child victim and provide treatment where appropriate. While the juvenile court's jurisdiction extends to the child victim and in some states to the child's caretakers, it does not extend to a perpetrator who is not a parent or caretaker of the child victim. However, a parent's failure to protect the child against a "third party" perpetrator may bring the issue to juvenile court.

The burden of proof in the juvenile court is either a preponderance of the evidence or evidence which is clear and convincing. This burden of proof is substantially lower than the criminal court which requires proof beyond a reasonable doubt.

There are two *major* hearings in a case of sexual abuse in the juvenile court. The first is the *adjudicatory hearing*. At this hearing there is only one issue to resolve. Can the child's injuries or the parents' behavior be classified as sexual abuse as defined by state law? In the juvenile court it is not necessary to show who did what to whom or to establish the guilt of the perpetrator. It is sufficient to demonstrate with the requisite burden of proof that the child has been sexually abused. If this cannot be demonstrated, all legal proceedings must cease. If it can be demonstrated that the child had been sexually abused, the juvenile court will order that the second proceeding be held.

The second formal proceeding is called the *dispositional hearing*. At this hearing there are two issues to resolve. To whom shall custody of the child be awarded, and what treatment should be provided?

Juvenile courts have the authority to hear three different types of cases involving children: juvenile delinquency, status offenses, and neglect. In a very general way, neglect might be construed to mean those cases in which the parents have grossly or unreasonably violated their duties of care, custody, and control. While most state statutes do not specifically mention sexual abuse in their neglect statutes, courts regularly intervene on this basis. Many states, for example, have a statute similar to California's which defines a neglected child as,

> "... a child whose home is an unfit place for him by reason of neglect, cruelty, depravity or physical abuse by either of his parents, or his guardians, or other person in whose custody or care he is ..."[13]

Colorado's statute defines a neglected child as a child

> "whose environment is injurious to his welfare ..."[14]

Although sexual abuse is not specifically mentioned in either one of these statutes, they are easily interpreted to include the element of sexual abuse.

There are some problems in juvenile court pertaining to its jurisdiction and decision-making regarding sexual abuse. First of all, although the juvenile court clearly has the right to intervene in cases of sexual abuse involving a child and his caretakers, there is no common agreement concerning the scope of this right. While acts of sexual intercourse, fellatio, masturbation, cunnilingus, anilingus, and oral intercourse would obviously be appropriate for juvenile court intervention, activities which fall within the non-touching category are not so easily resolved.

Secondly, it is sometimes very difficult to prove a case of sexual abuse in the juvenile court given the requisite burden of proof. In some cases the data which has been collected during the investigation is inadequate. All involved in case preparation must use all *appropriate* means of legal discovery, such as court-ordered mental evaluations of the parents or child. The greater the time differential between the sexual abuse and the time it is reported, the more difficult it is to collect relevant information. Also, there is sometimes a failure to conduct a timely and thorough medical examination of the child victim. Finally, it is often quite difficult to find any eye-witnesses to the attack or any eye-witnesses willing to testify. This is especially true of cases of sexual abuse involving family members or friends of the family. The perpetrator cannot, of course, be forced to testify. A spouse may also refuse due to fears of retaliation or break-up of the family. The child victim is often too young to testify. To determine if a child may testify most states use a two-pronged test:

1. Is the child old enough to articulate properly?
2. Does the child know what the truth is, and can s/he distinguish between right and wrong?

Even if the child is deemed able to testify by the juvenile court judge, s/he is often very unwilling or hesitant to do so. S/he may fear retaliation by the perpetrator, fear of being blamed or not believed, or feel ashamed or humiliated. If the perpetrator is a family member or a close friend, there can be a tremendous pressure for the child to amend his or her original testimony or refuse to testify at further hearings. Despite these difficulties, however, there is usually one individual, a social worker, a lawyer, or a doctor who has enough expertise or interest to insure that the court is provided at least baseline data.

Statutes are not the only guidelines available to the courts. Other cases of child abuse which have similar fact situations are often viewed by courts as precedents. The more similar the fact situation, the greater the credence the trial court will give it. All of the cases which cover the same subject, such as sexual abuse, are collectively referred to as the case law. The more extensive the case law, the greater the likelihood that the trial court will be able to find a similar case and the greater the guidance in reaching a decision. Good case law can compensate for poor quality statutory law. Unfortunately, there is not much case law concerning sexual abuse within the child protection system and the juvenile court. The decisions of juvenile courts are not routinely recorded and codified. Only decisions which have been appealed to a higher court are recorded and codified, and the vast majority of juvenile cases are not appealed.

The Criminal System

Sexual abuse of children is a crime in every state. Like the child protection system, however, there is no common agreement among the states concerning what constitutes criminal sexual abuse. At a minimum it might be said that sexual intercourse between children and adults is a crime in every state. Beyond this point, the lines of demarcation between acceptable and non-acceptable sexual behavior are often not clear. In general, the statutory enactments, the definitions, and the case law concerning sexual abuse in the criminal system are much more comprehensive than in the child protection system.

The successful resolution of a case of sexual abuse in the criminal system follows the same steps and procedures as it does in the child protection system, that is, identification, investigation, and intervention. There are only three major differences:

1. In the criminal system, the police, not the department of social services, receive the report of suspected sexual abuse and investigate it. The purposes of the police investigation are to determine if the child's injuries or the adult's behavior can be classified as sexual abuse under the state's criminal code, and to determine what charges, if any, should be lodged against the suspected perpetrator.
2. Unlike the child protection system, the investigator in a criminal case does not make the final decision. When the police complete the investigation, the data is forwarded to the district attorney's office, and it is he who decides if sexual abuse has occurred and whether or not it is possible and appropriate to prosecute the suspected perpetrator under the state's criminal code. In some of the larger district attorneys' offices there are investigators who can be used to complement the police investigation.
3. The primary purpose of the criminal system is to punish the perpetrator. While the district attorney may consider the child's safety, the unity of the family, and treatment when reviewing his options, his first responsibility is to determine if a crime has been committed and to prosecute the case.

Criminal Court

The jurisdiction of the criminal court extends only to the perpetrator, not to the child victim or parents, unless the suspected perpetrator is one of the child's parents. The burden of proof in the criminal court is beyond a reasonable doubt which is substantially higher than the burden required in the juvenile court. The result, of course, is that it is much more difficult to prove a case of sexual abuse in the criminal court than it is in the juvenile court. A successful prosecution in the criminal court requires a showing and proof of two elements. The district attorney must establish that the perpetrator committed an unlawful act and that the act was committed with an unlawful intent. In a case of sexual abuse in the criminal court the district attorney must establish with the requisite burden of proof that the child has been sexually abused, that the defendant is the one who committed the sexual abuse, and that the defendant committed the sexual abuse with the requisite intent. In contrast, in the juvenile court it is sufficient to establish that the child has been sexually abused.

In any state, a case of sexual abuse in the criminal court system may involve at least three separate legal hearings. The first is a *preliminary hearing* where probable cause must be shown. This means that the district attorney must present enough evidence to convince the court that an offense has been committed by the defendant. If the defendant is accused of a crime which is classified as a felony, the case may be sent to the *grand jury* whose responsibility it is to determine if the case will proceed to the criminal court for adjudication. The defendant in a criminal action has a right to be present and confront his accuser (the child) at a preliminary hearing, but there is no such right in a grand jury hearing. The defendant does not have a constitutional right to a preliminary hearing and, therefore, in some communities the district attorney will skip this hearing.

The third proceeding is the *trial* itself. At the trial the district attorney must prove beyond a reasonable doubt that the child has been sexually abused, that the defendant sexually abused the child, and that he did it with the requisite intent.

If a defendant pleads guilty or is found guilty, punishment can mean a fine, a jail sentence, or both. If the perpetrator is one of the child's parents, the sentence may be deferred by the court while attempts are made to provide for treatment and improvement in the parent–child relationship.*

Incest

In general terms, incest may be defined as "a sexual relationship between people of a kinship pattern for whom marriage is prohibited by law". Some researchers have suggested that in at least 50% of child sexual abuse cases the perpetrator is a natural parent while a significant percentage of the remaining perpetrators are other relatives of the child.[15]

While the definition of incest in the criminal statutes varies from state to state, most incest statutes attempt to do two different things:

1. They attempt to prevent marriages between individuals who are closely related.
2. They attempt to prevent the sexual abuse of children by their relatives. The purpose of the first is to protect the *genetic pool*. The purpose of the second is to protect the *child*. The tendency to mix both purposes in one statute can be problematic.

Every state except Vermont[16] has enacted a statute which specifically deals with incest. The majority of these states' incest statutes fit one of three patterns. The incest statute may prohibit marriage between closely related individuals and prohibit sexual activities with minor relatives.[17] The statute may only prohibit sexual activities between individuals who are closely related,[18] or the statute may prohibit sexual intercourse between persons who are prohibited by another statute from marrying.[19] The class of victims protected by these statutes varies substantially. In some states, incest is defined to include sexual activity between blood relatives only. In other states the scope of protected victims is broadened to include step-children, grandchildren, and adopted children. The prohibited sexual activity also varies from state to state. In some states only sexual intercourse is prohibited while in other states this is expanded to include other forms of sexual activity.

Colorado, for example, has enacted a statute entitled *Aggravated Incest*. This statute says:

> "Any person who has sexual intercourse with his or her natural child, stepchild or child by adoption, unless legally married to the stepchild or child by adoption, commits aggravated incest.
> "For the purposes of this statute only, child means a person under 21 years of age.
> "Aggravated incest is a class 4 felony."[20]

---

* *Editors' note:* Some perpetrators plead guilty for a deferred or more lenient sentence. Deferred sentencing is used extensively by the treatment program in San Jose, California. Deferred prosecution is an alternative course of action which is frequently used in Colorado. Criminal charges are filed but are not acted upon while the perpetrator is given a trial period for rehabilitation. This usually means he agrees to a prescribed course of therapy. If results are not favorable, the criminal charges still go forward.

The purpose of Colorado's Aggravated Incest statute is to protect children from sexual abuse by related adults. The prohibited activity is limited to sexual intercourse. The class of protected victims, however, covers not only natural children but adopted and stepchildren as well.

Other Statutory Sexual Abuse Crimes

There are, in addition to incest statutes, a plethora of other types of criminal statutes prohibiting sexual activity between children and adults. It is possible to arbitrarily divide these remaining statutes into two classes: non-codified and codified.

Non-codified Sexual Abuse Statutes. Non-codified statutory enactments are characteristic of how states used to deal with the problem of sexual abuse. Each statute deals with a different class of victim, a different class of perpetrator, and a different kind of sexual activity. The proscribed activities are usually not specifically defined, and the element of intent is defined in an oblique, broad manner. Since intent must be established in a criminal prosecution, the language of these statutes makes the crime more difficult to prove. For each type of criminal sexual activity, a punishment is listed. Although one state may have a number of these non-codified statutes, there is no cross-referencing and no standardization of terms. (See Appendix A for examples of non-codified abuse statutes.)

Codified Sexual Abuse Statutes. In recent years some states have reviewed, rewritten, and codified all crimes involving sexual matters into one Act.[21] Unlike those states which have a non-codified system for crimes of sexual abuse, these new Acts are characterized by:

1. A clear and concise definition of sexual abuse. These statutes are specific in detailing what is and what is not permissible sexual activity between an adult and a child.
2. A clear explanation of the required intent. These statutes make the element of intent easier to determine.
3. A recognition that children today are more sexually mature than they were a decade ago. These statutes characteristically lower the age requirements for certain types of consensual sexual activity.
4. A codification of all prohibited sexual activity in one place in the statute books. The sexual crimes are arranged according to the type of sexual activity, the age of the child, the age of the perpetrator, and the degree of force or threat of force used. (See Appendix B for an example and discussion of a codified sexual abuse statute.)

Problems in the Criminal Court and Case Law

Many of the problems that plague the juvenile court in cases of child sexual abuse also plague the criminal court. Additionally, there are problems which are indigenous to the criminal court.[22] Because the burden of proof and the penalties are much greater, there is a vigorous effort to thoroughly protect the defendant's rights. The

United States Constitution through the Sixth and Fourteenth Amendments guarantees the defendant the right of counsel, the right to a speedy and public trial, the right to confront the accuser (the child), and the right of cross-examination. The overall result can be a highly traumatic experience for the child. The child must once again, this time in open court, face the perpetrator, relate the details of the incident, and suffer through the cross-examination. As a practical matter, the criminal court has a cold and formal ambiance. The actual proceedings can drag on for months because postponements and continuances are common events. The longer the legal proceedings continue, the greater the pressure for the child. If the defendant is a relative or friend of the family, there is often a constant and insidious pressure for the child to recant his/her original testimony or refuse to testify at later proceedings. The criminal court process can inflict as much trauma on the child as the sexual abuse itself.

There is one positive difference between the child protection system and the criminal system. In the criminal court, because the penalties are so severe, more cases are appealed. The results of these appeals are compiled and listed in *State Reporters*, and the cases become the case law. In criminal cases of sexual abuse there is a great body of case law which can provide the lawyers and the court with guidance in rendering a reasonable and equitable decision. The value of these criminal proceedings must be questioned. There is no concrete evidence that the threat of incarceration itself is a deterrent to sexual abuse. However, in many cases the criminal process can be used as leverage to insure constant participation in a treatment program. In these cases the defendant is found guilty of sexual abuse, but sentencing is postponed on the condition that the defendant seek out and receive treatment. The child protection system may be actively involved in the same case. If the perpetrator cannot be helped, the least detrimental alternative may be incarceration.

Cooperation between Child Protection and Criminal Systems

It is not unusual for child sexual abuse cases to wind their way through the state's child protection system *and* criminal system. Table 1 traces the events in each system from the time the report is received. In some communities there is cooperation and coordination between the two systems, but in many communities there is not. Each system may function in a vacuum, jealously protecting its own perceived authority. The child is, in effect, victimized twice—once by the abuser and once by the system. S/he may be required to "relive" the abuse in the process of retelling it to authorities in each system and may be subjected to long delays in any action that is taken. There is no reason, either legally or practically, that there could not be more creative coordination and cooperation between the child protection system and the criminal system. It may be up to the child advocates to force this issue in the communities where it has not already happened.

The Youth Examiners of Israel

Several countries, including Scotland, Sweden, and Denmark, have been creative in their responses to child sexual abuse. Israel has been remarkably innovative and daring. In 1955, the Israeli Knesset enacted what is now known as the Protection of

Table 1
*A Simplified Comparison of the Child Protection System and the Criminal System in an Example of a Case of Child Sexual Abuse**

Incident of
Child Sexual Abuse

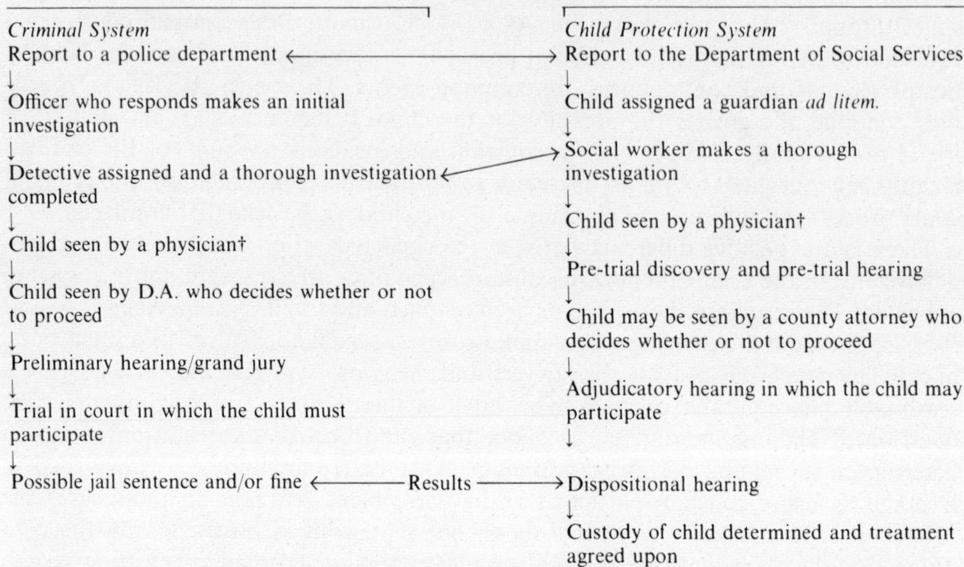

Criminal System	*Child Protection System*
Report to a police department ←→	Report to the Department of Social Services
↓	↓
Officer who responds makes an initial investigation	Child assigned a guardian *ad litem.*
↓	↓
Detective assigned and a thorough investigation completed ←→	Social worker makes a thorough investigation
↓	↓
Child seen by a physician†	Child seen by a physician†
↓	↓
Child seen by D.A. who decides whether or not to proceed	Pre-trial discovery and pre-trial hearing
↓	↓
Preliminary hearing/grand jury	Child may be seen by a county attorney who decides whether or not to proceed
↓	↓
Trial in court in which the child must participate	Adjudicatory hearing in which the child may participate
↓	↓
Possible jail sentence and/or fine ← Results →	Dispositional hearing
	↓
	Custody of child determined and treatment agreed upon

* Relatively few of all incidents of child sexual abuse are actually brought to the attention of society and reported to the police department and/or department of social services. For those which are, much of the activity in the child protection system and the criminal system is a duplication, regardless of the point of entry of the child into the process. Coordination of these processes is in the best interests of the child.

† The physician may be asked to see the child immediately after the report is made. Usually, it is the same physician who sees the child under both the criminal and child protection systems.

Children Law.[23] This law altered the basic rules of evidence in cases of sexual abuse and established new procedures for investigating those cases. The heart of this law was a new cadre of individuals who would serve as *youth examiners.*

This law took the investigatory powers away from the police in cases of child sexual abuse and gave them to the youth examiners. Today, police in Israel may not interview the child victim. The right and responsibility to interview the child is that of a youth examiner. There are only two exceptions to this rule. The police may interview the child if the late arrival of the youth examiner would impede the proper examination, and when it is necessary to prevent further crimes. To insure that the police do not abuse these two exceptions, the youth examiner has been given two additional rights. He may veto the admission of any statement taken by the police from the child without his permission, and he may forbid the police to perform any act which would require the presence and the participation of the child. The practical result of these two powers is to prevent a complete investigation and a successful filing in the court without the active participation and cooperation of the youth examiner.

When the police in Israel receive a report of suspected sexual abuse, they immediately notify the youth examiner who then begins his own investigation. S/he controls, by law, all aspects of the investigation including the interviews with the child, the medical examination, the process of identifying the perpetrator, and all appearances in court. At the conclusion of the investigation the youth examiner and the police will decide if court action is appropriate. If a decision is made to file the case in a court of law, the youth examiner will make a decision concerning the child's participation. If s/he feels that the child is capable of testifying, s/he will explain the legal process and the purpose of the proceeding and will provide moral support and reassurance in the courtroom. If s/he decides that it would be psychologically traumatic for the child to testify, the rules of evidence are relaxed, and the youth examiner may testify in the child's place. If there is an issue which the court believes is not resolved, it can ask the youth examiner to make an additional inquiry of the child. If the youth examiner believes that this would prove too traumatic to the child, s/he may refuse. Although the rules of evidence have been relaxed to allow the youth examiner to testify in place of the child, the law also states that the defendant cannot be convicted by the youth examiner's testimony alone. There must be some additional corroborative evidence.

Youth examiners are chosen by a committee consisting of a judge, a mental health expert, an educator, a child and youth expert, and a police official. Candidates are recruited from the fields of clinical psychology, psychiatric social work, psychiatry, social work, and probation. They are individuals who demonstrate knowledge of child development, sexual abuse, rules of evidence, legal procedures, trial techniques, and interviewing skills. They are non-threatening, empathetic individuals who relate well with children. They are paid a fixed fee plus expenses and may be dismissed if they prove to be ineffectual.

It is highly unlikely that this kind of a system would ever be accepted in America. The constitutional rights of confrontation and cross-examination are too jealously guarded to be abrogated. This is not to say, however, that portions of our current system could not be altered and improved. There is no reason why one individual like the youth examiner could not conduct the investigation with the child. The investigating data could then be made available to both the criminal and child protection systems. There is also no reason why the courtroom procedures could not be relaxed to soften the traumatic impact of confrontation and cross-examination of a child. Guardians *ad litem* are already assertively representing children in many juvenile courts, and victim-oriented programs are helping prepare children for the investigatory and judicial processes, especially criminal proceedings. *Above all, there must be cooperation between the criminal and child protection systems.* How this is to be done will vary from one area to another, for as yet there is no sure way of knowing what policies and procedures work best.

Conclusion

Legislation and the courts do not offer a solution to the problems of child sexual abuse, but they are a framework within which the problem can be addressed. Sexual abuse is primarily the responsibility of the individual states. Codification of sexual abuse laws has been a big step forward in many states. Currently, many attempts are being made to draft model laws for both the criminal and the juvenile courts which states can use as guidelines when they revise their legislation. In the end, however, what is needed is not more law but more services, both to offenders and to victims and their families.

Appendix A

Examples of Non-Codified Sexual Abuse Statutes

Mississippi has enacted a statute, *Touching and Handling a Child for Lustful Purposes*, which reads:

"Any male person above the age of 18 years, who, for the purpose of gratifying his lust, or indulging his depraved, licentious sexual desires, shall handle, touch, rub with hand or any part of his body or any member thereof, any child under the age of 14 years, with or without his consent, shall be guilty of a high-crime and upon conviction thereof, shall be fined in any sum not less than $10.00 nor more than $1,000.00 or be imprisoned in the state penitentiary for not less than one year nor more than ten years . . ."[1]

This statute demonstrates a lack of clarity; words such as "lust", "depraved" and "licentious" are oblique and unclear. The statute also incorrectly assumes that only males sexually abuse children.

Similarly, Alabama has enacted a statute entitled *Child Molestation* which reads:

"It shall be unlawful for any person to take or attempt to take any immoral, improper or indecent liberties with any child of either sex under the age of 16 years with the intent of arousing, appealing to or gratifying the lust of such person or of such child, or both such person and such child, or to commit, or attempt to commit any lewd, lascivious act upon or with the body, or any part or member thereof, of such child, with an intent of arousing, appealing to or gratifying the lust or passions or sexual desires, either of such person or such child, or of both such person and such child . . ."[2]

Again, in this statute neither the acts prohibited nor the requisite intent are clear. The non-codified statutes in other states range from: *Child Molestation*[3] in Alabama, to *Lewd and Lascivious Acts Towards Minors*[4] in Alaska, to *Sexual Conduct with a Minor*[5] in Arizona, to *Indecent Acts with a Child*[6] in Washington, D.C., to *Contributions to Sexual Delinquency of a Child*[7] in Illinois, to *Sexual Abuse of Minors*[8] in Maine, to *Indecent Assault and Battery on a Child Under Fourteen*[9] in Massachusetts, to *Touching and Handling of a Child for Lustful Purposes*[10] in Mississippi.

References

1. Mississippi: Miss. Code Ann. §97-5-23 (1972).
2. Alabama: Ala. Code §13-1-113 (1975).
3. See reference #2.
4. Alaska: Alaska Stat. 11.15.134 (1970).
5. Arizona: Ar. Rev. Stat. §13-1405 (1978).
6. Wash. D.C. Code Encyclopedia 22-1112 (1967).
7. Illinois: Ill. Rev. Stat. §38-11-5 (1978 Supp.).
8. Maine: Me. Rev. Stat. Title 17A, 254 (1978 Cum. Pamphlet).
9. Massachusetts: Mass. Gen. Laws Ann. (L265 #13)(B) (1968).
10. Mississippi: Miss. Code Ann. §97-5-23 (1972).

Appendix B

Colorado's Codified Sexual Abuse Statute

Colorado has enacted as part of its criminal code a section entitled *Unlawful Sexual Behavior.*[1] In part, this statute reads:

"18-3-401. *Definitions.*

(2) 'Intimate parts' means the external genitalia or the perineum or the anus or the pubes of any person or the breast of a female person.

(4) 'Sexual contact' means the intentional touching of the victim's intimate parts by the actor, or of the actor's intimate parts by the victim, or the intentional touching of the clothing covering the immediate area of the victim's or actor's intimate parts if that sexual contact can reasonably be construed as being for the purposes of sexual arousal, gratification, or abuse.

(5) 'Sexual intrusion' means any intrusion, however slight, by any object to any part of a person's body, except the mouth, tongue, or penis, into the genital or anal opening of another person's body if that sexual intrusion can reasonably be construed as being for the purposes of sexual arousal, gratification, or abuse.

(6) 'Sexual penetration' means sexual intercourse, cunnilingus, fellatio, analingus, or anal intercourse. Emission need not be proved as an element of any sexual penetration. Any penetration, however slight, is sufficient to complete the crime.

18-3-402. *Sexual Assault in the first degree.*

(1) Any actor who inflicts sexual penetration on a victim commits a sexual assault in the first degree if:

(a) The actor causes submission of the victim through the actual application of physical force or physical violence; or

(b) The actor causes submission of the victim by threat of imminent death, serious bodily injury, extreme pain, or kidnapping, to be inflicted on anyone, and the victim believes that the actor has the present ability to execute these threats; or

(c) The actor causes submission of the victim by threatening to retaliate in the future against the victim, or any other person, and the victim reasonably believes the actor will execute this threat. As used in this paragraph (c), 'to retaliate' includes threats of kidnapping, death, serious bodily injury, or extreme pain; or

(d) The actor has substantially impaired the victim's power to appraise or control the victim's conduct by employing, without the victim's consent, any drug, intoxicant, or other means for the purpose of causing submission; or

(e) The victim is physically helpless and the actor knows the victim is physically helpless and the victim has not consented.

(2) Sexual assault in the first degree is a class 3 felony, but it is a class 2 felony if:

(a) In the commission of the sexual assault the actor is physically aided or abetted by one or more other persons; or

(b) The victim suffers serious bodily injury; or

(c) The actor is armed with a deadly weapon and uses the deadly weapon to cause submission of the victim.

18-3-403. *Sexual assault in the second degree.*

(1) Any actor who inflicts sexual penetration or sexual intrusion on a victim commits sexual assault in the second degree if:....

(e) At the time of the commission of the act, the victim is less than fifteen years of age and the actor is at least four years older than the victim; or

(f) At the time of the commission of the act, the victim is less than eighteen years of age and the actor is the victim's guardian or is responsible for the general supervision of the victim's welfare.

(2) Sexual assault in the second degree is a class 4 felony, but it is a class 3 felony if the actor inflicts sexual intrusion on a victim by use of such force, intimidation, or threat as specified in section 18-3-402(1)(a), (1)(b), or (1)(c).

18-3-404. *Sexual assault in the third degree.*

(1) Any actor who subjects a victim to any sexual contact commits sexual assault in the third degree if:....

(e) At the time of the commission of the act, the victim is less than eighteen years of age and the actor is the victim's guardian or is otherwise responsible for the general supervision of the victim's welfare.

(2) Sexual assault in the third degree is a class 1 misdemeanor, but it is a class 4 felony if the actor compels the victim to submit by use of such force, intimidation, or threat as specified in section 18-3-402(1)(a), (1)(b), or (1)(c).

18-3-405. *Sexual assault on a child.*

(1) Any actor who subjects another not his or her spouse to any sexual contact commits a sexual assault on a child if the victim is less than fifteen years of age and the actor is at least four years older than the victim.

(2) Sexual assault on a child is a class 4 felony, but it is a class 3 felony if the actor commits the offense on a victim by use of such force, intimidation or threat as specified in section 18-3-402(1)(a), (1)(b), or (1)(c).

18-3-406. *Criminality of conduct.*

(1) If the criminality of conduct depends on a child's being below the age of eighteen and the child was in fact at least fifteen years of age, it shall be an affirmative defense that the defendant reasonably believed the child to be eighteen years of age or older.

(2) If the criminality of conduct depends upon a child being below the age of fifteen, it shall be no defense that the defendant did not know the child's age or that he reasonably believed the child to be fifteen years of age or older."

The first section of this codification is a list of definitions. The terms "intimate parts", "sexual contact", "sexual intrusion" and "sexual intercourse" are all specifically and clearly defined. The range of prohibited sexual activities between adults and children greatly exceed the scope of sexual intercourse. Each crime which follows in the codification is differentiated according to the type of sexual activity, the age of the child, and the degree of force. The more traumatic the sexual activity, the younger the child, and the greater the force, the greater the penalty. Colorado has drafted its codification (like most other states in this classification) in such a manner that the defendant's intent is *not* an essential element of the crime. Although the district attorney must show intent on the part of the defendant, this intent can be inferred from the defendant's actions. The language is couched in such a way that the district attorney does not have to demonstrate that the defendant acted with a purpose of sexual gratification. The language says that the action of touching the victim can "be reasonably construed as being for the purpose of sexual arousal, gratification or abuse". All the district attorney must establish is the fact that the defendant did indeed sexually abuse the child.

The Colorado codification uses the terms "victim" and "actor" (defendant) which are neutral terms. The statute has been drafted with the recognition that victims and perpetrators can be male or female. In a number of the sections the statute's language makes reference to the age differential between the child and the adult. The drafters of the Colorado codification were fully cognizant of the fact that children do mature sexually at a younger age today and are quite likely to experiment sexually with their peers. In order to exempt this kind of activity from the criminal courts, some provisions require that the defendant be at least four years older than the child before the activity is classified as a crime. Finally, if the criminal provision is one which requires that the victim be below 18 years of age, there are some affirmative defenses. If the child is below the age of 18, but above the age of 15, and if the defendant reasonably believed that the child was 18 years of age or older, s/he may use that as a viable defense. If, however, the criminality of conduct depends on the child being under the age of 15 years, it is no defense that the defendant thought the child was 18 years or older.

Reference

1. Colo. Rev. Stat. §18-3-401 to 18-3-406 (1978, Cum. Supp.).

References and Notes

1. Child protection statutes are *civil* in nature. These are statutes which do not have a criminal penalty attached. They may be found in a Children's Code, Family Code, Juvenile Court Code, etc.
2. These courts are the juvenile court, the family court, or the district court with juvenile jurisdiction.
3. The Child Abuse Prevention and Treatment Act, 42 U.S.C. 35101-35106 (1974).
4. Mann Act, 18 U.S.C. 2423 (1948).
5. S. 1585 Amending 18 U.S.C. 2423 (1948) passed both houses 1/24/77.
6. May, G. (1977) *Understanding Sexual Child Abuse*, National Committee for Prevention of Child Abuse, Chicago, Ill.
7. The states which do not specifically require that sexual abuse be reported are *New Mexico, North Dakota, South Dakota, Tennessee* and *Texas*.
8. The states are *Indiana, Iowa, Maryland, Minnesota, Nevada, New York, North Carolina, Ohio, Oklahoma, South Carolina, Virginia, Wisconsin* and *Wyoming*.
9. Burns Ind. Stat. Ann. §35.5.5-1-1(b)(2) (1978 Cum Supp.).
10. Ann. Code Md. §35A(b)(8) (1978 Cum Supp.).
11. Ala. Code Title 26 §26-14-1(1) (1975).
12. It should be noted that in an additional 11 states the term sexual abuse, sexual molestation or sexual assault used in the reporting statute is the name of a specific statutory criminal offense. These terms are defined in the criminal statute. It could be argued, but very weakly, that the term used in the reporting statute has the same definition as it does in the criminal statute.
13. Cal. Wel. and Inst. Code 600 (Wests, 1972).
14. Colo. Rev. Stat. Ann. §19-1-103(20)(c) (1973).
15. See: The crime of incest against the minor child and the state's statutory response, 17 *Fam. Law.* 93 (1978).
16. Although Vermont does not have a specific incest statute, it does have a statute which prohibits marriage between relatives. (Vt. Stat. Ann Title 15, §3252 [Cum Supp. 1978]) and statutes which prohibit certain types of sexual activity between children and adults.
17. For example: Alaska Stat. §11.40.110 (1970).
18. For example: Ky. Rev. Stat. §530.020 (1975).
19. For example: Hawaii Rev. Stat. §707-741 (1976).
    Hawaii Rev. Stat. §526-1 (1976).
20. Colo. Rev. Stat. §18-6-302 (1973).
21. The states which have adopted a codified approach to crimes involving sex include *Arkansas, Colorado, Connecticut, Delaware, Florida, Hawaii, Iowa, Kentucky, Maryland, Michigan, Minnesota, Missouri, Nebraska, New Hampshire, New Mexico, New York, North Dakota, Ohio, Oregon, Tennessee, Texas, West Virginia, Wisconsin* and *Wyoming*.
22. See: Libai, D. (1969) The protection of the child victim of a sexual offense in the criminal court. *Wayne L. Rev.* 15:977.
23. Law of Evidence Revision (Protection of Children Law) 5711-1955 (4-9) Laws of the State of Israel 102 (1955).

Editorial Note

This chapter clearly sets forth the difficulties encountered in the judicial process involving cases of sexual abuse of children. A combination of criminal and juvenile court or civil legal involvement can be most beneficial. Particularly in cases of father–daughter incest, interviews, after proper legal cautioning by a pair of preferably female and male police detectives who are not in uniform and preferably in the perpetrator's home, very often lead to rapid confession in over 90% of our cases. This is especially so after it is pointed out that legal criminal bypass procedures exist in the county. Such a procedure is described in detail in Chapter Nine by Topper and Aldridge. In these jurisdictions the district attorney and the child protection service authorities join the perpetrator in signing a contract which includes the requirement of not less than two years of treatment. Certain perpetrators are automatically not eligible for this program, but these, along with those who do not admit to the offense, constitute less than 10%. The rest, in fact, plead guilty as charged but know that the record will be expunged and no open court hearing will be held, thus guaranteeing privacy, preservation of jobs and social standing and, in most cases, keeping the family intact while giving the victim maximal protection from recidivism. In less forward-looking communities where pressure on child protective services is so very great and "three months of family therapy" and the early closing of the case by the authorities is resorted to, there results a very high rate of recidivism, depriving the victim of protection. In short, an alliance between the juvenile court, the criminal court, the district attorney, child protection services, and the therapists is essential for providing the required involvement in cases of sexual abuse.

Finally, the frequency of divorce and remarriage frequently brings non-blood related families together, and sexual abuse between a step-parent and child victim or between non-blood related minors pose additional problems for the judicial system. In each case of sexual exploitation of a child for the gratification of another individual at an age when the child is unable to understand the action and is unable to give proper consent by virtue of age, it is our belief that legal definitions of incest apply, regardless of blood relationship and the fact that family exists.

C. HENRY KEMPE

Chapter Six

Sexual Abuse of Children: An Examination of European Criminal Law

JACK E. DOEK

This chapter will review the similarities and differences in the punitive approaches to child sexual abuse in Western and Eastern European countries. The merits of and objections to penal regulation in this area will also be discussed.

The Place of Sexual Child Abuse in the Penal Code

In European criminal law, sexual child abuse is covered by two types of statutes. The first type, which relates to the mishandling of children, can be applied to some forms of sexual child abuse. Other statutes, however, deal more directly with sexual child abuse through sections which are aimed at protecting or maintaining morality. One of the consequences of using such a broadly defined statute is that statistical information about the incidence of sexual child abuse, to which the penal code is applied, is difficult to come by. The statistics from Western European countries are restricted to moral delinquency in general. Quantitative information about sentences passed on perpetrators of sexual child abuse, particularly those within the family unit, are not readily available. Statistics, as well as any material on child sexual abuse other than law texts, are generally impossible to obtain from Eastern Europe.

In all of the European books on criminal law which were consulted by the author, there are specific acts which deal with the issue of morality and cover all forms of punishable sexual behavior. Included in such statutes are:

1. Sexual contact including sexual intercourse and indecent acts between men and women who are not married to each other, which may be in combination with threats of violence.
2. Sexual contact between persons of the same sex.
3. The making, selling, and public display of pornography.
4. Prostitution.

The minor child is given special consideration in these statutes.

Western European Countries

In the penal codes of the Western European countries[1], there are detailed articles in which sexual contact with children is made a punishable act. In some countries, these articles are old, dating from the end of the 19th or beginning of the 20th centuries. There are penalty clauses augmenting parts of sections in which certain forms of sexual contact between adults, such as rape and homosexuality, are declared punishable. Some countries, such as Belgium, the Netherlands, West Germany, and Switzerland, have detailed and specific articles in their penal codes outlining which forms of sexual child abuse are punishable. These articles deal with minors of a certain age or in certain dependency relationships with the perpetrator.

During the past few years some European countries, such as Denmark, the Netherlands, and Western Germany, have begun discussions concerning the desirability and/or necessity for changing the penalty clauses regarding sexual crimes. These discussions have focused primarily on the articles in which homosexuality and the dissemination of pornographic writing and printed material were made punishable offenses. In some countries these discussions have resulted in partial changes. In Denmark, for example, the penalties for the dissemination of all kinds of pornography were abolished in 1969, and in the Netherlands an article in which homosexual contacts of an adult with a minor were made punishable was abrogated in 1971.[2] In the Netherlands more changes of the penal code are expected on the basis of reports of a governmental committee which is reviewing all sections of the penal code which deal with sexual crimes/offenses against morality. That committee, which has reported and suggested legislative proposals concerning pornography and homosexuality, is now working on a report concerning penalization of sexual offenses against children. Until now, there has not been extensive or systematic attention paid to sexual child abuse in penal law in the Western European countries with the exception of father–daughter incest. However, this is beginning to change.

Among the Western European countries, what has occurred in West Germany has the most significance, as a total revision of the penal code occurred there in 1973. In this chapter, Germany's revised provisions will be used as a basis for a comparison of penal codes among various countries.

The most important principle of West Germany's penal code in the matter of sexual crimes (including sexual child abuse) is that the degree of the immorality is *not* the basis for penalization. Rather, the punishment is related to the danger or the damage which the sexual behavior poses for the interests of the community and/or society, including the individual interests of the citizens.* In other words, the West German government no longer feels it is entitled to mandate strict rules for the sexual behavior of its citizens merely on the basis of moral considerations. Instead, penal codes are reserved for the protection of certain interests which can be formulated in concrete terms. This "protection worth" interest pertains to the sexual self-determination of an individual citizen.[3] This is comparable to the Swiss penal code in which protection of normal sexual development is the most important factor in determining the penalization of certain sexual activities with children.

In the West German penal code, there are two detailed articles which deal with various forms of sexual child abuse. One of these (Article 174) focuses on sexual abuse of children who have a dependency relationship with the perpetrator; the other (Article 176) deals with sexual child abuse in general. The latter article states that sexual acts committed with a child below the age of 14 are punishable. This also

* The West Germans are in this connection talking of "Sozialschädlichheit".

applies to the person who induces a child into indecent activities or sexual acts with others. The punishment is six months to ten years in a house of correction, but in some cases, an even heavier penalty is possible. This can occur if there has been sexual intercourse with a child who is below the age of 14, or if the child suffers serious physical damage or death. Sexual intercourse or serious physical damage results in a penalty of at least one year in a house of correction. If the child dies, the penalty is not less than five years in a house of correction. Persons engaged in activities designed to sexually excite the child or others[4] are penalized separately, with a maximum of three years in a house of correction or fine.

Sexual activities which are made punishable in Article 176 of the West German penal code can also be found in the penal codes of most other European countries, but they are in separate articles. In other words, the West Germans have a codification of sexual offenses that is similar to the codifications that have occurred in some of the American states. (See Chapter Five.)

The separate articles in other countries include, for example, the British Penal Code (Sexual Offenses Act of 1956, Sections 5 and 6) which makes an offense of unlawful sexual intercourse with a girl under the age of 13 and with a girl under the age of 16, with certain exceptions. The Dutch Penal Code makes the distinction between sexual intercourse with a girl below the age of 12 years (maximum penalty being 12 years imprisonment) and with a girl of the age of 12 but below the age of 16 years (maximum penalty being eight years imprisonment). The Penal Code of Belgium does not have a provision concerning sexual intercourse, but the "violation" of a minor, with or without violence or serious threat, is punishable. The years of penal servitude range from 10 to 20, dependent on the age of the child who was involved. Likewise, the Norwegian and Turkish Penal Codes have articles dealing with sexual intercourse with a minor.

In general, there is not much uniformity among these separate statutes in the various countries. This applies not only to the specific form of legislation, but also to the age limits of the child. However, common to all of the penal codes is the general rule that the younger the victim, the heavier the penalty.

Article 176 of the West German Penal Code is considered an overall provision, including all kinds of sexual acts with or before a child of a certain age. In addition to sexual intercourse which has already been discussed, the article is applicable to various forms of indecency. Again, other countries have separate provisions to deal with indecency, for example, the British Indecency with Children Act of 1960, Articles 372 and 373 of the Belgian Penal Code (indecent or immoral acts to a child with or without violence or threat) and Section 195 of the Norwegian Penal Code.

Article 174 of the West German Penal Code is considered a special provision, dealing with sexual child abuse committed within a special relationship. This applies to an adopted child of the perpetrator not older than 17 years and to a child not yet 16 years of age who is entrusted to the perpetrator for care (such as foster parents), education (such as teachers), and treatment. A separate provision is applicable when the perpetrator has misused the authority or power he derives from his relationship with the child. A second part of this article pertains to seduction of the child into sexual activities with the perpetrator for the purpose of sexual excitement. Similar provisions to Article 174 can be found in the penal codes of other Western European countries; for example, Sections 10 and 11 of the Sexual Offenses Act of 1956 of the

United Kingdom, Article 377 of the Belgian Penal Code, and Articles 198 and 199 of the Norwegian Penal Code.

As with the statutes on sexual intercourse and indecency, the special provision statutes of the various countries lack uniformity on the age limits of the child and maximum penalties for the perpetrator.

As mentioned earlier, it is most difficult to get a true picture of the incidence of sexual child abuse from the criminal statistics. The main problem is that the figures very often refer to a combination of sexual crimes. For example, in the Netherlands in 1960, 241 persons were sentenced because they had sexually abused a child who was entrusted to their parental power, care, education or treatment. In 1970, this total was 138. However, it is impossible to separate out from these figures how many children were sexually abused by their parents because the total group includes step-parents, foster parents, teachers, and others. The same problem occurs with figures referring to other forms of sexual child abuse. Also, these are only part of the cases, namely the cases that are recognized and prosecuted and have resulted in criminal sentences. Underreporting exists in all European countries. In France, it has been estimated that there are approximately 300 cases of incest per year known to the judicial authorities. Therefore, the incidence of incest is approximately six cases per 1,000,000 inhabitants.[5] In the Netherlands in 1975, 815 abused children were reported to confidential doctors (a non-mandatory system of reporting child abuse).[6] Of these children, 46 were considered to be sexually abused. In 1976, 896 abused children were reported and of these, 45 were thought to be sexually abused.

In general, the maximum penalties for sexual offenses to children are seldom applied. It would seem that most Western European countries are fairly tolerant concerning punishment of sexual child abuse.[7,8] This also can be concluded from the changing of the penal code of West Germany which resulted in a lowering of the age limits and a decrease in some maximum penalties. Also, the recent developments and discussions in countries such as Denmark, Switzerland, and the Netherlands have not resulted from a predominantly punitive attitude.

Eastern European Countries

It is generally known that after the Second World War, the judiciary systems of the Eastern European countries falling under the Russian sphere of influence were subjected to revision and were brought into line with the Soviet model. This means, among other things, at least in theory the judicial system is based upon the Marxist concept of rights. Justice in the Soviet-Russian society and in varying degrees in the other Eastern European countries is a means of bringing to realization a new kind of social and economic order. Protection of (subjective) rights is then dependent on the posed social purposes.[9] However, the statutes of various Eastern European countries are often quite different from one another. This can be explained in part by the fact that the Soviet-Russian model has not been put into effect equally in all countries. In addition, alignment with the Soviet-Russian model has had more to do with private or personal rights than with criminal law. Prior to the Second World War, vast differences existed because of the great divergence of legal forces and influence. Austro–German jurisprudence had, alongside its inborn law-of-custom, great influence upon the development of the justice system in the Balkan countries, with the exception of Rumania. Rumania's system is strongly influenced by French law which is based on Roman law whereas Polish law, in contrast, is reflective of Russian, German, and Hungarian jurisprudence.

Just as in the various Western European countries, there is much discrepancy in the penal codes of Eastern Europe as they pertain to child sexual abuse.[10] In most of these countries' statutes there is some confusion regarding punishment of the perpetrator of a crime of child sexual abuse. In some countries, the criminal laws give little attention to the matter of the child as victim of sexual abuse and exploitation. This is true, for instance, in Poland and Czechoslovakia. It is possible that in these countries there is no perceived need for a penal-code approach, but more likely the problem of child sexual abuse is being ignored. Other countries, for example, Rumania, Hungary, and Yugoslavia, are giving more attention to this social problem, and there are specialized statutes which pertain to sexual abuse of children by guardians and caretakers. These same countries often give particular attention to juvenile prostitution and/or child pornography.

Similarities in European Penal Codes

In reviewing the criminal codes of many Western and Eastern European countries concerning child sexual abuse, it is possible to conclude that there are many similarities among them, despite obvious differences.

1. There are usually one or more articles or sections in the criminal codes making sexual abuse a punishable act.
2. In many countries these articles are part of a more generally formulated section or article concerning indecent, immoral behavior. Sexual child abuse is apparently considered a serious kind of reprehensible sexual behavior, and sexual child abuse is made a punishable act because, from a moral point of view, the behavior is so reprehensible that punishment needs to be threatening and carry a higher maximum sentence than other sexual crimes.
3. In some countries, Western Germany and Switzerland in particular, the emphasis in the criminal code is primarily on the protection of the child against damage to his/her sexual development which might result from the sexual abuse. The protection of the child rather than the protection of public morals is the most important goal of such legislation. There is usually at least one article or section which deals with sexual child abuse in the dependency relationship. This means that parents or other caretakers, such as foster parents, step-parents, or teachers, who commit sexual abuse against a child who is subject to their authority or supervision are considered as a separate group for punishment. In some countries the maximum penalty which can be given in these cases is higher than in other cases of sexual child abuse. The intent of such statutes is to give the child, in his dependent relationships with caretakers, extra protection.
4. Most countries have laws pertaining to pornography and juvenile prostitution. The delivery of obscene writings, pictures, or similar materials to minors is punishable by extra-high penalties. (The age of those classified as "minors" differs from country to country.) In a few countries, such as Belgium, there is more

detailed attention given to the exploitation of children for pornographic purposes. There are separate articles with separate penalties for such exploitation.

5. The various criminal statutes apply to the child as a minor person, usually citing specific age limits. The most frequent age is 16, although 14 and 18 are also used. In a few articles the term "minor" is used without specific age limits.
6. The fact that most European countries can impose penalties in cases of child sexual abuse is explained by the traditional imposition of penalties against indecent sexual behavior dating from ancient times. In most countries child sexual abuse is still not a recognized social problem. There is little known about the extent to which the existing possibilities for prosecution have been or are applied. Similarly, there is little known about "non-criminal" possibilities which have been or are being used in practice. The only exception to this is in regard to father–daughter incest which has been dealt with more openly in some Western European countries. In general, the Western and Eastern European countries have not formulated clear and thoughtful policies concerning child sexual abuse, and they have not debated whether prosecution of the perpetrator in these cases is desirable or necessary. One result of this lack of attention is that there are no published reports of systematically organized treatment programs for child sexual abuse as are already in existence in the United States.

The Role of Criminal Law in Child Sexual Abuse

Although relatively little is written about child sexual abuse in criminal law in Europe, it is possible, on the basis of increased writings dealing with incest appearing in American publications, to raise the legal issues which must be considered by European countries in reviewing their statutes on sexual child abuse.

1. Police investigation is always necessary for the preparation of a prosecution of the offender. It is essential that law enforcement personnel have good interviewing skills which will enable them to gather the necessary information for the prosecution in a manner which will cause the child no further harm. Inasmuch as the child is often required to testify as a witness in open court, attention must be given to protecting him/her from further trauma, while at the same time protecting the rights of the perpetrator.
2. Sentencing the offender, particularly if s/he is a member of the family, can make the solution of the problem more difficult. Further consideration must be given to whether it makes sense to prosecute cases of child sexual abuse and, if so, to what extent and under what circumstances.

Do criminal proceedings (police investigations, court hearings, and sentences) provide the best solution to the problem of child sexual abuse or do they at least contribute as much as possible toward that goal? To consider this primary issue it is helpful to distinguish the damage which can be caused by child sexual abuse on two levels. First of all, there is the damage at the individual level. Not only is there the victim of the sexual abuse to consider but the other members of the family as well who can be adversely affected. Secondly, there is the collective or societal level. This has to do with the disturbance and fear which arise in a society when it acknowledges that children are sexually assaulted.

It is usually very difficult to diminish the individual damage by criminal justice. On the contrary, the shock to family life and the overall tensions and tragedy are merely amplified by such proceedings. Only the more indirect damage to the society-at-large stands to be neutralized by criminal justice. Citizens in society can, by the prosecution and sentencing of the offender, obtain a feeling of security from the fact that the state is willing and able to maintain a standard of safety and, thereby, give protection against other possible sex offenders. State intervention for the purpose of neutralizing social damage and disturbance is also important to curb revenge and "vigilantism". If the state were *not* to intervene in serious cases of sexual child abuse, it would not be unlikely that the citizens, with a mind to protecting their own children, would take the law into their own hands. Another advantage of criminal prosecution in these cases is that the state may be able to intervene with whatever means are at its disposal *without* being dependent on the consent of the victim, the offender, or any other involved persons such as the child's parents. It should be noted, however, that in many Western European countries, the state can also intervene in a mandatory/involuntary way without using penalty clauses of the criminal law to protect children who have been sexually assaulted and abused.

Criminal proceedings also offer leverage in urging or forcing the offender to accept treatment, for example, by offering a suspended sentence. In other words, if the offender is willing to cooperate in obtaining treatment and shows a willingness to do so, the penalty will be waived. In the Netherlands and some other Western European countries, it is also possible, by imposing the same conditions, *not to prosecute*. The prognosis of such non-voluntary treatment is not yet known.

Suggestions for Future Legislation

In a broad sense, the term "sexual child abuse" can be defined as including all kinds of sexual activities committed by an adult with or in the presence of minors; these are activities which are detrimental to normal development of the sexuality of the child or which curtail or inhibit his/her sexual self-determination. Further legislation must be willing to specifically define different categories of sexual child abuse and link specific penalties to those categories. The following categories are a guideline. Sexual child abuse which is:

1. Committed by someone who is in charge of the daily care and education of the child, for example, parents, step-parents, or foster parents.
   (a) Without serious physical harm to the child.
   (b) With serious physical harm to the child.
2. Committed by someone on whom the child is dependent and who has misused this relationship (or the authority he/she derives from this relationship) for the purpose of indecent sexual acts, for example, teachers or group leaders who provide residential care.
   (a) Without serious physical harm to the child.
   (b) With serious physical harm to the child.
3. Committed by someone whom the child hardly knows or has never seen.
   (a) Without serious physical harm to the child.
   (b) With serious physical harm to the child.

4. Committed by someone using or exploiting the child for the purpose of pornography and/or prostitution.

In most European countries the age of majority is 18 years, and many other statutes pertaining to child sexual abuse use 18 as the age limit. This author, however, suggests that the limit be lowered to 16 years. Those minors between the ages of 16 and 18 can still be protected by the application of general penalty clauses in the criminal law which give protection to the sexual self-determination of every citizen.

Finally, the merits of criminal prosecution must be carefully considered in each case. The protection of the child as an individual and as a member of a family must always be given first consideration. When criminal justice is directed only at avenging or appeasing the general welfare of the society and can yield no reasonable advantage to a particular child, criminal prosecution should not be the first option. However, if such prosecution clearly will protect other children from sexual attack or yield some advantage to the child, such as treatment for a parent, criminal proceedings may be quite necessary and should be instigated promptly.

Whenever the perpetrator of the sexual abuse is someone within the family, criminal prosecution may not be the best course of action. However, whenever there has been serious physical harm to the child, regardless of the perpetrator's relationship to the child, the penal statute may need to be invoked. It does seem entirely appropriate to use criminal prosecution with high fines and prison sentences for those who exploit children for pornographic purposes or prostitution.

Conclusion

Consideration must be given on an international level as to whether criminal justice is a sufficiently pragmatic means of solving problems created by child sexual abuse, not only with respect to the child as victim but to the perpetrator as well. Much more thought has been given to these matters in the United States than has occurred to date in most European countries.

References and Notes

1. Penal Codes of Western European countries:

   (a) *West Germany*
   Systematischer Kommentar zum Strafgesetzbuch, Rudolphi, Horn, Samson, Schreiber (Alfred Metzner Verlag, Frankfurt, 1978).

   (b) *Belgium*
   Wetboek van Strafrecht van 8 juni, 1867; nederlandse tekst laatstelijk vastgesteld bij wet van 10 juli, 1964.

   (c) *Netherlands*
   Wetboek van Strafrecht (loose-leaf commentary), Noyon-Langemeyer, 7th edition edited by Prof. J. Remmelink (Kluwer, Deventer).

   (d) *Norway*
   The Norwegian Penal Code (The American series of Foreign Penal Code no. 3, 1961).

   (e) *Turkey*
   The Turkish Criminal Code with an introduction of Dr. Nevzat Gürelli (The American series of Foreign Penal Codes, 1964).

   (f) *Switzerland*
   Schweizerisches Strafrecht Besonderer Teil II, Günther Stratenwerth (1974, Verlag Stampfli und Ge AG Bern).

2. Staatsblad, No. 212, April 8, 1971.
3. The 13th Section of the penal code of West Germany has been titled "Straftaten gegen die sexuelle Selbstbestimmung".
4. There are distinctions made in the West German penal code between sexual acts *to* ("an") and *before* ("vor") the child; for example,
   —committed to ("vornehmen an"); art. 176(1)
   —committed by the child to the perpetrator ("von dem kind an sich vernehmen lassen"); art. 176(1).
   —the same for "others".
5. J. P. Peigne (1978), L'Inceste: problemes poses et point de vue d'un juge. In *Family Violence.* (Edited by Ekelaar, J. M. and Katz, S. N.) Butterworth, Toronto.
6. For more on the system of "confidential doctors" see: Doek, J. E. (1978) Child abuse in the Netherlands: the medical referee. *Chicago Kent Law Rev.* **54:** 785.
7. Senaeve, P. (1978) Incest in Belgian criminal law. In *Family Violence.* (Edited by Ekelaar, J. M. and Katz, S. N.) Butterworth, Toronto.
8. Niemann, H. (1974) Unzucht mit Kindern, Eine kriminologische Untersuchung unter Verwendung Hamburger Gerichts akten aus den Jahren 1965 und 1967 (Verlag Otto Schwartz, Gottingen.) Two-hundred and two cases in which the perpetrators were sentenced. In 91% of the cases the penalty was not more than *two* years; the possible maximum was *ten* years.
9. Johnson, E. L. (1969) *An Introduction to the Soviet Legal System.*
10. Penal Codes of Eastern European Countries:

   (a) Soviet Criminal Law and Procedure; the RSFSR Codes Introduction and Analysis, Harold J. Berman (Second ed. Harvard Univ. Press, Cambridge, Mass., 1972).

   (b) The RSFSR Criminal Code and Code of Criminal Procedure of October 27, 1960; into force since January 7, 1961.

   (c) The American Series of Foreign Penal Code, No. 19 The Penal Code of the Polish People's Republic translated by William S. Kenney and Tadeusz Sadowski. This code came into force on January 1, 1970; see *Journal of Laws*, May 14, 1969, No. 94.

(d) Sammlung ausserdeutsche Strafgesetzbücher in deutscher Ubersetzung Max Planck Institut (Publ. Comp. Walter de Gruyter, Berlin/New York).
a. nr. 81. Rumanisches Strafgesetzbuch
Dr. Paula Tiefenthaler und Alois Provasi (Berlin, 1964).
b. nr. 83. Das Strafgesetzbuch der Ungarischen Volksrepublik.
Dr. Ladislaus Mezäfy (Berlin, 1964)
c. nr. 85. Das Tsechoslowakische Strafgesetzbuch
Dr. Erich Schmied (Berlin, 1964)
d. nr. 93. Das Bulgarische Strafgesetzbuch vom 16 März 1968
Dr. Thea Lyon and Dr. Anton Lipowschek (Berlin, 1973)
(e) Criminal Code of the Hungarian People's Republic translated by Pàl L'Amberg Corvina Press 1962, Budapest.

General References

1. Smith, J. C., and Hogan, B. (1973, 3rd edition) *Criminal Law*. Butterworth, London.
2. Simson, G., and Geerds, F. (1969) Straftaten gegen die Person und Sittlichkeitsdelikte in rechtsvergleichender Sicht, Munchen.
3. Würgter, W. (1976) Unzucht mit Kindern nach art. 191 STGB Verlag Ruëgger, Diessenhofen.

Part III.
PSYCHODYNAMICS AND EVALUATION

Introduction

Understanding the factors which contribute to the various types of child sexual abuse is an essential first step in the evaluation process. In Chapter Seven Macdonald reviews the present-day knowledge on exhibitionists, rapists, and child molesters, and in Chapter Eight Mrazek summarizes the literature on the various dyadic types of incestuous relationships. Macdonald also discusses the role of the forensic psychiatrist in the evaluation of adult offenders.

In Chapters Nine, Ten and Eleven specific guidelines are given for the assessment of the sexually abused child and his or her family. Topper and Aldridge describe a system of intervention, including investigation of the report and crisis intervention, which has been effective in a social services department. Kerns outlines the critical role the physician has in the diagnosis, reporting, and treatment planning in child sexual abuse cases. Mrazek discusses the specific expectations of the child psychiatric examination, contrasting the evaluation of a child who has been sexually assaulted by someone outside the family with the approach which should be used with a child who has been involved in an incestuous relationship.

The reader is encouraged to consider the following issues. What are the contributing factors which explain the onset and continuation of the various types of child sexual abuse? What are the essential components of a thorough assessment of a sexually abused child and his or her family? How can the evaluations made by various disciplines be integrated into a comprehensive view, leading to realistic treatment planning?

PATRICIA BEEZLEY MRAZEK
C. HENRY KEMPE

Chapter Seven

Sexual Deviance: The Adult Offender

JOHN M. MACDONALD

The purpose of this chapter is to review present-day knowledge of adults who commit sexual offenses against children. The exhibitionist, the rapist, and the child molester will be considered. Adults who commit incest are considered in Chapter Eight. Some offenders do confine themselves to one type of sex crime against children, but it is important to note that there are many offenders who commit a wide variety of sex offenses against both children and adults.

Exhibitionists

Indecent exposure, the most frequent sex crime against children, is important because of the alarm which it raises in some children or in their parents. Almost invariably the offender is a male, and the majority of these men are exhibitionists who expose their genitals for sexual pleasure, without any intention of further sexual contact with the viewer or viewers of the exposure. The exposure may be combined with masturbation. The exhibitionist is more likely than other sex offenders to continue his abnormal sexual behavior following arrest, conviction, and punishment. Although these men are properly regarded as posing slight risk of physical injury, a few of them also commit forcible rape and criminal homicide.

Others charged with indecent exposure include men detected urinating in public, usually while under the influence of alcohol. Occasionally a young man or group of young men will expose themselves, usually their buttocks ("shooting a moon") on a dare, as a lark, or as an expression of contempt. Persons with organic brain disease and schizophrenics under the influence of hallucinations or delusions may also expose their genitals.

Three out of four cases of indecent exposure occur in a public place, outdoors, and in daylight. Streets, alleys, parking lots, parks, and school playgrounds are frequent sites of exposure. The exhibitionist may expose himself from the doorway of his home or through a living room window. Other indoor sites of exposure include apartment houses, laundromats, offices, stores and movie theaters. Exhibitionists are most active between 8:00 and 9:00 a.m. and between 3:00 and 5:00 p.m., the hours when children are going to and from school.

The exhibitionist seldom makes any attempt to touch or to come very close to his victims. He will often draw attention to himself by clearing his throat or by calling out. When seated in a car, he will ask a young girl for traffic directions and then draw her attention to his exposed penis, perhaps asking her if she knows what it is, has she ever seen one before, what does she think of it? He may comment on the girl's physical appearance and make obscene statements. If any attempt is made to grab the victim, the offender may have in mind a more serious sex offense, even though no further action was taken.

If arrested, the exhibitionist may claim that he was urinating, having trouble with the zipper on his pants, was unaware that his fly was open, or drunk and unable to recall the incident. Usually the circumstances of the offense point clearly to deliberate exposure. For example, a man who said he was urinating was reported to have his pants lowered to his knees over a period of ten minutes.

The exhibitionist is usually a young man under the age of 30 at the time of his first arrest. He may have started exposing himself at the age of 19, but he was probably not arrested until he was about the age of 25. After the age of 30 there is a decline with each decade in the incidence of exhibitionism. Older men who start exposing themselves for the first time after the age of 40 often have organic brain disease from alcoholism, head injury, or other cause.

The majority of exhibitionists over the age of 20 are married or have separated, but many are childless or have only one child. They tend to have a higher intelligence than other sex offenders, and Mohr[10] found that the majority of exhibitionists are engaged in skilled trades or as laborers with a preference for "manly" occupations.

They have been described as immature, shy, young men with sexual inhibitions. The value of such a vague description is limited, but at least it indicates that these men are not usually sociopathic personalities. Rosen[14] noted that many of these persons pride themselves on their self-control and high moral standards in other spheres. All 37 exhibitionists treated by Hackett[5] tended to use obsessive-compulsive defenses as major coping techniques.

It is difficult to understand why men rape, plunder, and murder; yet these crimes, however abhorrent, seem to be more readily explicable than the illegal act of indecent exposure. Many men have fleeting fantasies of forcible sexual relations, robbery, and homicide, but thoughts of indecent exposure do not readily spring to mind. Fictional heroes may rob banks and cut down their enemies, but they do not lower their pants except in privacy for the purpose of sexual intercourse. James Bond would not sit in his car waiting to expose himself to a group of school-girls. Much has been written about the origins of exhibitionism, but still the puzzle remains.[7]

The psychoanalytic explanation of exhibitionism in men is that it represents an attempt to overcome castration fear, that the offender seeks reassurance of his masculinity through the expression of alarm on the face of his victim.

It is often said that the sex offender does not progress from minor to major sex crimes; nevertheless some offenders commit both minor and major sex crimes. Some exhibitionists, fortunately a minority, also molest children or commit rape. The writer has examined three murderers who gave a history of exhibitionism and rape or attempted rape.

Rooth[13] quotes papers which contradict the traditional view that exhibitionists are harmless and claims that a proportion of exhibitionists commit sexual offenses involving force while others molest children. Grassberger[4] examined the criminal records over a 25-year period of 220 Austrian exposers convicted in 1937 and found that 12% of them were subsequently convicted of serious sexual offenses, in particular assaults, while about 25% were convicted of non-sexual offenses involving violence. Dost[2] reported a series of 11 rapists who had a previous history of exhibitionism and Cabanis[1] referred to several notorious sex murderers whose careers began with exhibitionistic activities.

In Rooth's[13] series of 30 persistent exhibitionists, only one subject admitted to sexual violence, but a comparatively high proportion (1/3) had a history of pedophilia or hebephilia. There were three cases of incest. Rooth[13] concludes that the current disagreement over the relationship between sexual aggressiveness, child molestation, and exhibitionism may be the outcome of considering exhibitionists as though they were a homogeneous group of offenders.

Rapists

Rape, like many other crimes, is largely a product of youth and masculinity. In the United States men under the age of 25 have accounted for over half of the arrests for rape, and men under 30 have accounted for three out of four arrests for this crime.[3] Relatively few offenders are over 60 years of age. Some of these elderly offenders may choose child victims because they fear physical combat with a mature woman. Young adult males may also choose child victims because of their lack of self-confidence in the presence of adult women.

Many psychiatrists and psychologists regard rape as primarily an expression of hostility toward women rather than an act motivated by a desire for sexual gratification. This hostility may have been derived from anger at a rejecting, controlling, or seductive mother. The rapist may not be aware of the source of his hostility which is displaced onto other women. This explanation of rape has been over-emphasized in some circles, and there are even those who would deny a sexual motive in rape.

Another group of rapists is composed of men whose self-control has been weakened and their judgment impaired by the effects of alcohol or drugs. In a study of 77 rapists confined at Atascadero State Hospital in California, Rada[12] found that 50% had been drinking at the time of the commission of the offense, and 35% were alcoholic according to stringent criteria. Rada is careful to emphasize that although alcohol may be an important factor in the commission of rape, his data do not prove a cause and effect relationship.

A third group of rapists are those plundering sociopaths who may steal your wallet or rape your wife. The sociopathic offender is characterized by his antisocial behavior, disregard for the truth, impulsivity, unreliability, poor work record, poor judgment, failure to profit from experience or punishment, and apparent absence of remorse or guilt. Such a brief description is misleading because it highlights the negative aspects of the sociopathic personality. Not all these features are present in every sociopath, and few of the features may be in evidence at the time of a psychiatric evaluation.

Textbooks refer to the superficial charm of the sociopath, but they do not reveal how to distinguish charm from superficial charm. All too frequently false statements by these persons are accepted at face value. On the other hand, some sociopaths make no effort to conceal their wayward nature and may speak in a callous manner of the rape of very young children without any apparent concern for the welfare of their victims.

A fourth group of rapists consists of men who are defending themselves against homosexual wishes or against feelings of sexual inadequacy. This type of offender has to prove to himself that he is not a homosexual or not sexually inadequate by repeated acts of intercourse with willing or unwilling members of the opposite sex. Halleck[6] notes that quite frequently in our society latent homosexual fears are associated with paranoid attitudes toward the world and particularly toward females, who threaten the deviate's masculine image. The rapist tends to see all women as seductive, depriving, and dangerous. He frequently vacillates between perceiving them as frightening giantesses or as lesser beings. In his attacks upon women, he both conquers his fears and confirms their inferiority.[6] It is easy to see why persons so fearful of women should attack young girls.

Child Molesters

Child molesting, like indecent liberties, is one of those vague terms which covers a wide range of offenses against children. In this section adults who commit sexual offenses other than indecent exposure, rape, or incest will be considered. The term pedophilia, which means literally "love of children", has been used to refer to abnormal sexual attraction to young women. It has been defined as the expressed desire for immature sexual gratification with a prepubertal child.[10] Such offenders may be charged under laws which are applicable to victims of any age or which apply to victims under 14, 15 or 16 years of age. Many pedophilic offenses are covered under the indecent liberties statutes.

Child molesters are almost invariably men, who fondle, finger or kiss young girls' breasts or genitals (heterosexual pedophilia) or who fondle young boys and indulge in mutual masturbation or oral-genital contact (homosexual pedophilia). In contrast to exhibitionists, these offenders usually select as victims children they know rather than strangers. Thus, the offender is often a relative, such as a grandfather, uncle, or older cousin, or an acquaintance, such as mother's boyfriend, a family friend, lodger, neighbor, teacher, or scoutmaster.

When the offender is a stranger, he may pick up the child near a school, in a park, playground, or movie theater. Offers of candy, a ride in a car, or some other inducement may be offered to obtain the company of the child.

Mohr and associates[10] report that pedophilia occurs predominantly in three age groups: adolescence, where it signifies a maturational lag; middle age, with a peak at ages 35 to 39 where one can observe a regression from adult sexuality caused by negative life experiences; and in the late fifties and early sixties, at which point loneliness may lead to a close relationship with a child in the course of which erotic impulses, often unsuspected, break through.

Peters and Sadoff[11] also noted a peak in the mid-to-late twenties. These authors state that the pedophiliac usually manifests a passive-aggressive personality and has attempted in vain to establish a relationship with an adult female. He lacks the feelings of adequacy and emotional maturity to maintain an adult heterosexual relationship. When rejected by a wife or girlfriend, he may seek out a young child who is less threatening to him. These authors also note the role of the dominant wife who denies her husband sexually, berates him, and makes him feel less of a man. Possibly while under the influence of alcohol, he makes sexual advances to his young daughter or some other child.

Evaluation of Offenders

The courts and others concerned with the welfare of child victims of sexual offenses are most interested in those sections of the psychiatric report which deal with the dangerousness of the offender and the prospects of treatment. When the victim is a relative or neighbor of the offender, the risk of further victimization and measures for protection of the victim become especially important issues. It is in these cases that there is often an attempt to avoid or cut short criminal proceedings, especially when the child has not been physically harmed.

There is embarrassment over the sexual nature of the offense, and initial anger toward the offending relative or neighbor may have been replaced by the feeling that he is a sick person in need of treatment. In addition, there is the desire to prevent further trauma to the child and to avoid requiring testimony in court. It is not surprising that promises of the offender to obtain psychiatric treatment lead to withdrawal of all criminal charges.

At this stage the offender's interest in obtaining treatment may suddenly disappear. He may attend a few sessions or stay on a psychiatric in-patient service for a few days. He is quick to protest his innocence and to say that he does not need treatment but agreed to see a psychiatrist only upon the request of his attorney. (For more on how this affects the child and family, see Chapter Fifteen.)

If the charges are not withdrawn, the defendant may be willing to plead guilty, and the child does not have to testify. Treatment can be made a condition of probation. Sometimes the court will defer judgment so that if the offender completes a long period of psychiatric treatment and abides by other conditions imposed by the court he will be able to avoid the stigma of a criminal conviction.

As a condition of probation the pedophilic offender should avoid situations or activities which would bring him in touch with young children. If he was drinking at the time of the offenses or if he has an alcoholic problem, whenever possible he should be placed on Antabuse thereafter and required to attend meetings of Alcoholics Anonymous. Some offenders are able to avoid further offenses providing they remain sober. Treatment will also be required for drug abuse.

The likelihood of recidivism is greater when the behavior has been occurring since adolescence or the early twenties. Repetition is less likely when the behavior suggests regression from healthy sexual behavior in response to severe stress or to an accumulation of stressful circumstances. Expression of guilt or remorse is a favorable sign, but loud and prolonged expression of such feelings may be deceptive. Similarly enthusiastic demands for psychotherapy may represent an attempt at manipulation rather than a desire for change in sexual orientation.

A history of sadistic fantasies, sadistic behavior, firesetting or bombing, or other antisocial behavior suggests the need for care in assessing dangerousness. A chronic organic brain disease or functional psychosis is likely to be an unfavorable prognostic factor. As in any assessment of dangerousness, it is important to obtain information from many sources including police department records. If provocative behavior on the part of the victim contributed to the offense, this should be considered in the overall evaluation.

Dangerousness fluctuates and there should be a reassessment following a period of treatment. Family therapy, especially treatment of the wife, may lead to resolution of difficulties within the marriage which contributed to the offense. It should be kept in mind that good behavior within a security hospital or prison may not be a good indication of behavior upon release from custody.

Those mental health professionals responsible for the welfare of the victim of a sexual offense should attempt to obtain a copy of the forensic psychiatrist's evaluation of the offender. The suspect may be willing to sign a permit for release of the report or the court may make it available. This report might provide significant additional information regarding the circumstances of the crime, but accusations of seductive behavior on the part of the victim may represent an attempt to shift blame, rather than an accurate account of the offense. When offender and victim are relatives, consultation with the psychiatrist who examined the offender may be essential in treatment planning.

References

1. Cabanis, D. (1966) Medizinish-kriminologische untersuchung uber exhibitionismus. Unpublished Habilitationsschrift. University of West Berlin.
2. Dost, O-P. (1963) Die psychologie der notzucht. *Verl f. Kriminal Fschliteratur.* Hamburg, 293.
3. Federal Bureau of Investigation (1978) *Uniform Crime Reports.* U.S. Government Printing Office, Washington, D.C.
4. Grassberger, R. (1964) Der exhibitionismus. *Kriminalistik* **18:** 557.
5. Hackett, T. P. (1971) The psychotherapy of exhibitionists in a court clinic setting. *Semin Psychiatry* **3:** 297.
6. Halleck, S. L. (1967) *Psychiatry and the Dilemmas of Crime.* Harper, New York.
7. Macdonald, J. M. (1973) *Indecent Exposure.* C. C. Thomas, Springfield, Ill.
8. Macdonald, J. M. (1976) *Psychiatry and the Criminal.* C. C. Thomas, Springfield, Ill.
9. Macdonald, J. M. (1971) *Rape: Offenders and their Victims.* C. C. Thomas, Springfield, Ill.
10. Mohr, N. W., Turner, R. E. and Jerry, M. B. (1964) *Pedophilia and Exhibitionism.* Univ. of Toronto, Toronto, Canada.
11. Peters, J. J. and Sadoff, R. L. (1970) Clinical observations on child molesters. *Hum Sexuality.* Nov.
12. Rada, R. T. (1975) Alcoholism and forcible rape. *Am. J. Psychiatry* **132:** 444.
13. Rooth, G. (1973) Exhibitionism, sexual violence and pedophilia. *Br. J. Psychiatry* **122:** 705.
14. Rosen, I. (1964) *The Psychology and Treatment of Sexual Deviation.* Oxford Univ., London.

Chapter Eight

The Nature of Incest: A Review of Contributing Factors

PATRICIA BEEZLEY MRAZEK

Rigorous studies of the precipitants of incest are exceedingly rare. Those that have been done have often used biased sampling techniques or have reflected the investigator's own theoretical orientation. Other reports are simply case histories which have been compiled during diagnostic or psychotherapy sessions. This chapter will review three primary theoretical perspectives for understanding the contributing factors of incest. Also, the literature on the various dyadic types of incestuous relationships will be summarized.

While early studies tended to define incest as genital intercourse between relatives who are not allowed to marry, for the purpose of this chapter, the definition will be broadened to include sexual activity such as oral-genital contact, fondling of genitals and breasts, and mutual masturbation among blood relatives and also among those related through adoption.

Theoretical Perspectives

Generally, there are three theoretical perspectives for understanding the etiology of incest. These are: (1) the sociological viewpoint; (2) the role of organic factors such as alcoholism and mental subnormality; and (3) the psychodynamic perspective. While these views are not mutually exclusive, preoccupation with a single perspective does affect one's opinions about prognosis and recommendations for intervention.

Sociological Viewpoint

This perspective associates low socio-economic class, poverty, overcrowding, social isolation, subcultural values, and external stress with incest.[12,22,37] To assess the validity of such a perspective it is essential to review the samples from which the conclusions were derived. The studies of incest which used court and prison settings to obtain their samples found that the participants were from low socio-economic classes and lived in poor, overcrowded housing. Weinberg[37] criticized the overcrowding theory and showed that the ratio of rooms per person for his sample of over 200 incestuous families in Chicago was no worse than the average for the city. More recent work, like that of Giarretto[15] (See Chapter Fourteen) and Finkelhor,[12] has shown that incest also occurs among a large number of middle-class families.

Social isolation has also been seen as an important contributing factor to incest. From this theory have come stereotypes of incestuous families from, for example, backwoods Appalachia and rural parts of the United Kingdom. However, high degrees of social isolation can occur in large cities as well and may reflect as much about a family's style of functioning as it does of a sociological phenomenon.

The theory of subcultural values permitting or tolerating incest is similar. Lukianowicz[22] concluded from his study of 26 father–daughter incest cases that the action of some fathers should not necessarily be regarded as an expression of a real sexual deviation but rather as an expression of a morally and socially accepted type of behavior in some "oversexed" and underinhibited males in the subculture of certain social groups. Furthermore, he thought that the incest was precipitated in many of these cases by overcrowding and social isolation.

Also, stressful external events which directly affect the father, such as loss of employment, financial setbacks, diseases and injuries, have been associated with the onset of incest. Such events may result in the father spending more time at home and may make him more vulnerable, leading to increased drinking and decreased impulse control.

Because of the methodological problems in much of the research, there are no conclusive answers to the query of how sociological phenomena contribute to incest. In recent years the sociological perspective has been thought to be relatively unimportant in comparison with other viewpoints, but new data based on a sample of 796 college students has been published by Finkelhor.[12] His survey has shown that incestuous experiences were higher for girls and boys who had spent their childhoods on farms and that although incest is much more common in the middle class than was previously thought, it is still more common among the poor. Clearly, additional investigation is needed to assess the importance of all these factors and to determine how they interact with the effects of organic psychopathology and with individual and family psychodynamics.

Organic Psychopathology Viewpoint: Effects of Alcoholism and Subnormality

An alternative explanation stresses organic psychopathology of the perpetrator and/or child.[7,9,12,14,35,39] The organicity can be due to alcoholism, mental subnormality, or drug induced psychosis.

Virkkunen[35] has noted 12 studies of incest which emphasize the central role that alcohol plays on the part of the offender. In several of the studies, half of the offenders were alcoholics; one report found the figure to be as high as 80%.[9] Virkkunen studied 45 case reports of incest in Helsinki, Finland and found alcoholism in 48.9% of the cases. Compared with non-alcoholic incest offenders, the alcoholics had significantly more previous criminality and violence. That is, the incest offense was just one expression of a general pattern of crime. Seventy-seven percent of the alcoholics had been under the influence of alcohol at least at the beginning of the incest relationship. More recent reports by Browning and Boatman[7] and Finkelhor[12] have also indicated high rates of alcoholism in incestuous families.

A major problem with all of these studies has been the definition of alcoholism. The definitions vary from one report to the next, and in many of the studies the criteria are unreliable. The evidence relevant to the diagnosis has sometimes come from second-hand reports rather than from the offender himself. Also, the definition is sometimes broad, such as in Virkkunen's study, in which alcoholism is defined as "almost daily consumption of alcohol and long periods of drinking which has gone on for several years". With such a broad definition, the incidence of alcoholism at 48.9% must be questioned. Gebhard *et al.*,[14] defined alcoholic as "drinking a fifth or more per day or drinking to the extent that social and occupational adjustment were seriously impaired". Using this definition, nearly 25% of the fathers imprisoned for sexual relations with prepubertal (under 12) daughters were alcoholic; the percentage of alcoholic fathers lessened as the age of the daughter involved in the case increased. Gebhard noted that many other fathers had been drinking at the time of the first incest incident although they were not alcoholics.

The implication of all these findings is that alcohol may act as an inhibition-removing and triggering influence. The organicity associated with drug induced psychosis and other forms of toxicity may also act as a trigger for incestuous relationships. Although alcohol or drugs may contribute to the onset and perhaps to the continuation of incest, they are not a sufficient explanation; there must be other factors present as well.

Virkkunen's study also reveals some noteworthy data about intelligence. While 22.7% of the alcoholics had limited intelligence (IQ under 80), 43.5% of the non-alcoholics did. Other authors as well have found mental subnormality to be a primary factor, not only in adults but also in the children, especially sons in mother–son incest. Weinberg[37] classified nearly 65% of the fathers in his sample as being of dull–normal intelligence or below. Gebhard *et al.*,[14] noted that fathers of the "endogamic-subcultural" type tended to be of dull–normal or marginal intelligence as were imprisoned older brothers.

While mental subnormality might result in an inability to understand which sexual relationships are forbidden by law or what the consequences of incest would be, this seems to be rather atypical of retarded individuals. They usually are quite able to comprehend that some actions are illegal or immoral. The high incidence of subnormality which some authors report may simply relate to a detection bias; retarded individuals may be less careful in keeping the incest a secret.

Psychodynamic Perspective

The psychodynamic perspective has highlighted the individual psychopathology of the offender, the victim, and other family members, such as the wife. In addition to this individual focus, it has become increasingly recognized that it is important to view the family as a system in which each member has a contributing role (See Chapter Thirteen) in order to more comprehensively understand the etiology of incest.

In general, the psychodynamic perspective has stressed the interaction of a variety of contributing factors to incest.[8,16,18,23,24] These include personality disorder of the individual, marital discord with sexual estrangement, loss of an important relationship or fear of family disintegration, and emotional deprivation leading to a search for nurturance through sexuality by the adult and/or child. While this viewpoint is potentially promising, at the current time the number of potentially contributing dynamics is so large and the conclusions so contradictory, that there is no consensus within the field as to the most critical interrelationships. The same or similar dynamics exist in many families who do not go on to become incestuous. What the essential differences between these families and the incestuous ones are remains a controversy.

A Review of Various Types of Incestuous Relationships

The following descriptions of the various types of incest are summarized composites of the psychodynamics which have been written about for the last 50 years.

Father–Daughter Incest

Of all the types of incestuous relationships, father–daughter has been the most thoroughly studied.[10,14,19,22,23,28,31,32,37,40] Descriptive typologies have been formulated by Weinberg,[37] Gebhard,[14] and Meiselman[28] while most other authors have discussed dynamic criteria. The following summaries of the possible contributing factors are taken from descriptive and dynamic approaches.

Father. Often the father has had a background of emotional deprivation, experiencing rejection by his mother and abandonment by his father. If his own father had not left the home, he was often harsh and authoritarian. The psychological disturbance in the father ranges from minimal abnormality to psychotic disorder. Common diagnoses include sociopathy, pedophilia, dependent personality, and paranoid personality disorder. Several authors[14,22,37] have described at least some of the fathers as being "oversexed", "loose", and "pathologically obsessed with sex". Some men have frequent sex with their wives and several of their own children, but they are unwilling to seek sexual partners outside the nuclear family because of a need to maintain the public facade of a stable and competent patriarch. For some fathers the incest occurs only during a high-stress period, and the incest may be triggered by excessive drinking. When marital tension is so high that there is sexual estrangement and minimal communication between husband and wife, the incest may continue for many years because it actually serves to reduce tension in the family. It has often been thought that the fathers have unconscious homosexual tendencies and have difficulty in achieving a stable heterosexual orientation. While domination and brutal violence against the children and wife characterize a subgroup of these fathers, others are best described as ineffectual, gentle men who are seeking nurturance and approval from their daughters.

Daughter. The oldest daughter in a family is most vulnerable to becoming a participant in father–daughter incest, especially if she and her mother have a role-reversal relationship and if she, like mother, is passive, dependent, and masochistic. Younger daughters are more at risk if the mother has allowed the sexual relationship between father and eldest daughter to continue. A daughter may agree to the incest at the point she realizes her mother has abandoned her. Frightened and lonely, she may accept the sexual advances from her father as signs of affection and "specialness". In turn, she gets revenge against her non-nurturing mother. If the daughter is particularly attractive with well-developed secondary sexual characteristics and/or if she has been sexually promiscuous, this may influence a father who was predisposed to incest. Some daughters play an active, initiating role in the sexual relationship. Generally, the daughter is of average intelligence but may be doing poorly in school.

Mother. There has been considerable debate as to the extent of the mother's participation in the incest. While rarely actively involved, she has usually been described as colluding and actually "setting up" the sexual relationship between father and daughter. Because of her own deprivation during childhood, she is unable to show much affection and love to her husband and children. She may also have been sexually abused as a child but is reluctant to discuss this. Her frigidity and hostility toward her husband have often resulted in marital estrangement, with little sexual involvement. She has come to accept a rather full role reversal with her daughter who assumes the responsibilities and privileges of the "woman of the house". Mother's absence from home, due to death, divorce, separation, illness, extensive work hours, or unwillingness to accept the role of wife or mother, increases the chance for a sexual relationship between father and daughter. The mother has also been described as dependent, infantile, masochistic, and pathologically attached to her own rejecting and hostile mother. Through identification with her daughter she fulfills in fantasy her childhood incestuous attachment to her own father. Even if the mother has not colluded in the onset of the incest, she is usually seen as partially responsible for its continuation through her failure to take any action that would terminate it.

Mother–Son Incest

In 1960, Wahl[36] noted that in all the literature up to that point, only four cases of mother–son incest were reported and these were mentioned rather than described. Wahl gave detailed histories of two adult schizophrenic men who had had incestuous relationships with their mothers. Since that time, there have been less than a dozen isolated clinical reports of one or two cases,[2,4,6,19,27,33,36,40] and larger studies, such as those by Lukianowicz,[22] Meiselman[28] and Weinberg[37] have provided only a few examples.

From these case reports the following picture of the contributing factors to mother–son incest arises.

Mother. The mother may be alcoholic or have other severe character problems. Typically, she had rejected her son during his formative years, but this may have alternated with gross overprotection. She is likely to have been overtly promiscuous or have had multiple lovers and husbands. Loss of internal control may have resulted in nudity and coitus in front of her son as well as overt seduction of him prior to the incest. Usually she denies any harmful influence she has had on him.

Son. The son often has a variety of problems subsequent to the maternal rejection and had these prior to the incest. He may have nightmares of a persecuting nature, poor school performance, and other behavior problems, including delinquency. He often has had a variety of sexual experiences, including incestuous relationships (heterosexual and homosexual) with other members of his family; these may have served to weaken his taboo against maternal incest. His homosexual fears may be a defense against his anxieties about the potential for or actual sexual involvement with his mother. In son-initiated incest, case histories suggest that the son is likely to be mentally subnormal or disturbed, possibly schizophrenic.

Father. The father has often been absent from the home since the son was a young boy, and they have not kept in contact although the son may have attempted to find his father. If the father is at home, he is often ineffectual and passive in face of a rigid, controlling wife.

Father–Son Incest

The psychodynamics of father–son incest are much less clear than they are for father–daughter incest, primarily because only two dozen cases have ever been reported in the literature.[1,3,4,20,25,27,28,30,31,38] The primary controversy of these reports has been on how much the overt incestuous behavior is an expression of interactional family difficulties and how much results from the intrapsychic conflicts of the father. While both Langsley[20] and Awad[1] have concluded that family interaction is not as important in father–son incest as it is in father–daughter incest, Raybin[30] and Machotka[25] see the incest as resulting from a combination of individual and family disturbances.

Father. The father frequently has had severe problems with his own mother, being rejected and deprived during his formative years. His problems with women continued with inhibited relationships with girls during his teens and severe marital problems, sometimes including sexual estrangement, with his wife. Latent or conscious struggles with homosexual impulses usually have been a major determinant for some of the father's long-term behavior and character style. Frequently, there have been other homosexual incestuous experiences with brothers, uncles, cousins or even fathers during childhood and adulthood. Homosexual relationships outside the family are less common. The homosexual incest is a living out of the father's own adolescent conflicts. The father often is intelligent, successfully employed, and without a history of severe psychological disorder. Often he is under the influence of alcohol during the incestuous episodes. Half of the cases in the literature report simultaneous physical and sexual abuse of the child. The father may also foster other incestuous relationships, such as between siblings, or a son and an uncle, or engage in additional sexual activities himself with his other children, both male and female.

Son. Even if the son has no history of emotional disturbance during his early years, a variety of problems usually occur as a result of the incest or other severe family tensions. There are no reports of a son's seductive solicitation of incest with father as there are of sons with mothers and adolescent girls with fathers. However, mutual exercising and massaging during a son's adolescence have been reported to result in sexual incidents. The son may also have simultaneous and/or subsequent homosexual experiences with brothers, male cousins, and peers.

Mother. The mother's role in father–son incest has been discussed less fully than it has in father–daughter incest. Although she often has marital problems with her husband, it does not appear that she has completely abdicated her role as wife and sexual partner. There is not necessarily the role-reversal with her son which often occurs with a daughter involved in incest. Despite this, she usually colludes in the incest by not making her awareness of the sexual incidents known; at times she may completely repress what she has seen and heard. The mother has been described as much more powerful than she acknowledges. With a castrating attitude toward men, she lets them think they are in charge but then manipulates situations behind their backs. Mothers often take action to protect their sons, including divorce from the sons' fathers, only after the incest becomes known to the community.

Mother–Daughter Incest

The reports of mother–daughter incest[17,21,27,38] are so exceedingly rare that little is known about contributing factors. Weiner[38] has described an intense homosexual relationship which occurred between a mother and her 26-year-old daughter, whom she had not seen since she placed her in a foster home in infancy. The mother initiated the incest which lasted for four months. At the time, both women were separated from their husbands due to severe marital problems including sexual difficulties. The incest terminated when the mother returned to live with her husband.

Goodwin and DiVasto[17] described another mother–daughter incestuous relationship which began in childhood. The mother was a controlling and jealous woman who slept with her daughter rather than her husband. Occasionally, the mother also had a homosexual lover. The father was overshadowed by his wife and was frequently away from home on business trips. The daughter responded, in childhood and adulthood, to her mother's demands that she comfort her when the mother was lonely or ill.

Medlicott[27] has described a case in which the mother slept with the daughter to avoid father, and then the mother initiated sexual activity. Lidz and Lidz[21] have examined the adverse influences of a mother's homosexual tendencies toward a daughter. In three cases, the erotic relationship involved matters such as skin contact, anal preoccupations, and physical intimacy while asleep, but this closeness alternated with aloofness which increased the child's insecurities. In adulthood all three daughters became schizophrenic.

Brother–Sister Incest

Even though brother–sister incest is often said to be the most common type of incestuous relationship, valid documentation of this assumption is lacking. However, much has been written of the dynamics and contributing factors to this type of incest.[5,11,13,19,22,26,28,29,34,37]

Brother and Sister. Often the sister has had prior sexual experience, either an incestuous relationship with her father or a multitude of relations with peers. The youngest sister in a family with several older brothers is at particular risk. The brother may have assumed a father role in the family, especially if the biologic father is absent from the home, and insisted on having sexual relations with his sister. If the father is at home, he may have urged his son to engage in incest. The sister who idolizes her older brother may go along with his sexual requests and experience relatively little guilt at the time.

Father and Mother. Obviously, the parents of incestuous siblings have not provided adequate supervision of their children. With young children, it is the mother who is absent or unable to provide a restraining influence, while with older children, especially a son, it is the father who is absent, physically ill, or incapacitated by emotional disturbance or old age and thereby unable to act as a prohibiting influence. Also, the mother has often been described as rigid and puritanical in her attitudes about sexuality. Through her excessive repression, her children's interest in the "forbidden" may have increased. On the other hand, some parents are excessively permissive about sex in the home with considerable discussion of sexual matters, nudity, and acceptance of their children watching parental intercourse.

Incest Among Other Relatives

There are a few reports in the literature on homosexual incest between brothers.[28,30,31] In cases described by Raybin[30] and Rhinehart[31] such incest occurred in addition to the father–son incest. Meiselman[28] found one case of brother–brother incest in her psychotherapy sample: a 10-year-old boy was anally raped by a 15-year-old stepbrother. There do not appear to be any reports on incestuous relationships between sisters.

There are also scattered clinical publications on incest between grandmothers and granddaughters,[2] uncles and nephews,[25] aunts and nephews,[22] uncles and nieces,[28] and children and even more distant relatives, but the infrequency of cases makes any composite picture impossible.

Multiple Incest

Several authors have noted that multiple incest sometimes occurs within the same family.[3,7,11,25,26,28,29,31,37] Meiselman[28] has reported that nearly 30% of her psychotherapy sample had either been sexually involved with more than one family member or knew of other incestuous affairs within their families. This finding indicates that once the incest taboo is broken in a family, it is quite likely to be broken again. Berry[3] and Raphling *et al.*,[29] have emphasized that incest should be thought of as a transmissible phenomenon. Indeed, previous incestuous experience or knowledge of it may be the most significant factor in the continuation of incest with new family members.

Conclusion

Incestuous families are clearly much too complex to be described in any unilateral way, and there does not appear to be any single necessary or sufficient contributing factor which explains its onset or continuation. Rather, a complex interaction of many events and psychodynamics must exist before incestuous thoughts become actualized. With further research, the contributing factors to various types of incest may become clearer. Meanwhile, the clinician would do best to consider sociological factors, possible organic psychopathology, and individual and family psychodynamics when assessing a family and planning intervention. Of all the contributing factors mentioned in the literature, the most predictive are likely to be the absence of a strong, satisfying marital bond and *prior* incestuous behavior somewhere in the family.

References

1. Awad, G. A. (1976) Father–son incest: a case report. *J. Nerv. Ment. Dis.* **162:** 135.
2. Barry, M. J., and Johnson, A. M. (1958) The incest barrier. *Psychoanal. Q.* **27:** 485.
3. Berry, G. W. (1975) Incest: some clinical variations on a classical theme. *J. Am. Acad. Psychoanal.* **3:** 151.
4. Bender, L., and Blau, A. (1937) The reaction of children to sexual relations with adults. *Am. J. Orthopsychiatry* **7:** 500.
5. Bonaparte, M. (1953) *Female Sexuality.* International Univ., New York.
6. Brown, W. (1963) Murder rooted in incest. In *Patterns of Incest.* (Edited by Masters, R. E. L.) Julian, New York.
7. Browning, D. H., and Boatman, B. (1977) Incest: children at risk. *Am. J. Psychiatry* **134:** 69.
8. Burton, L. (1968) *Vulnerable Children.* Routledge & Kegan Paul, London.
9. Cabinis, D., and Phillip, E. (1969) The paedophile homosexual incest in court. *Dtsh. Z. Gesamte Gerichtl Med.* **66:** 46.
10. Cormier, B. D., Kennedy, M., and Sangowicz, J. (1962) Psychodynamics of father–daughter incest. *Can. Psychiatry Assoc. J.* **7:** 203.
11. Eist, H. I., and Mandel, A. U. (1968) Family treatment of ongoing incest behavior. *Fam. Process* **7:** 216.
12. Finkelhor, D. (1979) *Sexually Victimized Children.* Free Press, New York.
13. Fox, J. R. (1962) Sibling incest. *Br. J. Sociol.* **13:** 128.
14. Gebhard, P. H., Gagnon, J. H., Pomeroy, W. B., and Christenson, C. V. (1965) *Sex Offenders: An Analysis of Types.* Harper & Row, New York.
15. Giarretto, H. (1976) The treatment of father–daughter incest: a psychosocial approach. *Children Today* 34.
16. Gibbens, T. C. N., and Prince, J. (1963) *Child Victims of Sex Offences.* Institute for the Study and Treatment of Delinquency, London.
17. Goodwin, J., and DiVasto, P. (1979) Mother–daughter incest. *Child Abuse and Neglect* **3:** 953.
18. Gutheil, T. C., and Avery, N. C. (1977) Multiple overt incest as family defense against loss. *Fam. Process* **16:** 105.
19. Kubo, S. (1959) Researches and studies on incest in Japan. *Hiroshima J. Med. Sci.* **8:** 99.
20. Langsley, D. C., Schwartz, M. N., and Fairbairn, R. H. (1968) Father–son incest. *Comp. Psychiatry* **9:** 218.
21. Lidz, R. W., and Lidz, T. (1969) Homosexual tendencies in mothers of schizophrenic women. *J. Nerv. Ment. Dis.* **149:** 229.
22. Lukianowicz, N. (1972) Incest: I. paternal incest; II. other types of incest. *Br. J. Psychiatry* **120:** 301.
23. Lustig, N., Dresser, J. W., Spellman, S. W., and Murray, T. B. (1966) Incest: a family group survival pattern. *Arch. Gen. Psychiatry* **14:** 31.
24. Macdonald, J. M. (1971) *Rape: Offenders and Their Victims.* C. Thomas, Springfield, Ill.
25. Machotka, P., Pittman, F. S., and Flomenhaft, K. (1967) Incest as a family affair. *Fam. Process* **6:** 98.
26. Magel, V. and Winnik, H. Z. (1968) Role of incest in family structure. *Isr Ann. Psychiatry* **6:** 173.
27. Medlicott, R. W. (1967) Parent–child incest. *Aust. NZ J. Psychiatry*, **1:** 180.
28. Meiselman, K. C. (1978) *Incest: A Psychological Study of Causes and Effects with Treatment Recommendations.* Jossey-Bass, San Francisco.
29. Raphling, D. L., Carpenter, B. L., and Davis, A. (1967) Incest: a genealogical study. *Arch. Gen. Psychiatry* **16:** 505.
30. Raybin, J. B. (1969) Homosexual incest. *J. Nerv. Ment. Dis.* **148:** 105.
31. Rhinehart, J. W. (1961) Genesis of overt incest. *Comp. Psychiatry* **2:** 338.
32. Riemer, S. (1940) A research note on incest. *Am. J. Sociol.* **45:** 566.

33. Shelton, W. R. (1975) A study of incest. *Int. J. Offender Ther. Comparative Criminol.* **19:** 139.
34. Sloane, P., and Karpinski, E. (1942) Effects of incest on the participants. *Am. J. Orthopsychiatry* **12:** 666.
35. Virkkunen, M. (1974) Incest offences and alcoholism. *Med. Sci. Law* **14:** 124.
36. Wahl, C. W. (1960) The psychodynamics of consummated maternal incest. *Arch. Gen. Psychiatry* **3:** 188.
37. Weinberg, S. K. (1955) *Incest Behavior.* Citadel, New York.
38. Weiner, I. B. (1962) Father–daughter incest: a clinical report. *Psychiatry Q.* **36:** 607.
39. Williams, J. E. H. (1974) The neglect of incest: a criminologist's view. *Med. Sci. & Law* **14:** 64.
40. Yorukoglu, A., and Kemph, J. P. (1966) Children not severely damaged by incest with a parent. *J. Amer. Acad. Child Psychiatry* **5:** 111.

Chapter Nine

Incest: Intake and Investigation

ANNE B. TOPPER AND DAVID J. ALDRIDGE

During the past several years each of the United States has enacted legislation to facilitate and mandate the reporting of abuse and neglect of children.[1,15] (See Chapter Five.) This is a giant and preliminary step in the right direction accomplished only after years of pressure and education of state legislators. The best reporting laws in the world, however, will only compound the problems of the abusive family if those responding to the reports do not know how to intervene effectively. It is important that the intervention provide protection to the endangered child and be of assistance to the family, though all concerned may not recognize it as "assistance" at the time. Such intervention also must be within the framework of the law of the locale. This is particularly important in cases of sexual abuse when the power of the law can, through court order or by stipulation, require that perpetrators, their families, and their victims become involved in treatment.

The intent of this chapter is to describe a system of intervention for sexual abuse which has proven effective in a state-regulated, county-administered social services department. The system will be described in two sections: investigation of the report and crisis intervention.

In this chapter the reader will note that the references to "perpetrator" will generally indicate that the perpetrator is a father, step-father, or father surrogate, that the victim is characterized as a daughter or step-daughter, and that the sexual assault is regarded as an incestuous liaison. The overwhelming majority of cases with which we have dealt have been consistent with this configuration, hence this generalization. We are very much aware that sexual assault is *not* limited to this group, and there are increasing indicators of mother–son and homosexual abuse as well as sibling sexual abuse. Many of our observations may be applied to these groups as well. Time, space, and our own experiences have limited specific references to these groups, but we are cognizant of them and of some of the special problems faced by the individuals who are involved.

In referring to caseworkers, we have used masculine and feminine pronouns interchangeably for two reasons: first, because we prefer to think that we are not chauvinists; and second, because workers of each sex are needed to provide the necessary treatment. A great deal of the treatment in such cases involves modeling, and assignment of workers of the appropriate sex may allow such modeling to get off to an early start though the initial impact may be superficial.

Investigation of the Report

Under Colorado law, reports of child abuse and neglect, including sexual abuse, may be made to either the appropriate law enforcement agency or the county department of social services. When the law enforcement agency is the receiving agency, it must make every effort to notify the social services department which shall then conduct an investigation itself and/or coordinate an investigation by others.[3] It has been our experience that *conjoint investigations* conducted by trained caseworkers and juvenile officers or specialized forces such as victim service staff are efficient and effective. They generate a good deal of information that might not be elicited by only one individual with training in one profession. Furthermore, the varied interpretations of the findings stimulated by different professional backgrounds tend to keep staff from becoming too rigid in one system. The additional resources appended to the several agencies represented may be utilized on behalf of victims and families more easily than if handled by a single individual. Such conjoint investigations can only be successful when the agencies involved subscribe to a policy of cooperation based on mutual respect and open communication, cultivated carefully and consciously by all levels of agency personnel. Such conscious cultivation should be made a part of the job descriptions of staff members so that administrators do not make the error of considering such contact as time wasted. (The importance of the golf course in consummating business deals has long been recognized, but it is often thought that agency personnel lack the subtlety to use informal contact to good advantage on behalf of those they serve.)

In these days when budget appropriations for human services are under heavy fire, such cooperation may extend the capabilities of limited personnel by avoiding repetitious reports and duplicated effort. The benefit to the family and victim who may thus be able to avoid at least a few repetitions of their stories is considerable.*

Honest cooperation between social services and law enforcement, including the district attorney's office, is so rare in most areas of the United States that our system has elicited expressions of disbelief. Typical reactions have been: "Social workers don't talk to punitive law enforcement personnel who are only interested in prosecution and destruction of families", and "Law enforcement personnel don't talk to 'bleeding heart' social workers who mollycoddle undeserving felons". Obviously, such oppositional stances will not be as beneficial to agency staff or to the families served as will a cooperative interagency approach.

Colorado County Departments of Social Services are required by law since 1976 to provide emergency child abuse response capability on a 24-hour basis.[3] El Paso County Department of Social Services had developed such a program prior to the enactment of this legislation. We have found that our contract with law enforcement has now provided protection to some of our young and vulnerable caseworkers who may need to check on a volatile situation at 2:00 a.m. In other instances law enforcement alone has been able to act effectively and decisively to provide a temporary solution which will protect the child and hold the family over until morning.

---

* Repetition of the story in a therapeutic setting may assist the victim in dealing with the trauma of her experiences as opposed to having to repeat the story to varied investigative persons.

The Intake Worker: Who and Why

Those social workers who receive initial reports of alleged abuse and neglect are designated as child welfare intake workers. They constitute one or more separate and distinct units with their own supervisory head. In our experience the best possible intake worker may not be the best possible ongoing worker and vice versa though they possess and require many skills in common. The skills needed and the basic orientations for both these important tasks vary, though of course the two functions must be compatible and allow easy flow of case material from intake to ongoing units specializing in provision of child protection services. Some of the important areas of competence of those workers engaged in intake will now be detailed.

*Personal Feelings**. As a society we are notably conflicted about sex and sexuality. Sexuality in children is denied at any point beyond determining whether pink or blue booties are the more appropriate. We have inquired of some audiences while lecturing around the country, "How many of you have children?" Many raise their hands. The people are asked semi-seriously, "And how many of you have felt like really clobbering those children at one time or another?" Hands are raised again. Then, "How many did it?" People turn and smile at each other in recognition of the fact that indeed the potential for physically abusing a child lies in all of us. We early recognized, however, that we could hardly expect the same response and achieve the same recognition by asking, "How many of you have felt like fondling your child's genitals?" The incest taboo is still strong among us.

Our conflicted reactions are increased virtually geometrically when the sexual activity we notice is aberrant sexual activity such as sexual abuse in general and incest in particular.[7,12] All of us are angered, disgusted, and saddened by such incidents. To remain "horrified" limits one's ability to be useful to the family experiencing trauma produced by sexual abuse. The worker must come to terms with his own sexuality and his own fears and experiences. He certainly must examine his value system before working with victims of sexual abuse and their families. If he cannot achieve an attitude of acceptance toward the involved individuals to accompany his position of authority, his ability to initiate successful intervention is seriously limited, for individuals in families caught up in these often tangled and convoluted relationships are extremely sensitive to nuances of judgmentalism and rejection. Thus, the worker who has not resolved his own feelings of revulsion and ambivalence should not be assigned such cases. Even the worker who has achieved a favorable resolution must re-examine his attitudes periodically and/or be given the freedom to reject the occasional case that for some reason triggers attitudes that would hamper his work with the family. For example, one of the authors was given a sketchy report of an alleged sexual assault on a very young infant that was so disturbing to her that she was immediately aware that she could not participate directly with the family in the case and so withdrew. The investigation finally established that no family members were involved in the abuse, and they were provided with counseling to remediate the trauma and the family disruption. But had the author not withdrawn as worker on the case, her revulsion as perceived by the family could have caused them to isolate themselves from therapeutic

* *Editors' note:* See Chapters Twelve and Fourteen for further discussions of this topic.

assistance. More importantly, her investigative reports, even if she had tried to accommodate for bias, might have had a negative impact on the ultimate determination of innocence; in fact, it was the social worker who did work with the case who pressed for further investigation which eventually cleared the family.

Knowledge of Psychodynamics. The ability to work constructively with the problem of incest further requires that the worker acquire as much knowledge as possible—both theoretical and practical—about characteristics, dynamics, and behaviors likely to be present in incestuous circumstances. There may be no stereotypes of either victims or perpetrators, as some authorities state,[6] but we and others[9,13] have found that certain characteristics do pertain in enough cases to provide a basis for some general observations.

Authority as An Element of Problem-Solving. The intake worker must be able to convey an impression of competence in problem-solving. The appearance of competence must be bolstered by sufficient authority delegated to this individual to enable participation in decisions in emergencies without falling afoul of red tape. For example, when a child is removed from the home by law enforcement with or without concurrence by the social worker, authority to place the child must be granted to the social worker as well as the authority to permit, with concurrence of the court in the locale, medical examination or whatever other emergency measures are required. The social worker and others working in such circumstances must not be caught in the double bind of being criticized or even threatened with a law suit for not providing immediate emergency services and conversely being called upon to explain at great length why they did not obtain prior administrative approval in each case, despite the emergent nature of the problem.

Assessment Skills. The intake worker must have an ability to interview effectively, to assess what he hears and sees, and to make quick determination of what is needed at the moment to protect the child, if indeed that is a consideration. Assisting the family, the victim, and/or the reporter will be of greatest importance in the beginning construction of a case plan which may determine the eventual outcome of the total intervention. In order to make as accurate an assessment as possible under the time constraints imposed by the law, the worker should be knowledgeable of procedures which will provide physical examination, psychological/psychiatric evaluations, legal custody, placement facilities, and law enforcement investigation.

Because our agency procedures are such that the intake unit transfers the case to the ongoing protective services unit for continuing services, the assessment by the intake worker is necessarily brief and incomplete, but the quality can be excellent. Furthermore, because of the training and experience these people develop, they will generally include their conjectures and assumptions—clearly labeled as such—about the family. These have been found to be helpful and amazingly near the mark. The ability to size up a family and a situation while under pressure and in a short period of time is a distinct talent not possessed by everyone.

Knowledge of Resources. The intake worker in general public social service systems also has the structure, as does no other worker in a single agency that we know of, to provide a battery of auxiliary crisis services to the victim and to the family that highly specialized or single-focus agencies typically lack. Services for the victim and for other children at risk could include foster placement and medical attention. Services for the family must include arrangements for evaluations such as medical, psychiatric, psychological, or social, and may encompass provisions for food, emergency housing, referrals for legal services, and so forth. In virtually all cases a multitude of community/county facilities need to be utilized. In urban areas such resources usually exist although they may not be readily available or may be difficult to coordinate. The intake worker must be fully aware of and knowledgeable about such resources and have the ability to get the needed services for the family. Constant updating of this knowledge should be overseen by supervision. Furthermore, administrators and planners must be kept informed of what is needed and is not available. Intake people can and should be a primary source of information about gaps in services and frequency of use.

In small and/or rural communities cooperative arrangements with larger centers of population for consultation and contractual arrangements are vitally necessary if treatment is to be provided. Though each small populated area cannot support all needed services, shared planning and shared funds for training and consultation will go far to meet some of the needs.

Respect for Confidentiality. Treatment in a small community may be very difficult because of the gossip grapevine, but attempts must be made to safeguard confidentiality. Understandably, the sensation and drama surrounding cases of sexual abuse cause such cases to be quite attractive to the media. While the minor child's name cannot be printed, the name of the perpetrator can be and is. The family name can be routinely picked up through the law enforcement channels as soon as the offender has been charged. Although this is regular procedure, it is obvious that such publication contributes serious and unnecessary burdens of stress to a family already overwhelmed by their situation.

In one recent case of alleged incest the father, who happened to be a widely respected businessman, was arrested right after his daughter voiced her accusation. The press, having access to the summons and complaint, published the father's name and address as well as his alleged offense in the local paper. This was long before the merits of the case were investigated, let alone tried in court! In this particular case, criminal and social investigations found the daughter's claims to have been untrue. The fact that the case was dismissed was never published, and there is little doubt that many individuals in the commuity continue to hold the first story as being true. The ongoing damage to this particular family cannot be measured. In addition to the social damage to the family, a permanent splintering of the family unit persists. The parents decided that the child should not be returned to the home out of fear that the girl might use such vindictive tactics again. If there had been some means to keep the matter confidential, at least until after the evidence was presented at trial, the child might be safely back in the home today.

As a general rule, the incestuous father, almost by definition, practices sexual assault only in his own home. Since he is unlikely to jump out from behind a bush to attack a casual passerby, the public does not require protection afforded by publication of his name and alleged misdeed in the press.

In cases of child abuse, including sexual abuse, the privilege of confidentiality is largely abrogated due to the combined jurisdiction of social services, law enforcement, and the courts. Appropriate planning for services to the victim and the family requires that agencies coordinate their efforts; however, the family's privacy must be respected to the extent that is concomitant with the protection of the child.

A healthy respect for confidentiality includes the judicious sharing of information. Such sharing must be based on the needs of the family, provisions of the law, and professional ethics. Knowledge should only be shared when the agencies involved have achieved status as reliable, resourceful, conscientious, and cooperative. Good working relationships with other agencies promote communication and exchange of ideas. Again, these do not just "happen". Recognition of the importance of such efforts can be regularized by their inclusion in job descriptions and by screening for appropriate attitudes at employment interviews.

Good interagency relationships should not be an accidental bonus but must be planned for and worked toward. No one agency, even a multi-purpose agency, can be all things to all people, nor perhaps should it try to be. The complex treatment required in these cases necessitates an involvement of various people with various skills and resources. Cooperation in case planning is essential and sharing of information is vital.

In Colorado, the law specifically states that the physical record may not be shared in its entirety with other persons unless subpoenaed in a formal court proceeding. However, reports and information in the case record may be verbally shared with persons providing adjunct services or who were involved in making decisions regarding the family.* Through this formal court proceeding, the force of the legal system can be brought to bear to aid in gathering information from reluctant sources, but this should only be done when a good case cannot be made without certain relevant information.[14]

Preparation for Court. We have found that social workers in general are not particularly comfortable with lawyers nor with working in judicial territory.[2] Few fully understand the adversary judicial system, even diluted as it may be in the juvenile court hearings. Training, knowledge, and experience will help workers retain their poise in court and thus be better able to achieve desired results for the family. Thorough preparation of the case with as much documentation as possible, plus prior consultation with the agency's specially designated attorney, will do much to alleviate this tension.

Assessment of the Family: Specific Intake Investigative Inventory

Assessment of the family, including its problems and strengths, is of primary importance. The worker's skill and attitude will affect the quantity and quality of information gathered and will set the tone for the family's relationship with the agency.

---

* In order to clarify the Colorado Children's Code regarding confidentiality and related matters, the authors conferred with the Honorable John F. Gallagher, District Court Judge, Fourth Judicial District, Colorado Springs, Colorado, on December 18, 1978.

Especially if there have been no other contacts with any other official organization, this initial contact may be the most important in the entire proceedings.

In the assessment process, time may be severely limited due to legal constraints. As a result, initial interviews may not contain as much clinical information as will be developed later. However, the assessment must include a great deal more than the recording of demographic data, the narrative about the sexual abuse, and a brief social history.

Planning an effective treatment program cannot be accomplished until a detailed assessment of the parents as individuals and as a couple, and of the family as a whole (See Chapter Thirteen) is completed. The mother's background should be explored:

1. Was she an incest victim herself?
2. How does she relate to men in general and her husband in particular?
3. How does she feel about sexual expression?
4. How does she feel about herself, her role in the family, and her children?
5. Does she want to be a parent?
6. What does she want to happen to the family?

Much of the same information should be gathered about the father's background:

1. What were his childhood experiences?
2. What were the sexual behaviors in his family?
3. When and how did he first become aware of his sexual urges?
4. What seemed to trigger his interest in his daughter as a sexual being?
5. How adequate does he feel as a male, a husband, a father?
6. What would he like to see happen, and what is he willing to do to reach that goal?

Commitment of the parental couple to each other, to the marriage, and to the family, is of the utmost importance for the therapeutic course is often long, arduous, and painful. Without such commitment, maintenance of the family as a unit is not a realistic goal and alternatives should be sought.

There are circumstances which make conventional therapeutic intervention with the parent(s) futile. These range from psychosis to lack of commitment. Our mandate remains: protect the child and save whatever else can be managed.

Because so many cases of incest are not reported, it has occurred to many therapists and others that part of the problem is that the right questions are not being asked. The intake worker must ask the "right" questions with forthrightness, not only in cases where sexual assault may have been the presenting problem but also in other kinds of cases where family dysfunction is a primary concern. Such "right" questions include asking directly, depending upon the age of the child, whether he or she has been sexually assaulted and repeating this at intervals by asking more specifically detailed questions about sexual activity. When convinced that this is not an area of concern, this approach should just as directly be dismissed and noted in the record.

Because there seldom are witnesses to incestuous incidents, the child's story of what happened may become the best available legal testimony and provide the best possible information for effective intervention in the family processes. Therefore, the initial and other early interviews with the child are of paramount importance. The worker who is interviewing a victim of sexual assault may be hearing the child's story before it has become crystalized by repetition, and thus it may be much more revealing than later versions. It may even be possible to determine whether the story being told by the child is true. Body language, descriptive material about the sexual activity, family roles, and so forth, may actually reveal that the child has not been sexually molested but that the family has other problems which may require intense intervention, but not necessarily child protection. Sensitivity to such nuances of language and physical presence, along with an eye and ear for congruence of affect with emotional status, may not be "hard" court evidence but will certainly give the worker a much more accurate picture of the victim's situation. It may also give many indications about what other questions might be asked.

The setting for the interview(s) should be geared to the child's comfort and characteristics. Freedom to move about and explore should be allowed. Privacy and avoidance of interruptions are needed since these divert an already short attention span and may produce apprehensiveness and self-consciousness. The presence of supportive and familiar people may be allowed if the child is frightened, but having the parents present, even the non-active perpetrator, is seldom a wise choice.

Establishment of a relationship with the child will help to ease the tense situation, and the worker should first explain her role and the purpose of the talk. This, followed by some random and general conversational exchanges, will usually help to ease the tension and allow the interviewer an opportunity to begin to assess the developmental level of the child.

The worker should make some determination about cognitive and emotional developmental status. (See Chapter Eleven.) She also should review the circumstances of the assault with the child: what, where, when and by whom. Additionally, the worker should determine to whom the incident was reported, to whom the child has spoken, and how many persons have interviewed the child. Throughout this process, the worker should carefully note the child's exact words. Obtaining the history of the sexual assault can be facilitated by using language the child can understand and by dealing forthrightly with her fears for herself and her family. Reassurance that she is not "bad" and is not seen as an accomplice is important. The questions should be simple, direct, as open-ended as possible, and non-accusatory. Sensitivity towards the child's feelings about herself, her family, and the perpetrator should be demonstrated by the worker's affective responses to her.

The child's statement about the sexual assault needs to be very specific on factual matters for legal purposes. Some of this data will also be useful in planning for the family. Information about family functioning and structure will also be revealed in the course of the statement even though primary focus will be on factual descriptions about what happened, who was involved, when and where the incident occurred, and what degree and kind of coercion was used.

Assessment of the accuracy of the report and the credibility and the competency of the child should be made:

1. Would the average child have had the described experience?
2. Does the experience include any archetypal circumstances?
3. Is the history given now consistent on basic facts with the previous recital(s)?
4. Is information spontaneously given; does it sound rehearsed; how much prompting is required?

The worker should ask about what has been happening in the family since revelation of the assault(s):

1. Have the parents been supportive, blaming, angry or ambivalent?
2. How does the child feel about these reactions and any changes in the family unit?
3. What, if any, emotional signs of distress (nightmares, withdrawal, regression, acting out) have occurred?

The interview should be closed by thanking the child for her cooperation and for the information given. The child is told what is most likely to happen next. Projections into the future only confuse her and arouse her fears. It is extremely important to provide reasonable reassurance about her security.

These guidelines are used by criminal justice system personnel as well as by social services. As noted, a conjoint interview, if it does not intimidate the child, will generally provide a broad spectrum of information and will eliminate some reiteration of the story.

The participant with the social services perspective in the interview described above should be the more active questioner in the areas heavily weighted with psychosocial impact, while the questioner about basic facts and details could well be the agent of the law. Such role differentiation should help the child understand that many people are working on her behalf, and she will know more clearly which sources to turn to for what type of assistance.

In addition to the police–social services report, other reports on the child and perpetrator which should be obtained include: medical reports, psychological and psychiatric evaluations, school reports, and information from any other agencies who have previously been involved.

The age of the victim will make a great deal of difference in much of the immediate questioning and planning. All victims should be medically examined as soon as possible by a physician who is well aware of sexual abuse and can answer possible questions or give information without further embarrassing or alarming the child.[11] It is not a given that such an examination may only be adding trauma. Not only may the physical report be essential for legal reasons but also it will determine whether other medical needs exist. A really "tuned-in" physician can be one of the best possible early remediators of the abuse by providing the child, in addition to whatever medical treatment is immediately indicated, with certain basic assurances about the child's body and its functioning. (See Chapter Ten.)

We have been told and have read about the difficulty encountered in having a child victim examined by a physician due to the fact that the parents may be reluctant to give their consent for the medical examination. Such a physical examination conducted as quickly as possible after the child has been taken into temporary custody constitutes a part of the legally required investigation and therefore must be done. If heavy opposition develops, the physician, the intake worker, and the hospital may feel more secure if a protective order is issued. Ongoing medical treatment must be approved by the parents whenever possible and/or by the court-ordered legal custodian.

We recommend a routine staffing between intake and ongoing personnel to facilitate the bridging process between investigation and treatment. This staffing must consider every aspect of the case including all unrecorded feelings that the participants may have about the family and the situation. Once this is accomplished and the intake worker has passed on all available information and completed his court commitment, he must retire from the case completely. The family and the victim must be prepared for this withdrawal and be able to interpret it as a progression through a system, not as a rejection. If the worker does not withdraw in good style and in good time, he could be instrumental in establishing a manipulative situation that could enable the family or victim to avoid some aspects of the treatment that they found unpleasant.

Shared Decision-Making by the Child Protection Team

In October 1972, the El Paso County Department of Social Services initiated child protection teams which functioned to clinically assess each case within 48 hours after the report. These first teams consisted of social service staff members, medical, public health, law enforcement personnel, and any other professional who had information concerning the history of the case. In 1975 the Colorado State Legislature passed a bill which mandated every county in the State reporting 50 or more child abuse cases per year to appoint standing child protection teams.

Colorado Statutes define the Child Protection Team as:

> "... a multidisciplinary team consisting, where possible, of a physician, a representative of the juvenile court or the district court with juvenile jurisdiction, a representative of the local law enforcement agency, a representative of the county department, a representative of a mental health clinic, a representative of a public health department, an attorney, a representative of a public school district, and one or more representatives of the lay community. In no event shall an attorney member of the child protection team be appointed to represent the child or the parents at any subsequent court proceedings nor shall the child protection team be composed of fewer than three persons. When any racial, ethnic, or linguistic minority group constitutes a significant portion of the population of the jurisdiction of the child protection team, a member of each such minority group shall serve as an additional lay member of the child protection team. At least one of the preceding members of the team shall be chosen on the basis of representing low-income families."[3]

After considering all of the information presented during the team conference the team moves to certain conclusions and recommendations concerning the case. Of primary concern is whether the team can conclude that abuse actually occurred (not in a fault-finding manner nor to necessarily identify the perpetrator) or, if in doubt, what factors might identify high-risk potential within the family. The recommendations are then presented as a remedial design for the family. Recommendations often include what custody actions might be pursued.

Within 90 days of the team meeting a standard review form is filled in by the social worker. This form details the history of the implementations of each team recommendation and an account of the current status of the case. Any member of the team, including the social worker, may call an additional team meeting, if there is disagreement concerning the original conclusions and recommendations or about whatever actions were taken in response to them.

The existence of these teams has greatly facilitated the reaction and response capabilities of the community while safeguarding the rights of individuals and families through a more thorough consideration of the case than could be conducted by any individual of one discipline in such a brief period of time. Unilateral condemnatory decisions can seldom be made in such a setting.

Another obvious advantage of the team concept is that the burden of having to make final decisions in these matters is no longer borne by the doctor or any other one individual. Finally, the child protection team serves as an excellent training forum for professionals in the community. As individuals from various disciplines rotate off the team, they take valuable experience into their practices.

Crisis Intervention

Most states mandate that the protection of the child be of primary consideration in any abuse and/or assault situation.[15] Following this first concern the law usually requires that any course of action be designed to reunify the family and to maintain the family intact.

When we consider the fragile condition of these families resulting from years of marginal and pathological functioning, it is apparent that insensitive and unprofessional investigation and intervention could well shatter any remaining structural strengths. Sometimes family disorganization must precede a period of rebuilding. Nevertheless, the basic issue of incest must not be avoided nor clouded, particularly if the family is dealing with the confrontation through denial.

Keeping the Family Informed and Preventing Family Disintegration

The initial investigation must be coupled with crisis intervention if the family is to feel that others want to help them. One way to do this is to be sure that the family knows what is happening. It is important that all family members as well as their attorneys be briefed on whatever legal, social, and therapeutic planning is being done. The uninformed family caught up in complex legal and social service systems very often can only react with anger and stubborn resistiveness to the frustration of feeling powerless in the planning process.[4] The adversity created through the lack of communication and cooperation between social service personnel and the family's legal counsel can easily cause the "curtain to be pulled", that is, a lawyer's refusal to allow his clients to talk to anyone except through himself. Legal proceedings, whether criminal or civil, are usually and by design, adversary in nature. This adversary stance which is so deeply rooted in American jurisprudence can be detrimental to the family's rehabilitation. The workers must develop negotiating and conciliatory skills to use the judicial system to help the family rather than to disrupt it.

Family Separations

Hospitalization and Foster Placement. One of the most crucial decisions made in an incest case is whether to remove the child from her home. The evidence to corroborate the sexual abuse may be only a child's story of her experience. Such evidence is often so insubstantial that unless medical testimony, an admission from the perpetrator, or a witness is produced, no case can be made. Even this information will become available in some cases only after the child has been removed.

The *authority* to remove a child from home rests solely with law enforcement. The *decision* to remove the child is often made jointly with others, such as the social worker on call, victim service division personnel, a physician, or a nurse. The decision is, according to law, based upon whether the child can stay at home in safety, which is a difficult legal determination to make. The decision is most often made under circumstances of great stress; information and evidence are woefully incomplete. The child who is being "saved" from danger is herself reluctant and fearful of leaving familiar surroundings for the unknown place of safety. Nevertheless, the decision must be made.

Hospitalization of the child, under a police hold or an order of protection until a temporary custody hearing can be held, is an available legal option in Colorado which has proven effective. Psychological/psychiatric evaluations generally are not accomplished until after the temporary custody hearing, but arrangements can be started and some preparations of the child can begin.

If it is determined that the child is at great risk in returning to her home, foster placement is made. Foster parents who receive sexually abused children need to be specially selected and trained about the needs and behaviors of such children. They need to examine their own behaviors and expectations. Sexually abused children may indulge in sexual behavior or exhibit provocative mannerisms that will be troubling or misunderstood to uninstructed though well-meaning foster parents. The worker making an emergency placement must check and double check to make sure the foster parents have an understanding of the most probable behaviors of the child to be placed. Furthermore, the worker must share pertinent information so that the foster parents can be full team members rather than merely custodial caretakers.

Removing a child from her home, though traumatic for all concerned, does accomplish a number of objectives. First, of course, the child is protected. Then the family and especially the adult couple are confronted with the inescapable fact that society, through the law, can intervene in intimate family relationships when such relationships are deemed dangerously inhumane. The disruption engendered by the removal then forces the family into some action to preserve itself as a unit or to regroup into distinct segments. This momentary lack of family homeostasis will often provoke an admission of guilt and a commitment to treatment which is needed so desperately. Foster placement is often necessary even when the father/perpetrator is not in the home, through his own choice on a voluntary basis because the remaining family members, especially the mother, will often pressure the child to change her story to save the family from shame, separation, and financial hardship. The victim may be scapegoated in such subtle, subconscious ways that neither she nor the family knows what is being done. In such cases the victim can become so overwhelmed by guilt and depression that she will indeed retract her story.

Even though the victim has been removed from the home, she remains a family member. She must not be separated from the flow of activity on the erroneous assumption that having been protected she can be spared the pain and discomfort of the ongoing investigation and decision-making process. Depending on her age, the victim usually needs to feel some sort of control over her situation even through someone else. Manipulative behavior can also be minimized if the child understands, shares in, and to some extent identifies with the investigative process and ensuing program for the family.

Some authorities feel that removal further victimizes the victim.[17] In certain cases this is assuredly true, but we hold to the premise that a short-term placement during which investigations and evaluations are continued predisposes the family and the child to greater efforts to restructure and rehabilitate themselves.

In one instance a 14-year-old girl was not removed from her home because the father had moved out. She made a very serious suicide attempt shortly afterward because she felt that her mother, who had made the initial report of incest, really believed the sexual activity was all the girl's fault. The mother had conveyed this message repeatedly by such statements as, "You knew how your daddy was; you should have stayed away from him". This girl had really tried to "stay away from him" by running away from home.

The child may be left in the home for several reasons. There may be insufficient evidence to remove her. The mother really may not have known what was transpiring and may have barred the home to the perpetrator. The court may order the child to be left at home. In such cases, protection is still essential. The child must be given as much support as possible. She must be given a contact number to call should trouble arise again, and treatment referrals should be made.

Voluntary Absence from the Home and Incarceration. Occasionally, the father's voluntarily removing himself from the home is seen as a signal of a favorable outcome for eventual family reintegration. The motivation behind such a move must be examined extensively. If done only to impress the court, if his moving out of the house is a product of a manipulative agreement between the parents, or if such a move is interpreted as positive by a therapist who is particularly naive about the dynamics and repetitive nature of incest, the father's voluntary absence from the home may be a persuasive method of pacifying the intervening authorities.

The father who with understanding and sensitivity removes himself from the home to spare his family additional anxiety and to allow the daughter the security of staying home is a prime candidate to succeed in therapy. The treatment plan should allow a relatively speedy reunification in his family if that is the intent of all concerned.

A decision by the couple to legally separate (generally instigated by the mother) should also be examined carefully by the worker. Such a decision may be an emotional one made in anger or sorrow and may not be maintained. Or, it may be a manipulative gesture to "tell them what they want to hear". Early assessment of such decisions is of necessity speculative, but an exploratory foray can be executed which will contain some basic information about how the family responds to stress and crisis.

It is not uncommon for the perpetrator of sexual assault to be incarcerated which places a family already in shock into a situation of more tangible insecurities, particularly financial. Upon his release from jail, the perpetrator may be unable to return to the home; this decision might be made by himself, the worker, his spouse, or the court. In these situations it is important that the individual working with the family marshal every resource available to keep the family afloat. With the victim removed from the home, the father in jail or out of the home, and the stresses of practical and legal pressures brought to bear, it is not difficult to understand why family members perceive the family as being destroyed. The worker must outline with confidence to the family the future course of events. Indecisiveness at this time may be detrimental to the plan for reuniting the family. The worker must be seen as a person in a position of authority who can help resolve the situation.

Visitation. Another issue of sensitivity and concern is whether the family members, particularly the perpetrator, should be in contact with the child after removal from the home. We feel that the key factor in this decision is the attitude of the victim. If the child verbalizes a genuine desire to have contact with her family, such contact should be arranged in a controlled setting with such supervision as to allow for immediate termination if the interaction tends to get out of hand. Such a termination is particularly advisable if the family and/or perpetrator attempts to foster or to magnify guilt in the victim with the idea of pressuring her to change her story.

Providing Needed Services

To the Child. During all of the hullabaloo of the investigation, a strange and almost cruel thing can happen to the child victim. In previous years, once her story was told, she had simply been ignored. In our more enlightened times, she may be placed safely away in a foster home or a friend's home—and still be ignored. This can occur despite the fact that she has been the central focus of concern that generated all the action. Obviously, this only increases the trauma and strong sense of separation and worthlessness the child might feel. A child who has been sexually abused may well have become shamed and guilt-ridden. Having dozens of people poking around in her life is often most distressing. The worker assigned to the case can be the connecting link, the constant, encouraging, accepting individual who gives the child a feeling of continuity and a reference point through the early stages of the process. Contact must be reasonably maintained until additional linkages with relatives, friends (carefully screened), foster parents, guardian *ad litem*, and therapist can be introduced by the pivotal worker.

Provision of supportive, therapeutic counseling for the child should be immediate and on a one-to-one basis. Such therapy is generally provided by a same-sex therapist. Additionally, referrals to victims' groups and to family therapy are certainly of value, although family therapy is often best delayed until some basic issues such as commitment to treatment by the whole family and acceptance of responsibility for the problem are settled. During early stages, particularly, the child needs an advocate to help prepare her for the polygraph,* court appearances, and confrontation by the family. A victims' group led by individuals knowledgeable about the court system is a most effective method for dealing with such problems. (See Chapters Fifteen and Sixteen.) Our victim services division is adjunctive to the local police department and is staffed

---

* *Editors' Note:* Even though the perpetrator's defense attorney may be eager for polygraphy tests on both the victim and perpetrator, such tests are not admissible in court. Further, polygraph tests for children under 12 years of age are not advisable. Far better information is obtained in even younger children utilizing projective testing such as the Rorschach and TAT.

by psychologists and social workers. A system of early referral and of automatic consultation between these two agencies has proven very effective.

To the Family. During the initial contacts with the parents or adult custodians, the intake worker must stress the possible legal repercussions, the rehabilitative aspects and the need for commitment to evaluation and treatment of both parents. Unless both individuals are committed to treatment little can be accomplished if the family intends to mend itself. The passive partner, usually the mother, must see herself as an active partner in restructuring the family. The eventual focus of treatment will, in most cases, be the family as a whole, as well as its constituent parts and combinations.

Assessment of blame—who did what to whom—is not of basic importance to the social worker though it certainly is to the law enforcement personnel. Indeed, in many cases, culpability for incest may never be clearly established. However, if an admission of guilt is made by the perpetrator, this may be the first and most important step in keeping the perpetrator and family in treatment.[5,6] Such admissions are most easily obtained during the intake or assessment phase though they may be recanted later. Even a tenuous admission can be utilized quickly by the intake worker and the agency legal staff to strike a bargain for *deferred criminal procedures* providing that the perpetrator enters fully into a recommended evaluation and treatment program. Such full participation must involve the other adult partner and relevant family members.

The El Paso County Department of Social Services, in conjunction with the District Attorney's Office of the Fourth Judicial District, the Colorado Springs Police Department (juvenile and victim service divisions), the El Paso County Sheriff's Office, the Public Defender, and the Pikes Peak Children's Advocates (represented by a defense attorney), has instituted an *Incest Diversion Program* which offers the non-violent, first offender an opportunity to be diverted from the judicial process if he is willing to undergo treatment of his problems and to follow through on the programs set up by professional counselors. If admitted into the program, the individual must adhere to the treatment and family counseling programs planned for them for up to two years. Failure to complete the program or dismissal for failure to cooperate can lead to the filing of criminal charges by the District Attorney. If the program is successfully completed, no criminal charges will be filed. An important aspect of this program is that all proceedings will be handled in a confidential manner. (For further details and the actual contract see Appendix 1.)

Through an extensive public information campaign, it is anticipated that knowledge of the existence of this program will overcome the reluctance to report incestuous activities so that treatment can help to rebuild a healthy family unit.

Perhaps the argument that an "arrangement" among the court, social services, the prosecutor, adult probation and the family smacks of collusion cannot be totally refuted. However, the practice of immediate rehabilitation and remediation prior to or instead of full criminal proceedings has been successful.

Appendix

Adult Diversion Program

The District Attorney's Office and the El Paso County Department of Social Services have developed and started an adult diversion program for the supervision and treatment of incest offenders.

Background

Incestuous activity is not only a criminal offense, but more specifically a symptom of serious family problems. It causes fear and humiliation for the victims. It creates secrecy and shame in the family. A child has fear and guilt that "telling" may cause a parent to go to prison. A wife fears exposure will destroy a marriage and leave her family without support. These factors strongly hinder discovery and correction of the problem.

And, if the criminal conduct is prosecuted through the judicial system, those same emotional responses are devastating to a child who must testify in court to incestuous acts with a parent.

For these reasons, the Adult Diversion Program was created.

Purpose

The Adult Diversion Program offers the non-violent, early stage incest offender an opportunity to be diverted from the judicial process if he or she is willing to undergo treatment of his or her problems and to follow through on the programs set up by professional counselors. If admitted into the program, an individual must adhere to the treatment and family counseling programs planned for them for up to two years. Failure to complete the program or dismissal from the program for failure to cooperate can lead to the filing of criminal charges by the District Attorney. If the program is successfully completed, no criminal charges will be filed. All proceedings will be handled in a confidential manner.

Knowledge of the existence of this program will overcome the reluctance to report incestuous activity, and treatment can help to rebuild a healthy family unit.

Eligibility

The Adult Diversion Program was established to provide a non-judicial alternative to non-violent incest offenders with a recent limited history of incestuous conduct. Individuals who use threats or violence against victims or who have a long-standing history of incestuous conduct will be handled through the criminal justice system. Only individuals who are willing to acknowledge their problems and voluntarily submit to the program will be accepted.

This program was modeled after the District Attorney's Juvenile Diversion Program with input from members of the following groups:

1. District Attorney's Office
2. Department of Social Services
3. Colorado Springs Police Department
4. El Paso County Sheriff's Department
5. Public Defender's Office
6. Children's Legal Advocates

Reporting

Incest is a form of child abuse which must be reported and which is subject to criminal penalty for failure to report.

Report incest/child abuse to the following agencies:

Department of Social Services	471-5951	(office hours)
	or 475-9593	(after hours)
Victim Services	471-6616	(office hours)
	or 471-6611	(after hours)
Any Law Enforcement Agency	911	(24 hours)

Adult Diversion Program Parameters

A. Persons excluded from considerations by District Attorney's Office:

1. Persons charged with Sexual Assault crimes on victims not related to the suspect by blood, marriage, or adoption, or victims with whom the suspect has resided for 12 months or less.
2. Persons who use physical violence, overt threats or intimidation which imply or state threats of bodily harm to the victim during or subsequent to the Incestuous Activities.
3. Persons who have been previously convicted of any Sexual Assault crime, or who are currently charged with any Sexual Assault crime or who have been granted Deferred Prosecution on any Sexual Assault crime.
4. Persons who have been involved in incestuous activities over an extended period of time, on multiple victims to whom the suspect is related by blood, marriage, or adoption, or multiple victims with whom the suspect has resided for more than 12 months, or a combination of such victims.
5. Persons previously accepted into and/or discharged from the Adult Diversion Program.

B. Persons excluded from consideration by the Department of Social Services:

1. Persons who do not desire to participate in the Adult Diversion Program.
2. Persons who are insane as defined in 16-8-101 C.R.S., 1973, as amended or who are certifiable under 27-10-105 or 27-10-106 C.R.S., 1973 as amended.

Adult Diversion Agreement

Name .... DOB ....
Address .... Phone ....
Employment .... Address ....
SSN or Military ID # ....

I, ... have been advised of my right to speedy prosecution and to have a speedy trial and I hereby waive those rights for a period of two months until the date of .... for consideration by the Adult Diversion Program. Upon acceptance into the program I give an unconditional waiver of those rights.

I, ... admit responsibility for the situation which brought this matter before the Adult Diversion Program, and I understand that such admission will not be used against me in any criminal prosecution, including impeachment but this will not extend to any new offenses admitted to.

I, ... agree to give a release to the Adult Diversion Program for medical or psychosocial information from any physicians and counselors whose services are secured as a requirement of this program.

I, ... agree to participate in any counseling or therapy that is recommended as a requirement of my Adult Diversion Program or any counseling or therapy approved by the Adult Diversion Program and I agree to pay any costs incurred by these requirements.

I, ... understand that if I fail to cooperate or comply with any requirements or conditions placed upon me by the Adult Diversion Program that I may be removed from the Program and criminal prosecution may be instituted against me.

I, ... understand that in any proceeding to remove me from the Adult Diversion Program, I will be informed of the recommendation for removal from the Program. I will be notified of the date on which the Child Protection Team will review the recommendation and I may be present to hear the reasons for removal from the Program and I may respond to the Child Protection Team on those reasons.

I, ... understand that the duration of this Agreement is to be no more than 24 months and that upon successful completion of the Program, that the District Attorney agrees not to prosecute me upon the incident which brought me into the Adult Diversion Program.

I, ... understand that the date of the signature of the District Attorney's Office will be the effective date of my acceptance into the program.

I, ... understand that I will inform the Adult Diversion Program of any change in address or employment.

I, ... have read this Agreement and understand the statements and requirements it contains and agree to abide by those statements and requirements.

....	....
Date	Dept. of Social Services
....	....
Date	Applicant
....	....
Date	Deputy District Attorney

References

1. American Humane Association (1974) *Child Abuse Legislation in the 1970's, Revised.* Denver, Colorado.
2. Barton, W., and Sanborn, C. (Eds.) (1978) *Law and the Mental Health Professions.* International Univ., New York.
3. Colorado Revised Statutes (1973) *Children's Code.*
4. Gentry, C. (1978) Incestuous abuse of children: the need for an objective view. *Child Welfare*, June.
5. Giarretto, H. (1976) Humanistic treatment of father–daughter incest. In *Child Abuse and Neglect: The Family and the Community.* (Edited by Helfer, R. E. and Kempe, C. H.) Ballinger, Cambridge, Mass.
6. Giarretto, H., and Giarretto, A. (1978) Urban League Workshop, Colorado Springs, Colorado.
7. Herman, J., and Hirschman, L. (1977) Father–daughter incest. *Signs*, Summer.
8. Helfer, R. E., and Kempe, C. H. (Eds.) (1966) *The Battered Child.* University of Chicago, Chicago, Ill.
9. Lustig, N., Dresser, J. W., Spellman, S. W., and Murray, T. B. (1966) Incest: a family group survival pattern. *Arch. Gen. Psychiatry* **14:** 31.
10. Schmitt, B. (Ed.) (1978) *The Child Protection Team Handbook.* Garland, New York.
11. Sgroi, S. (1978) Comprehensive examination for child sexual assault: diagnostic, therapeutic, and child protection issues. In *Sexual Assault of Children and Adolescents.* (Edited by Burgess, A. W., Groth, A. N., Holstrom, L. L., and Sgroi, S. M.) Lexington, Lexington, Mass.
12. Sgroi, S. M., Burgess, A. W., Groth, A. N., and Holstrom, L. L. (1978) Introduction: a national needs assessment for protecting child victims. In *Sexual Assault of Children and Adolescents.* (Edited by Burgess, A. W., Groth, A. N., Holstrom, L. L., and Sgroi, S. M.) Lexington, Lexington, Mass.
13. Summit, R., and Kryso, J. (1978) Sexual abuse of children: a clinical spectrum. *Am. J. Orthopsychiatry.* **48:** 237.
14. Talan, T., DeFrank, C., and Gamm, S. (1978) *Child Abuse and Neglect Legal Handbook*, Child Advocates Assoc., Chicago.
15. U.S. Department of Health, Education and Welfare (1978) *State Reporting Laws*, U.S. Government Printing Office, Washington, D.C., May.
16. Yelaja, S. (1971) *Authority in Social Work: Concept and Use.* University of Toronto, Toronto, Canada.
17. Zaphiris, A. (1978) *Incest: The Family With Two Known Victims.* American Humane Assoc., Englewood, Colorado.

Acknowledgments

We acknowledge our indebtedness to the El Paso County Department of Social Services, Alfred L. Gillen, Director, who has given us much support, and all of our co-workers, especially those in Child Welfare Intake. Special appreciation to John P. Kelley and J. Worth Linn, critics, and to Lola Barbur, typist.

Chapter Ten

Medical Assessment of Child Sexual Abuse

DAVID L. KERNS

The physician plays a critical role in diagnosis, reporting, and treatment planning in child sexual abuse cases. Commonly, the physician's office is the site of first disclosure of incest. The child who has been the target of an extra-familial assault is usually taken directly to a medical facility for an examination. Protective services and juvenile court personnel will often turn to the physician as the sole potential source of physical evidence in incest cases. The child's physician is a natural advocate for the protection and treatment of sexually mistreated children. It is encumbent upon physicians who care for children and adolescents to acquire the skills and knowledge necessary to appropriately respond to these very difficult cases.

Clinical Presentations

Disclosure of Extra-Familial Sexual Molestation

In most instances, the child will tell his or her parents that sexual activity has occurred with a "stranger" outside of the home. This is virtually always true when the molestation has been accompanied by physical force. In some instances, coercive but non-violent assaults will not be disclosed by the child in response to bribes or threats by the perpetrator. Upon disclosure of the incident to the parents, immediate medical and law-enforcement interventions are sought. While some children will not perceive a non-violent, non-penetrating molestation as terribly disturbing, most of the victims will be in an acute and serious emotional crisis when they present to the physician.

Disclosure of Incest

Disclosure of incest following a first incident is rare. In most instances, incestuous behavior has been occurring for months or years when discovered by a non-family member. The "incest secret" may be disclosed for many reasons. The younger child or adolescent may inadvertently or out of anger tell someone such as a friend, neighbor, extended family member, babysitter or teacher. The mother, in anger at the father or other adult male figure, may attack him by disclosure. The mother, in genuine conflict over her daughter's needs, may finally act on the child's behalf. In some families, as the daughters enter adolescence, the fathers become very "protective" and jealous of their daughters' potential sexual relationships with peers. As the father becomes more restrictive, the daughter, now more influenced by peers than family, may disclose the incestuous relationship in order to free herself.

The physician may be the person to whom the disclosure is initially made. More commonly, the physician will be asked to evaluate the child by protective services or law-enforcement personnel after disclosure has taken place by another route. It is crucial that immediately following disclosure the child is absolutely protected from contact with the alleged perpetrator. Likewise, no professional should confront the alleged perpetrator without police protection. Such confrontations have resulted in extreme violence and, on occasion, homicide.

Venereal Disease

Venereal disease, particularly gonorrhea, may be the presenting problem of a child or adolescent who is being sexually abused. Clinical gonorrhea will usually present as vaginitis in young children, with manifestations of vaginal discharge, vaginal itching, and burning on urination. Children may also acquire gonorrheal infections of the eye, throat, and rectum and, rarely, may have generalized infections with involvement of the joints.

There has been much controversy about the mode of transmission of gonorrhea in children. It is clear that the gonorrheal eye infections seen in infants can be transmitted non-venereally. Several authors[5,6,7] have concluded that, since no history of sexual contact was elicited in some families where children had clinical gonorrheal infections of the vagina, the gonococcal organism could be transmitted non-venereally to sites other than the eye. From these studies and from the reluctance to confront the possibility of sexual abuse in families has grown the belief that towels, bedsheets, and toilet seats are vectors for this organism. However, in the only study that employed a skilled, experienced, and aggressive approach to contact investigation, Branch and Paxton[2] found strikingly different results. Of 20 children with genital gonorrhea in the 1-to-4-year age group, 19 had a history of sexual contact; of 25 children with genital gonorrhea in the 5-to-9-year age group, all 25 had a history of sexual contact. All of these children's contacts were in the nuclear or extended family. While it is not inconceivable that genital gonorrhea could in a rare instance be transmitted non-venereally, the initial presumption of sexual contact should be made, and only after the most experienced investigation has taken place should the possibility of non-venereal transmission be considered. Acceptance of the "mythology of bedsheets and toilet seats" removes the physician from a most stressful situation but surrenders the child to continued sexual activity.

Behavior Problems

The child who is being sexually abused may manifest any number of behavior problems as an expression of anxiety, depression or guilt over the sexual activity. The physician should consider the possibility of sexual abuse as an underlying cause for apparently inexplicable behavioral changes. It is clear that runaway behavior in adolescents is commonly in response to sexual mistreatment at home. Young children may demonstrate a wide range of regressive behaviors and expressions of anxiety such as night terrors and tantrums. The school-age child may have unexplainable and erratic changes in school performance. While no particular behavioral patterns are characteristic and a myriad of issues other than sexual abuse will lead to behavioral problems in children, sexual abuse should be included in the differential diagnosis of underlying causes.

Selection of Appropriate Personnel for Case Assessments

The assessment of child sexual abuse cases is complex and time-consuming. It cannot be accomplished within the pace and routine of the private office or hospital clinic or emergency room. The professionals involved with the case will probably have to stop all their other activities for at least 1 to 2 hours. In terms of attention and priority, it should be viewed as a medical emergency, with re-allocation of staff and re-scheduling of patients if necessary.

Skillful assessments demand time, special interviewing skills, facility with pediatric and adolescent gynecologic examinations, an understanding of the psychodynamics of incest and other forms of child sexual abuse, and an awareness of legal requirements regarding physical evidence of sexual abuse and protective services reporting responsibilities. In addition, the physician performing the assessments will be likely to have testimonial responsibilities in juvenile and/or criminal court proceedings. If there is inexperience or insecurity in these areas, the physician should form an *ad hoc* assessment team with selected professionals with experience in these cases, for example, pediatrician, psychiatrist, gynecologist or psychiatric social worker. If the services of an established child protection team with medical diagnostic capabilities are within reach, referral would be appropriate. It is of critical importance that physicians who do not have easy access to such consultations and referrals acquire the skills necessary to perform these assessments on their own.

It is often recommended that female physicians should conduct sexual abuse evaluations. If a female physician who is knowledgeable and experienced with these cases is available, the option should be given to the victim. In general, male physicians who are gentle, empathic, and experienced do not add additional trauma for the child. The recruitment of an inept female physician, because she is a woman, is not required, but the presence of a sympathetic female nurse as well as a relative, such as mother or sister is necessary, especially with children involved with forcible sexual rape. If the child continues to be very fearful, waiting for an experienced woman physician is worthwhile.

Interviewing Parents and Children

On rare occasions, fathers will openly seek help for their incestuous behavior. In most instances, the daughter will be accompanied by the mother or an adolescent will visit the physician alone. In some instances, incestuous fathers repeatedly accompany their daughters to the physicians' offices as a technique to enforce secrecy. As emphasized above, if the father is not openly seeking help and if sexual abuse is known or suspected, the physician need not confront the father with an accusation. This is potentially dangerous to all concerned. It is important to interview mothers and daughters separately in known or suspected incest cases. If there has been an extra-familial molestation, it is quite important not to separate the pre-adolescent child from her parents during the interview. The adolescent victim should be allowed to make her own choice in these instances; she may choose to be interviewed alone or have her parents present.

Interviewing the Mother

If the mother is acknowledging incestuous behavior in the family at the onset, allow her to tell her story and ventilate her feelings. Responses should be supportive and non-judgmental while attempts are made to elicit as much objective detail as possible about sexual activity. After obtaining the sexual information, the child's general medical history should be taken, and an assessment of family functioning, as outlined below, should be done.

If there is a consideration of incest which the mother is not acknowledging at the outset, sexual information should be sought in the context of the child's medical history and a family functioning assessment. Questions should proceed from the least sensitive to the most sensitive. The assessment of family functioning should include the following:

1. Who lives at home? Elicit marital status, duration of relationships, and ages of family members.
2. Determine the make-up of the extended family and identify regular visitors to the household, including family, friends, and those employed for child care.
3. Identify chronic stresses in the household, such as physical health problems, unemployment, low income, or housing problems.
4. Identify any recent acute stresses or crises in the family, for example, recent deaths, recent onset of illness, new pregnancy, recent job loss, or change of residence.
5. Elicit a description of how the mother views the family members. If a general question does not stimulate a descriptive response, ask about the mother's views of strengths and weaknesses, likes and dislikes, and attractiveness and unattractiveness of individual family members.
6. Inquire into intra-familial relationships in terms of friendship, supportiveness, activities, mother's availability and responsibility for housekeeping and parenting tasks, decision-making, areas of disagreement, and discipline. These issues should be assessed in child–child, child–parent, extended family–parent, and parent–parent dyads.
7. Ask the mother if she feels if anyone in the family has a serious emotional problem.
8. Determine if any family members have a problem with alcohol or other drugs.
9. Ask if anyone at home ever loses control and physically hurts anyone else.

In seeking sexual information, directly and supportively inform the mother of the reason for the questions, for example, the child has evidence of venereal disease, a third party (school teacher, friend, neighbor) was told by the child of sexual activity, a serious emotional or behavioral problem can be an expression of a child's anxiety, depression, or guilt stemming from illicit sexual activity. The author uses the following questions to elicit sexual information:

1. What are the sleeping arrangements at home?
2. Is the physical relationship between you and your husband satisfying?
3. Are you concerned that your husband may be having extra-marital relationships?
4. Is your child frequently alone with male family figures?
5. Is there any possibility that your child is participating in sexual activity?

If the mother denies the possibility, further questioning regarding sexual activity is not likely to be fruitful and probably will be agitating. If knowledge of the child's sexual activity is confirmed, questions should then be directed toward the identity of the perpetrator, the presence or absence of physical force or threats, the child's age at onset, the frequency of activity, and the types of sexual contact.

Interviewing the Child

The physician's interview with the child or adolescent sexual abuse victim should have four phases: (1) establishing a relationship; (2) eliciting general personal and family information; (3) eliciting details of sexual activity; and (4) preparation for the physical examination. Observations of the child's affect and behavior during the interview should be documented. These interviews may vary from those yielding easy and direct responses to those "running into a stone wall".

1. *Establishing a Relationship.* With the young child, a brief period of time should be spent in introductions, play, and "small talk". With the older child or adolescent, likewise a brief period of time should be spent to introduce yourself and convey a gentle, non-threatening demeanor. The verbal and non-verbal cues given during the interview will have a great effect on the degree of trust and communication with which the child or adolescent will respond. An even, pleasant temperament should be maintained throughout and surprise, revulsion, or anger should never be communicated by words or facial expressions.

2. *General Personal and Family Information.* As in the parent interview, inquiries should proceed from the least sensitive to the most sensitive areas. Begin with questions about friends, school, hobbies, and sports. Ask about siblings and how they get along with each other. Ask the child to describe her parents. How does she get along with them? What do they do when they are upset? How do they show affection? What does she like about them? What does she dislike about them? Elicit similar observations of male figures other than the father who are in the family network.

3. *Details of Sexual Activity.* Specific details of each case will determine the approach to sexual information. If incest or extra-familial molestation has already been established by the victim, the direct documentation of physical details may not be difficult. With all victims, but especially the young child, the level of anatomic sophistication should be determined. The use of dolls may be helpful, and a mutual understanding of a child's particular vernacular should be established. (See Chapter Eleven.) This will also be helpful in the preparation for the physical examination. Do not expect that the child will necessarily have experienced sexual activity as painful or

unpleasant or that there will be anger at or fear of the perpetrator. If vaginal penetration has not occurred and physical restraint was not necessary, the child may not have any negative feelings toward the experience.

The age of the child will determine the way in which questions regarding sexual activity will be asked. If the victim is an adolescent, a careful menstrual history should be taken. An attempt should be made to determine the precise kinds of sexual behavior that were experienced: exposure, kissing, fondling, masturbation, fellatio, cunnilingus, vaginal penetration, or anal penetration. With the young child, the use of dolls and drawings may be essential in eliciting these physical descriptions. The onset and frequency of activity should be elicited, and it should be determined if ejaculation has occurred or not. It is important to learn if threats or use of physical force are part of the activity. Once the victim has identified the perpetrator, there is no need for the child to repeatedly name him. The discussion can then focus on the activity, not the person.

4. *Preparation for the Physical Examination.* At this point the young child should be reunited with the mother, or other relative, and the details of the physical assessment should be explained to both of them. The adolescent should be given the option of having a relative present for her examination. In all cases a female (nurse or other personnel) must be present during the pelvic examination period. The physical examination should be described, with the use of media if necessary. Unless there has been genital or anal injury, the child should be reassured that the examination will not be painful. It may be prudent in the young child to delay telling her that there will be a blood test and possibly an injection until after the physical examination is completed.

In some cases, this may be the point of greatest resistance by the patient and greatest difficulty for the physician. If the sexual activity has been physically traumatic, the victims may be especially terrified of the examination or even fantasize that they are about to be sexually assaulted again. The messages that have been conveyed by the physician during the interview will greatly affect the child's responses at this point. If the physician has been perceived as gentle and caring throughout the interview, it is likely that the victim will be more amenable and less traumatized in anticipation of the examination. A brief hospital admission may be needed if a general anesthesia is required to repair injuries such as vaginal tears.

Physical Examination

The physical assessment of child sexual abuse should be done in the context of a complete general physical examination. Since it is highly likely that positive findings will ultimately be used as evidence in civil and/or criminal court proceedings, it is crucial that all findings be carefully and quantitatively detailed in the medical record, all visible positive physical findings be photographed, and all laboratory specimens and material evidence be meticulously labeled and handled. A forensic collection kit available from the police department should be employed exclusively for the collection of specimens discussed under "Diagnostic studies. Forensic material." Directions should be observed meticulously and the collection witnessed and countersigned, generally by a nurse.

Skin

The child's entire body should be examined for the presence of skin injuries. If bruises are present, the following guidelines[8] will help to determine the approximate age of the injuries: (1) initially—red to purple; (2) within the first week—dark purple; (3) within the second week—yellow-brown, and (4) complete resolution after 2-to-4 weeks. Dried semen or blood on the skin can be scraped free with a tongue blade and collected and held for laboratory studies (for example, acid phosphatase and blood group antigens).

Mouth

The mouth should be examined for any signs of trauma and for the presence of sores which might be venereal in nature.

Abdomen

The abdomen should be carefully palpated for tenderness or the presence of masses. With forceful vaginal or rectal penetration, internal tissue injury and bleeding may occur in the absence of specific physical complaints by the victim.

Genital and Rectal Examination

Males. Signs of genital or anal trauma should be noted and the presence or absence of urethral discharge determined. If there are any signs of anal trauma or a positive history of anal penetration, a digital rectal examination should be done to determine the presence of tenderness, masses, or blood.

Pre-pubescent Females. Careful inspection should be done to document bruises, abrasions, or lacerations of the labia, vagina, hymen, anus, and adjacent skin. The size of the vaginal and hymeneal openings should be measured and documented. These observations, in the absence of injury, can be made by painless manipulation of the labia. A small, sterile plastic medicine dropper can be inserted painlessly into the lower vagina for the collection of laboratory specimens. In the absence of history or signs of vaginal or rectal penetration in the pre-pubescent child, it is generally not necessary to use a speculum or perform a bimanual pelvic examination. It is crucial to keep in mind, however, that the absence of penetration does not rule out sexual abuse. The majority of young children do not experience forceful penetration.

If there is historical or physical evidence of penetration, it will be necessary to do both vaginal speculum and bimanual examinations, primarily to rule out internal injuries. The bimanual examination can be done rectally. In most instances, the child's cooperation can be elicited for this examination. On occasion, particularly with significant penetration injuries, it will be necessary to hospitalize the child for an examination under brief, general anesthesia.

Pubescent Females. In the pubescent female, the physical examination is the same as for the pre-pubescent female except that the speculum and bimanual examinations are done routinely, unless the hymen is intact. Aside from the collection of laboratory specimens and inspection and palpation for injuries, special attention should be given to signs of pregnancy, that is, increased uterine size or bluish discoloration and softness of the cervix.

Diagnostic Studies

Evaluation for Gonorrhea

Specimens from throat and rectal swabs and from the vaginal aspirate should be cultured for the gonococcal organism. A "dirty" (first ten drops) urine specimen also should be cultured. It is crucial that these specimens be immediately placed in special media (Thayer-Martin or Trans-Gro) and incubated properly. If a urethral, vaginal, or rectal discharge is present, culture and Gram stain should be performed. The microscopic presence of gram-negative intracellular diplococci will immediately confirm the diagnosis of gonorrheal infection.

Evaluation for Syphilis

A venipuncture for baseline serology for syphilis should be done.

Presence of Sperm or Semen

The vaginal aspirate should be examined microscopically for the presence of sperm. This test will generally become negative 24–48 hours after ejaculation. If semen is present, a high level of acid phosphatase will be found in the specimen. This is strong indirect evidence that ejaculation occurred.

Pregnancy Tests

In pubescent girls, a *blood* test for chorionic gonadotrophin should be obtained to rule out early pregnancy. This test becomes positive seven to ten days after conception.

Urinalysis

When there has been traumatic penetration, a urinalysis may reveal bleeding secondary to urethral or bladder injury.

Forensic Material

Stained clothing and scrapings of dry blood or semen from skin should be collected and turned over to the police. If there is any collected material beneath the victim's fingernails, scrapings should likewise be collected and given to the police. The forensic laboratory can perform a variety of studies including acid phosphatase, blood group antigens, and hair analysis.

Radiologic Bone Survey

In children under six years of age with signs of physical trauma, a radiologic bone survey (skull, ribs, pelvis, and long bones) should be performed to rule out occult old or new bone injuries.

Diagnostic Considerations

When there are hard physical findings of sexual activity, for example, presence of sperm or penetrating anal or vaginal injuries, this constitutes *prima facie* evidence of sexual abuse in the pre-adolescent child. The adolescent, of course, may have been a consenting partner with another adolescent, and the diagnosis will be dependent upon the history given. In most cases of incest, however, there will be no positive physical signs, and the diagnosis will be entirely based on historical information. The child or adolescent who tells us he or she is being sexually abused should, in almost all instances, be believed. While adolescents may occasionally fantasize or angrily fabricate sexual activities at home, younger children rarely do so. Kempe[4] contends that the sexual allegations of pre-adolescent children should be taken at face value. When the allegations of an adolescent are not supported by physical evidence or corroborating statements of others, careful and experienced psychological or psychiatric assessment will be helpful in distinguishing the true incest victim from the angry, aggressive adolescent who is attacking the family. In interviews and on projective testing, primarily the TAT and Rorschach, the incest victims usually see themselves as guilty, threatened, powerless, and yearning for a happy, cohesive family; the adolescent who is lying will generally reveal anger, aggression and withdrawal from the family.

The following are diagnostic indicators which provide direct or supportive evidence of possible child sexual abuse:

1. Positive histories from the perpetrator, victim, or witnesses
2. Venereal disease—primarily gonorrhea in sites other than the eye and syphilis
3. Pregnancy
4. Signs of physical abuse
5. Genital or anorectal trauma not consistent with accidental injury
6. Vaginal or rectal foreign bodies
7. Microscopic confirmation of sperm in the vagina or rectum or on skin or clothing
8. Vaginal aspirate with high acid phosphatase content (indicates semen)
9. Forensic material evidence such as blood or hair of perpetrator on victim's body or clothing.

Disposition

Post-Evaluation Interview

Following the completion of the evaluation, the diagnosis and treatment plan should be thoroughly discussed. Both the mother and the adolescent or young child should have the opportunity to ask questions and clarify any confusions about the findings and the proposed disposition. The therapeutic process can begin with the victim at this point. The implicit and explicit message to the victim should be: "This was not your fault. You are not to blame for what has happened to you." The victims often will feel disruption caused by disclosure as well. The communication that the child was indeed a victim should begin immediately and will continue as a major theme in follow-up therapy.

Immediate Child Protection

There should be immediate concern for the incest victim in terms of absolute protection from further molestation. Unless the perpetrator has been taken into custody and there is certainty that he will not be released, the child should not return home. Contact with the perpetrator will not only render the child vulnerable to repeated sexual activity but will also endanger the child in terms of possible physical assault. If the safe home of a relative or an emergency foster home is not available, the child should be hospitalized until the perpetrator is in custody. In those cases where there is irresolution diagnostically, it is best to err on the side of the child and provide protection until a complete investigation by police and protective services has taken place.

Case Reporting to Child Protective Services

It is a legal requirement that physicians report all known or suspected child sexual abuse to the county or state protective services agency. These cases require an immediate response by a protective services caseworker. (See Chapter Nine.)

Police Involvement

If there is not already absolute protection of the child from the perpetrator when the child is seen, the police should be immediately involved in the case.

Prevention of Venereal Disease

If there is no clinical evidence of venereal disease at the time of evaluation, it is reasonable to wait for laboratory results. If there is a vaginal, urethral, or rectal discharge at the time of the examination, the following treatment for gonorrhea should be given: Procaine Penicillin G, 100,000 units per kilogram intramuscularly (up to 4.8 million units) followed by Probenecid, 25 milligrams per kilogram orally (up to 1 gram). If one wants to avoid injection therapy, a single oral dose of Ampicillin, 50 milligrams per kilogram (up to 3 grams), may substitute for intramuscular Penicillin. In this case, the Probenecid should precede the oral Ampicillin. If the patient is allergic to Penicillin, Spectinomycin should be given intramuscularly, 40 milligrams per kilogram (up to 2 grams).

Prevention of Pregnancy

Serious consideration should be given to the use of oral diethylstilbesterol (DES) in pubescent girls who have just experienced vaginal intercourse. It is clear that DES, given orally in a dosage of 25 milligrams twice a day for five days within 48 hours of vaginal intercourse, will virtually always (99.9% of cases) prevent pregnancy. The single contraindication for use of DES is pre-existing pregnancy. If the pregnancy test (*blood* chorionic gonadotrophin) is negative and there are no historical or physical indicators of pregnancy, DES therapy is indicated in pubescent girls. If the DES fails to prevent pregnancy (1 in 1,000 cases), therapeutic abortion should be recommended because of the risk, albeit small (0.14%), of eventual vaginal cancer if the fetus is a female.[3]

Surgical Intervention

In cases where there has been forceful vaginal or rectal penetration, there may be lacerations which require surgical repair. Rarely, a victim will have signs of injuries to the urinary tract, gastrointestinal tract, or peritoneum and will require hospitalization for observation or exploratory surgery.

Referrals

Long-term mental health follow-up for family members will generally be planned by the protective services agency alone or in conjunction with a multidisciplinary child protection team. In some instances, the victim will require acute psychiatric intervention, and referral should be made on an emergency basis. In those instances where there is irresolution regarding the truth of a child's or adolescent's allegations of incest, referral to an experienced psychologist or child psychiatrist is appropriate. Combined interviewing and projective testing will generally lead to the correct diagnosis. When there has been significant trauma from penetration, early involvement of a gynecologist is necessary.

Medical Follow-up

The child or adolescent should be seen again within several days for a general physical evaluation. At this time, the results of cultures for gonorrhea and the blood serology for syphilis will be known, and treatment can be instituted if necessary. It is possible that the child will only now be manifesting signs or symptoms of venereal disease acquired by the sexual activity occurring prior to the previous visit. The follow-up will also provide the physician with the opportunity to elicit additional history, perform a baseline developmental assessment of the young child, be available to the family to respond to unanswered questions, and continue to reinforce therapeutic messages to the child. Arrangements should be made for physical and developmental assessments of siblings in the household. Medical information obtained should be shared with the protective services worker, either directly or through the child protection team mechanism.

Conclusion

The thorough and thoughtful medical assessment of child sexual abuse is technically and emotionally demanding and obviously time-consuming. Even the most experienced physicians are uncomfortable with difficult cases. To a large extent, the physician's responses will determine both the quality of the supporting evidence (thus the justification for child protection) and the degree to which the child is further traumatized by the evaluation itself. Refined responses can only take place once the physician acknowledges that child sexual abuse exists, that it is not a rare occurrence, and that these cases deserve all the time, skill, and sophistication that are applied to any other serious medical problem.

References

1. *American College of Obstetricians and Gynecologists Technical Bulletin* (1970), No. 14, American College of Obstetricians and Gynecologists, Chicago, July.
2. Branch, G. and Paxton, R. (1965) A study of gynococcal infections among infants and children. *Public Health Reports* **80:** 347.
3. Herjanic, R. and Wilboss, R. P. (1978) Sexual abuse of children: detection and management. *J. Am. Med. Assoc.* **239:** 331.
4. Kempe, C. H. (1978) Another hidden pediatric problem: the 1977 C. Anderson Aldrich lecture. *Pediatrics* **62:** 382.
5. Michalowski, B. (1961) Difficulties in diagnosis and treatment of gonorrhea in young girls. *Br. J. Vener. Dis.* **37:** 142.
6. Shore, W. B. and Winkelstein, J. A. (1971) Non-venereal transmission of gonococcal infections to children. *J. Pediatr.* **79:** 661.
7. Tunnensen, W. W. and Jastremski (1974) Prepubescent gonococcal vulvovaginitis. *Clin Pediatr.* **13:** 675.
8. Wilson, E. F. (1977) Estimation of the age of cutaneous contusions in child abuse. *Pediatrics* **60:** 750.

Acknowledgments

The author acknowledges the support of the Robert Wood Johnson Foundation and is grateful to Marion R. Rex for her able secretarial assistance.

Chapter Eleven

The Child Psychiatric Examination of the Sexually Abused Child

DAVID A. MRAZEK

Even though there has long been recognition of the psychological consequences of sexual abuse,[9] the role of the child psychiatrist in the evaluation of these cases has remained obscure. The subject has not been addressed directly in current child psychiatric textbooks,[1,16] despite an increasing awareness of the problem. Morrison[13] has documented the occurrence of referral for sexual assault and incest to a child psychiatric emergency service after identification in the emergency room, but specific guidelines for evaluation of these children and families have not been available until recently.[4]

This chapter will address special considerations necessary for the psychiatric diagnostic evaluation of the sexually abused child after identification of the occurrence of abuse has been made. Issues related to problems of definition are dealt with elsewhere. (See Chapter One.) However, for the purpose of this discussion a simple dichotomy of sexual abuse into sexual assault and incest will be made. The primary differentiation is whether the adult perpetrator is a first degree relative. While it is becoming increasingly well documented[8] that all possible patterns of incest do occur, this chapter will primarily address the most frequent pattern, father–daughter incest. Thus, when the term "incest" is used, it will refer to this pattern unless otherwise specified.

This focus on assessment after identification does not imply that a child psychiatrist may not be the initial individual to uncover a sexually abusive situation. Quite the contrary, it may well be a child psychiatrist who, through the understanding of concomitant emotional symptomatology, learns of the sexual experience of the child. The fact that these children do indeed experience concomitant emotional symptoms is documented in a review of the presenting problems encountered by a child psychiatric emergency service.[12]

The child psychiatrist can help provide an understanding of the psychological impact of the event or experience on the child and family. However, the question of whether psychiatric referral is always appropriate still arises. Certainly it must be acknowledged that there is a limited availability of child psychiatric services, and in some circumstances referral is not possible. However, this shortage should not obscure the reality that a greater understanding of the etiology and psychological consequences of the problem would be an important contribution in coping with these cases. While there have been reports that non-coercive sexual contact between adults and children does not have negative psychological repercussions, a review of long-term prognosis[11] suggests that some concern for these children's future adaptation is appropriate. (See Chapters Seventeen and Eighteen.) Certainly clinical studies have tended to identify those children who have later suffered from these experiences. In fact, emotional problems have been reported to have been present in more than two-thirds of the child victims at the time of the initial evaluation.[3] While it is true that many of these children may have had some emotional difficulties as a result of family disorder prior to the actual incest, this would probably be indication for even more concern for their later development. Until better methods of predicting difficulty in future psychological adjustment are developed which could be used to identify the minority of the children who are at minimal risk of both immediate and later emotional disorder, child psychiatric assessment should be a part of a team evaluation of the child's emotional adjustment.

This chapter will address five aspects of the psychiatric referral of a sexually abused child. Often a referral will focus on one of these areas in the form of a question. In these situations it is entirely appropriate to address all pertinent aspects of the problem. The five general questions are as follows:

1. Are either the *parents* or *child* suffering from an emotional disorder? If so, what is the prognosis and what psychotherapeutic intervention is indicated?
2. Has an appropriate *immediate* intervention been made in order to protect the child from further trauma? This is always a major concern of those responsible for the child's welfare and is often the primary reason for the urgency of many of these referrals. After a *safe* short-term placement has been secured, possible more permanent future living circumstances can be thoroughly investigated.
3. What is the likelihood of a *recurrence* of a sexually abusive situation if the family continues to remain intact? Specifically, should the child or father be removed from the family?
4. Are there any means of *confirming the occurrence* or extent of the sexual experience in question? Specifically, is there a possibility that the sexual act did not occur but is rather the product of the child's fantasy or an intentional distortion?
5. Are there psychological considerations which have a particular importance for *long-term planning* for the care of the child, and can the psychiatrist provide supporting evidence to justify and facilitate these plans? Specifically, this should include a long-term involvement with later re-assessments when changes in the original planned decisions are contemplated.

Each of the questions will be dealt with separately and the different implications for sexual assault and incest will be discussed.

Diagnostic Process

A practical consideration in organizing the psychiatric evaluation is that the child psychiatrist must have adequate time with the involved members of the family for him to elicit sufficient information with which to make the required judgments. The first goal of referral is to rule out the presence of overt psychiatric illness in any member of the family. During this investigation a central objective is to define the specific family dynamics which allowed the sexual abuse to have taken place.

The standard child psychiatric diagnostic process is well described in the literature.[2,6,17] In the evaluation of sexually abused children the usual assessment of the child's development, interpersonal relationships, and adaptive capacity which are part of the general child psychiatric examination must be done. This would include a thorough understanding of the child's relationships with parents and siblings as well as clarification of the child's defensive mechanisms and coping strengths. However, the assessment of the child in a family in which an overt incestuous relationship has been occurring requires some specific inquiry and awareness of particular problems. Still other issues arise during the assessment of a family in which sexual assault of a child by a person outside the family has occurred. It is these special diagnostic considerations which will be highlighted in this chapter.

Some basic principles are common to assessing both forms of sexual abuse. A primary consideration is to provide a setting in which the child can feel safe. Only after a sense of security is established can the child be expected to trust the examiner sufficiently to be able to describe the events which took place as well as his or her emotional reaction to both the sexual relationship and its subsequent discovery and exposition. The setting for the evaluation should be private and provisions made to prevent interruptions. It is essential that at some point in the evaluation the child be seen alone to provide an opportunity to discuss sexual matters without censorship from either parent. In this regard, it is often advantageous to have a family session or a session with the mother and child prior to the first individual session to allow the parent to give the child explicit permission to discuss sexual experiences. One individual session often may be an insufficient period of time for the child to begin to trust the child psychiatrist. Therefore, it is usually best to see the child for a short series of sessions. It is helpful to establish early in the interview that the child psychiatrist is a different kind of doctor than those whom the child was dealt with in the past. Specifically, the permission to play as part of the diagnostic process may facilitate communications. Some discussion regarding the limitations which exist on the confidentiality of the child's communication is also important. Frank acknowledgment is necessary of the inevitability of the parents learning about the content of the child's description of the sexual experience. However, reassurance that only a limited number of individuals will have to know what happened and that the child will be protected from any retaliation is often very facilitating.

Assessment of the developmental age of the child is important for multiple reasons. Most basically, the mode of communication employed with the child will be in part determined by the child's developmental maturity. Judgment of the child's capacity to deal directly with the abusive incident is also dependent upon this understanding. Additionally, the nature of the proposed therapeutic intervention with the child will be determined based on developmental considerations, specifically, more verbal and cognitive approaches being considered appropriate with children with greater emotional maturity.

After the individual evaluation of the child, it is often very revealing to see the child's differential response to being with each parent. It is particularly helpful if the entire family can then be seen together to determine how the more complicated family dynamic patterns influence the interaction seen between the child and his/her parents. In summary, the child psychiatrist's evaluation should be an assessment of the child's individual functioning and the strengths and interactional patterns of the family. This requires that the child be seen alone, independently with each parent, and within the whole family context. While this intensive involvement may not always be feasible, the specific advantages should not be minimized.

Another general consideration in the psychiatric assessment of these children is the role of psychological testing. Two types of tests may provide helpful additional information. The first of these is intelligence testing which may provide an additional perspective regarding the validity of the child's report and highlight special needs which must be taken into consideration in deciding upon an appropriate long-term disposition. Certainly intelligence testing should be requested if there is any question of mental subnormality. Secondly, projective testing may allow indirect assessment of emotionally charged areas of conflict as well as providing some estimate of the degree of the child's psychological disorganization. Projective tests can be particularly useful for children who are either very inhibited or exhibiting considerable emotional psychopathology. Additionally, the child's differential response to a male and female diagnostician can provide interesting insights regarding his or her current coping as well as past interactions with parents. Providing this contrast should be a consideration in making a psychological referral.

The question of whether the child psychiatric diagnostician ideally should be male or female often arises. While some clinicians feel that the diagnostic process is facilitated if the evaluator is the same sex as the child, this need not be the case. It is usually far more important for the diagnostician to be patient, gentle, and non-critical than be a particular gender. However, in cases where a girl has been physically traumatized in addition to being sexually abused, the child's response to a male stranger may be so strong that immediate evaluation by a male child psychiatrist is indeed not possible.

Evaluation of Incestuous Families

An important consideration in the assessment of incestuous families is the issue of family loyalty. The child involved may be under considerable family pressure both implicitly and explicitly to keep the incestuous relationship a family secret in order to assure that the family remain intact. This pressure may be particularly strong if the incestuous relationship is a long-standing one rather than an isolated act resulting from temporary loss of impulse control. In the former case, the family has made an internal adjustment to the situation, the sexual nature of the daughter–father relationship has become fixed, and the legal consequences are more prominent. The specific issue in these cases becomes whether the father will remain a part of the family unit. If the possibility of imprisonment exists, this concern should be directly addressed with the family. Additionally, the potential impact of the child's interview on the father's future must be dealt with at some point in the process. While it is desirable for the father to be interviewed, it is probable that he will be defensive and reluctant to become involved, particularly if prosecution is likely. Similarly, mothers of these children may be quite ambivalent about the course of the evaluation if the possibility exists that their husbands will be separated from the family.

A variety of pathological characteristics have been ascribed to parents who have permitted overt incestuous relationships to develop.[13] (Also see Chapter Eight.) These include psychotic illness, alcohol and drug abuse, mental subnormality and a wide variety of characterological disorders.[3] It follows directly that clarification of parental pathology is one of the goals of the evaluation. While this assessment may evolve as part of a thorough family approach, individual sessions with the parents are often indicated. These individual assessments can be accomplished by the child psychiatrist who is involved with the child and family. However, an alternate strategy is for an adult psychiatrist to meet with the parents separately to arrive at an independent diagnosis. If this latter strategy is employed, it is imperative that adequate communication take place between the two evaluators to assure an integrated picture of the family's functioning.

The individual interview with the child should include an unstructured period during which affect and anxiety can be assessed, as well as a more structured interaction during which events related to the development and discovery of the incestuous relationship with the parent can be explored. While it is usually necessary to ask directly about the incidents, the psychiatrist should avoid taking the position of an interrogator. By the time the child is referred, she has usually been asked to repeat her "story" on a number of occasions. Unfortunately, this may have been done in a stressful, insistent, and often critical manner. A repetition of this negative approach to "getting the facts" is certainly contra-indicated. Instead, the direct inquiry related to the events should be guided by the level of anxiety of the child and may actually serve as a means to further assess the child's current capacity to cope with her situation. If the child is reluctant to discuss the sexual events or flatly denies their occurrence, no attempt should be made to coerce her to supply this information. In summary, the evaluator should allow the child an opportunity to raise the topic of sexual abuse. If this does not occur spontaneously, he should inquire about it directly but should not persist with a "cross-examination" if the child is in acute distress. The following clinical example illustrates some of these issues.

Melinda

Melinda was a six-year-old girl who had been sexually abused by her father eight months prior to my seeing her. He had been convicted of sexual assault and sent to the state prison. Assessment was requested in order to determine whether her current behavior problems might be related to the incident and whether psychotherapy might be appropriate.

Melinda showed little hesitancy upon meeting me in the waiting room although she was distinctly coy, often turning her eyes away from me for a moment. She was a very pretty little girl although she was brought for the evaluation in a tattered and stained dress. She had long, attractive blonde hair, but it was neither clean nor combed. Despite her frequent glances away, she was not shy and took my hand to go to the playroom with surprising confidence.

On arriving in the playroom, Melinda was delighted to see an array of toys. She waited politely while I suggested we could play as we talked and then immediately began to take inventory of the playthings. Among a collection of animals, dolls, and puppets, there was a complete family of plastic people as well as a plastic bull, cow, and calf. After a period of play together, which might be best described as a time of introduction to both the toys and to each other, I asked her if she understood why she had been brought to see me. She was initially evasive but rather quickly stated that it was because of her daddy who was now in prison. She then became silent.

A period of play with farm animals followed. She began by describing each animal until she eventually came to the bull. She identified his genital area and told me in the manner that a secret would be revealed that "this part would get hard like a stick" and that "white stuff would come out". She then added that her daddy had a "do do" like that, which was the reason he had been sent to prison. At that point she threw the bull down and turned her attention to the family of plastic dolls. She was then able to use the dolls to reveal the drama of her own seduction and the ensuing family chaos. My role during this retelling of her story was essentially to ask questions of clarification and to assume a studied non-judgmental posture despite a strong emotional reaction to what she was telling me. After a second session with Melinda, I recommended she receive individual play therapy with one primary goal being a better understanding of her ambivalent feelings toward both her parents. Additionally, I hoped that she would be able to develop a less sexualized manner of interacting with adults and be able to improve her self-esteem as a result of mastery of more age-appropriate accomplishments and relationships. Her mother was also evaluated and psychotherapy recommended to help her to deal more effectively with her own feelings towards her husband as well as to receive direct support in providing better care for Melinda.

As the preceding case illustrates, one of the central aspects of the psychiatric diagnostic process is often the evaluation of the indications for psychotherapy. Clearly, practical considerations such as the availability of psychotherapists must be taken into account when making a recommendation. However, the documentation of the indications for psychotherapy may be one of the factors which will be central in determining an appropriate long-term disposition. Therefore, it is important to establish the need for psychotherapy whether or not resources are currently available. This is particularly true as the long-term consequences on development of even a non-coercive incestuous relationship may be quite serious. (See Chapters Seventeen and Eighteen.)

This emphasis on thorough diagnostic assessment is in contrast with the alternative approach of referring all children who have been involved in an incestuous relationship for psychotherapy on at least a "trial basis".[4] It is surely a mistake to minimize the emotional impact of an incestuous experience and deny the child an opportunity to deal with current observable psychological distress. However, a "trial psychotherapy" without specific indications serves little purpose if adequate coping mechanisms are in effect.

In making the determination of whether psychotherapy is appropriate and if so, what type and duration of therapeutic help is indicated, the specific circumstances of the case must be analyzed. For example, if the family is to remain intact and demonstrates a high level of motivation for change, family therapy has been shown to be an effective mechanism for shifting pathological patterns after initial work with individual family members has taken place.[7] (Also, see Chapter Fourteen.) If, however, the family is not amenable to such an approach and the child's primary areas of symptomatology include guilt about her involvement in the relationship and withdrawal from normal peer interactions, a specialized group setting of similar sexually abused children may be an ideal treatment modality (See Chapters Fifteen and Sixteen.) Alternatively, if the child is demonstrating considerable neurotic symptomatology with evidence of family and social withdrawal and internalized unresolved conflicts, an individual treatment setting may well be most appropriate, particularly if family availability is limited. Should individual psychotherapy be indicated, a parallel psychotherapeutic involvement with the child's mother or both parents is advisable to support changes within the child herself as well as helping the mother or both parents to understand the family patterns which allowed the initial situation to develop. This arrangement may well evolve into a conjoint family treatment after gains have been made with either the parents or child.[7] Even in those cases where the incestuous relationship was confined to a single incident and understood as a reaction to a stressful precipitant, a short-term psychotherapeutic involvement may be appropriate if the family or child is experiencing distress. However, focused intervention of a time-limited nature with stated goals, such as the alteration of the circumstances which led to the initial abuse, may be sufficient to help the family deal with the incestuous incident. Specifically, some assurance as to the unlikelihood of serious psychological sequelae following a single isolated incident may be helpful in relieving the guilt and anxiety of both parents in such families.

Evaluation of the Sexually Assaulted Child

While the issues of security and trust are equally important in approaching these children, concerns of family loyalty and betrayal are not central, nor is there usually the reality concern of dissolution of the family. However, guilt may still be a primary aspect of the family's reaction. This may take the form of the child being seen as partly responsible and subsequently blaming herself for the assault. Alternatively, parents often express the feeling that they should have taken steps which would have in some way prevented the occurrence. It may be true that some parents have been negligent, but this is not the case for others. Helping the parents deal with their guilt, however justified, is an important aspect of the initial encounter with the family. If the child was physically injured during the assault, this will compound the negative impact of the experience for both the child and family. A key factor which contributes to the emotional state of these families is the intense rage directed towards the perpetrator. This anger may be experienced by the family as both frightening and uncontrollable and can result in a state of acute disequilibrium. An estimate of their capacity to cope with what is often seen as an overwhelming crisis is a central aspect of the evaluation. The following clinical example highlights some of the special needs of the younger child.

Anita

Anita was a five-year-old Spanish-American child who lived in a large family with strong ethnic and cultural traditions. Her parents had left her in the family's home with a teenage cousin and had gone to a party in the neighborhood. The cousin was preoccupied with the other children and did not carefully supervise Anita. At nearly midnight, she was surprised to hear Anita screaming from the back yard and found her there with her clothes torn, bleeding, and frantic. Anita's parents were called, rushed home, and were horrified by what had happened. The police were called and Anita was taken to the emergency room. Medical examination revealed vaginal lacerations, and she was taken directly to the operating room for surgical repair.

Child psychiatric consultation was immediately requested. The parents were interviewed in the emergency room, and an interview with Anita was arranged for the next day. The initial concern of the parents was a fear that Anita had been permanently damaged. However, guilt about having left her with her cousin and a feeling of disbelief that the assault had taken place were prominent issues in the first session. Clearly, the parents were appreciative of the opportunity to express their fears about Anita and rage at the rapist. The following afternoon, Anita was seen with her mother on the pediatric ward of the hospital. It was clear that she had a strong attachment to her mother whose presence was highly reassuring to Anita. Initial attempts to engage Anita verbally were unsuccessful, but through the use of puppets she was able to respond. After a period of play, Anita was asked if she had slept on her first night in the hospital. She acknowledged that she had and that she remembered a dream. Rather than telling the story of the dream, Anita was asked to draw a picture of it. She proceeded to draw a forest path with a small girl on it and a huge bear with fangs and claws lurking just around the bend. The detail was exceptionally good, and the emotional tone was vividly clear. Overestimating the capacity of the child to deal with so recent a trauma, the interviewer observed that "the little girl in the picture must be frightened with so terrible a bear so close by". This resulted in the child becoming acutely distressed and throwing herself upon her mother who was sensitively able to comfort her despite the intensity of her reaction.

Two aspects of the situation became immediately evident. The first was that even this indirect confrontation of the child with the assault was too overwhelming so soon after the event. Secondly, the mother had the ability to respond to her daughter in a very therapeutic manner. Intervention was thus focused on helping the mother to gradually deal with the child's anxieties and fears. Additionally, the mother was allowed to work through her own guilt about having left Anita on the night of the assault. The parents' guilt about the incident persisted for some time, and repeated reassurances to the entire family were necessary that this one traumatic attack need not leave a lifetime scar on Anita's emotional development.

Assessing the Immediate Response of Social Services

Incestuous Relationships

Assuring that the child is not in danger of repeated sexual abuse is directly the responsibility of social services. (See Chapter Nine.) However, this concern often results in an urgent request for psychiatric involvement. It is certainly true that an understanding of the family's dynamics can provide a better basis for making a decision concerning the return of the child or father to the home. However, a valid assessment of the family's capacity to change requires time. Here the child psychiatrist can play a helpful role in differentiating the short-term priority of safe placement from long-term decisions regarding the future of the child.

The immediate strategy for protecting the child usually involves either placing the child outside the home or removing the father. If the child is placed, her feelings of rejection and separation must be dealt with. If the father is removed, his loss may turn the family temporarily against the child and result in increased guilt and impulses to flee the family. Yet another alternative is to allow the family to remain together under close supervision. Again, the decision must arise from the specific family situation. This is best achieved when social services has an opportunity to discuss these issues in the light of the family assessment. Assurance of protection for the child from recurrence of the sexual abuse is a necessary condition. Ultimately, the decision should be made considering the best interests of the child.

Sexual Assault

Placement of the child outside the home is less often a central issue in these cases. An urgent referral is more often the result of a concern about the immediate psychological impact of the event on the child. Often this concern is most acutely felt by the parents as demonstrated by Anita's family. In fact there is more of an immediate worry if the parents seem only mildly concerned or indifferent about the event. In these cases, specific support for the family and further clarification of the parents' paradoxical reaction are imperative. It has been suggested that this indifferent response, which has been documented in an alarming number of identified cases,[3] is a specific indicator of family pathology.

Recurrence

While the use of therapeutic measures to deal with the impact of previous trauma is an important goal, the prevention of future episodes of sexual abuse should be seen as an even higher priority. It is the central question to address once the immediate safety of the child is secured. This is particularly true in the light of an increasing appreciation that chronic exposure to moderately abusive or even neglectful parenting has more serious impact on emotional development than an acute, severe episode of abuse which is an isolated event.[5,10] Unfortunately, recurrence is not a rare circumstance, and thus this issue must be addressed in each case. One study[3] found that in 41% of the families evaluated, there was a history of previously documented sexual abuse. In more than 20% of the families assessed, two children were being sexually abused, and in two families the incestuous involvement extended to all five children in the family. This data highlights the need to be concerned not only with recurrence involving the same child but also with assessing the sexual abuse risk for all siblings.

While it is impossible to predict with certainty those families where future sexual abuse will occur, the decision should be based on two factors. The first is the documentation of the previous history of the family and assessment of whether the factors which allowed the incestuous or assaultive situation to occur originally are still present. The second is an assessment of the parents' personality structure and their motivation and capacity for change.

The first factor is of critical importance and has been shown to be the most valid predictor of recurrence with other impulsive deviant behaviors.[17] The immediate practical implication is at least twofold. First, if there has been no change in the family situation except the removal of the child, there is a high likelihood of recurrence. Second, if the incestuous relationship or the sexual relationship with an adult perpetrator outside the home was of a longstanding nature, there is a greater risk of recurrence, and more concrete steps must be taken to assure the child's safety.

The second factor is related to the first. Verbal assertion that change is desired must be treated with caution for while it is an indicator that the family is willing to begin psychotherapy, it must be coupled with behavioral change before it can be established with a high degree of certainty that abuse will not recur. The psychiatrist's understanding of the severity of the parents' characterological defensive structure and an appreciation of their needs and alternative mechanisms for having these needs met can help in determining the likelihood of initial positive changes in family interaction being sustained.

Fact or Fantasy

In most sexual abuse cases, there is some question as to the extent and nature of the sexual experience. Only in a minority of cases does physical evidence remove any doubt about occurrence. Many families present a confusing array of accusations and denials. The child psychiatrist is often requested to clarify the event through exploration of the child's perceptions of the experience and to help determine whether the abuse did occur or is the product of an overactive imagination.

This anxiety about the reality of the event must be acknowledged to have some basis. There have been cases where children alleged that sexual contact had occurred in a conscious attempt to punish an adult for some perceived transgression. Additionally, unconscious mechanisms can play a role in distorting the perception of reality. In addressing this question, the child psychiatrist must deal with subjective reports and relative certainties. There are specific indications which may support the child's story.

For example, the child may have a sophisticated knowledge of sexual activities or the sexual characteristics of the parent in question. Other considerations are the accuracy of the child's recall of the details of the incident and the consistency with which these details are remembered with subsequent retelling.

Understanding family dynamics may also help in this clarification. An overstimulating sexual atmosphere in the home may lead to increased sexual preoccupation on the part of the child. This may result in either the child masturbating excessively or becoming increasingly sexually active outside the home as well as with family members. While some distortion may be understood as related to unconscious impulses, another concern for the evaluator is that the child may be intentionally lying. When parents are involved in a custody battle for the child, it is particularly important to carefully consider the possibility that accusations may be untrue. However, in most instances the child is not fabricating the reported incident.

Still, in some rare cases, there may never be an absolute resolution of doubt about the actual occurrence of the event. In these more clouded cases or even in cases where the sexual assault is proven to be fictitious, there is a need to understand the motivation for the development of such a fantasy as well as to provide help for the child in coping with the impulse and its consequences.

Role in Long-Term Disposition

The handling of these cases requires the involvement of a team of professionals. The child psychiatrist has a variety of responsibilities to the team. The first is the presentation of the findings of his evaluation which pertain to the placement of the child. This should involve both an estimation of the risk of recurrence and an assessment of the developmental needs of the child. Usually a written report directly addressing these areas is necessary, and in cases where psychological considerations are central in arriving at the recommended disposition, direct testimony in court may be required.

The second responsibility is the determination of the need for psychiatric intervention, the type of psychotherapy indicated, and an estimation of the duration and prognosis of treatment. Documentation of the specific indications and initial focus of the treatment will facilitate implementation of the recommendations. This documentation is particularly important when a specific course of action is necessary to assure that treatment will be available.

These responsibilities of the child psychiatrist to the team are not always clarified. Uncertainty regarding the commitment of the child psychiatrist to be involved throughout the evaluation and disposition can lead to a variety of problems. One of the most serious is a misunderstanding related to the need for a court appearance. The recognition of the possibility of testimony and an agreement to appear in court if necessary is an important condition for the inclusion of the child psychiatrist in the team effort. The minimal commitment of the evaluator must be the adequate presentation of his findings. However, the further commitment to be available to the team and family in the future to make re-assessments of the child's development provides continuity which can be critically important in effectively making decisions in the child's best interest.

The psychiatric assessment of sexually abusive families can be an intense emotional experience for the child psychiatrist just as other professionals can experience their work with these families as stressful. An appreciation of this reality for both himself and others is an important aspect of the evaluation. Recognition of the specific reactions of team members and providing support to them in dealing with these emotional situations can be an important indirect contribution to the entire process of helping these children and families.

Conclusion

All the consequences of sexual abuse are not clear. However, some general principles are emerging. For example, isolated incidents of abuse are almost certainly less damaging than sexual abuse which continues over a prolonged period of time. The impact of involvement of a member of the family as the perpetrator poses special problems of loyalty as discussed, but even in those circumstances the impact may be influenced by the amount of affection and the degree of coercion within the relationship. A more serious prognosis is likely if physical abuse accompanies the sexual exploitation. Similarly, the immediate reaction to this concurrent physical and sexual abuse is more severe.

While many questions still exist, some guidelines are clear. A supportive team approach with mutually recognized commitment to implementing the team's recommendations is an effective vehicle for helping these children and families. The child psychiatrist not only plays a role in deciding upon the most appropriate short- and long-term dispositions for the child and family, but he is called upon to clarify possible distortions which may occur in these emotionally charged situations. The process by which these goals are achieved is through exploration of the family's past experiences and careful assessment of their defensive mechanisms and coping capacity in order to develop a better understanding as to how the team should proceed. This conservative approach to what is often a difficult problem coupled with a primary concern for the best interests of the child and a developing appreciation of the important clinical issues will hopefully lead to increasingly effective ways of predicting and influencing psychological outcomes.

References

1. Chess, S. (1969) *Fundamental Child Psychiatry: An Introduction to Child Psychiatry* (2nd Ed.) Grune & Stratton, New York.
2. Cox, A. and Rutter, M. (1976) Diagnostic appraisal and interviewing. In *Child Psychiatry: Modern Approaches.* (Edited by Rutter, M. and Hersov, L.) Blackwell Scientific Publications, London.
3. De Francis (1969) *Protecting the Child Victim of Sex Crimes Committed by Adults.* American Humane Assoc., Children's Division, Denver.
4. Farley, G. K., Eckhardt, L. O. and Hebert, F. B. (1979) *Handbook of Child and Adolescent Psychiatric Emergencies.* Medical Examination Press, Garden City, N.Y.
5. Gaensbauer, T. J., Mrazek, D. A. and Harmon, R. J. (1980) Emotional expression in abused and/or neglected infants. In *Psychological Approaches to Child Abuse* (Edited by Frude, N.) Batsford Academic & Educational Ltd., London.
6. Group for Advancement of Psychiatry (1957) *The Diagnostic Process in Child Psychiatry.* GAP, New York.
7. Giarretto, Henry (1976) Humanistic treatment of father–daughter incest. In *Child Abuse and Neglect: The Family and the Community.* (Edited by Helfer, R. E. and Kempe, C. H.) Ballinger, Cambridge, Mass.
8. Green, B. E. and Manz, M. (1979) *Same Sex Incest: A Case Series.* Presented at the 26th Annual Meeting of the American Academy of Child Psychiatry, Atlanta, Georgia.
9. Kanner, Leo (1935) *Child Psychiatry.* C. Thomas, Springfield, Ill.
10. Martin, H. P. and Beezley, P. (1977) Behavioral observations of abused children. *Devel. Med. Child Neurol.* **19:** 373.
11. Meiselman, K. C. (1979) *Incest: A Psychological Study of Causes and Effects with Treatment Recommendations.* Josey-Bass, San Francisco.
12. Morrison, G. C. (1969) Therapeutic intervention in a child psychiatry emergency service. *J. Amer. Acad. Child Psychiatry.* **9:** 595.
13. Morrison, G. C. (1975) *Emergencies in Child Psychiatry—Emotional Crises of Children, Youth and Their Families.* C. Thomas, Springfield, Ill.
14. Mrazek, P. B. (1980) Annotation: sexual abuse of children. *J. Child Psychol. Psychiatry* **21:** 91.
15. Rosenfeld, A. A., Nadelson, C. C. and Krieger, M. (1979) Fantasy and reality in patients reports of incest. *J. Clin. Psychiatry* **40:** 159.
16. Rutter, M. and Hersov L. (1976) *Child Psychiatry: Modern Approaches.* Blackwell Scientific Publications, London.
17. Scott, P. D. (1977) Assessing dangerousness in criminals. *Br. J. Psychiatry* **131:** 127.
18. Werkman, S. L. (1965) The psychiatric diagnostic interview with children. *Am. J. Orthopsychiatry* **35:** 764.

Part IV.
TREATMENT

Introduction

The authors of the chapters in this section on TREATMENT share some values and beliefs upon which their clinical work is based. First, sexual child abuse is often harmful not only to the child but also to his or her family. Therefore, treatment must be offered, and even court-ordered if necessary, following comprehensive evaluation of all family members. Second, while the initial and primary goal of therapy is to stop the sexually abusive behavior, there are many other psychological difficulties of the individuals and families which must be addressed. Third, not all families can be helped to stay together with marked improvement in their interactions. Even so, the children and adolescents in these families should be offered treatment in their own right. Fourth, treatment of sexually abused children and their families is extremely taxing clinical work which requires considerable self-awareness.

Each of the chapters in this section is based on clinical experience and contributes to our understanding of what the therapeutic process entails. In Chapter Twelve Mrazek discusses some of the technical and counter-transference issues; these are elaborated on in the later chapters. In Chapter Thirteen, Mrazek and Bentovim conceptualize the incestuous family as a dysfunctional system and offer suggestions for the treatment of the family unit. Giarretto, in Chapter Fourteen, describes the components and process of a comprehensive community intervention program in San Jose, California. This model, which utilizes multiple therapies and emphasizes cooperation with the judicial system, is being adopted throughout the United States. The next two chapters, Fifteen and Sixteen, are based on group psychotherapy with sexually abused children and adolescents; both projects took place at The National Center for the Prevention and Treatment of Child Abuse and Neglect in Denver, Colorado. Mrazek, using diagnostic and group process material, highlights the importance of early intervention with young children. Gottlieb and Dean offer useful insights into the emotional complexities of the co-therapy relationship when treating an adolescent group.

The ideas offered in this section will not provide the reader with an "ideal treatment package", for as yet little is known about the long-term success of any intervention. In many ways, the chapters raise more questions than they answer. What criteria should be used for determining who should be treated and how? What standards should be applied in assessing improvements in individual and family functioning? When treatment fails to successfully reunite a family, what are the alternatives? When a therapist's personal life circumstances negatively affect his or her clinical work, what options are there for the family, agency, and community?

PATRICIA BEEZLEY MRAZEK
C. HENRY KEMPE

Chapter Twelve

Special Problems in the Treatment of Child Sexual Abuse

PATRICIA BEEZLEY MRAZEK

To believe that expertise and comfort in dealing with physical child abuse adequately prepares one for working with a sexually abused child and his family is a false assumption. Despite the similarities in the two types of abuse and the co-existence of physical and sexual abuse in some families, the clinician who is just beginning to work with sexual abuse has new issues to face, not only in the treatment process but also with himself as a responsive human being with a whole host of emotions. Other matters more directly parallel those in physical child abuse, but even these must be addressed again and clearly thought through. This chapter presents only some of these technical and counter-transference issues as a means of introduction to this section on TREATMENT. The areas to be addressed are: attitudes about sexuality and sexual abuse; the timing of interventions; choosing who will be treated and how; compassion and external control; specific personal reactions; and coping with community resistance.

Attitudes about Sexuality and Sexual Abuse

Accepting the idea that some adults have sexual relationships with children is often more difficult for professionals and the lay public than is the recognition of how some children come to be physically abused. In part, this is because it is usually easier for adults to accept their own aggressive feelings toward children than their sexual feelings toward them. Being angry with a child and having the impulse to strike out and hurt that child is well within the understanding of most parents and child caretakers. But what about erotic, sexual feelings? Western culture has gone so far with its spoken and unspoken taboos that adults feel guilty about any sexual feelings they may have toward children. Pincus and Dare[4] have clearly pointed out in their book *Secrets in the Family* that "incestuous feelings and fantasies within the family are universal and play an important part in the healthy development of the child". They go on to remind us that "the child whose parent is not a bit in love with him or her is in danger of feeling rejected and uncared for. It will be hard for that child in later years to believe that anyone else could love him either".

But, as with aggressive feelings, the incestuous impulses can be too strong for the adult to cope with and can result in chaotic and direct expression. The clinician must be able to understand and accept that erotic feelings toward children are part of human nature; it is only when the impulses are acted upon to the extreme that the situation warrants societal intervention.

The clinician must also carefully think through his or her own values, feelings, and experiences in relation to sexuality. A puritanical repressive upbringing or personal experiences with sexual assault as a child or an adult may make this type of work more difficult or impossible unless the experiences are understood and worked through. During an intensive inservice training program with 60 social service workers, a well-known educator found that 25% of the females and 15% of the males had been sexually assaulted as children.[3] Many of these probably have gone on to become highly skilled and sensitive clinicians, but others may have found themselves needing to talk about their own assaults and come to some resolution about what happened during their therapy sessions with sexually abused children and/or their families. It is then that one questions who is receiving the treatment.

Other therapists may have difficulties drawing boundaries and making decisions regarding sexual matters with their own children. For example, if there is conflict between a therapist and his or her spouse regarding nudity in their home, working in the area of sexual abuse may be more difficult. He may find himself unreasonably angry or so unsure about his personal ethics that his professional judgment is impaired. (For more on psychosexual development within the family, see Chapter Two.)

Thus, personal experiences may make it impossible, either temporarily or permanently, for some clinicians to treat sexually abused children and their families. The professional community must respect these feelings by letting these therapists turn down referrals and requests for service.

The Timing of Interventions

Mental health practitioners usually do not deal with issues of life and death. For them to begin dealing with physical child abuse a decade ago required a shift in orientation and a willingness to provide quick, decisive intervention, often supporting recommendations to remove children from potentially lethal situations. Those same practitioners, if now beginning to work with sexual abuse cases, must make another shift. Despite the critical nature of a sexual assault on a child or adolescent, it is *not* an issue of life or death *unless* physical violence has also occurred or is likely to occur. Therefore, the timing of particular decisions and actions will vary depending on the child and family. If the sexual assault was made by someone outside the family and the family is concerned about the child, immediate short-term intervention may be all that is necessary. If the family reveals an incestuous relationship while already in treatment or makes a self-referral because of such a problem, there may be no need for emergency measures. Some time can be taken to unravel the complexities of the family situation and decide with the parents and child what should be done. However, if only one family member reveals the occurrence of sexual abuse and the others either deny or angrily admit to such behavior, there is justification for taking immediate actions which actually create a crisis for the family. Investigations by the police and social services, hospitalization, and foster placement may be necessary not only to protect the child but also to make the entire family aware that the incestuous relationship must stop. Likewise, if it seems that the family might flee from the community, quick, decisive intervention is necessary.

The mental health practitioner must balance a sense of immediacy with the long-term consequences of his actions. If he is going to intervene, he must be sure that the timing is appropriate. We must always keep in mind who is really having the crisis—the child, the family, or the professional who has just learned about a relationship which may have been occurring for many years. With the latter, the primary justification for dealing with the case as though it were an emergency is to unsettle the family enough that they might be open to help.

Although sexual abuse may be a family's presenting problem, there are usually other difficulties as well. A clinician who works exclusively with child sexual abuse cases is in danger of compartmentalizing the issue, seeing it as the major, if not the only, issue. The opposite may be true of the therapist who does not usually deal with sexual abuse; he may ignore the problem and concentrate on more familiar difficulties. Although it is necessary to focus initially on the assault and discuss who did what to whom and why, there must be room in the therapy for the clarification and resolution of the other difficulties as well. There often becomes a point in treatment when it is appropriate to move on and leave the sexual abuse behind. The family or individual who has resolved some of the primary issues involved in the abuse no longer need see themselves as a sexually abusive family or victim. A shift to new personal identities is easier to conceptualize than to obtain, but it is a worthwhile goal to keep in mind.

Choosing Who Will be Treated and How

As yet, there is no evidence that any one particular unit of treatment, such as individual, marital couple, or whole family, is specifically indicated in the treatment of child sexual abuse. Likewise, there is little reason to believe that any particular theoretical orientation, such as humanistic or psychodynamic psychology, is more helpful than another. The therapist is therefore left with his own clinical judgment as his guide. He will use his own theoretical framework to understand causation, and his decision as to who to treat will follow from that. If he sees the intrapsychic abnormality of the adult offender as the locus of the pathology, he is likely to offer individual treatment to that person. If he sees the family as a system whose interactions are faulty, he is more likely to treat the family as a unit. The danger with these approaches, particularly with a therapist using a single treatment method, is that all families will be expected to fit the same theory of causation and the same method of treatment. Such singular or specialized professional interests do not allow for rational evaluation of treatment effectiveness.

Another danger is that communities which are in a rush to establish treatment programs for child sexual abuse will adopt the present-day approaches to physical child abuse, which have become quite standardized, without adequately considering whether these interventions are transferable. For example, even though lay therapists and parent aides have been quite successful with physically abusive parents, it is questionable how effective they would be with sexually abusive parents, especially when a family claims to be comfortable with the incestuous behavior.

Until adequate research with controlled studies indicates which methods of treatment are most successful with child sexual abuse, the clinician must be careful to assess adequately the needs and the accessibility of all family members and consider various treatment alternatives before deciding on a particular course of action. In the end, the choice must be based on the family and on the therapist's competencies, not one or the other.

Combining familiar treatment methods with innovation is a legitimate practice and may help prevent emotional "burn-out" of therapists by providing outlets for creativity. However, too often this has meant that every family is given a trial with every new program that comes along. This can easily mean that the family becomes overwhelmed by having too many therapists to relate to, too much conflicting advice, and too many expectations placed upon them. It is far better for the family if only one therapist or one co-therapy team assumes primary responsibility with one or two additional therapists, using their innovative and/or specific intervention, brought in very cautiously and only after some progress has been made with the family.

Compassion and External Control

Rosenfeld and Newburger[5] have addressed the need for a balance between compassion and control when working with physically abusive families.

> "The compassionate model derives from the need for insight and the formation of a helpful professional-parent relationship to understand and to improve the functioning of abusive families.... The control model refers to the aggressive use of intervention to limit and, if necessary, to punish deviant behavior."

This balance between compassionate understanding and external control is just as crucial when dealing with child sexual abuse. Yet, many clinicians find the dual role difficult if not impossible. In cases of physical abuse these functions are often assigned separately to different professionals, but this has often resulted in additional problems. The families may continue to split the persons involved with them into "good" and "bad", never integrating these aspects into a whole. Also, professional collaboration is often difficult when roles are assigned so rigidly; the professional with the responsibility for the external control can end up feeling that he has nothing to offer the family.

For some professionals the compassion which is so necessary in treating sexually abusive adults and child victims does not come easily. Anger, over-identification, or helplessness can all get in the way. For others, it is impossible to use their own authority to seek external controls, even when appropriate, because such actions feel too judgmental and punitive. Those clinicians who are most successful in their work with these families are able to combine these functions to whatever degree is necessary with a particular family. For example, it is often crucial to take firm stands regarding who gets evaluated and treated, who remains in the home and who leaves, and who, if anyone, gets prosecuted. Giarretto[1] and the Kempes[2] have maintained that the law enforcement authorities must be involved in cases of incest, but they advocate the use of deferred prosecution or probation while rehabilitation efforts are being made. Only if treatment is unsuccessful would the criminal process resume, leading perhaps to incarceration. (For more on this see Chapter Nine.)

In a study of 71 physically abusive families referred to a treatment program which emphasized child management skills, Wolfe *et al.*[6] have shown the importance of adjudication. Parents who were court-ordered to complete treatment as a requirement for full return of child custody were approximately five times more likely to complete treatment successfully than families who were not required by the court to participate (voluntary). It seemed to be those parents who had little choice but to comply with the court order who began the process of change.

As yet, there is no comparable study of sexually abusive parents, but control by society through the court may be just as pertinent. Other methods of increasing parental compliance with treatment, such as parenting salaries and contingency contracting, have been addressed by researchers in related areas of parent training but have not been reported with sexually abusive parents.

Some therapists are uncomfortable with mandatory treatment ordered by the court and consider it a major interference with the development of a positive therapeutic alliance. Indeed, it does place an extra burden on the clinician to be honest about his recommendations to the court, to be alert to various forms of resistance, and to try harder to establish a working alliance with the parents.

Specific Personal Reactions

Treating sexually abused children and their families engenders intense and specific personal reactions in therapists. Some of these feelings and responses can best be understood through the application of the traditional definition of counter-transference, that is, emotional responses including unresolved conflicts and problems which are aroused in the therapist by the specific qualities of the patient and can hinder the therapist's effectiveness. It is important to remember that not only the internal problems of the clinician are involved. Sexually abused children and their families can induce or evoke particular types of responses in the professionals with whom they have contact. It is remarkable how similar these responses can be. Three of these will be addressed: collusion with the family system, responding to the sexual milieu, and having unrealistic expectations.

Collusion with the Family System

When recognition of sexual abuse occurs, families often are quick to blame one member of the family unit or, with third party abuse, to blame the outsider while refusing to look at the contributing roles played by the rest of the family. If the clinician does not understand the whole system, there is a danger of scapegoating one particular member such as the "seductive" adolescent or the alcoholic father while overly protecting or rescuing other family members. The therapist will almost always be pushed by the family to collude with their splitting. Unfortunately, there is often just enough truth in what the family is saying to make the splitting difficult to resist. This often leads to simplistic solutions such as removal of the problematic family member from the home and treatment for only that individual.

The family's dynamic equilibrium is usually greatly upset when the sexual abuse becomes known to outsiders. Attempts will be made by the family members to recreate old patterns of interaction with which they are comfortable. It is at this point of crisis that there is the possibility that healthier realignments could be initiated. The therapist is in a precarious position. He must enter the family system as it is and has been so that he knows it and becomes accepted by the members, but he must be separate from it so he can affect some change. The family, both intentionally and unintentionally, will try to draw him into their familiar interactions as they struggle to recreate the psychodynamics they had before discovery. The therapist may go along with the family's splitting and scapegoating of a particular member, or he may find himself representing an absent member to the rest of the family. Additionally, he may begin saying and doing things which are not part of his usual therapeutic approach and with which he is uncomfortable following the treatment sessions. Alternatively, he may find himself liking the family and looking forward to meeting with them but then realizing that they have changed very little if at all. All of these are indications that the therapist is colluding with the family system and may need some consultation with a colleague to acquire some objectivity and distance.

Responding to the Sexual Milieu

The milieu of the treatment of sexually abusive adults or sexual abuse victims is often highly erotically charged. The verbal content and the non-verbal behavior of the client or patient is at times intentionally provocative. The adolescent girl who arrives for her first appointment in a see-through blouse, the father who uses slang terms for sexual organs and acts, the mother who strokes her young son's body during a family interview, and the preschool child who climbs into her male therapist's lap during group therapy and begins to rub against him while calling him "cute" are all continuing behaviors which were accepted and rewarded in their family setting. Even clinicians who are highly skilled and experienced may find themselves uneasy with such blatant behavior.

Alternatively, the family members may put tremendous pressure on the therapist to accept their sexual practices which they consider to be "open", "liberal," and "modern". They want his or her approval of what others have termed sexual abuse. They may present logical, intelligent arguments, and, indeed, no one in the family may seem "damaged" by the incestuous practices which have occurred. The therapist may begin to feel he is being moralistic and rigid not only in relation to that family but also in his broader views of the world. This is especially difficult for the therapists who are supposed to be "experienced" and "knowledgeable".

Because of the sexual fantasies and conflicts which this work engenders in therapists, it is essential that we spend adequate time trying to understand why a family or victim is behaving a particular way, staying alert to our own responses, and consulting with colleagues.

Unrealistic Expectations

There are those therapists who are convinced they can succeed in rehabilitating persons and families with whom no one else has ever been able to make any progress.

Such eternal optimism only rarely proves to be justified. But there are those families who are so likeable and seemingly so sincere in their wish to change that a therapist is willing to give them a try. If, after a reasonable amount of time, no progress has occurred, some hard decisions must be made. Sometimes the therapist's own self-image and personal investment make it impossible for him or her to give up with a particular family even when it is obvious to everyone else that it is unrealistic to expect any change. This is especially unfortunate when a young child is involved and it is the parent who is being treated. Years can be spent trying to rehabilitate the parent while the child waits in foster care, uncertain whether s/he will ever be returned home.

Although unrealistic optimism can do considerable harm, unfounded pessimism can do likewise. An error which is sometimes made by clinicians, especially those with a psychoanalytic orientation, is to assume that all incestuous relationships only have negative effects of a most serious nature on at least the younger of the two participants. This can lead to a belief that only a long course of intensive psychotherapy will begin to mitigate the damage that has been done. In victims who have made satisfactory life adjustments by their own standards, such unrealistic pessimism can generate guilt and self-doubt.

Coping with Community Resistance

The reluctance of the professional and lay communities to acknowledge the existence of child sexual abuse and to financially support treatment programs for these children and their families places a strain on the clinician which may not be adequately appreciated. It is not only the families who are affected by this resistance. Those who work in the field begin to wonder where the rewards are, for personal validation through positive feedback from the community is minimal. One social service worker whose caseload was primarily incestuous families was dismayed at the reaction to her work from her family and friends. "It is as though I were treating lepers. The rest of the world is relieved someone else is doing it, but they would prefer not to know about it." Many clinicians have felt depreciated when their work has been referred to as "kinky", voyeuristic, or even immoral.

Some of the job satisfaction for the therapist must be self-generated, for example, feeling good about professional abilities such as the thoroughness of an evaluation or the quality of the treatment that is offered. But the support, respect, and appreciation which can be provided by an interdisciplinary team can be even more important. To have one's work scrutinized, discussed, and then validated can bolster self-esteem and make it possible to go on. Also, team members can use a type of humor and view of the world with each other which may not be understood or tolerated by those outside of this professional network. This ability to lighten things up occasionally is essential in preventing emotional "burn-out".

As there is increased publicity and public education about child sexual abuse, similar to what has occurred with physical abuse and domestic violence, there may be more acknowledgment of the important role therapists have and, therefore, more community appreciation of their efforts. However, this will always be an uncomfortable area to work in because child sexual abuse will never become comfortable. To work in this area too exclusively for too long can take its personal toll.

References

1. Giarretto, H. (1976) Humanistic treatment of father–daughter incest. In *Child Abuse and Neglect: The Family and the Community*. (Edited by Helfer, R. E. and Kempe, C. H.) Ballinger, Cambridge, Mass.
2. Kempe, R. S. and Kempe, C. H. (1978) *Child Abuse*. Fontana/Open Books, London.
3. Moulton, Joyce. Personal communication. June 7, 1979.
4. Pincus, L. and Dare, C. (1978) *Secrets in the Family*. Faber and Faber, London.
5. Rosenfeld, A. A. and Newburger, E. H. (1977) Compassion vs. control: conceptual and practical pitfalls in the broadened definition of child abuse. *J. Am. Med. Assoc.* **237:** 2086.
6. Wolfe, D. A., Aragona, J., Kaufman, K. and Sandler, J. (1980) The importance of adjudication in the treatment of child abusers: some preliminary findings. *Child Abuse and Neglect* **4:** 127.

Chapter Thirteen

Incest and the Dysfunctional Family System

PATRICIA BEEZLEY MRAZEK AND ARNON BENTOVIM

While there is no unitary explanation for the occurrence of incest, there are many stereotypes regarding etiology and family constellation. Some of these, whether they are derived from sociological, organic, or psychodynamic perspectives, have a basis in fact. (See Chapter Eight.) However, to look for single and/or static characteristics is to fail to understand the complexity of the family system. Even though some incestuous families are quite dissimilar on the surface, their underlying family dynamics, motivations, and needs may be remarkably comparable though multifactorial.

This chapter will use some of the principles of systems theory to understand why incest occurs and continues, often for long periods of time. These conceptualizations will then be linked to ideas for treatment.

The Family as a System

Systems theory originated in the work of von Bertalannfy[20] as a way of conceptualizing the nature of relationships within living systems. Only later was the theory applied to the pathology of families (See Chapter Two). Understanding the family as a system includes, but goes beyond, an individual model of diagnosis and treatment to focus also on the other family members and their context as well as on the feedback loops that connect them. In the systems model, the locus of pathology is the individual in context.[18] A systems understanding includes not only the behavior of the family members but also their perceptions and memories which change over time as interactions occur. A "healthy" system is never static but rather is always changing and evolving.

Recently, the second author has described the way that a family's system or *surface action* (that is, its characteristic pattern of communication, alliance, parental function, boundary integrity, atmosphere, affective status, and relationships with the outside world) serves to give psychosocial support to all family members and to provide nurturance and socialization for the children.[10] Such "healthy" surface action depends on a *depth structure* in the family where stressful events in the family of origin (that is, which affected the parents as children) and in the family of procreation (that is, affecting the parents as adults) have been accepted, integrated, resolved, and worked through. This gives rise to a functional way of being for the family and to a web of common and inter-subjective meanings to these events which enables the family to respond creatively to normal life-crises and to the developing needs of all members of the family.

Without such working through and integration of stressful events, the family system appears to be required to develop a characteristic surface action which is repetitive and circular and which develops a compulsive, dominating, urgent pattern of interactions which cannot be stopped on request for more than a brief time despite obviously destructive consequences. Such a dysfunctional action appears to be required as a way of either avoiding, denying, or deleting the meaning of unassimilated stressful events, or repeating and generalizing them so that past stressful events are constantly being replayed in various forms. Alternatively, there is an attempt to deal with stressful events by a massive attempt to overcome the event or deposit it on some other person as the "source of all bad things". Thus, the family develops a number of pathological meaning systems which underlie the surface action, and this handicaps the family's ability to respond creatively to new significant external stresses or the internal demands of the family life cycle.

Analysis of a Dysfunctional Family System

An incestuous family is one where the surface action of the family does not meet the needs of family members for nurturance, care, and warmth in an appropriate way relative to the maturity of those individuals. Instead, a sexualization of what should be nurturant physical contact is substituted. This "solution" itself adds to the dysfunctional surface action, and the resulting possessiveness, secrecy, and guilt can pervade the family's life, and the "solution" becomes a problem in its own right.

There are many different "routes" to this incestuous family surface action from the depth structure of the family whether resulting from events experienced by the parents as children in their family of origin, such as deprivation and incestuous relationships, or in the family of procreation, such as absence of a parent or marital breakdown. Whatever the original stressful events, incestuous families seem to share a belief that on the one hand close relationships and intimacy in adult relationships cannot be risked, and on the other that any separateness leads to disintegration and abandonment. Such pervasive and shared meaning seems to maintain the pathological surface action which contains incestuous behavior and perpetuates it over such long periods. To understand how this works in detail specific aspects of the family system will be examined.

Boundaries and Roles of Subsystems

Individuals and dyads are subsystems within a family. Subsystems can be formed by generation, sex, interest, or function. Thus, every individual belongs to several subsystems in which he has different levels of power and where he learns differentiated skills.[17]

The boundaries and roles within an incestuous family have become confused. Intergenerational boundaries have been crossed in relation to sexuality and often in other areas as well, such as decision-making or household management. A parent whose primary closeness is with his child rather than his spouse is acknowledging that the marital subsystem is askew. Paradox[21] and incongruity[2] are operating in that relationship, with members constantly being qualified and disqualified, leading to a sense of confusion and perversity between parent and parent, parent and child, and child and child.

The parental subsystem or coalition has also failed for it has not carried out two of the primary functions of parenting, that is, *nurturance* has been minimal and caring has become sexualized, and the *socialization* of the child has, at least in part, become deviant. One parent may be doing better in this role than the other; for example, an incestuous father may provide more emotional support to a child despite the sexual exploitation than a mother who is unavailable for any kind of attention or caring. Parents whose children are involved in sexual relationships with each other have failed to provide adequate supervision and alternative social experiences.

Rapid reversals of roles are also common in incestuous families. For example, a mother may solicit sexual relations with her adolescent son and then infantalize him by demanding he ask her permission to watch television. Although he may expect this type of reversal, it makes it exceptionally difficult for him to consolidate an identity.

Symptoms, Myths and Fears

We have described incestuous behavior in the family's surface action as a symptom which has become a sort of compromise between the need for expression of a family problem (that is, repetition) and attempts to avoid it. Lustig, *et al.*,[12] and Gutheil and Avery[8] view incest as one of many socially deviant behavior patterns which may be employed by a dysfunctional family in the maintenance of its own integrity and existence. The incest reduces tension and serves as a defense against fears of disintegration and abandonment.

While incest may help a family temporarily avoid facing painful realities, its continuation is dependent on a multiplicity of factors and complex interactions. For example, Mr. B's anxiety about his declining sexual potency and his fears that his wife will leave him contribute to his decision to approach his daughter, Pamela, sexually. Pamela, 9 years old, has an idealized image of her father and needs his attention and approval for her own image to be maintained. Her positive response to Mr. B's sexual advances reassures him about his masculinity. This father–daughter dyad is mutually dependent and reinforcing. The incest temporarily helps each of them avoid his/her problems with identity and self-esteem; it also prevents Mr. B from having to face the quality of his marital relationship. Mrs. B may well be spared meeting her husband's sexual needs, and the family shares a meaning or a myth that sexuality between father and daughter is an acceptable and necessary part of the family's life together.

The idea of family myth was first put forward within the context of systems theory by Ferreira[6,7] and has been elaborated by Byng-Hall.[3,4] They view family myth as a defense mechanism which, like any other defense, can be used excessively. A myth represents a family's common and intersubjective meaning; it is a body of beliefs that a family has about itself which are repeatedly confirmed by family consensus over the years rather than being challenged from within the family. Myths result in individuals being locked into role images which are often maintained without ever testing them against reality.

Most incestuous families are deeply embedded in mythology. At times the myths are readily apparent to the outside observer and can be directly related to life events and painful experiences as was described earlier. At other times, the origin of the myths has been lost, but the beliefs continue to guard against unconscious fears, taboos, or wishes.

A common myth is the idea that the mother in the family is weak and vulnerable. A 15-year-old girl defended keeping her incestuous behavior a secret by saying, "Mom doesn't know about dad and me, and we won't be telling her. It would kill her if she found out". But both the daughter and her father realized that at some level her mother already knew. The myth defends against a worse fear: "If I told my mother about dad and me, she'd do nothing. So, I feel better thinking I'm protecting her".

Homeostasis and Feedback Circularity

A feedback circularity within the incestuous family is established which permits the pathological surface action to continue its pattern. As long as everyone assumes his or her same role, or an acceptable variation, a homeostasis is achieved. But this requires continuous complex interaction. If time were frozen after observation of only a few steps of the sequence, it might appear that the homeostasis had been disrupted even when it had not been. For example, protest by one of the family members may be an essential component to the continuation of the incest.

The R Family

Mr. and Mrs. R have not spoken to each other for a week, and neither can remember the last time they had intercourse. They have not made any attempts to resolve their differences, but Mr. R has found some consolation with his adolescent daughter, Terri, sharing late-night meals in front of the television set and occasionally going on outings. Eventually, he approaches her sexually, and she responds because of her concern for her father and the excitement of keeping a "secret" from Mrs. R. But Mr. R becomes very possessive and demands intercourse several times a day. Eventually, Terri complains to her mother who in turn chastises Mr. R. The marital fight that ensues has a quality of sexual excitement to it, and Mrs. R seems more alive than she has been for months. Mr. R, however, finally breaks down in tears, asking his wife's forgiveness. He promises to leave Terri alone and to spend more time with his wife. This results in a dramatic withdrawal from Mrs. R who cannot tolerate even the potential for closeness in the marriage. In the following days, she avoids her husband. The system is left open for further incest.

This system is homeostatic, which does not mean it is without discord, but disagreements are kept *within* the family. The sexual interactions are kept within the family as well, to the exclusion of others. This equilibrium would be drastically upset if the daughter complained to a boyfriend or school teacher rather than to her mother. If the family was reported to social service authorities, the homeostasis could no longer exist. The external intervention would throw the family into chaos or "system runaway". The parents' initial response might be to scapegoat their daughter, denying her allegations and labeling her as the "problem" and source of all "badness".

Figure 1 shows the sequences of the family's homeostatic process while Figure 2 shows the disequilibrium which occurs when the daughter reports the incest outside the family.

The Evolution of Functional Systems

The evolution of functional family systems, that is, how they adapt to new situations and cope with severe stresses, has been of interest to social scientists for quite some time, and we have described some common responses earlier. Families do not

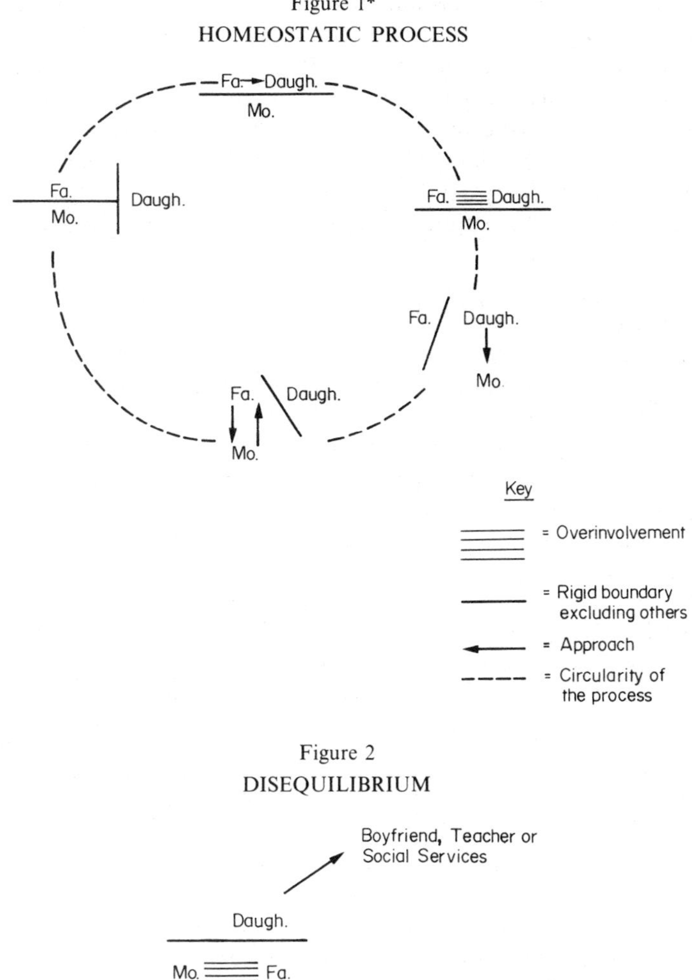

Figure 1*
HOMEOSTATIC PROCESS

Figure 2
DISEQUILIBRIUM

necessarily assess their interactions, decide to make changes, and then implement their ideas into actions, carrying them through to success. They usually maintain their status quo in relation to beliefs and interactions which are most important to them. Rather, families usually change, like all systems, when all other options, including maintaining the status quo, are blocked.[9] The normal crises which present with the various stages of the family life cycle (see Chapter Two) are enough to decrease resistance and put the system in flux. The family must accommodate, and the very same pattern of interactions is unlikely to return. If the family can rally, a new and satisfying level of adaptation can be achieved. If surface action absorbs so much energy that the family cannot marshal whatever resources it does have, it will still change but maladaptively, such as one of the members developing a psychiatric or physical symptom or the family maintaining destructive behavior such as incest.

* Idea based on work by Minuchin.[17]

Interventions with the Incestuous System

Applying these conceptualizations to incestuous families, we can see that the overall task is a difficult one. Stopping the sexual abuse, while a worthy and necessary goal, is not enough. The underlying family dynamics must be addressed.

If someone outside the family knows about the incest, someone within the family has had some level of discomfort with the incestuous behavior. Either consciously or unconsciously, one of the family members, perhaps even a sibling of the abused child, may be delegated to reveal enough of the "family secret" that eventually the homeostasis will be upset and the depth structure of the family more open to change. He or she can then easily become the family scapegoat by destroying what the others had perceived as working. Exceptions to this include the very young or retarded child who cannot voice his objections and has been used repeatedly by other family members.

Now is the time for the social service worker, therapist, or judge to intervene and assume the role of family disequalizer or "psychoshaker". The task is a complicated one. First, the equilibrium must be disturbed sufficiently so that the usual retreats are blocked; the family then has to move in a different direction. Creating a crisis in the therapeutic session or through temporary removal of a parent (preferably) or child, even for a brief period of time, can achieve this. (See Chapter Nine.)

This is a powerful position, and the intervenor must be aware of the potential impact. The initial complainer must be given relief; the therapist must work against the family attacking him or her. Likewise, the child must be protected, even if he was not the initial source, against being a scapegoat. The child may be willing to assume this role and may not take kindly to the therapist's blocking of this familiar pattern.

The therapist must be active, almost intrusive, and determined to participate in the family system so he can modify it. The tight, incestuous system often has worked well for many years, so the family members will not easily let him in, and when they finally do, initially it will be on their terms so they can manage the interactions. Lengthy, frequent appointments may be necessary, and much active work is needed to balance the complex activity involved in assessing family interaction yet creating a positive rapport with *each* individual.

Incest has often been labeled a crime or a sin, and the family is well aware of this. In treatment, the situation can be redefined or reframed in such a way that the family members take notice and perhaps begin to see themselves. The therapist cannot lie, but he can exaggerate one side of an ambivalence or conflict and help the family members become more aware of their myths and shared meanings which separate them as a family from the outside world. For example, to a family with a father who has been sleeping with and fondling two young sons, the therapist can say, "Dad's a cuddler, is he? Does he ever give mom a cuddle, too?" This puts the focus back on the spouse subsystem. To a family with a mother who claims she knew nothing about the incest and is a passive victim in it all, an unexpected intervention would be: "This is a powerful woman here—to have accomplished all this and avoid sex herself. She's rather like an orchestra conductor, creating lots of sound without playing an instrument herself".

Identifying how everyone in the family is involved can be a delicate matter; it must be done carefully. The intent is *not* to distribute blame evenly but to help each member understand his or her role. For example, a child, while certainly not to blame, can perpetuate the system and may feel guilty about his/her sexual involvement. To seek a solution it would be helpful to stress the positives and use the notion of "positive connotation" of behavior which helps the individual stop far more effectively than condemnation and negative connotation which only provoke a continuation of behavior to prove it could not be helped.[19] For example, "Mary has been trying so hard to keep the family together and not cause any upsets. She has sacrificed a lot, including not dating boys her own age, so she could help her mom and dad not have to confront each other". If the child has been playing an important part in the triangulation of mother–father–child, as is usually the case, she may be somewhat conflicted about giving up her role, even if it was she who first told about the incest. It then becomes important to find her another role in the family. "Now that Mary will not be sleeping with dad anymore and will not be keeping secrets from mom, she'll have a lot of time on her hands. What could we figure out for you, Mary, so you could have some fun in this family?"

Using siblings in the treatment can help take pressure off the designated child.[17] An older sibling who has moved out of the family and is no longer involved in the incest can often serve as a kind of "co-therapist", quickly pointing out patterns and vulnerabilities.

A Sense of Timing

Minuchin, *et al.*,[16] in their early development of structural family therapy with disorganized and disadvantaged families, gave a detailed case study of their attempts to work with a family where the father attempted to have intercourse with an older daughter. They described a treatment approach with the whole family in various combinations where problems are "enacted" by confrontation of participants, excluding and including family members according to the boundaries and alliances of the family map. For example, in the R family described above, Terri might be taken behind a screen and the parents would be helped to confront and deal with avoided problems without access to Terri and familiar pathways. Providing rules for communication and blocking disqualification would be necessary. A variety of tasks would be set to change pathological surface actions to more functional interactions. In addition, we feel historical stressful events which have been repeated, avoided, or overcome falsely in the family meanings need to be worked through and dealt with in a way which frees the family's creativity.[11]

While Giarretto (see Chapter Fourteen), Meiselman,[15] Anderson and Shafer,[1] and others[5,8,13] have advocated the use of family therapy with incestuous families, they have been cautious about the timing of its introduction. Most commonly, it is used as a last stage of treatment, after interventions with individuals and various dyadic combinations, although an initial family interview may be held. The reasons for this approach have not been adequately addressed, although the potential destructiveness in family interviews is often mentioned.

Certainly, family treatment does not necessitate seeing all of the family at every session. Subsystems can be contracted with for specific purposes and lengths of time. For example, a child can be told that his parents will be coming without him for the next four sessions because they have problems of their own which are not related to him. This serves to bolster the spouse subsystem and reinforce the child's natural position in the family. Whether family treatment is the primary intervention or whether most treatment is done with subsystems, it is the therapist's comfort and skill as well as the family dynamics which must be taken into consideration. However, a systems orientation will help in understanding the incestuous family.

Clinical Example: The B Family

Referral

The B family was referred by a social services department. Acting in its child protection role, the department was having to provide for the needs of five children ranging from 10 to 15 years of age. The mother had left the family three years before, and the father had been imprisoned six months before for having had intercourse over a lengthy period with his daughter, Joanne, who was 14 at the time of referral. There was a younger girl, Janet, age 13, and three boys—Gerald, age 15, Matthew, age 12, and Richard, age 10. Social services was proposing to set up a "home" for these five children with professional housestaff who would take on parental functions. Help was requested for the staff who had to deal with the children's needs, the case management team who had to make long-term plans for the children and parents, and the family group who had to cope with separation and crises.

The Family Before Discovery of Incest

The exploration of this case in its early stages illustrates some of the issues in a dysfunctional family with incestuous behavior and demonstrates how "solutions" can become problems of far greater magnitude than the original problems themselves.

The B family had been known to social services for 11 years—since 1969 when the family was threatened with eviction for non-payment of rent. A comment was made at that time that the house was like an adventure playground by day and a brothel by night. The family was taken into a family rehabilitation unit four years later for a two-year period. The mother was described as a small, untidy lady with straggly hair, tight mini-skirts, and a mouth full of dirty jokes. She left for a time with the two girls, and there was concern about her promiscuity, her "nights off" with soldiers, two or three at a time from a local barracks, with children being around at the time. She left because she disliked her husband's unhygienic habits, such as "masturbating in the kitchen". The father was described as a small, apathetic man, compliant and semi-literate.

Mother returned the girls to the rehabilitation unit when she "couldn't cope", and after being hit by her new cohabitee, she returned herself. She petitioned for divorce, but after they left the unit the whole family was rehoused. Father had the custody of the children, and social workers were to supervise mother to act as the "housekeeper". Mother had no sexual relationship with father at that time but had other men friends and ran what appeared to be a brothel. The children and father "staggered on" with the children being described as "gypsies" and "waifs". The father complained that threats were being made that he would be shot, and the family was moved to a different part of the town. Social services saw the father as close and caring despite his poor budgeting.

The Process of Discovery of Incest

After another two years, there was concern when the father was noted to have a black eye caused by Janet, the younger sister. Three months later the father complained to the social worker that Joanne would not go to school and alleged that he was being accused by Joanne of "touching her up" and "touching her knees" which he had not done. Joanne told the social worker that she had not accused her father but that she did not want to live with him. The father also said he was being accused by a neighbor of assaulting her, and she had "suicided" as she was unbalanced and guilty.

When the social worker saw Joanne the next day, she cried and said there was no time when her father had *not* been touching her. She remembered it first when she was age six, and from the age of 11, when her mother had left, there had been regular sexual intercourse. When the father was confronted, he said, "I've been trying to tell you; I'm relieved it's come out in the open".

The girls were removed to a children's home; the father was criminally charged; and although the mother wanted to take over the children's custody, it was discovered that her new husband had a history of violent crimes, a child in care due to brain damage, and no professional visited without a chaperone for fear of his violence. The mother quietly dropped her attempt to take over the children.

The Family's Dysfunction

It is clear that a familiar scenario has occurred in this family's depth structure. Both parents have emerged from their families of origin repeating the poor parenting skills, shallow emotional relating, and chaotic operations they had experienced as children. Their attempts to reverse and overcome such deficits led to mother being "required" to become involved in a surface action of promiscuous sexuality, excitement, and violence, while father is "required" to involve one of the children in an inappropriate sexual relationship.

There is a family myth or inter-subjective meaning that Joanne was not the father's child so that a sexual relationship with her completes the cycle. This maintains an interlocking belief that father cannot get a woman, so that the only way he can participate in the mother's exciting sexual activities is through the bastard product which maintains the mother's activities and so forth in a never-ending circle. It is interesting to speculate why it broke down at the time it did, since social workers and homemakers had been in constant contact with the family, unwittingly helping to maintain the family system. Perhaps Joanne's adolescent development or Janet's rejecting her father's sexual advances had played a part.

The ramifications of the family surface action emerged from the professionals' family observations, and the requirements and pressures locking family members into roles became clearer once the secret had been revealed. Family boundaries both with the outside world and between family members were diffuse and easily crossed. The family home was filled with stray kittens and dogs, wet beds and chaos; yet, there was no food or saucepans in which to cook. Father, although "warm" outside the home, was unavailable inside.

The notion that the children could be separated and live with relatives was quite inconceivable after their father's removal from the home. They clung to their social worker in a mass with moods of fear and rage sweeping around the family without variation. The social worker, feeling very responsible for what was going on under her eyes, felt compelled to enter the system to attempt to provide for the absence of nurturing, and four capable professionals with the full backing of the social services department took on the task that had been carried out so ineffectively by one "inadequate", semi-literate man.

Family and Labeled Roles

Inevitably a variety of roles had been shared among the rest of the family to compensate for the father's difficulties. Such labeled roles maintained the "labeled" and "labeler" in the same position, contributing to the stereotyped rigid circularity of the system and its homeostatic function.

Gerald (15) took his role very seriously. He sorted out squabbles and disagreements, inevitably using physical force and violent language in a parody of the absent parental authority and control. He was obsessed with soldiers and had some transvestite tendencies, possibly his attempt to give some meaning to his parents' sexual actions. Joanne (14), quiet and plump, was the second "parental child" and was the little mother to the family. Many factors came together to make her father's consort. Janet (13) had some aspects of her mother's role in the latter's absence. Slim, blonde, quick-witted, verbal, and volatile, she even looked like her mother. She was a warm, cuddly girl, provocative and demanding, particularly of women. She had relationships with "outside" friends, and it was not surprising that when father tried to extend the boundary of sexuality to her she rejected him. Matthew (12) took the role of the person who had to bear the conflict of whether control was possible or not, and he was terrified of losing control of his temper. He had an alliance with Gerald and hero-worshipped him. He was also the one who had to mourn his mother's loss, demanding physical contact, particularly from women. Richard (10) represented the family's deprivation, the baby who demanded constant contact, particularly from Janet.

The pattern of alliances and labeled roles and boundaries can be seen to interlock and mesh. They provided the release from tension and individual psychic pain which once meant that continuation was inevitable.

System Changes After Intervention

It is also interesting to see the system changes that followed intervention, that is, the "new" family system. Joanne was treated as the "source of all bad things" when her father was imprisoned; she was alternately blamed and then forgiven by the family. Although much changed superficially with the father's absence, the surface action reasserted itself in unexpected ways. Instead of stray cats and dogs, stray children were "sucked" into the home, perhaps being attracted by the presence of competent care staff. The news of the court case attracted excitement in the form of boys interested in the girls, and there was a suspicion that they were being drawn into adolescent sexuality prematurely with a good deal of squabbling over boyfriends. Gerald seemed to be taking his father's role by becoming more withdrawn and silent and involved in his soldiers, while Matthew had the violent outbursts which demanded control from the staff. He also became very interested in young girls who visited the house. Richard was constantly seeking physical contact with an increasingly physically aggressive edge.

The staff at times feels utterly overwhelmed by the sheer physical work, the lack of professional space in the children's home, and the impulsive, demanding, squabbling needs of the children. They have to live with fears of becoming sexually involved by the children. If they are to avoid being pulled into a repetition and reproduction of the family's surface action, they certainly require help to maintain their own boundaries. They have to provide a model of parenting that can control without undue punishment and sexual misuse and an open system of communication and respect for individual needs that can counter the pervasive pull of the incestuous family system.

Conclusion

In this chapter an attempt has been made to apply the concepts emerging from a systems/dynamic view of family functioning to the dysfunctional incestuous family. Incestuous behavior is only one aspect of what can be a widespread disturbance of boundary functions, alliances, communication, labeled roles, and parenting within the family. The family and societal response to the emergence of incestuous behavior can both add to the family's dysfunction, and professional/family systems can help foster change or unwittingly maintain problems. It is only by maintaining a contextual view of the whole interacting system of individual, family, and professional groups that the correct intervention emerges—or at worst, the least harmful.

References

1. Anderson, L. M. and Shafer, G. (1979) The character-disordered family: a community treatment model for family sexual abuse. *Amer. J. Orthopsychiatry* **49:** 239.
2. Bandler, R. and Grinder, J. (1976) *The Structure of Magic II: A Book About Communication and Change.* Science and Behavior Books, Palo Alto, Calif.
3. Byng-Hall, J. (1973) Family myths used as defence in conjoint family therapy. *Br. J. Med. Psychol.* **46:** 239.
4. Byng-Hall, J. (1979) Re-editing family mythology during family therapy. *J. Fam. Therapy* **1:** 2.
5. Eist, H. I. and Mandel, A. U. (1968) Family treatment of ongoing incest behavior. *Fam. Process* **7:** 216.
6. Ferreira, A. J. (1963) Family myth and homeostasis. *Arch. Gen. Psychiatry* **9:** 457.
7. Ferreira, A. J. (1963) Family myths: the covert rules of the relationship. *Confin. Psychiatry* **8:** 15.
8. Gutheil, T. G. and Avery, N. C. (1977) Multiple overt incest as family defence against loss. *Fam. Process* **16:** 105.
9. Hoffman, L. (1976) Breaking the homeostatic cycle. In *Family Therapy* (Edited by Guerin, P. J.) Gardner, New York.
10. Kinston, W. and Bentovim, A. (1980) Creating a focus for brief marital or family therapy. In *Forms of Brief Therapy* (Edited by Budman) Guilford, New York.
11. Kinston, W. and Bentovim, A. (1980) Conceptualising pathological family interaction in the light of family history. (In preparation.)
12. Lustig, N., Dresser, J. W., Spellman, S. W. and Murray, T. B. (1966) Incest: a family group survival pattern. *Arch. Gen. Psychiatry* **14:** 31.
13. Machotka, P., Pittman, F. S. and Flomenhaft, K. (1967) Incest as a family affair. *Fam. Process* **6:** 98.
14. Magel, V. and Winnik, H. Z. (1968) Role of incest in family structure. *Isr. Ann. Psychiatry* **6:** 173.
15. Meiselman, K. C. (1979) *Incest: A Psychological Study of Causes and Effects with Treatment Recommendations,* Jossey-Bass, San Francisco.
16. Minuchin, S., Montalvo, B., Guerney, B. G., Rosman, B. L. and Schumer, F. (1967) *Families of the Slums.* Basic Books, New York.
17. Minuchin, S. (1974) *Families and Family Therapy,* Tavistock, London.
18. Minuchin, S., Rosman, B. L. and Baker, L. (1978) *Psychomatic Families: Anorexia Nervosa in Context.* Harvard Univ., Cambridge, Mass.
19. Palazzoli, M. S., Cecchin, G., Prata, G. and Boscolo, L. (1978) *Paradox and Counter-Paradox.* Aaronson, New York.
20. von Bertalannfy, L. (1968) *General System Theory.* Braziller, New York.
21. Watzlawick, P., Weakland, J. H. and Fisch, R. (1974) *Change: Principles of Formation and Problem Resolution.* Norton, New York.

Chapter Fourteen

A Comprehensive Child Sexual Abuse Treatment Program

HENRY GIARRETTO

A father–daughter incestuous relationship is usually extremely damaging to the victim, the offender, and the entire family both during the sexual phase and after it ends. The daughter suffers emotional trauma which often leads to self-abusive behavior that may last a lifetime; the father's life goes into sharp decline; and the marriage, weak to begin with, becomes intolerable and often ends in dissolution. If the situation is reported to the authorities of a typical American community, their reactions aggravate the family's troubled state even more. The victim's accusations are often ignored by law enforcement officials if the evidence is weak and the parents deny the charges, thus leaving the child feeling betrayed both by her parents and by the community. On the other hand, the officials become harshly punitive if they have a court provable case. They separate the child from her mother and family and incarcerate the father, often for several years. This way of coping with father–daughter incest prevails in most communities in the United States and was the way officials reacted in Santa Clara County, California before the Child Sexual Abuse Treatment Program (CSATP) of that county was started and proven effective.

This chapter, a case study of a comprehensive community program, will discuss the component parts of the CSATP and the processes of case management and treatment with a special focus on self-help groups.

The CSATP

In 1971, I began to counsel sexually abused children and their families for the Juvenile Probation Department of the county. During the first year, 26 cases were referred. I soon discovered that the traditional weekly session was inadequate and that each family needed much more attention than I could provide alone. It was this realization that led to the development of the community-based effort which was eventually named the CSATP. In 1978, the program provided services to more than 600 families, receiving by far the largest number of referrals recorded by any comparative population area in the country. This sharp increase in the referral rate must be attributed to the growing reputation of the CSATP as a resource for help rather than punishment for sexually abusive families. In all, the CSATP has served more than 2,000 families. Of those families who received full treatment and formally terminated, about 90% of the children have been reunited with their families, and the recidivism rate in these is less than 1%. I estimate that more than a quarter million children are being molested in their own homes each year; most of the molestations would stop if a CSATP were established in every community in the country.

The CSATP is composed of three interdependent components: a professional staff, a cadre of volunteers, and self-help groups. To provide a full complement of services, responsive to the special needs of sexually abused children and their families, all three are necessary. Together they generate the humanistic, community-rooted climate in which sexually abused children, perpetrators, and other family members are supported during the crisis period and go on to learn the attitudes and skills needed to lead self-fulfilling lives and to develop social responsibility. The CSATP copes with all forms of child sexual abuse, both familial and extrafamilial, including not only children recently molested but also adults molested as children. However, the majority of the clients referred to the program are for father–daughter incest under current investigation.

The Professional Component

The professional component of the CSATP subsumes all the officially responsible members of the community: police, social workers, mental health workers, probation officers, defense and prosecuting attorneys, judges, and rehabilitation officers. To enable the community to treat abusive families successfully (humanely and economically), this group must agree in substance on a consistent treatment approach and work cooperatively to implement this approach. Interagency cooperation does not come about by chance. Someone has to take the lead in convincing the other interveners by sound rationale and demonstration that a CSATP approach is more effective than a punitive one in coping with parental child molestation. That person is usually a member of the county agency officially responsible for the child-victim, such as Child Protective Services (CPS). Santa Clara County is an exception to this rule in that the Juvenile Probation Department is the jurisdictional agency. In a few instances CSATPs have been started by mental health people. Regardless of how they begin, all CSATPs must eventually win recognition and support from the local CPS agency and the criminal justice system.

Typically, the CPS worker, acting as coordinator, begins a CSATP by forming a core group composed of other CPS workers and counselors from the mental health agency and/or private agencies. Eventually they meet with representatives of juvenile and adult probation, policemen assigned to sexual assault cases, and deputies of the district attorney's office. As the program gains strength and credibility, interagency cooperation is gradually achieved. Concurrently, the self-help component is formed, and as the caseload increases, the core group begins to organize a cadre of volunteers.

It must be stressed that a typical CSATP does not supplant or interfere with the functions of existing official agencies. Rather, the paid staff of a CSATP is drawn from these agencies and taught to perform their tasks in a more productive manner. Thus, a CSATP can be organized and operated with little additional cost to the community. As the caseload increases, new hires may be necessary, but these added costs are easily offset by considerable savings in welfare payments, upkeep of offenders in jails, payments to temporary shelters, foster homes, and group homes.

The Volunteer Component

The volunteer staff of the Santa Clara County CSATP consists of about 40 people. One-fourth of this number are administrative interns, usually undergraduate students who perform office duties, provide transportation to the children, and in general relate to them as big brothers and sisters. The balance of the staff is made up of graduate students working towards licenses in marriage, family, and child counseling. They are supervised by the licensed counselors and frequently see the clients in their own homes. A few of the volunteers are seasoned members of Parents United whose dedication exceeds that of the average member. They provide countless hours of intense companionship to the new clients and perform a variety of administrative tasks. The volunteers, ranging in age from the early twenties to late fifties, do much to give the CSATP its community-based character.

The Self-Help Component

Parents United and its adjunct, Daughters and Sons United (PU/DSU), constitute the self-help component of the CSATP.

A Parents United chapter is usually started the way the one in Santa Clara County was started. In 1972, I asked the mother of one of the first families treated to make a telephone call to another mother who was caught in the early throes of the crisis. The ensuing conversations went on for several hours and had a markedly calming effect on the new client. I continued to couple old and new clients by telephone, and a month later three of the mothers met together for the first time. As expected, they found it very helpful to talk things out personally with others who had been through the same experiences, and they began meeting regularly in their homes with a juvenile probation officer, a public health nurse, myself, and my wife, Anna.

At one point, I suggested that these women get together with the mother of a physically abused child; perhaps they could start a chapter of Parents Anonymous in San Jose. The women found, however, that although they could discuss general family problems with this woman, they did not feel completely at ease discussing intimate details of their particular problem of incest with her.*

Their own weekly sessions continued, however, with rewarding results. After a few more such meetings, to which several other women were invited, the group known as Parents United was formally designated and launched. To celebrate this event, the three charter mother-members wrote the following creed:

> To extend the hand of friendship, understanding, and compassion, *not* to judge or condemn.
> To better our understanding of ourselves and our children through the aid of the other members and professional guidance.
> To reconstruct and channel our anger and frustrations in other directions, *not* on or at our children.
> To realize that we *are* human and do have angers and frustrations; they are normal.
> To recognize that we do need help, we are all in the same boat, we have all been there many times.

---

* In the spring of 1979 leaders of Parents Anonymous and Parents United started a series of meetings for developing a plan of action for collaboration between the two organizations.

To remember that there is no miracle answer or rapid change; it has taken years for us to get this way.
To have patience with ourselves, again and again and again, taking each day as it comes.
To start each day with a feeling of promise, for we take only one day at a time.
To remember that we *are* human, we will backslide at times. To remember that there is always someone willing to listen and help.
To become the *loving*, *constructive* and *giving parents* or *persons* that we wish to be.

The primary purpose of the meetings was group therapy, but from the very beginning the group performed many other important functions. For example, as the members became aware that some of the new mothers did not have jobs, money, or transportation, they investigated resources to fill those needs and invited different agency people to come and talk to their group. As people from various agencies found out about the small group and what they were trying to do, they would ask the mothers to speak to their groups. This public relations function of Parents United is now known as the Speakers Bureau. Besides the obvious benefit of spreading the word about the program, it gives client-members an important opportunity for social action. Many of them have been loners and have limited social skills. They have felt helpless and unable to have any effect on "the establishment". Through Parents United they know that they can have a definite, positive effect on the community and can pave the way for helping other troubled families.

An important development in the history of Parents United came when fathers began to enter the group. The first father to do so was serving a sentence at a rehabilitation center. The father's rehabilitation officer became interested in what the CSATP and particularly Parents United were accomplishing and started meeting with them. He was instrumental in gaining permission for the father to be allowed to meet with the mothers' group. This development, in late 1972, opened the way for fathers from the rehabilitation center to attend the meetings.

The Santa Clara County chapter of Parents United has grown rapidly. The chapter now has over 200 members with an average attendance of 125 members at the weekly meetings. Meetings begin with a group centering exercise, followed by a brief conference to discuss progress in growth and effectiveness. The membership then breaks up into smaller groups jointly led by a staff member and a trained member of Parents United. The smaller groups include five couples' groups limited to five pairs each, a men's group, a women's group, a mixed gender group, an orientation group primarily for new members but including older members as well, a group for women who were molested as children, a social skills group, and a group for training group leaders. The number and focus of the small groups change periodically according to the needs expressed by the membership. The groups are started at the same time and run for eight sessions after which the members are encouraged to join other groups.

The group process provides clients an opportunity to compare their view of reality with that of their peers since all clients in the group have a common, highly stigmatized problem. This peer interaction also has the effect of emphasizing increased self-direction and personal accountability instead of reliance on authority figures who will "cure" them. To prepare members for positive social attitudes and confidence in their ability to effect changes in the attitude of the official community toward families troubled by incest, Parents United welcomes police, probation officers, prosecuting and defense attorneys, judges, and other professional interveners to the meetings.

Parents United provides for many of the urgent emotional and practical needs of its members. The independent evaluation team who studied the CSATP[3] estimated that incoming families receive an average of 20 hours per week of support over the crisis period by Parents United members. In some areas, such as babysitting and transportation for the nondriving parent, members of the program are able to assist one another directly. Parents United keeps a list of jobs available for women who have been out of the work force for many years; it also helps them brush up on job skills or obtain training for new vocations. The group also maintains a list of companies who are willing to hire a parent with a felony record and uses its influence to help get work furloughs approved. Parents United has drafted a form letter to send to lawyers who exploit the vulnerable emotional state of the offender by inflating their fees. The letter protests the exhorbitant fee, suggests a fair fee, and insists that the fee be adjusted either voluntarily by the attorney or by determination by the Santa Clara County Bar Association. Parents United now has a list of lawyers with proven competence who charge reasonable fees. The organization has outgrown its present quarters and will soon move into a facility especially renovated for its requirements. To reduce the rent on these new quarters, the members have contributed over 5,000 hours of labor to the renovation project. One of the members has opened his home to fathers who may not live in their own homes. About six members live on the average in his home, and the men are on call on what, in effect, is a 24-hour hotline. These are a few examples of the many ways Parents United helps its members help themselves through this difficult passage in their lives.

The following statement describes the impact of Parents United on a new member.

HELLO ME!

Hello Me seems like a strange thing to be saying, especially when you're saying it for the first time to the person that's lived inside you for almost 38 years.

As far back as I can remember, I've felt dislike, disgust, and displeasure. Hell! I downright hated myself most of the time.

Oh, I managed to project a desirable image of myself which I considered socially acceptable—self-confident, dependable, understanding, honest, brave—a lily-white pillar of respectability. That was me.

Suddenly! Out of nowhere, I had been discovered, my protective covering had been penetrated. The world would know who and what I really was. I would be destroyed. There I stood naked and ugly, the likeness of a Dorian Grey. I wanted to hide, to run, to somehow disintegrate.

The phone rang. "Hello, I'm with Parents United. I'm a member of a group of people who've been through the same thing you're going through". "My God", I thought, "not only am I not the only one this has ever happened to—Hell! They've got their own club". The voice on the phone continued, "We understand your pain. We share your pain with you. We want to help you". I didn't believe any of this was possible. How could anyone understand my pain? How could anyone want to help *me*?

What I could have easily believed was that this Parents United was a colony on an island off the coast somewhat like a leper colony where they sent people like me so we wouldn't be able to contaminate the rest of the people in the world.

Well, I came to Parents United's Wednesday night meeting. I don't have to tell any of you what I expected to find. However, what I found was a room full of normal, everyday looking people—hugging and kissing, smiling and greeting each other as if they were all family and hadn't seen each other for years.

What I discovered that first night was that they were a family, a very special family held together by a common bond of unconditional love and understanding, of honest truth and caring. I began to feel warm inside. I felt alive again. I began to feel that "I, too", might be a worthwhile person.

The success of the self-help component of the CSATP is a tribute to the power of, and the need for, caring; it is due most of all to the dedication of its members to fellow human beings in crisis. That so many members remain to help others even after their own treatment has been successfully completed underscores the vigor of the self-help concept as defined by Parents United. Again, it must be stressed that PU/DSU is not as autonomous as other self-help groups such as Alcoholics Anonymous and Parents Anonymous. PU/DSU is an organic part of the CSATP and grows as the CSATP grows.

In June 1975, Parents United became incorporated and gained status as a nonprofit organization. Formal bylaws were written and a Board of Directors was formed. The directors include several Parents United members, some representatives of other chapters, a member of Daughters and Sons United, two lawyers, three psychiatrists, two members of the San Jose Police Department, and two community leaders. The Santa Clara chapter of Parents United continues to grow, with two or three new families joining each week. In addition, the chapter has had a major role in the formation of 23 new chapters in California and several throughout the nation.

Daughters and Sons United

This organization, an adjunct of Parents United, is composed of children 5 to 18 years of age, the majority of whom are girls. The two organizations work together and share many similarities. I formed the first DSU groups in 1972, a play therapy group for children up to the latency period and the other one for adolescent girls. Both were co-led by juvenile probation officers. The children's groups require much more professional attention and guidance than the adult groups, which, of course, are more self-sufficient. Because of the pressure of an increasing caseload on a small staff, the children's groups did not grow as rapidly as the adult group. However, in late 1977, two young interns were assigned the task of improving and expanding DSU. Since then, the membership of DSU has grown to about 120 members, and its organizational structure has been considerably strengthened.

DSU's decision-making body is the Task Force Committee which is composed of six members who meet weekly with a Parents United representative and the Daughters and Sons United coordinators. The committee establishes goals and projects geared to enhance the development and unity of the DSU program. DSU coordinators and the interns under their supervision implement the Task Force Committee's decisions. The self-expressed goals of the committee are:

1. Alleviate trauma experienced by the victim through intensive emotional support during the initial crisis.
2. Facilitate victim and/or sibling awareness of his/her individual feelings.
3. Promote personal growth and communication skills.
4. Alleviate any guilt the child may be feeling as a result of the sexual abuse.
5. Prevent subsequent destructive behavior such as running away, heavy drug abuse, suicide, child prostitution, and promiscuity.
6. Prevent repeats of the offenses by increasing victims' independence, assertiveness, and self-esteem.
7. Prevent subsequent dysfunctional emotional/sexual relationships.
8. Break the multi-generational abusive and dysfunctional pattern which is evident in many of these families.

The Task Force Committee assesses all new group formats and sees to it that the group facilitators who work with the professional group leaders are carefully selected and trained. DSU helps to organize and conduct an adolescent girls' orientation group, four adolescent girls' groups, an adolescent boys' group, a pre-adolescent girls' group, a pre-adolescent boys' group, a play therapy group, and a transitional group for young women.

DSU provides or becomes involved in the following services:

1. Children's Shelter Liaison, which makes initial contact within one or two days after admission for crisis intervention, introduces the children to DSU groups, and continues to provide support and counseling throughout protective custody.
2. Juvenile Hall Liaison, which performs the same functions for children in juvenile hall.
3. Home Liaisons, in which DSU coordinators make initial contact during the crisis period with those children who remain in the home.
4. Sponsorship Program, in which seasoned members facilitate new members' entry into the group.
5. Time-Out Corner, which is an area designed specifically for DSU members where resources and reading materials are available to improve the children's understanding of drug abuse, birth control, and other adolescent problems.
6. Big Sister/Big Brother Programs which provide one-to-one friend relationships for those children demonstrating the need for sustained support.
7. Supportive people who accompany the children through the various steps in the criminal justice system process.
8. Transportation for about 30 children to weekly groups and counseling sessions.

The DSU task force also organizes fund-raising activities and administers the money collected. The members are active in the public education effort of the self-help component by participating in talks to schools and private organizations, appearing on radio and television, and publishing and distributing various information packages. To build *esprit de corps*, birthdays are celebrated and visits are arranged to entertainment and cultural centers.

The members are becoming increasingly assertive in defense of children's rights in general; they often come to the adult groups to argue for their specific rights within the CSATP. It is gratifying to see that DSU does not regard itself as the lesser half of the self-help component but as a full partner in the aims and purposes of the CSATP.

Donna

The CSATP has treated many women, molested as children by their fathers, who were not helped during childhood. Their stories of lives devastated by parental rejection, promiscuity, drug addiction, inability to keep jobs, and broken marriages are repeated in the several hundred letters we have received from women with similar childhood histories. In each of these letters is the message explicitly stated or implied: "Where were you when I needed you?" The women molested as children who come to the CSATP receive individual counseling and couple counseling if they are married or living with someone. If their parents are available, they come for joint sessions with their fathers and mothers. These sessions occur infrequently and only later in the therapeutic process. The most progress usually develops in the group sessions of Parents United, first in the group made up exclusively of women molested as children and later in the orientation group where they gradually learn to understand the confusion and guilt suffered by mothers and father-offenders of sexually abusive families. In role-playing exercises with these parent-members, the women prepare themselves for future confrontations with their real parents. It seems that alienation from one's parents is intolerable at any age and is particularly painful when the mother–daughter bond is broken. In these women who eventually are able to re-establish emotional ties with their parents a remarkable transformation takes place. Their life postures, formerly withdrawn and fear-ridden, are now patently confident, even exhuberant, and are clearly manifested in the improvement in their marriages and careers. When this breakthrough occurs, they usually want to help others, and several of these clients work with young victims individually or serve as facilitators in the group sessions of Daughters and Sons United and Parents United, recognizing that helping others is an important phase in their own therapeutic process. Another critical step in this process is the realization that their present ability to identify sensitively with the feelings of others and to articulate them precisely is in a large part a compensatory reaction to the severe trauma they had experienced during childhood.

One such client, Donna, has been in the program for about two years. Donna was molested as a child, and the situation had not been exposed and dealt with. Her adolescent and early adulthood periods were marked by typical self-destructive behavior including promiscuity, drug abuse, and sabotage of intimate relationships, schooling, and career. She was in her early thirties and still in the self-abusive phase when she joined the CSATP and PU. Since then, Donna has received in-depth individual counseling and participated in the group for women molested as children and in the group which is made up of current offenders and their spouses. She now serves as a volunteer counselor, and a few months ago she took another big step when she enrolled in a graduate program leading to a master's degree in marriage, family, and child counseling. The following are excerpts from a paper Donna wrote for a classroom assignment:

> This paper and my 35th birthday coincided. The combination promoted a long reflection. Who am I, who was I, what do I need, what do I have to give, what do I

> require of myself, of others, of life? I'm in charge of my life for the first time this past year. I'm a real neophyte in the world of the really living. I still have to assure myself I'm no longer the young woman who lay in bed for days at a time, refused to drive a car, couldn't operate a washing machine, was terrified to live so decided not to. I have freed myself from practically a lifetime career of sitting on the secret that I was an abused child. Keeping a secret and living a lie is a true energy drainer. The stamina I expended projecting the image I wanted passersby to see was tremendous. I now spend that stamina building, brick by brick, a constructive, honest, serene life... I'll keep taking in as much of the world and as much experience as my energy limits allow, because I'm determined to make up for all those wasted years when I was Sylvia Plath's understudy.

Donna began to turn away from her self-sabotaging behavior when she finally was able to fly home and to confront her mother successfully. Past attempts had failed because she had met with both parents and was angrily accusative and vindictive towards both. She would become incoherent when her father denied the charges and she saw her mother side with him, countering that Donna's disastrous marriage and career were the true cause of her craziness. This time Donna took my advice and talked to her mother alone. She was able to communicate her story clearly, incontrovertibly, and with sadness rather than anger at her mother's inability to see what was going on right under her nose and at her father's obsessive but unconscious need to exploit her sexually. That encounter went on for hours, ending with the embrace and plea for forgiveness that Donna had long sought from her mother. Later they met with the father, who, seeing that his wife believed Donna's story, acknowledged that something must have happened between himself and Donna because he could not remember a thing about that period in his life, probably because he had been drinking heavily at that time.

Donna's relationship with her father remains partly unresolved, but in being able to re-establish her bond with her mother, she returned to the program truly a new woman. She continued to communicate with her parents by telephone and letters. Recently her parents came to visit her in California and, as a result of counseling sessions in which they all participated, the father finally was enabled to face his fear and guilt. He recovered his memory and made a full admission of his offenses to his wife and daughter. This encouraging outcome, however, probably would not have taken place if Donna had not prepared herself with the cooperation of Parents United members. In the group sessions, she was able to ventilate her terrible anger towards her parents. Once this was discharged she gradually began to realize that the parents of sexually abusive families are themselves victims of a dysfunctional family system. (See Chapter Thirteen.)

It is heartening to know that lives blighted by untreated incest can be salvaged with the help of the CSATP. However, far more rewarding is the knowledge that the victims and their families can be spared long years of alienation and pain if they are treated while the victims are still children. During the early stages of treatment some of the adolescent girls, in particular those who feel they have been abandoned by their mothers, begin to manifest the anticipated self-abusive behavior: truancy, promiscuity, and drug abuse. Girls rejected by mothers who deny the charges or blame their daughters for the incestuous situations are the most difficult to treat. But here, too, the maladaptive behavior usually stops, largely through the influence of the adolescent group sessions which are often attended by women molested as children, the extra individual attention given by the staff and volunteers, and, in essence, the surrogate family formed around the girls by foster parents, the CSATP staff, and members of PU/DSU. A surrogate family, of course, is a poor substitute for the child's natural family, and if there is any hope at all of reuniting the child with her mother and family, the CSATP perseveres towards that end.

The Treatment Process

The Humanistic Attitude

The success of a CSATP depends on how well the leaders have internalized what may be called a humanistic attitude in coping with sexually abusive individuals and families and how well they are able to transfer this viewpoint to co-workers, the various interveners, and the clients. Because this attitude has been discussed in previous articles,[1,2] it will only be summarized here.

Persons who form abusive relationships with their mates, children, and other important people in their lives do so because they are incapable of developing trusting and mutually beneficial relationships. Abusive parents typically were raised by punitive and generally uncaring parents. As children and later as adults they seem to court rejecting and even hostile responses from siblings, relatives, acquaintances, teachers, and others. They persevere in this lifestyle when they form their own families. Abusive parents are incapable of leading self-fulfilling lives. Consequently, they stew in a state of chronic resentment which can be discharged only through hostile acts *unconsciously* intended to be self-punishing.

It must be emphasized that this essentially self-abusive behavior is an *unconscious* reaction to inner malaise. The sexually abusive father does not use his child primarily for sexual gratification but principally as a means of reconfirming and discharging his low self-worth. He approaches his child sexually without full awareness of the needs, drives, and motives fueling his behavior nor of its consequences to his child, family, and himself. The negative emotional energy that impels parental child abuse is similar to that which leads to substance abuse. Conversely, the greatest personal rewards come from satisfaction (not negation) of traditional human values; we would all prefer to be loved and respected by our children, mates, and peers. When we cannot attain these commonly desired goals, we simply are incapable of doing what we must do to attain them; they are beyond our life coping abilities.

When abusive parental behavior becomes severe enough to warrant intervention by the authorities and they react by harshly punishing the offender, his self-hate/destructive energy syndrome is reinforced once more.

Despite their schooling, members of the helping professions are not entirely free of punitive emotional reactions to abusive parents. The image of a 5-year-old girl performing fellatio on her father in submission to his parental authority does not engender compassion for the parents. Instead, the images evoke spontaneous feelings of revulsion and hatred that shatter any reason and capacity to function as a therapist. CSATP counselors still experience these feelings when they read the details of the offenses in police reports despite the large number of cases that have come to their attention over the past eight years. Although these feelings are normal reactions, if they persist, the counselor cannot hope to help the clients. He cannot claim to be working for the best interests of the child-victim if he destroys her father. Normally a positive direction is given towards family reconstitution when the counselor actually faces the father and senses his desperate helplessness and confusion. The hateful reactions of the counselors toward abusive parents must be replaced with productive interventions based on understanding of the complex psychological dynamics that led to the abusive acts.

Another key realization that came during the early stages of the CSATP was that although traditional counseling is important, one person cannot attend to the multitudinous needs of the family. Many persons took part in the negative socialization of the family, and many must contribute to the positive resocialization process. People immobilized in low self-worth can be taught the attitudes and skills for high self-esteem and thereby the ability to lead self-fulfilling lives. This aim is best accomplished if such people are given the opportunity of helping one another towards that end by professionals who themselves take part in the process.

Case Management

The case management of a family referred to the CSATP for father–daughter incest illustrates how the professional, volunteer, and self-help components work together. The procedure is more or less replicated in the other CSATPs in California with the exception that child protective services workers perform the duties of the juvenile probation officers in Santa Clara County.

The initial referral of the sexually molested child in Santa Clara County often comes to the patrolman on duty within the jurisdiction where the child lives. The child may go to her mother, relative, or friend who usually reports the situation to the police. If she relates her plight to a school nurse or another professional, all are required by law to call the police department. A patrolman is on round-the-clock duty to receive and immediately respond to these referrals. The officer takes the initial statement from the girl and any witnesses concerning what has happened and, if he believes that the child is in jeopardy, places her in protective custody in the Children's Shelter. That occurs much less frequently than it did before the CSATP got started. A police officer from the Sexual Assault Investigation Unit (SAIU) of the San Jose Police Department, who has had special training in sexual abuse cases, investigates the case to decide whether or not there is sufficient evidence to warrant an arrest and referral to the District Attorney for prosecution.

An intake juvenile probation officer may also receive the referral directly via a telephone call from the school, a neighbor, or another agency person and takes appropriate action for the child. The juvenile probation officer is a member of a special unit specifically set up to investigate cases of child neglect and abuse. The probation officer may bring the child to the attention of the Juvenile Court by filing a petition under Section 600 of the Juvenile Court Law which applies when the minor resides in a home "which is unfit by reason of depravity".

Generally, the police and probation officers work together during the investigative stages, coordinating their efforts to minimize the trauma to the child and family during this process and to maximize services to the family. The Juvenile Probation

Department completes an exhaustive inquiry into the family situation to determine if the case requires the attention of the juvenile court.

The family is referred to the program coordinator of the CSATP who assigns the family to a counselor. The counselor and the responsible juvenile probation officer confer and agree on a plan of emergency and long-range supportive action for the family. Thereafter, they meet when necessary. It is important for the CSATP to maintain continual contact with the policemen and the juvenile probation officers servicing the cases.

About 40% of referrals to the CSATP come from the clients directly. Prospective clients, who are often very upset, call in for information about the program. The program coordinator usually takes these calls although other staff members and Parents United members may get them. The callers are listened to carefully and given information about the program and the services available to them. However, no identifying information is taken until they agree that the situation must be reported. Those who do not want to report are listened to, talked to about their alternatives, and asked to call back if they want further help. If they decide to come forward, they are given the names of agency persons, such as the juvenile probation officers and police officers to contact for reporting purposes. They are given a counseling appointment as soon as possible. If a client is very disturbed and needs immediate services, a counselor or intern and a Parents United member are assigned to the family and particularly to the victim during or immediately after the reporting interview.

When girls are placed in the Children's Shelter, they also often need immediate services, and an intern or staff member tries to go out right away to see them. In cases where the situation is not critical, the girl will see a counselor in a few days and is invited to come to the girls' group. An intern trained as a liaison worker between the CSATP and the Children's Shelter goes twice weekly to see the girls.

As much as it is possible, crisis needs are met immediately. These initial crisis interventions markedly influence the way clients orient themselves to the program. (For more on crisis intervention, see Chapter Nine.)

Order of Treatment

The counselor's first step is to design a treatment program for the family. Conjoint family therapy was found to be inappropriate for families in the early throes of the crisis, but the fundamental aim of family therapy which is to facilitate a harmonious familial system has not been discarded. Incestuous families are badly fragmented as a result of the original dysfunctional family dynamics, which are further exacerbated upon disclosure to civil authorities. The child, mother, and father must be treated separately before family therapy becomes productive. Consequently, the treatment procedure is usually applied in this order:

1. Individual counseling, particularly for the child, mother, and father.
2. Mother–daughter counseling.
3. Marital counseling, which becomes a key treatment if the family wishes to be reunited.
4. Father–daughter counseling.
5. Family counseling.
6. Group counseling.

The treatments are not listed in order of importance, nor followed invariably in each case, but all are usually required for family reconstitution. In general, the objective of the treatment plan is to rebuild the family around the essential mother–daughter core. The counselor usually meets first with the mother to help her deal with her distraught state and to assure her that the CSATP will help her through the family's crisis and in time hopes to bring her family together.

The mother and, in most cases, the father are contacted by telephone by a member of Parents United. The purpose here is to put the parents in touch with a "sponsor" who has been through a similar experience. In addition to personal contacts, the sponsor invites the clients to PU and prepares them for the initial group sessions.

In the first meeting with the child, the counselor helps to quiet down her fears, assures her that she has a responsible and sympathetic team working for her, and arranges the important early counseling sessions between the child and her mother. The child is also assigned a sponsor and invited to attend one of the groups conducted for DSU. If necessary, transportation is provided by interns.

Mother–daughter counseling is the key first step towards re-establishing a sound mother–daughter relationship. The child's overwhelming fear is that she has placed her father and family in serious jeopardy. The thrust at this point is to return the child to her home and her mother as soon as possible.

With few exceptions, most child victims wish to return to their mothers who in turn want them back. This may not be apparent at first because the child often feels she has betrayed her mother and family just as she feels anger for having been betrayed. The mother, too, often feels badly let down by her daughter. In some cases the alienation between them is so acute that the child and mother must be counseled several times separately before they can be brought together for treatment. The aim of the early counseling sessions is to convince the child that she indeed was victimized by her father and that it was her mother's duty to protect her. She must hear this not only from the counselor but convincingly from her mother before she will be ready to return home. She must also learn from her mother that her father has assumed full responsibility for the sexual activity. If the mother–daughter relationship cannot be resolved and it is necessary to place the child in a foster home, she is still persuaded to attend group sessions and individual counseling. Persistent effort is maintained to return her to her home.

While working with the mother and the daughter, the counselor also sees the father as soon as he is free on bail or placed on his own recognizance. Generally the father is not allowed to make contact with the daughter at this point, but in most instances it is possible to start marriage counseling. In any case, it is important to provide therapy to the father as quickly as possible during the pretrial period. If the offender is discouraged by his lawyer from attending counseling sessions because this may be construed as an admission of guilt, the lawyer is contacted and usually convinced that it is to his client's advantage to come for counseling. It will help his marital and familial relationships, and this in turn will have a positive effect on the decision of the juvenile probation officer and the courts regarding the return of the child-victim to the home and on the adult probation officer regarding his recommendations to the court. The father continues with his treatment throughout the prosecution period. The counseling continues by special arrangement with the rehabilitation center even if he is given a jail sentence. Counseling and participation in Parents United goes on after the sentence is served; participation in the CSATP is often a condition of his probation or parole.

By now the mother and the daughter usually are reunited in the home. The main thrust of the counseling at this point is to save the marriage and get the father back into the home. It must be repeated that this is not desirable if the child still feels that her parents are blaming her for the family's crisis. When the child and her father are ready to confront each other, counseling sessions are scheduled. The sessions eventually include the mother and, finally, the entire family.

The professional counselors supervise the treatment plan and use PU/DSU members and counselor interns to assist them in providing services to the family. The counselor determines on an individual basis whether or not to release the family to an intern for gradual termination of the counseling. The counselor continues to be responsible for monitoring the progress of the family and to determine when the family can be released from treatment.

The Court Process

During the early parts of this procedure, the father is facing the court process which lasts, on an average, about three months. If the offender is charged with a felony (usually the charge is child molestation or statutory rape; incest is seldom the charge), he is instructed to contact two court-appointed psychotherapists to determine if he is a mentally disturbed sex offender (MDSO). If, on the basis of their reports, the judge finds the offender to be a MDSO, the offender is sent to the psychiatric state facility for such people. Incest offenders in Santa Clara County, however, are now rarely diagnosed as mentally disturbed, owing to the growing acceptance of the CSATP by the psychiatrists and judges as an effective alternative to the psychiatric facility. If the offender is judged not to be a MDSO, then he can be sent to a state prison, but this has never happened to a CSATP client. As a rule the offender is given a suspended sentence or is sentenced to the local rehabilitation center for a few months. His rehabilitation officer is contacted and urged to hasten the client's work furlough and to permit him to come for individual counseling and to the Parents United weekly meetings. The officials at the rehabilitation center have been releasing offenders who have employment immediately upon incarceration and also allowing attendance at counseling sessions and Parents United meetings. In a growing number of cases the judges, in lieu of jail, order the offenders to contribute several hundred hours of work to Parents United.

Criteria for Termination of Treatment

If the client or family remains in counseling with the CSATP, then the decision to terminate the case takes these criteria into consideration:

1. Is a court order for counseling still in existence?
2. Do the family members, in particular the parents, feel they have made sufficient progress in their communication, parenting, and self-management skills to need no further regular counseling?

3. Does the counselor who has been seeing the family feel they have made sufficient progress to terminate counseling?
4. If a supervising probation officer or social worker is involved, does he or she feel the family has progressed sufficiently to recommend termination of the counseling to the court?

The following questions are usually considered to determine sufficient progress:

1. Is a molestation likely to recur? In other words, has the marital and home situation improved enough to prevent recurrence of molestation and ensure a safe home environment for the child-victim?
2. Has the offender taken responsibility for his behavior and become aware of the formerly unconscious impulses which preceded the molestation of his child? Is the offender able to control them if they recur?
3. Have the feelings and conflicts between family members (mother, daughter, father, siblings) been dealt with openly and completely so that the family environment is nurturing for the child and other family members?

In cases where only the adult is being counseled, as in the case of an adult woman who was molested as a child or in cases where only the child-victim is being seen, perhaps in conjunction with his or her foster family, these same questions will be considered but in relation to the client's particular circumstances.

If there is an existing court order, that order must be modified before termination. The court usually respects the recommendation of the CSATP counselor in this regard. If no order exists, the decision is made jointly by the client, counselor, and supervising agency.

The above description of case management describes the treatment cycle for most, if not all, incest cases. Generally, family members receive intensive individual, couple, and family counseling as well as group counseling in PU/DSU. The average family stays in the CSATP for about nine months, but each family is encouraged to stay with the program as long as it is deemed necessary.

Growth and Accomplishments

The success of the Child Sexual Abuse Treatment Program can be assessed by the rate of increase of referrals and by the percentage of families who are helped. As mentioned earlier in this chapter, the referral rate has increased drastically since 1971. Since it is reasonable to suppose that the actual rate of incest itself has not changed appreciably in Santa Clara County during the past few years, the significance of this growing referral rate is all the greater. It means that many families are now receiving help who would not have received such help were it not for the CSATP and its ability to gain the cooperation of the criminal justice system and a positive reception by the press and public. Hundreds of families are being treated each year for a family problem that has always plagued society but has heretofore largely been ignored.

In 1977, the success of the CSATP was measured by the staff, and the findings were considered by some to be questionable because of potential bias. In mid-1977, however, a review committee appointed by the California State Director of Health assigned an independent investigator to collect and analyze data on the performance of the CSATP. An evaluation team, led by Dr. Jerome A. Kroth, surveyed comparable groups of clients at three stages in the treatment program: intake, midterm, and near termination. "*The evaluator's overall conclusion is that the impact of CSATP family therapy in the treatment of intrafamilial child sexual abuse is positive, conclusive and unmistakable!*"*[3] The following are some of the evaluation team's key findings.

The Daughter. Child victims of incest in Santa Clara County who were removed from their families by the authorities are being returned to their families much sooner than they were before the CSATP was formed and sooner than in other communities throughout the nation. Based on a sample of 127 active cases, the median time out of the home for these girls was 90 days, and 92% could be expected to return home eventually. Although not objectively measured, it was clearly apparent to the evaluators that there was a decline, both in intensity and in duration, in the typical self-abusive behavior of child-victims. It appeared that the coordinated approach of the CSATP prevents truancy, decline in school performance, promiscuity, and heavy drug use by helping the girls overcome their strong feelings of betrayal and guilt. The evaluator measured this absence of self-abusive behavior as a "failure to deteriorate". He found, from a sample of 70 incest victims, that during the prior two months only 4% had gotten drunk or high on drugs; only 3% had shown signs of sexual promiscuity; only 1% had stayed out overnight without permission or run away from home, and only 6% had become involved with the authorities. These figures are extremely low compared with any other figures in the literature of child sexual abuse.

> Put, perhaps, in strong terms, if one supposes that children who experience incest have an increasing tendency towards social maladjustment and are, as a consequence of the molest, more prone toward delinquency, sexual actingout, substance abuse, etc., receiving family therapy intervention entirely contradicts such a prognosis.[3]

The psychological health of the girls also improved during the course of treatment. The percentage with symptoms such as bedwetting, nail biting, and fainting declined from 47% at intake to 6% by termination. The girls' relationships with their peers and the other members of their families, particularly their fathers, showed marked improvement. Whether these gains can be sustained remains to be seen.

The Father. The father-offender in the incestuous family has also benefitted greatly from the Child Sexual Abuse Treatment Program. Men who formerly would have received long jail or prison sentences are now being given shorter terms or even suspended sentences as a result of increasing reception of the CSATP by the judiciary as an effective alternative to incarceration. Indeed, many fathers initially come to the CSATP primarily because they assume that participation in the CSATP and in Parents United is likely to soften the court's decision on their sentence. Before long most realize that the CSATP tries to keep them out of jail so that they can be taught to become effective husbands and parents and, in general, to lead more rewarding lives.

---

* Emphasis in original.

For successful treatment to take place, the father must accept full responsibility for the molestation. In the evaluator's sample, 89% are ready to accept most or all of the responsibility for the molestation at termination of the study period. Significant, too, is the finding that feelings of extreme general guilt are reduced at the same time. The number of parents feeling "strong guilt" declined from 65% of the sample at intake to 24% near termination. This ability to distinguish between responsibility and guilt is one of the most important goals of therapy. The former is necessary for self-management; the latter is only destructive.

The CSATP has significantly speeded up the process of rehabilitation for the offender. Before the program started, individual or marriage counseling did not occur, if at all, until after the offender was released from jail. Now counseling is started soon after his arrest and continues during and after incarceration. It is reasonable to assume that this early counseling has been vital in helping to restore the licenses of two pilots and two real estate men, to reinstitute the security clearances of two engineers in the aerospace industry, to have a discharged postal service employee return to his civil service position, to save the jobs of numerous men in private industry, and to save the careers of four military servicemen.

Even more important, in terms of the victims and their fathers, the CSATP has been successful in developing normal relationships between them. This goal, once considered by many to be undesirable and/or impossible, has proven to be vital to the future mental health of the child and the family as a unit. The evaluation found in a sample of 23 that by the end of treatment worsening relationships between father and daughter decreased from 17% to 4%, while improving relationships increased from 22% to 50%. (Not all of the relationships fell into these two categories.)

The Mother. In the typical incestuous family treated by the CSATP, the mother is the first to receive tangible help in the form of immediate counseling and emergency assistance with housing, employment, and financial aid. Before the program existed, mothers usually found themselves alone and devastated. The bureaucracy was badly fragmented, and the mother had no guidance in securing the various kinds of help available. The CSATP has been able to mobilize typically disjointed and often competitive services into a cooperative effort.

While the mother's strong sense of guilt declines during the course of treatment, as does the father's, she, too, learns to accept her share of responsibility for the conditions leading to the molestation. By termination, 50% of the evaluator's sample admit that they were "very much responsible" as opposed to none who admitted this at intake. This change of attitude comes from learning that incest is in large part due to a failing marriage for which both spouses are responsible.

The Marriage and the Family. The positive effect of the CSATP on both parents is revealed in the evaluator's measure of "attitudinal changes". Near termination, 82% of the parents agreed with the statement, "I feel more open, honest, and in control of myself", and all affirmed that "Things are a lot better than they used to be". The percentage of those who disagreed with the statement "Right now I feel devastated emotionally" rose from 0% at intake to 76% near termination. Similarly, the percentage of those who felt "Not close at all to a nervous breakdown" rose from 12% to 88%.

The evaluator determined that 78% of the couples were still married at the end of the study period and 14% were separated. Many of the separated couples will probably be reunited after the early turmoil subsides. Near termination, 59% of the sample reported that their relationships had improved, whereas only 6% reported that their relationships had deteriorated. They reported that their sexual activity increased both in frequency and quality. There is a corresponding marked improvement in the husband's sense of his own sexual health. Those marriage partners who argued "quite a lot" at the beginning of the study argued much less at the end; the decrease in arguments ranged from 38% at intake to 0% near termination. In many instances, the husbands and wives confided that their relationships are better now than they were before the crisis, or, for that matter, better than they had ever been. As one couple put it, "This is the first time in our marriage that we have ever been able to communicate".

As an indication of the CSATP's success in achieving the goal of repairing the relationship between father and daughter, *no recidivism has been reported among the more than 600 families who have received a minimum of ten hours of treatment and whose cases have been formally terminated.* The evaluator determined that the overall recidivism rate for CSATP client families is 0.6% compared to an average of 2% rate reported by other studies. However, the recidivism rates on incest offenders cited by a recent study of recidivists treated at Atascadero State Hospital ranged from 8% to 11%. It must be noted that the typical recidivism rates reported in professional journals are based on populations in which about 50% of the fathers do not return home. Kroth points out, however, that the recidivism rate is not as significant as the number of the referrals to the CSATP:

> However admirable the recidivism rate may be at CSATP or elsewhere, it is difficult to place a great deal of emphasis on such small percentages and draw substantial conclusions from them. With or without therapy it appears that 98% of incest offenders will not repeat the offense *once coming to the attention of the criminal justice system**... In effect the single most important statistic which reflects on the efficacy of treatment is not recidivism or anxiety level, or the grade point averages of victims in treatment, but the rate at which victims, offenders and families come forward! In this regard the CSATP referral record is superb... Since 1974, for example, there has been *an average increase of about 40% in the number of clients coming forward each year, and it is likely 98% of these new clients will not repeat the offense merely on the basis of the fact** that the molest has been reported and the family secret broken.[3]

In the future, it will be possible to measure the success of the CSATP's case management in terms of quantitative data. A computerized system for data collection has been developed and is now being tested which allows the CSATP to gather a wealth of demographic and case history information at intake on each family referred to the program. The present system is designed for intake information only, but the use of data processing has opened up the possibility of future computer programs which will be able to monitor the progress of each case to termination.

The need for computerized data collection in the field of child sexual abuse is great. Until now there has been no effective way to gather information on incest, and the

---

* Emphasis in the original.

statistics offered by the literature have been speculative, inconclusive, conflicting, and biased by meager samples. Weinberg's[4] study, for example, although it was based on a retrospective survey of 203 cases (an exceptional number when compared to the majority of other studies), led to conclusions that already appear deceptive in the light of the extensive first-hand experiences of the CSATP. Undoubtedly, other treatment programs will emulate this system and improve on it, making possible a network of reliable and valid data on child sexual abuse.

Conclusion

This chapter has described the approach developed by the Child Sexual Abuse Treatment Program of Santa Clara County, California, for treating the casualties of father–daughter incest—the victims, the offenders, and their families. My faith in this method leads me to hope that one day CSATPs or agencies like them will be commonplace, so that all families—not only those troubled by incest—will have available to them a humanistic, caring environment in which to rebuild their lives.

References

1. Giarretto, H. (1976) Humanistic treatment of father–daughter incest. In *Child Abuse and Neglect: The Family and the Community*. (Edited by Helfer, R. E. and Kempe, C. H.) Ballinger, Cambridge, Mass.
2. Giarretto, H., Giarretto, A. and Sgroi, S. (1978) Coordinated community treatment of incest. In *Sexual Assault of Children and Adolescents*. (Edited by Burgess, A., Groth, A., Holstrom, L., and Sgroi, S.) Lexington, Lexington, Mass.
3. Kroth, J. (1979) *Child Sexual Abuse: Analysis of a Family Therapy Approach*. C. Thomas, Springfield, Ill.
4. Weinberg, S. (1955) *Incest Behavior*. Citadel, New York.

Note:

In 1980, nine two-week training courses on the principles and methods of the CSATP will be conducted by the Institute for the Community as Extended Family (ICEF) at San Jose, California. This new CSATP training project will continue through 1982 and is funded by the National Center on Child Abuse and Neglect, Department of Health and Human Services. Qualified applicants will be drawn nationwide from child protective services agencies (or equivalent agencies) and/or their appointees who wish to establish CSATPs in their communities. The trainees will participate in the administrative and treatment functions of the Santa Clara CSATP and will be instructed by the developers of the CSATP who also conducted the recently completed California training project that resulted in 25 new CSATPs throughout the state.

For enrollment information contact:

Training Coordinator
National Child Sexual Abuse Treatment Training Project
ICEF
P.O. Box 952
San Jose, California 95108
408/280-5055.

Editorial Note

While the San Jose model has been highly successful both there and in other locations, alternative approaches can also be effective. All kinds of professionals and volunteers can help in the therapeutic process depending on the location, the style of the treatment programs, and the financial support available.

C. HENRY KEMPE
PATRICIA BEEZLEY MRAZEK

Chapter Fifteen

Group Psychotherapy with Sexually Abused Children

PATRICIA BEEZLEY MRAZEK

Despite concerted efforts in recent years to provide treatment for abusive and neglectful families, many children reach primary school age without having received adequate intervention for their emotional problems. There is increasing documentation of how limited the changes in parent–child interactions often are, despite therapy for the parents.[5,6] Therefore, some type of direct help for these children is often necessary. While individual psychotherapy or play therapy is one alternative,[1] group psychotherapy is a better choice for some children. Group sessions can be useful both diagnostically and therapeutically with early latency-age children,[2,4,11] including those who are deprived and ego-impoverished.[3,8,9,10] However, documentation of the usefulness of groups with abused and neglected children is limited, especially with those who have been sexually abused.[7,12]

This chapter is a report of the use of group psychotherapy with young sexually abused girls. The process of the treatment will be described, and the data from pre-post diagnostic evaluations and eight-month and three-year follow-up will be summarized. Detailed case histories will be presented to demonstrate how the group psychotherapy interrelated with the overall treatment for the family and with the legal actions which were taken.

Method

Setting and Population

Evaluation and treatment of the children took place at The National Center for the Prevention and Treatment of Child Abuse and Neglect of the University of Colorado Health Sciences Center, Denver, Colorado. Referrals came from protective service workers in three metropolitan counties.

The group consisted of seven girls (including two sets of siblings) who ranged in age from 4 to 7 years. Six of the children were white, and one was American Indian. All but one were from lower socioeconomic families. All of the girls had experienced sexual contact, ranging from inappropriate fondling and manual stimulation of the genitals to intercourse, with their biologic fathers. Five of the seven children were in foster placement at the time of the referral; the other two lived with their mothers, but their fathers were not in the home.

Diagnostic Measures

An attempt was made to assess the important domains of the child's life: social, academic, cognitive-language, and affective. Evaluations were made by a child psychiatrist, a speech therapist, a trained para-professional, and the co-therapists. The standardized measures which were used are listed in Appendix 1.

The psychiatric assessments included free play, structured family doll scenes, sentence completion regarding the children's group, fables, wishes, and dream material. Historical and current information was obtained from protective service workers, biologic parents, and foster parents. Home visits were made to each residence where the children were currently living; school visits were also made.

The diagnostic measures were completed prior to and near the termination of the group. Videotapes of the psychiatric interviews were made both times for comparison. Teacher, parent, and self-assessment measures were repeated at eight-month follow-up. Information was obtained from protective service workers and foster parents at three-year follow-up.

Treatment Method

Treatment for the girls consisted of weekly group therapy sessions of one and one-half hours duration over the course of six months. Each session was led by the author and a male co-therapist and was videotaped by a trained para-professional who also provided transportation for some children and occasionally substituted for one of the co-therapists.

The therapy was modeled on the modifications of activity group therapy which Frank[3] has described in her work with ego-impoverished children. Each session included a talking and sharing time, a structured activity to initiate further fantasy and discussion, free play, and a snack. Individual goals for each child were based on diagnostic assessments. Over-all group goals included:

1. Providing a safe setting in which the girls could talk and play through their feelings about individual and family problems, including the sexual experiences with their fathers.
2. Providing male and female adult role models which were different than those the girls had experienced in their biologic homes, that is, providing a caring relationship without exploitation.
3. Providing an opportunity for the girls to relate with peers who had similar sexual experiences.
4. Helping the girls improve their social skills.

Even though treatment for the parents was to occur through community resources, generally, the parents did not follow through with specific recommendations. Gradually, the co-therapists began meeting with some of the parents to provide them some feedback regarding their children. Requests for such sessions were often motivated by the parents' wish to have increased visitation with their children. Eventually, this led to a weekly parents' group, lasting for two and one-half hours with dinner provided. Five parents participated; they constituted three families, involving four children from the group. The parents' group was active for three months and terminated simultaneously with the children's group.

Consultation with protective service workers and probation officers occurred throughout the six-month period. The written reports and recommendations to the juvenile and criminal courts were always openly shared with the parents, and discussion of these matters occurred with the girls in the group sessions.

Observations and Interventions During the Therapy

In the initial sessions of the group, all of the girls except one pair of sisters appeared to be rather self-sufficient and sophisticated. They listened calmly and politely as we told them about the purpose of the group and talked with them openly about the sexual contact that each of them had had with their fathers and the subsequent separations, either through foster placement or father leaving the home. Although it was many weeks before the girls could discuss these issues, they knew from the start why they were in the children's group and what they had in common.

Some of the girls' behavior was deceptively mature and was based on very strong dependency needs which were being defensively denied. As the girls came to trust the therapists in the group experience, the pseudo-maturity lessened and very basic helplessness and neediness were expressed. Rather than continuing the sexualized play, in which the girls dressed up in high heels and paraded around in front of the male co-therapist, they pretended they were babies to be loved and taken care of by the therapists. They drank out of baby bottles, sucked their thumbs, and asked to be rocked. They also began to show problems around eating and sharing during the miniature dinner which was served as a calming down period just after the hectic playtime. Food was served family style, and the few extras that were left became an important ground on which sibling rivalries were worked out. The children grabbed food and filled their pockets, so they could take something home from the group. Frequent limit-setting by the therapists was necessary, but this was done in the spirit of protection of the children, not punishment.

As time went on, the girls talked more and more about the separations from either both of their parents or at least from their fathers. When it was appropriate, we helped arrange supervised visitation, and with all of the children we attempted to deal with the bond disruption which they were experiencing. Discussion of the sexual abuse played a relatively small part in the six months of treatment. However, there was a comfort, even a safety, in being with children with similar problems. When one of the girls would share a dream or a memory or express her fears about having to go back to her parents, the others could nod in agreement and understand what she was going through.

The parents chose to focus their group on themselves rather than on the progress of their children. Initially the fathers denied or said they could not remember the incestuous behavior. Gradually, they confronted each other, and their defenses were less strong. One father said, "With me, I'm sure I didn't do it, but there is that doubt". The next week he told the group he had dreamed about the incest, and the following morning he had total recall of what had happened. Following assurances about confidentiality, the therapists videotaped some of the sessions. Replay of portions of the tape was a considerable help in getting the parents to realize there were inconsistencies in their explanations about the past and in their plans for the future.

Case Histories: The Children in the Group

The following seven case histories describe the children who were in the group and their families. All of the names have been changed to assure confidentiality.

Mary R.—"The Leader"

Mary was seven years old when her older sister ran away from home in an attempt to avoid further sexual assault from her father. The sister told of repeated emotional, physical, and sexual abuse in the family of 12 children, with the older brothers abusing the younger siblings just as father was doing. All 12 children were adjudicated dependent and neglected, and the father was charged with felony child abuse and sexual assault. A deferred prosecution arrangement was worked out whereby the criminal charges were dropped because the father agreed to cooperate with treatment recommendations. Mary was told about the children's group, and a week before it began she told her foster mother the details of the sexual intercourse her father forced her to have with him.

On the standardized pre-tests, Mary showed significant variation in her language sub-test scores; some of the lags seemed due to deprivation while others reflected central processing difficulties. In school, she was two years behind (she had never spent much time there before) but made significant progress. She was seen as a very compliant child, overly eager to please, and shy with other children. The foster mother, to whom Mary felt very close, described her as sensitive, not liking herself very much, and extremely malnourished. Mary's worries about being hurt were reflected in nightmares about monsters and in a constant need to be reassured. During the day and especially at bedtime she masturbated excessively, sometimes in front of people. After visits with her biologic parents, she became withdrawn, vomited at meals, and occasionally had nighttime wetting. On self-report, Mary stated she worried more than others; her feelings were easily hurt; she had sleep problems and headaches; and she wished she could run things in her life. She was extremely positive about her relationship with her biologic parents, appearing to be unable to say anything negative about them. The psychiatric assessment showed her to be an anxious, depressed child whose pseudo-precociousness and excessive talking were temporarily helping her compensate for a lifetime of deprivation and abuse.

Mary immediately became the leader in the children's group. She talked not only about current events but also of her feelings about her biologic parents and the physical and sexual abuse she had received. Her openness helped the other girls be more comfortable, but her willingness to take care of them only reinforced her pseudo-maturity. The following dream material was shared with the group when another visit with her biologic parents was imminent.

> "I was playing at my house when these men came with knives. They called us over. The girls followed. Then they were cutting us in the neck. Annie (her sister) was there. Paul (her brother) and daddy tried to chop my head off, but I pushed them back. We ran to the queen's home and went swimming and out to play, but a couple men were still there with razor blades. They were running after me and almost caught me. The queen's door was shut. I ran to another house, but the door was locked. That's when I woke up, but I was afraid to open my eyes".

When asked who the queen was, Mary said it was her foster mother. This dream material led to an intense group discussion. One girl said the moral of the dream was "never play with men"; another said, "It means you can't trust any moms or dads".

Mary came to look forward to the group and was sad when it came to an end. On self-report, she now described herself as excitable, sensitive to criticism, fearful of new places and people, and daydreaming a lot. The problems she reported prior to the group were now improved. She volunteered to the examiner, "I was unhappy but not anymore". Regarding her biologic parents, she was now much more realistic. She described the attention she had received from her father as "only the other kind", meaning sexual. In regard to her foster parents, there was a great deal of attachment on both sides. The foster mother saw Mary as much improved; she was less pseudo-mature, masturbated less compulsively, and was genuinely affectionate. However, she was daydreaming a lot and still had problems sleeping. These difficulties were related to her tremendous fear of being returned home. Her school report at that point showed her to be doing well, catching up in the academic material, and relating better with peers although still overly eager to please the teacher.

The co-therapists agreed with the social service department's recommendation for termination of parental rights, but at eight-month follow-up little progress had been made because of legal technicalities. The foster mother and school reported that Mary was doing quite well. However, she still did have some difficulty getting to sleep, was fearful of rejection, and was too grownup although all these problems were lessening. On self-report, the only problems Mary was concerned about were daydreaming and not doing well in social studies. She seemed much more secure and was hoping she could stay with her foster parents forever. During the sentence-completion test, however, she talked of her concerns about how the past would affect her. Although she no longer was having nightmares about her father taking her to bed, she could not get it out of her mind. Sometimes at night when she was trying to get to sleep she thought about it, and then she would masturbate. She felt guilty about the self-stimulation and said she did not ever want to get married because she was embarrassed about the sex with her father. When she felt sad about these things, she kept it to herself, not wanting to make anyone else unhappy. Still trying to please, she told the author she loved her and the male co-therapist almost as much as her foster parents. Any anger about the termination of the therapeutic relationships seemed to be consciously suppressed.

On three-year follow-up Mary had been adopted by her foster parents, as had a younger biologic sister. They had taken new first names of their choice and had no contact with any of their other siblings. Now in the sixth grade, Mary was doing above-average work but needed considerable push and direction from her teacher. She no longer was overly polite but still was very sensitive to criticism and anything she perceived as rejection. She had some loving feelings toward her biologic parents and occasionally shared such thoughts with her new parents. Because Mary was developing physically and reaching puberty, her adoptive mother was sensitive to the possibility of a resurgence of memories about the sexual abuse and was prepared to seek further therapy if necessary. Since the adoption was a subsidized one,* this would not be at the parents' expense. Mary and her adoptive parents perceived the group therapy as having been very helpful and still occasionally talked about it.

Mary's biologic father did not serve a jail sentence for the sexual abuse nor did he follow through with psychotherapy. He did, however, serve time for a later kidnapping of two of the children from foster care. He and his wife have since had two more babies, both of whom were removed from parental custody through court action at which the eldest sister gave testimony.

Annie R.—"The Leader's Little Sister"

Annie, Mary's biologic sister, was six years old at the time of referral. Her older siblings reported that she had been fondled by father, including digital manipulation of her genitals and anus. She had also observed her father having intercourse with her older sisters. At the time of referral, Annie had many untreated medical problems including a speech defect and a serious eye disorder. Despite these, she was an attractive, appealing child though a bit shy.

The standardized tests showed her to be functioning in the mildly retarded range in language. How much of this was innate and how much due to cultural deprivation was unclear. The school quickly realized she may have had no prior education and moved her from first grade to kindergarten where her self-esteem and interest in learning quickly improved. She was affectionate and eager to please the teacher, using excessive talking as a way of engaging adults. In the foster home, she initially acted like a three-year-old and was fearful of everyone. She denied that the sexual abuse happened to her, saying that only her older sisters were involved. On several occasions she took off all her clothes and layed on top of a young boy until the foster mother intervened. She masturbated daily and tried to get other children to touch her as well. She also had frequent stomach aches and night waking, was fearful of new situations and people, told stories which were not true, had occasional day-time wetting, and was restless and unable to concentrate. On self-report, Annie described herself as unhappy, worrying more than others, getting into more trouble than others her age, and crying easily, such as when her biologic brother hit her. Although she described her biologic mother as giving care and attention only when she behaved, she was generally very positive about her and missed her very much. Although she was also positive about her father, she told of a time when she and her mother cried when the father ripped up the mother's Bible. Sometimes Annie had dreams about being punished by boy angels. The child psychiatrist described her as being frightened and unhappy but defended. The potential for regression, withdrawal, or religious preoccupation was great, especially if she felt guilty about her behavior.

In the group it took considerable effort to draw Annie out; her rambling about material possessions was her protection. She and her sister, Mary, looked forward to seeing each other in the group. Gradually, as she heard Mary express some negative feelings about their parents, she was able to share some of the memories which had been troubling her.

When the group treatment terminated, Annie had received medical attention, was making progress in school, and seemed attached to her foster parents. The only problems the foster mother reported were an inability to get along well with her brothers and sisters and telling lies on occasion. Annie was now more

---

* Through a subsidized adoption, the state pays certain expenses for the child until age 21.

negative about her biologic father though still quite positive about her mother. She was still eager to please adults, answering most items on the sentence-completion test as "It's nice". On self-report she mentioned problems with eating, stomach aches, and vomiting as well as feeling she was disobedient and fighting more and getting into more trouble than others her same age.

On eight-month follow-up the foster mother reported Annie as being very well-adjusted with no specific problems. During a recent visit with some of her sisters, the sexual abuse was discussed. Annie told them, "That was nasty of daddy to do that; that's why I don't like to be with him anymore". Annie described how much she liked her foster parents and how she wanted to continue living with them, but she was not really sure her foster mother liked her all that much. Her responses to the sentence-completion test were now more spontaneous and appropriate. Even though she had made significant progress in school, she was still in a remedial reading class and still made excessive demands for her teacher's attention.

On three-year follow-up Annie had been adopted but not by her foster parents. Her separation from them had been difficult and had resulted in increased emotional problems. After some psychotherapy, which was paid for by the state, she was beginning to make a satisfactory adjustment. She was also receiving special tutoring and medical care.

Emily K.—"The Rejected Hoarder"

Emily, age seven, was referred to the group following a series of sexual incidents with her father involving genital manipulation. On the last occasion he had attempted to insert an aspirator into her vagina. Although Emily told her mother what was happening, her mother took no action until she complained of physical pain. Prosecution of the father was deferred on the condition that he obtain psychiatric help. Two months later, following the psychiatrist's recommendation that visitation with Emily be allowed, the father left town. Meanwhile Emily continued to live with her mother who sued for divorce. Mrs. K. was unwilling to become involved with her daughter's therapy although she did obtain some supportive help for herself.

On the standardized tests Emily was functioning at average levels, but the school report showed her to be having significant problems. She was restless, distractible, and failed to finish her work. Preoccupied with problems at home, she daydreamed and craved attention from adults and peers. Her mother was perturbed with her, agreeing with the school's report but adding that Emily was also sassy and quarrelsome. Emily's self-report showed she was aware of her behavior problems, but she stressed her difficulties with sleeping, stomach aches, fearfulness, and sensitivity to criticism. Generally she was positive toward both parents but realized it was only her father who ever set effective limits for her. During the psychiatric assessment, she sexualized the interaction with the male examiner through her body posture and the content of her conversation. For example, she put her hand on his knee and talked about a romantic movie she had seen on television.

During the group it became clear how angry Emily was at her mother for the rejection that had occurred since she was a baby. She sexualized her relationship with the male co-therapist and was resistant to any attempt to help her understand the meaning of her behavior. Following the divorce of her parents, she was again sexually assaulted by her father; this time he attempted to put powder inside her vagina. The father angrily denied her accusation, and her mother did not want to be bothered. The therapists filed a child abuse report to assure that all further visitations would be supervised. Emily was surprised and relieved that such protection was possible.

At the close of the group Emily was extremely ambivalent about her parents. The group had become a substitute family for her, and she talked openly of her wish that the co-therapists could actually be her parents. She had hoarded food from the group more than any of the other children and wondered how she would do without these "love supplies". She reported improvements in some areas, that is, fewer somatic and sleep problems and less fearfulness and sensitivity, but behavior problems at home and school had become worse. She was not finishing her school work and was no longer getting along with peers. Emily attributed much of this to her mother's absences from home due to long work hours and a new romance. Even though many of the issues of the sexual abuse had been worked through, the maternal rejection had not been dealt with. Efforts were made to refer Emily and her mother for family therapy, but Mrs. K. would only agree to individual psychiatric treatment for her daughter. She refused to acknowledge her own role in Emily's problems.

Eight months later Emily was in individual treatment but was continuing to have the same types of problems. Her father had remarried, and his second wife had two sons. Emily had an overnight visit with them once a week. Even though there had been no further sexual abuse, Emily seemed preoccupied with sexuality. On the self-report, her greatest wish was to have a baby of her own—"maybe 14 of them". On three-year follow-up, the family could not be located, but the social service worker who had last seen the family reported that mother was now having serious problems with her son, but that Emily was doing better.

Jane F.—"The Waif"

Jane's mother left the family and moved out of state and four months later, Jane, age five, was placed in foster care. Her father was arrested for molesting several five- and six-year-old girls in his apartment building. It was only then that it became known that he had molested Jane as well. "He was messing with me and hurt me. I was bleeding and wanted a bandaid, but he said I didn't need one. He did it to my friend, Sally, too." On testing, Jane was above average intellectually and linguistically. Her school report was basically positive although she was somewhat behind in her work due to frequent family moves. Also, she was easily led by other children. On the parent questionnaires, Jane described her mother very negatively and her father positively. She felt that he cared about her, listened to her, and she missed him terribly. The social services worker reported that mother had lost control over Jane, and this was one of the precipitants for her leaving the home. Jane described herself as excitable, worrying more than others, dreaming about death, fighting constantly, and easily hurt by others. The foster mother reported that Jane had made a good adjustment but was unhappy when she did not get her own way.

During the group sessions Jane talked a lot about missing her father. At times she curled up with her thumb in her mouth, feeling sad about not being with him. Other times she was gregarious and coquettish with the male therapist who had to set firm limits for her. Due to her depression regarding the separation, visits with the father were arranged; they were held in the office and were supervised by the co-therapists. Mr. F.'s inappropriateness with his daughter continued. He had erections when he held her and treated her more like a sweetheart than a young daughter.

When Mrs. F. returned to town, she and her husband attempted to reconcile and joined the parents' therapy group. Mr. F. was found guilty of sexual assault and given a deferred sentence on the condition that he receive psychiatric care. Although he was severely disturbed and possibly schizophrenic, he did not follow through with individual treatment. He eventually admitted in group that he had molested the other children, but he continued to deny any sexual involvement with his daughter.

Based on the lack of progress with the parents, the therapists of the children's group recommended to social services that parental rights be terminated.

When the children's group concluded, both the foster mother and the school described Jane as being better adjusted. Jane, however, reported that she had many more problems than at the time of the first evaluation, including distractibility, fearfulness of new situations, and difficulty making friends. On the parent questionnaire, she was still more positive toward her father than her mother despite the weekend visitations she was having with Mrs. F. She was somewhat more realistic about her father than she had been prior to the group. On the sentence completion about the group she said the activity she had liked most was "playing baby". She also indicated how much she did not like the female therapist but liked the male therapist. She was fearful of all fighting and wished most for her whole family to be back together again.

Her parents sporadically attended a different parents' group for the next eight months, but her father avoided all individual psychotherapy. Mrs. F. continued with individual therapy just long enough to regain custody of Jane. The return of physical custody was on the premise that the father stay out of the home except for visitation. At the first follow-up Jane was doing fairly well in school with only a mild learning problem and some difficulties concentrating on her work. Jane, however, reported 15 issues which she felt were very serious ones for her, including eating problems, nausea, nightmares, headaches, fearfulness, excessive worrying, and daydreaming. She idealized her relationship with her biologic parents and still was wishing her parents would be reunited.

Four months later a neighbor of the family reported that Mr. F. was again sexually mistreating Jane and Mrs. F. was allowing this to continue. The parents' group therapist found this hard to believe and suggested social services check this out with another therapist the parents had seen for a few joint sessions. At three-year follow-up the family had fled the state even though social services technically still had legal custody of Jane and only mother was to have physical custody. Despite a police pick-up order, they have not been found.

Tina L.—"The Grown-up Baby"

Tina, age four-and-a-half years, was the youngest child referred to the group. One evening when Mrs. L. arrived home from buying liquor for her husband, who was already intoxicated, she saw him attempting to have intercourse with Tina. Mrs L. called the police, and Tina was taken to the emergency room of the hospital where it was discovered that she had genital injuries including bruises, abrasions, and some bleeding. Mr. L. was charged with second-degree sexual assault and aggravated incest. Although it would have been possible for him to have posted bail, he refused to do so and stayed in jail and suffered indignities and verbal abuse from other prisoners and guards. Eventually he was released and sent for evaluation of his alcoholism which had been a long-standing problem requiring hospitalization on several occasions.

Mrs. L. was an intelligent, articulate woman who filled her time taking care of Tina, a two-year-old son, and a baby who was born a few months after her husband was arrested. In some ways she was a good mother in that she was nurturing and caring and she did, in fact, call the police and report her husband.

However, she had difficulty setting appropriate limits with her children, tended to foster pseudo-adult behavior in Tina, and colluded in the ongoing problem with alcoholism which Mr. L. had. She began seeing her husband as "sick and in need of treatment" and was hoping that he could be quickly cured so that he could be reconciled with her. She was reluctant to have Tina join the children's group because she wanted to deny the sexual abuse and because she was worried that Tina would be discriminated against because she was an American Indian.

On the testing Tina was found to have above-average intellectual ability, but she appeared as a child older than her chronological age. Despite this pseudo-maturity there appeared to be some sadness and sensitivity to criticism. Tina basically saw herself as a very good child but occasionally impulsive and not sleeping well.

When Tina first began the children's group, she was somewhat fearful and inhibited. Part of this was due to her lack of experience in relating with other children, but she also seemed extremely sensitive to anything that she perceived as criticism or rejection. At times she refused to come back to the group, and her mother had to be persuaded to bring her. She was uncomfortable in relating with the male co-therapist until he demonstrated to her that they could have a relationship that was not sexualized. On the recommendation of the therapists Mrs. L. enrolled Tina in a special preschool for Indian children.

Mr. L. remained sober while he was taking Antabuse, and he looked forward to a permanent reunion with his family which social services was willing to allow. The therapists, however, put pressure on the juvenile court to prevent this from happening so that the family could be reunited more gradually. Meanwhile, the father stayed at a half-way house and seemed to be relieved at having such external controls placed on him.

Individual treatment for the father and marital treatment for the parents were recommended, but they did not follow through. They did, however, attend the parents' group and made excellent use of it. Initially, Mr. L. denied that he had molested Tina; then he claimed that he had amnesia for that entire period of time, but eventually, through confrontation from other group members and through the actual reading of the medical report when Tina was seen in the pediatric emergency clinic, he admitted that he had assaulted her on numerous occasions. The parents were able to work through some of their marital and sexual difficulties, and father became re-employed. Even though this necessitated a move out of state, social services agreed but kept the case open. At Tina's termination in the children's group she appeared to her parents and school as doing quite well. However, she saw herself as having quite a few difficulties, including daydreaming, problems with making and keeping friends, getting into more trouble than others her age, failing to finish things, and having problems with eating and fearfulness.

Eight month follow-up was not possible because the family was still out of state, but Mr. L. periodically called the male co-therapist to discuss the family's progress. According to father, Tina was doing well in school; he was remaining sober, and there was no further sexual abuse. The family could not be located for three-year follow-up.

Molly and Amy V.—"The 'Little Woman' of the House and Her Battered Sister"

Molly, age seven and Amy, age five, were placed in foster care after Mr. V. broke Amy's jaw for not getting ready for school quickly enough. Only later did relatives voice their concerns about the sexual abuse they felt was occurring. Although father never admitted it, it is likely that he fondled his daughters, especially the older one. Because Mrs. V. had abandoned the family when Amy was only a baby, Mr. V. had tried to manage alone. Not only were the girls severely deprived, but Molly became the "little woman" of the house, cooking, cleaning and taking care of Amy as best she could.

No formal charges were filed against Mr. V. for the sexual abuse because of lack of evidence, but physical abuse charges were made. He was found guilty, served a month's sentence on a day-release program, and then was placed on probation on the condition he receive psychiatric help. He attended the parents' group and joined Parents Anonymous but never received individual psychotherapy despite numerous promises that he would. He wanted his daughters back, especially Molly, and he tried to give the impression that he was cooperating.

The girls were seriously disturbed and almost unmanageable. This was related to years of deprivation, rejection, and physical abuse, rather than to the sexual molestation. A series of foster parents could not cope with them, and in the group they needed constant attention and limit-setting and preferred to pretend they were babies, sitting in the female therapist's lap and calling her "Mama". Molly talked openly with her sister about the morning Amy's jaw was broken, helping her, for the first time, show how angry she was.

On the standardized tests both girls showed they were of average intelligence, but they were not performing well in school according to their teachers. On the pre-tests Amy saw herself as basically unhappy, disobedient, and bullying other children. The foster mother saw her as immature, demanding, and having severe nightmares. The psychiatric assessment revealed that she was quite unsocialized and was somewhat preoccupied with sexual material. Molly's behavior problems were more severe. She refused to cooperate with anyone. She saw herself as shy, sensitive to criticism, daydreaming a lot, and having headaches and stomach aches. The psychiatric assessment showed her to be an extremely needy child with an intense unresolved Oedipal bond. Both girls were quite ambivalent in their feelings toward their father although Molly openly talked about her wish to marry him.

Amy's behavior improved somewhat over the course of therapy, especially after the girls were placed in separate foster homes so Molly no longer was assuming a caretaking role with Amy. Molly's emotional problems became even more severe, and finally she was expelled from school.

When the group terminated, Molly was referred for individual psychiatric treatment which continued for over a year. The recommendation to social services was that both girls remain in long-term foster care with visitations with their father.

At eight-month follow-up Molly was doing poorly in her foster home and was afraid of being hit. Her three wishes were "to go home with her real dad, marry a movie star, and get a baby who won't let go". Amy's foster mother reported many of the same problems she had always had but overall felt there was some improvement. Amy felt, too, that things were somewhat better.

On three-year follow-up Amy was at a residential treatment center where Molly had also been for over a year. Molly had made little progress and had engaged in repeated sex play with peers. She was now living with her father, his new young wife, and their baby. The public school system could not manage her and wanted her placed elsewhere. Father had contined to use a belt on Molly and on Amy during visitations.

Discussion

These case histories and follow-up reports have been presented in detail because there are no similar examples in the literature. While some treatment programs are presenting remarkable success rates, these cases highlight the dimension of the problems these children face.

It is necessary, initially, to place the group psychotherapy with these young girls into perspective. Relatively short-term treatment for them was only one aspect of the overall intervention with the family. Group therapy with the parents and criminal and juvenile court actions also had effects on the children. But first of all, let us consider the effects of direct treatment for the children. Because of the sexual over-stimulation which these girls had experienced, it was hypothesized that they would be unable to enter into latency with its focus on mastery in peer relations. In fact, this was the case, but the reason was not only the sexual abuse but also the prior years of neglect and deprivation which these girls had experienced. Within the group setting all of these girls except the V. sisters appeared to make improvements. However, as the post-testing and follow-up reports indicate, most of them continued to have emotional difficulties. Because of this, it is necessary to look at what could have been done to have helped them even more. Ideally, the treatment should continue for two to three years with individual therapy being provided by the co-therapists if necessary. While all of the children were average or a bit below average in intelligence, five of the six school-age children were having school difficulties. It is noteworthy that the girls frequently reported more problems, which represented internalized difficulties such as somatic complaints, worrying, and sensitivity to criticism, than the adults around them reported. This indicates that the assessment of a sexually abused child's adjustment must be made very carefully.

Direct treatment of sexually abused children can only be helpful in the long term if the child's life situation changes as well. It can either change through significant improvements being made by the parents or by permanent living arrangements with adults who are more responsive and caring than the biologic parents. Although all of the fathers in this study received either deferred prosecutions or deferred sentences on the condition they receive psychiatric treatment, none of them followed through with this for more than two months. Some of them did attend the parents' group, but they used this to avoid any more intensive therapy for their long-standing, severe emotional disturbances. There appeared to be no one in the system who had the power to re-enact the prosecution or the sentences when the fathers did not follow through on their agreements.

As therapists for the children and after contacts with most of the parents, we recommended termination of parental rights for three children, long-term foster care with visitation with father for two children, a gradual reunion of another family, and supervised visitation for another child whose parents were divorced. This does not speak highly for the parents' willingness to make the necessary changes to have their children home again. On the other hand, the three-year follow-up showed that, except for the family with multiple incest, the children did end up back home with parents who had not received the intensive therapy that they needed. The children's long-term prognosis is thus quite guarded, as it seems likely that all of them will continue to have some degree of difficulty in the areas of self-esteem, sexuality, and dependency.

Appendix

STANDARDIZED DIAGNOSTIC MEASURES

Peabody Picture Vocabulary Test
Illinois Test of Psycholinguistic Abilities
Spontaneous Language Sample Scored According to the Laura Lee Developmental Sentence Score System
Templin–Darley Test of Articulation
Conner Teacher's Rating Scale
Schaefer Children's Report of Parental Behavior
Conner Children's Self-Rating Scale
Conger Children's Sentence Completion Test
Conner Parent's Rating Scale
Schaefer Parent's Rating Scale

References

1. Beezley, P., Martin, H. P. and Kempe, R. (1976) Psychotherapy. In *The Abused Child: A Multidisciplinary Approach to Developmental Issues and Treatment.* (Edited by Martin, H. P.) Ballinger, Cambridge, Mass.
2. Frank, M. G. and Zilbach, J. (1968) Current trends in group therapy with children. *Int. J. Group Psychother.* **18:** 447.
3. Frank, M. G. (1976) Modifications of activity group therapy: responses to ego-impoverished children. *Clinical Social Work J.* **4:** 102.
4. Gratton, L. and Pope, L. (1972) Group diagnosis and therapy for young school children. *Hospital and Community Psychiatry* **23:** 40.
5. Jones, C. O. (1977) A critical evaluation of the work of the NSPCC's battered child research department. *Child Abuse and Neglect* **1:** 111.
6. Martin, H. P. and Beezley, P. (1977) Behavioral observations of abused children. *Devl. Med. Child Neurol.* **19:** 373.
7. McMillen-Hall, N. (1977) The focus of group treatment with sexually abused children. "Child Abuse: Where Do We Go From Here?" *Conference Proceedings.* Children's Hospital National Medical Center, Washington, D.C. February 18–20. pp. 99–100.
8. Scheidlinger, S., Douville, M., Harrahill, C., King, C. H. and Minor, J. D. (1959) Activity group therapy for children in a family agency. *Social Casework* **XL:** 193.
9. Scheidlinger, S. (1960) Experiential group treatment of severely deprived latency-age children. *Am. J. Orthopsychiatry* **30:** 356.
10. Scheidlinger, S. (1965) Three group approaches with socially deprived latency-age children. *Int. J. Grp. Psychother.* **15:** 434.
11. Sugar, M. (1974) Interpretive group psychotherapy with latency children. *J. Am. Acad. Child Psychiatry* **13:** 648.
12. Zilbach, J. J. and Grunebaum, H. G. (1954) Pregenital components in incest as manifested in two girls in activity group therapy. *Am. J. Grp. Psychother.* **14:** 166.

Acknowledgments

The author wishes to express appreciation to Lloyd Eckhardt, M.D., Florence Berman Blager, Ph.D., Catherine Augsburger, B.A., and especially to Robert Schrant, M.S.W., who was my co-therapist, for their help with this project.

Chapter Sixteen

The Co-Therapy Relationship in Group Treatment of Sexually Mistreated Adolescent Girls

BRUCE GOTTLIEB AND JANET DEAN

The male–female co-therapy model used in group treatment of sexually abused adolescent girls can be an effective therapeutic agent. Adolescents who have been involved in incest become very confused about relationships between men and women and can benefit from a healthy male–female role model to help them disengage from disturbed family relationships and begin to establish appropriate peer relationships and solid sexual identities. It is advantageous to them to see a male and female interact as equals with the ability to resolve conflicts between themselves. Co-therapists who are comfortable with their own sexuality and have a positive orientation toward the opposite sex can provide such a model. (See Chapter Twelve.) A female or male therapist whose attitude is radically oriented against the opposite sex would be detrimental to a group of sexually mistreated adolescents as this situation would not allow the girls the opportunity to observe the positive dynamics that can operate in a supportive relationship between a man and a woman.

This paper addresses some of the many issues that arose in the course of the co-therapy relationship between the authors while treating two consecutive groups of sexually mistreated adolescent girls. The girls in the first group were between the ages of 12 and 14; in the second group they were 13 and 14. The girls in both groups represented a wide range of socioeconomic classes and were referred to therapy by local county departments of social services. The girls reported incidents ranging from fondling to intercourse, and for the most part the sexual relationships had been ongoing for several years.

The purpose of the groups was to provide the girls with a social learning model as well as to help them understand some of their behaviors and family situations. Interpretations of the girls' projections were made to the groups; the aim was to connect the girls' past life experiences and patterning to how they were perceiving and responding to present situations.

It is not our intention to discuss the specific treatment process in our groups except as it relates to the co-therapy relationship. The sexually mistreated adolescent girl brings to treatment some difficult and unique problems that require increased openness and honesty between co-therapists. The nature of the transference was such that we found ourselves having to examine our own sexual beliefs individually as well as with each other.

Sexual Mistreatment during Adolescence

Adolescence can be a period of difficult adjustment even for the relatively "healthy" individual.[1] The physical and emotional changes present much confusion to the adolescent who on the one hand wishes to be more independent by establishing deeper peer relationships and autonomy while, at the same time, unconsciously wishes to remain dependent. The uncertainty of having an adult body with physical drives, yet oftentimes not having adequate outlets for these drives, puts the adolescent in a dichotomous holding pattern. These difficulties may be greatly amplified and separation-individuation issues may become distorted if the adolescent is also a victim of incest. Although mother–son and sibling incest can occur during adolescence, the focus of this paper is on sexual mistreatment experienced by young females.

Many of these girls are slowly patterned into becoming seductive, provocative adolescents. The patterning can come from fathers or stepfathers giving them sexualized attention from an early age through inappropriate fondling and sexual caressing. This often becomes a way of life for many years before the girl feels enough desperation to tell anyone what is happening. Collusion and secrecy are primary rules these enmeshed and minimally distant families follow.[2] (See Chapter Thirteen.) As the adolescent reaches out for primary supports to come from peers as opposed to family, the family then takes on a secondary role in terms of importance. Because of this, these girls do not feel as compelled to operate within their family rules. This often leads them to confide in someone about the incestuous relationship.

It is difficult for the adolescent who has been involved with incest to adequately work through the appropriate developmental tasks of adolescence. The coping styles she uses might be related to the time of onset of the sexual mistreatment and to the quality of the earlier parenting she has received. She may show more confusion around appropriate affection-seeking behavior and may be more afraid to seek support from adults.

One of the primary tasks for the normal adolescent is the progression from being appropriately sexually repressed during the latency period to becoming sexually expressive and learning how to cope with this positively in society. The sexuality of abused adolescents becomes confused because they may not derive pleasure from sexual relationships. This is due to their being exploited and dealt with not in terms of their needs but in terms of how they could satisfy others. The absence of tenderness and appropriate nurturing has deprived the adolescent of gratification that is possible in non-erotic love. This can only confuse the erotic lovemaking and its meaning. The child who receives a poor quality and/or inconsistent nurturing is less likely to be able to deal adequately with any sexual mistreatment or with appropriate developmental tasks.

The relationship between the sexually mistreated adolescent girl and her father/stepfather was oftentimes one of the few relationships in which the girl was receiving any type of attention. Just as some physically abused children prefer negative attention to being ignored, similar dynamics can operate with sexual abuse. It becomes very confusing for the child or adolescent because at one level she feels that her father at least cares enough for her to be giving her attention, but at the same time, the girl can be overcome with guilt, shame, fear, and often, physical pain. Although many fathers say they act in a "loving" way with their daughters, and many daughters perceive this relationship as a giving one on one level, it is not a positive relationship that will establish the foundation for future reciprocal relationships. Oftentimes, the mothers of sexually mistreated girls were unavailable to their daughters and were not able to offer the appropriate type of physical and emotional affection and protection. This lack of emotional and physical availability also dominates the marital relationship with sexual dysfunction being a common symptom between spouses.

Establishing a Co-Therapy Relationship

Certainly the single most important feature of a successful co-therapy relationship is trust. Some essential components of a trusting relationship are a basic liking and respect for one another. For the authors, co-therapy became a relationship with closeness and attunement of thought, compromise, and support. With basic trust existing, co-therapists are less inhibited and less fearful of asking questions or bringing up concerns. The concerns can often center around group behavior as well as their own behavior.

Within the confines of a trusting relationship, the element of competition can be greatly reduced, allowing for a better exploration of meaningful and effective treatment modes. If co-therapists cannot establish a trust with one another, the level of communication will be defensive and this can be counter-therapeutic for the adolescents.

For the most part, it can be difficult within society's structure for a man and woman to establish a close, platonic relationship which allows for the sharing and discussing of sexual beliefs. To each other the authors were friends as well as colleagues and co-therapists. The male author was married and had a child; the female author had a steady boyfriend. It is common to approach a co-therapy relationship with concern about the development of sexual attraction within the relationship. The process of working through potential sexual attraction becomes a very important step, and one needs to develop a framework in which this can happen. The authors feel that if these feelings exist and are not acknowledged, the therapists will have to be exerting much energy into a denial process that can be counter-productive in treatment.

Before beginning treatment with the sexually abused adolescent, there are many issues that the therapist needs to deal with both on a personal level and within the co-therapy relationship. It is important to keep in mind that the adolescent will respond not only to the therapists' conscious words and actions but also to the therapists' unconscious thoughts and feelings. These adolescents as children needed to cue in to the external world for survival; consequently, they are hypersensitive to both verbal and nonverbal messages given by important people in their lives. For this reason it becomes essential that certain sexual issues be discussed and worked through so that the therapists are able to give consistent, clear messages, both verbally and nonverbally, to the wary adolescents. The relevant issues for introspection and reflection include:

1. Societal and religious views on sex
2. Birth control—female and/or male responsibility
3. Masturbation

4. Appropriate outlets for sexual drives of adolescents
5. Sexual deviancy
6. Incestuous feelings and acts
7. Sexual vocabulary—terms and definitions
8. Feelings and possible sexual fantasies toward the co-therapist
9. Potential adolescent fantasies about the therapists' private lives, especially in regard to mates and spouses.

This list should not be viewed as all-inclusive nor should all of these topics be viewed as imperative in terms of sharing with a co-therapist. The sharing of past experiences or attitudes should only be done to the degree comfortable to both therapists. Equal to the importance of sharing is the setting of limits for individual privacy. Each co-therapy dyad needs to establish its own equilibrium in regard to these issues.

If one of the therapists has a real problem about any of the issues on the list, recognition of it will help determine what role the co-therapist might play in resolving the potential negative effect on the group. Because the authors as co-therapists had discussed and were comfortable with these issues, the girls were less inhibited in bringing these subjects up in group. For example, in the area of sexual vocabulary, we developed clear and consistent terminology and definitions which established a more relaxed atmosphere. The adolescents did not need to feel fearful that we would be unable to handle certain words and concepts.

The importance of discussion around these issues cannot be overemphasized. Entering the field of sexual mistreatment inevitably raises uncomfortable thoughts and feelings in the therapists which should be examined in a supportive setting, possibly with a consultant or supervisor who has had experience dealing with sexual issues.

When the co-therapists have gone through the experience of sharing with each other, they are more able to help the adolescents be able to bring their own material into the group. The girls raised many questions directly or indirectly concerning sexual mores in general and basic relationships, both heterosexual and homosexual. They also had a great need for role models who could demonstrate trust with one another.

When mutual trust and the open discussion of sexual issues are not a part of treatment preparation, important transference issues within the group are ignored due to the therapists' own counter-transference. If this happens, group process will be impeded and the already significant confusion of the adolescent increased.

Not only is it important for the therapists to prepare before the first group session but also to continue a dialogue throughout treatment. Time should be spent before and after the group sessions to help establish an overall cohesiveness to the treatment and also to share the insights and numerous frustrations in working with adolescents. A joint review of process notes made immediately after sessions is helpful in understanding the intensity of group transference and leads to discussion of counter-transference issues.

The Effects of Transference Issues on the Co-Therapy Relationship

One of the major transference issues for the girls in the first group was a confusion about the relationship between the co-therapists. They wanted to believe it was possible for a man and a woman to relate in a positive and warm fashion without the relationship being sexual. However, they saw the male therapist as a sexual threat to the female therapist and wanted to believe that she had the strength to withstand his supposed aggression. To deal with this question was an early treatment goal. Only after the group openly displayed curiosity about the co-therapy relationship were we able to work through this issue. We acknowledged to each other that this area might be a problem, but initially it was too threatening to deal with so we denied that there could be any sexual fantasies toward each other. Knowing though that this was a primary curiosity for the group, we acknowledged the need to look at the reality of our relationship and what we wanted it to be. In order to do that, and for treatment to work, there had to be a non-threatening atmosphere in which to deal with this material. With the establishment of these conditions, we were able to work through the feelings we had about one another and the conflicts between us.

Once this was accomplished, we transmitted to the group *why* we could relate comfortably with each other without there being any fear of sexual advances by either of us. This, then, became an important model of a positive, platonic relationship between a man and a woman which allowed the group the freedom to express some positive and negative feelings towards the therapists.

The potential for specific transference to develop is high. Regardless of the therapists' personal situations, such as marital status or age, each adolescent will find a personal point to focus on in order to act out her fantasies. Because of the girls' fantasies, the dynamics of the co-therapists' relationship could be misconstrued and distorted. In the therapy group there were many comments by members about the co-therapists' relationship. The adolescent girls fantasized the relationship to be a sexual one and verbalized their ideas about the therapists kissing each other. They wondered how the male's spouse would respond if she found out.

It is not unusual for male and female therapists to represent the client's mother and father in the transference. However, in this situation the male was seen as a representation of the girls' aggressive fathers, and his wife became their absent mothers. The female co-therapist became a representation of themselves, that is, a potential victim. The girls wished, on one level, for the therapists to replicate the acting out which had occurred between the girls and their fathers, but on an even stronger level, they wished for the therapist not to succumb to this situation and to help establish a resolution for them.

In order to deal more adequately with this transference issue which was shared by all group members, we needed to find out what the male's spouse actually did feel about the co-therapy relationship. All three people met and discussed the level of involvement, intimacy, and privacy in each of the three dyadic relationships. The co-therapists were then better equipped to explain to the group how it was possible to have a close working relationship, yet each person be able to keep parts of his/her life private. This was a very important process and actually dictated the success of the group. The power and importance of the male therapist's spouse was great even though she was not involved in the treatment process. Because she had a comfort level with our relationship, we were able to concentrate on group issues. If the absent spouse had not been comfortable with the co-therapists' relationship and level of information sharing, the female therapist would probably not have felt as open due to her fear of creating an uncomfortable situation for the male therapist. The male therapist would not have put as much effort into the relationship, thus the communication would have been curtailed. The therapeutic process would have been adversely affected in that it would have been impossible to provide an open, honest model for the group.

After we communicated to the group the level of trust we shared with one another, the transference shifted. The female therapist became the representation of the idealized mother rather than of the girls themselves. We felt that this was because the female therapist was perceived by the group as someone who was able to set limits. She was seen as a protector from the aggressive male as well as a strong female to idealize and identify with. For example, during one session the girls were throwing crumpled paper at each other, and one of the girls literally hid behind the female therapist and threw several wads of paper hitting the male therapist in the groin.

It can be a difficult situation when the female therapist is the idealized object in the transference and the male is the negative object of the group's splitting. It could have become an easy setup for the female therapist to encourage the group's anger toward the male. This should be carefully monitored and discussed if therapists feel this is a potential problem.

Part of the difficulty of being the object of the anger of some of the members of the group was the tension that was created between the therapists. The male felt a reaction toward the co-therapist for being the positive object, and this certainly could have been a potentially destructive situation for the therapists. This, in fact, was part of the transference as the girls' underlying rage was at their mothers for being unavailable to them, but since it was too threatening for them to express that directly to their mothers, we felt they tried to place the male therapist in a position of acting out their anger against their mothers. The anger that the girls were able to express directly to the male therapist indicated that they were perhaps less threatened by fantasized potential repercussions. This was in contrast to what they possibly fantasized would happen if their anger was directed to the female as a representation of their mothers. What was obvious, though, were the girls' attempts to provoke each therapist to act out his/her anger at the other therapist. Displacement and projection were safer ways for the girls to express aggressive feelings.

In experiences such as these, it is essential to analyze the transference/countertransference and the reality of the situation. In essence, we were both responding to the girls in a similar fashion—both of us confronting and supportive to equal degrees, but each was perceived very differently. The female took on the role of interpreting to the girls their behavior and questioning them as to why they needed to see the male as a negative object and the female as an all-positive one. Much of the discussion centered around helping the girls make the connections between their own pasts and the ways in which they viewed us. In one particular session, two of the girls argued about which of them would be stuck sitting next to the male. This type of blatant response to the male served as an excellent opportunity for us to help them begin to understand their fears and difficulties in establishing close relationships with adult men. At this point we began talking about how some of the girls' past situations perhaps dictated to them how they should behave.

Through this process and with the passage of time, the male no longer was seen as a primarily negative entity. It is important to note, however, that underlying the positive transference to the female was the unconscious anger towards the mother for being unavailable to both father and themselves. This was never directly expressed to the female therapist during the course of the group. Since the group continued only seven months, it is speculated that more time would have brought this issue to the surface.

This first group of sexually mistreated adolescent girls needed to deal with their life situations through the transference. To talk about their families was too threatening for this meant opening up the conflict and pain they were experiencing at home. There were very definite, though different, transference issues in the second treatment group as well. However, these girls, all of whom more directly had sought treatment for themselves, were much more able to deal with the realities of their families. Therefore, it was not necessary to use transference issues as the primary medium of therapy.

As the comfort level between us as co-therapists was far greater at the start of the second group, the intensity of discussion regarding general sexual issues lessened. We continued, though, to share our thoughts about transference and counter-transference phenomena.

The second group was seductive with the male therapist from the beginning of treatment and viewed the female therapist as passive and ineffectual. This was in contrast to the first group who viewed the male therapist as an aggressor and the female therapist as a potential victim. Dealing with the seductive behavior became a difficult issue. When one of the girls put her breasts up against the male therapist's back, no interpretation was made because such a comment might have been viewed as a rejection of her need for close physical contact. By modeling the ability to be physically close through touching which was not sexualized, the girls could still feel cared about without being exploited. At the same time, the female therapist started reaching out physically and touching the girls. They, in turn, started to view her, not as a passive woman, but as a woman who could acknowledge their needs.

Conclusion

Although adolescents may have similar backgrounds and may have experienced similar types of exploitation, both physically and psychologically, their needs in treatment will be different. Co-therapists who are planning to do group treatment with sexually mistreated adolescents must first begin a process of self-exploration in an attempt to resolve possible conflicts in attitudes or concepts regarding the various issues of sexuality. With this done, it will be possible to establish an honest role model and to be sensitive to the transference and counter-transference in the treatment process.

References

1. Group for the Advancement of Psychiatry (1968) *Normal Adolescence: Its Dynamics and Impact*. C. Scribner, New York.
2. Solomon, M. A. (1974) Typologies of family homeostasis: implications for diagnosis and treatment. *J. Fam. Therapy Inst. of Marin.* **1**: 9.

Part V.
PROGNOSIS AND OUTCOME

Introduction

As noted in the preceding section, treatment for the sexually abused child and his family has focused on strengthening the whole family unit while ensuring that the child is protected from further sexual assault. As yet, however, few treatment programs have reported their results. An exception is the Child Sexual Abuse Treatment Program in Santa Clara County, California, which reports virtually no recidivism of father–daughter incest in the families who have received a minimum of ten hours of treatment and have formally terminated. (See Chapter Fourteen.) However, Gibbens, *et al.* have documented, on much longer follow-up, similar low rates of recidivism with incestuous fathers who have been convicted and have served prison sentences. Therefore, it is obvious that recidivism cannot be the sole index of outcome. What recidivism rates may tell us is that whenever incest is brought to the attention of authorities (social services, police, the court), there is less chance that it will occur again *or* if it does, that society will hear about it. In other words, it is difficult to know whether the recidivism really is lower following detection or if families just become more cautious so that authorities do not learn about the recurrences. Regardless, outcome measures must become more sensitive just as they have had to do with physical abuse. Difficult though it is to assess finer aspects of family functioning, especially parent–child interaction, it is in this direction the field must move. The CSATP of California has begun to do this, but comparative data from other programs with alternative clinical approaches is necessary. As yet, there is no evidence that any one particular unit of treatment (individual, marital, couple, or whole family) or theoretical orientation (such as humanistic or psychodynamic psychology) is specifically indicated in the treatment of child sexual abuse. Therefore, there is a tremendous need for a range of diversified and innovative programs, thorough evaluation of each, and an objective comparison of the results.

The area of prognosis has had much more attention than that of treatment outcome. There have been numerous studies and clinical reports of the short- and long-term effects of early sexual experiences with an adult. Clinicians are well aware of the possible long-term effects of child sexual abuse for every day they see patients whose problems, which range from neurotic depressions to severe characterological disorders, are related to childhood sexual trauma. Chapter Seventeen by Steele and Alexander includes condensed life histories which describe many of the elements commonly seen in cases of sexual abuse as they are recalled in later life. It also clearly illustrates the difficulty that exists in separating those later effects which can be specifically attributed to the sexual abuse from those which can be more closely related to the co-existing physical abuse. These studies on prognosis have often utilized questionable methodology, equated types of child sexual abuse of varying severity, and yielded contradictory results. Chapter Eighteen by the Mrazeks addresses these issues through a critique of some of the published reports on the short-term and long-term effects of child sexual abuse.

In summary, the following issues are raised in this section. How can the validity of the numerous reports on short- and long-term effects of child sexual abuse be assessed? What methodological issues should be considered? Is a negative outcome related more to the sexual assault or to the other adverse factors in the environment? How do variables such as age of the child and type of sexual experience correlate with long-term outcome? How do personal biases affect the research investigations which are made?

PATRICIA BEEZLEY MRAZEK
C. HENRY KEMPE

Chapter Seventeen

Long-Term Effects of Sexual Abuse in Childhood

BRANDT F. STEELE AND HELEN ALEXANDER

There are various theoretical frameworks in which the establishment of long-term effects of sexual abuse in childhood can be understood, for example, social learning theory, conditioning, family role-modeling, and psychoanalytic concepts of drives, defenses, and adaptations. In general, this chapter will follow the psychoanalytic model, discussing the difficulties of assessing long-term effects and reviewing specific sequelae.

Assessing Long-Term Effects

The first thing to be said concerning the long-term effects of sexual abuse is that we do not know nearly enough about them. The literature contains few retrospective evaluations of persons who have been sexually abused in childhood and even fewer reports of the longitudinal observation of sexually abused children followed during the ensuing years of childhood. Even among those who have been followed, the effects of abuse have been significantly modified by the concern and intervention from the environment, thus distorting what would have been the "natural history" of sexual abuse.

A subtle and prevalent reason for our lack of knowledge is the reluctance of sexual abuse victims to discuss their problems, even with professionals, many years after the abuse occurred. Such reluctance is further abetted by professionals who, for whatever reasons of their own, are very hesitant to deal with the problem of sexual abuse, even during long-term counseling or intensive therapy. We know of many young adults who have had significant therapeutic contact during which the subject of incest or sexual abuse was either never brought up or, if once mentioned, was assiduously avoided thereafter. This phenomenon is not unrelated to the very strong admonition to the child victim to never tell about his/her experience, often accompanied by the threat of severe punishment if this prohibition is broken. Also involved is the great personal insecurity of the sexual abuse victim and the fear that revelation of the past activities will stir up unbearable shame, guilt, and social disapproval.

The later effects of sexual abuse cannot be simplistically related to the sexual nature of the abuse. The impact of such events upon the child will be markedly different according to the child's age, stage of psychosexual development, the nature of the abusive act, the frequency of repetition, the amount of aggression involved, and the relationship of the abused to the abuser. There are also the profound effects of the kind of relationships existing with non-abusing caretakers and with other significant figures in the child's life, both before, during, and after the sexually abusive episodes. In addition to these factors, the response of the environment when abuse has been revealed has a significant impact on the ways in which the child understands his/her experience.

The family setting in which sexual abuse occurs is of crucial importance. Incest occurring in the relatively well-ordered life of an economically stable suburban family may be quite different from similar acts of incest occurring in the haphazard, unstable life of a poverty-stricken, multi-problem family in the ghetto. It is our impression that sexual abuse is likely to occur earlier, more frequently, and often with more accompanying aggression or physical abuse in the multi-problem family in which *all* interpersonal relationships are likely to be more disturbed and distorted. While such multi-problem families may well be more common in the lower socioeconomic classes, they also occur in both middle- and upper-class families.

Physical and sexual abuse may occur concurrently or quite separately at any time in children's lives. In the first two or three years, physical abuse is more common than sexual abuse. However, they may occur simultaneously, and it is usually the physical abuse which draws attention to the problem and is reported, rather than the sexual abuse itself. Sexual abuse tends to become more frequent during latency, puberty, and adolescence and may then often occur without co-existent physical abuse.

There are many similarities between physical and sexual abuse. In physical abuse it is not the immediate physical act or damage itself which causes long-term effects as a rule. It is not the broken leg or arm which leads to the long-lasting distortions of development and emotional states but rather the non-empathic, uncaring climate in which such physical trauma has occurred. There are, of course, physical traumas such as brain damage and sexual traumas such as genital laceration and venereal disease which can themselves cause more permanent damage. But, in sexual abuse as well as in physical maltreatment, it is the emotional climate in which the sexual trauma occurred that is the most potent instigator of long-lasting effects. It is our impression that less severe sexual abuse occurring in the bosom of a disturbed family is much more traumatic than the sexual abuse of a child perpetrated with greater aggression by a stranger, completely outside the family. In a healthy family, a child abused by an outsider can be immediately comforted, supported, and helped to deal with the trauma, thereby minimizing later difficulties.

The following condensed life history describes many of the elements commonly seen in cases of sexual abuse as they are recalled in later life. It clearly illustrates the difficulty we have in separating those later effects which can be specifically attributed to the sexual abuse from those which can be more closely related to the co-existing physical abuse, and what elements of both physical and sexual abuse can be understood as variations on the themes of the co-existing family pathology.

Laura S.

Laura S. was the elder of two children of semi-alcoholic parents living in marginal economic circumstances on the outskirts of a small rural town. Her parents frequently argued and fought. Laura felt her mother was not interested in her and seemed far away when Laura tried to talk to her. The younger brother was mother's favorite to whom she gave all her love.

Laura was attached to her father. She felt close to him and believed he returned her warmth. The father, however, often beat her with his hands or a belt until she was black and blue, and his favorite saying was

"I'll knock you through the wall!" Sometimes he would make her hold two electric wires in her hands while he turned on the current to give her a shock in order to remind her that he was the boss, and she must obey him. By age seven, father was having regular sex-play with Laura, some fondling having occurred earlier, possibly at age four. He would ask, "Do you want me to make it feel good down there?" And Laura would answer, "Yes". This soon progressed to intercourse which continued for several years. Laura enjoyed the closeness of the sexual activity but also felt it was wrong because her father admonished her not to tell.

Mother was very rejecting of the father sexually and repeatedly told him to leave her alone. Mother was aware of the incest because after an argument with the father she would encourage Laura to go to him, sleep with him, and bring back several dollars so that she could buy a bottle of liquor.

When Laura was 13, her father committed suicide by blowing off part of his face and the top of his head with a shotgun in the bedroom while Laura and her mother were cooking dinner. After the funeral, on a cold, gray day, Laura came back home and went into the bedroom. She recalls, "There I saw bits of flesh and hair on the wall and ceiling—all that was left of my father. He was the only man I ever loved, and the only person who ever loved me".

Laura's first boyfriend, at 14, was someone who made her feel beautiful and fine. She began having intercourse with him frequently and enjoyed it. However, in public he fought with her and treated her as "something to wipe his feet on". Years later, she still dreamed and fantasized about him even though she realized life would not have been good with him. At 15 she began dating cadets at an Air Force base and loved being treated "like a lady". Between ages 18 and 21 she describes having affairs with 32 different men and, at times, "carrying on" with as many as three men in one day. She married at 22, a man who was patient, kind and considerate of her. Nevertheless, she continued to have some affairs and, at times, found her husband physically repulsive. She felt she had "ruined" her husband by avoiding sex with him, thus making him become cross, angry and critical. Toward Jimmy, the older of her two sons, Laura has been extremely ambivalent, at times feeling love for him, but more often feeling disgust and hatred. She often wished that she could get rid of him or that he would die. For various misbehaviors she would beat him with her fists or whip him with a belt or a board. She said, "He has all my faults. I've tried to beat all his phobias out of him. I know it's not sensible, but I can't control myself. I think he must be me, and I'm a combination of my mother and my father. My mother wouldn't pay any attention to me, and my father would beat me. I say to Jimmy, 'I'll knock you through the wall', just like dad said to me". Laura felt she had brainwashed her husband into also yelling and screaming at this boy to whom he had previously been very good. She felt she had ruined them both and felt very guilty about it. "I want to get rid of them both. I want them both to die. But I've thought of suicide myself because I've been ruining them."

Toward a younger son, Benny, she felt quite differently. She loved him dearly and felt a warmth and affection for him that she had not known before that she was capable of feeling. She surmised that he was like her younger brother to whom her mother had given all her love and attention. This relationship encouraged Laura to believe that inside her somewhere there was something good and decent.

Laura was puzzled about her own identity. She said, "I think Jimmy must be me, and I'm a combination of mother and father. When I would talk to mother, she would be far away and not answer. I do the same thing with Jimmy. It was father who used to beat me; now Jimmy is me, and little Benny is my brother, Joe. Mother gave all her love and protection to Joe". Another time, she said, "I don't know yet who I really am. I am beginning to think I am somebody and know a little bit about who I am, but I am having trouble becoming it and being something. I don't know whether I am mother or father or Joe or a combination of all of them, or whether I am my children".

In this tragic history, we see all the themes of economic difficulty, alcoholism, parental conflict, maternal deprivation, sibling rivalry, physical abuse, father-loss by suicide, and social isolation. Incest was just one more event in a complex drama of disturbed, unhappy family life. To the casual observer, Laura was an attractive, popular, young married woman with two children, not too different from other young matrons who lived on a military base with their armed-service career husbands. Yet, beneath the surface of her life, she is seriously troubled—psychologically and behaviorally.

With unusual clarity, she describes many of the features commonly seen in those who have been sexually or physically abused. Her low self-esteem, chronic depression, inability to find satisfactory pleasure in life, and bewilderingly unintegrated sense of identity are all quite obvious. The physical abuse of her older son seems related to her identification with a father who beat her as a child, and this is reinforced by identification with an unloving, unempathic, uncaring mother. Her desperate, frantic, compulsive search for a man to love and be loved by, beginning at age 14 and continuing in various forms up to the present, appears to be related to the memories of the warm closeness she had with her father, including the incest, and the unresolved grief-reaction to his suicide when she was 13. She over-idealized the loving side of her ambivalence toward him and has never been able to find an adequate replacement. Her promiscuous, sexual pattern with men is undoubtedly related to the sexualization of the love relationship with her father, but the desperateness of the search itself has more potent, deep roots in the effort to find somewhere a replacement for the lack of basic, caring love from the mother in her early life, and the need to find some way to get approval and acceptance. Her inability to enjoy sexual activity is at least partly the result of residual guilt in relationship to her father. Yet, this guilt is not so much the feeling of having done something wrong sexually with him, but much more that she was not able, even in her sexual relationship, to make him happy enough to prevent the suicide. Laura was aware that her sexual behavior was not really acceptable in society, which led to some feelings of low self-esteem, but she did not exhibit a true sense of guilt about it. This is understandable if we consider the fact that her earliest, most potent superego identifications are with the mother who encouraged the sexual relationship with the father, and with the father who accepted, approved, and appreciated the sexual activity. Laura's recurrent, futile attempts are a distortion of the normal, healthy hope of having a sexual relationship with a true love object. She hopes that through sex she will find love, rather than the reverse. Unfortunately, she became fixated to the sexual father of her childhood to whom she is still unconsciously attached and whom she can never find again. She has also had the recurrent tendency to attach herself to men who are cruel to her, fight with her or even attack her physically, as was true of the father who also loved her. She relives another part of her childhood drama in the sense that she gets her husband to dislike their older child, as she tried to get her father to dislike her brother because her mother favored him. At the same time, she herself favors the younger boy, as mother did her brother.

Specific Sequelae

There are several characteristics commonly present in people who have suffered childhood abuse—either physical or sexual or both. There is a lack of basic trust that develops out of a poor attachment to mother and a sense of little interest or involvement from her. This is usually associated with a tendency for social isolation and difficulty in establishing close human relationships. There is often a long-lasting, pervasive sense of inadequate loving care from an unempathic mother. This produces, as well, low self-esteem and a poor sense of identity, both general identity and specific sexual identity, especially for those who have suffered sexual abuse. Frequently, mothers of sexually abused daughters are described as vague and remote. One young woman aptly stated, "My mother would have been just as effective if she had been stuffed". Another described how her father had taught her all she knows; she could remember nothing her mother had ever taught her—not a single thing.

Especially common in formerly sexually abused persons is a feeling of having been exploited, abandoned, and never listened to. They seem quite aware, either consciously or unconsciously, that they were used to solve parental difficulties rather than cared for in an age-appropriate fashion. Although often very conscious of anger toward the person who sexually abused them, sooner or later, under therapy, they also become aware of an equal or greater anger toward the caretakers who failed to protect them. There is a feeling of being trapped because to talk about these problems or to seek help is forbidden or even dangerous. Even when they report the incest, they are frequently not believed or their story is discounted. This discounting of the child's views and perceptions may be pervasive, leaving the child unable to trust his/her own judgment or feelings in a variety of situations. Self-doubt can be complicated in those situations in which a child's story of incest has been ridiculed when the child discovers later that caretakers had known about the incest and done nothing to protect or help him or her. This may be associated with a long-lasting sense of helplessness and inability to control his/her own life or destiny. At the same time, the child may be used by the parents throughout life in attempts to solve the parents' own difficulties. One woman told us of how, when she was 16, she was used by mother for advice in relation to mother's boyfriends. Another woman describes a poignant scene which occurred when she was eight, of hearing mother and father fighting, and mother calling to her repeatedly for help. She still feels guilty because she did not know what to do and pretended to be sleeping.

Obviously, there are many factors which may be associated with sexual abuse and which are likely to have profound effects on the later lives of the victims. It is difficult to separate the sequelae of the sexual abuse *per se* from the effects of other noxious family situations. There are, however, some behaviors and emotional states in older children and adults which can be more specifically related to the sexual maltreatment of earlier years. Sexual seductions in childhood have been considered of etiological importance for the neuroses of later life since the early work of Freud[6] in 1896. He soon abandoned his first conviction that the seductions had actually occurred and based most of his later work on the concept that the usual fantasies of incest occurring during the Oedipal period had been distorted and elaborated on and could not be trusted as real occurrences. It is only within recent years that the actual frequency of incest and other forms of sexual abuse have been increasingly recognized. It has always been recognized, however, that abuse in infancy and early childhood involved excessive stimulation beyond the ego's capacity to manage and resulted in various psychosexual developmental disorders, including psychosomatic illness, hysterical conversions, and excessive passivity. Lewis and Farrell[11] stressed the pathogenic effect of the ongoing and often mutually sadistic, ambivalent, seductive relationship existing between parent and child.

Most obviously, sexual abuse is likely to distort the development of a normal association of pleasure with sexual activity. In abuse, the biologically normal, pleasurable, shared satisfaction in sexual relationships with peers in adult life is to some degree delayed, altered, inhibited or perverted. In some cases, both male and female, there are complete retreats from sexual activity and an avoidance of all close interpersonal relationships throughout life. Less severe manifestations of the poorly integrated pleasure responses are recognized in women in the form of frigidity, vaginismus, nymphomania, and promiscuity, and in men, in the form of impotence, premature ejaculation, exhibitionism, and compulsive sexual conquests. It must be borne in mind that the symptoms of sexual dysfunction are limited in number, and all cases in which such symptoms are exhibited do not share the same causes. That is, many factors besides sexual abuse can be involved in the development of sexual dysfunction. The same is true in homosexuality and perversion. In some cases, the experience of early seduction or abuse is apparently an important element in the formation of such patterns, but certainly it is not a universal or necessary precursor.

In the classical masochistic pattern of experiencing pain as part of sexual pleasure, the phenomenon is usually understood as the result of intrapsychic conflict and complex interactions of drive and defense. We observe in cases of sexual abuse that later masochistic behavior is not only related to intrapsychic processes but also is often the result of adaptation and fixation to real abusive events and exemplifies the masochism described by Berliner[3] as attachment to a sadistic love object in early life. In the case quoted above, Laura was pleasurably sexually involved with the father who also beat her; this relationship was symbolically repeated with the first boyfriend and in later relationships with men. It is not uncommon to find women who were physically or sexually abused as children repeatedly involved as sexual or marital partners with men who abuse them physically or emotionally. We believe that the same is true of men although it is less commonly described. It is impossible in such cases to disentangle the threads of sexual, physical, and emotional abuse which have been woven into the adult's patterns. One pervasive thread is the inability to find or develop adequate means of getting pleasure in ordinary living.

There are other aspects of pleasure which must be considered. In general, the more the sexual abuse is essentially pleasurable and the less it is abusive, the less deviation there will be from normal development. There is always the danger that, since the stimulation may be greater than the child's ego can manage, this will result in real psychic trauma, which is inversely proportional to the age of the child. In older children, especially adolescents, sexual activity without undue coercion or violence is less likely to be harmful. Sex with age peers or with unrelated adults also seems to be more pleasurable and less damaging, and incest between brother and sister less upsetting than between parent and child, as a general rule.

Brother–sister incest occurring as a "natural progression of early childhood curiosity and exploration" and accomplished in an atmosphere of mutual pleasure and caring can be relatively innocuous. A clear example is given by Bonaparte[4] of a pubescent girl who was seduced by a much-adored, older brother with whom she had coitus for some time. When discovered by the parents, the boy was sent away. The girl never felt she had done wrong; the brother was such an ideal that his approval and permission for the sexual act seemed to outweigh parental disapproval. Bonaparte suggests there may be less stringent incest prohibition in such a situation, and there is a predeliction for the brother who can love as opposed to the Oedipal father whose rejection is never forgiven. The brother can replace the father and direct the girl more effectively to men of her own age. Lukianowicz[12] also noted that brothers and sisters involved in incest did not, as a rule, develop feelings of guilt and later "find it easier to substitute for their siblings new sexual partners from outside the family". In 15 cases of brother–sister incest, two of the boys and one girl became aggressive psychopaths, but 13 of the brothers and 14 of the sisters were essentially normal, that is, "free from gross personality disorders, neurosis or psychosis".

Such is not always the case. Bonaparte[4] described another girl, seduced by a very dominant older brother who enjoyed caressing without coitus. On discovery, the brother was punished and the girl retreated from sexuality. In later life, she had orgasm only with clitoral masturbation, became somewhat promiscuous and, although never actually a prostitute, would often get money from rich lovers to give to her indigent lovers. More serious consequences are described by Sloane and Karpinski[18] in the cases of three girls who had experienced incest with their fathers and two girls with their brothers, all in adolescence. All five girls became somewhat promiscuous and felt quite guilty about their sexual activities even though promiscuity was not unusual or unacceptable in their communities. Such guilt was felt to be related to the breaking of the incest barrier during the adolescent period when the superego was more firmly established. It should be noted, however, that the family background of these girls was distinctly disturbed and chaotic. The following histories are indicative of some of the various difficulties evolving from brother–sister incest:

Anna M.

Anna M. was involved in an incestuous relationship with her brother when she was about 12 or 13 which continued for about two years. She was afraid of her brother then and remains so now, describing him as a very aggressive, provocative man. Both her father and brother referred to her in very derogatory terms, calling her "whore" and "slut". She recalls an incident prior to the incest when, at a public park, her brother urinated on her in front of her peers. She was deeply humiliated by this and felt it was symbolic of her feelings in relation to him. Subsequently, she became pregnant by a man who was physically abusive, and she finally left him. She was somewhat promiscuous for a while, then married a man who was basically kind and supportive to her but had some problems with alcohol.

Following the birth of a daughter, she found herself for a time disinterested in sexual contact with her husband. Some ambivalence about men and insecurity about her own sexual identity is indicated by her definite disapproval of homosexual men. She feels that their lack of response to her threatens her feminine identity.

Betty J.

Betty J., too, was sexually involved with an older brother with whom she has had a significant but ambivalent attachment during the ensuing years. He was physically aggressive to her during their childhood, and she felt their parents excused this by saying, "That's the way he is showing his love". When he approached her sexually, she did not resist but later felt he had violated her trust because he was aware of the consequences of the act (possible pregnancy) and she was not. She is now in her 20's and has not been involved in any significant relationships with men. She seems, on the one hand, to have declared a moratorium on the development of a clear sexual identity. She became very anxious and confused when her closest woman friend began to date her brother. She was angry at both of them and apparently felt deserted. This may well have been a re-enactment of her mother's preoccupation with her brother and Betty's sense of exclusion and lack of interest from her mother.

Betty finds herself very uncomfortable when a male expresses sexual interest in her. She is, however, very comfortable with "gay" men and maintains "pal" relationships with men very comfortably.

Information about the past history of male prostitutes, both adolescent and adult, is meager although previous seduction, usually homosexual, has been noted. There is, on the other hand, considerable data on the relationship between female prostitution and previous sexual abuse. Certainly, only a small proportion of sexually abused girls eventually end up as prostitutes, but viewing the data from the other direction, namely the histories given by prostitutes, one gets a clear-cut picture of the very close association between sexual abuse and later prostitution. Flugel[5] found that 71 out of 103 women arrested by a Chicago vice squad had been introduced to sexuality through incest with their fathers. More recently, James and Meyerding[7] found that 65% of the adolescent prostitute population they studied had been victims of coerced sexual activity, including incest. They also reported that 57% of a sample of 136 adult prostitutes had been raped.

We believe it is a common experience for young boys and girls to run away from home to escape either sexual or physical abuse, going to larger cities where they find it harder to survive and then taking up prostitution to make a living. Such behaviors are not the simple result of sexual abuse alone but usually develop out of the whole spectrum of disordered, chaotic family relationships. Sexual promiscuity and later prostitution are only a part of a developing pattern of delinquency.[21]

Kaufman, *et al.*,[9] reporting on 11 girls who had incest with their fathers, noted that depression, learning difficulties, sexual promiscuity, running away, and somatic complaints could be related to the previous sexual abuse. They felt that the lives of these girls were dominated by a craving for an adequate parent and that the children's experiences of guilt were related more to breaking up of the family than breaking of a social taboo. Rosenfeld, *et al.*[16] concluded that patients with previous experiences of incest presented with symptoms of frigidity, promiscuity, and depression but that the intense sense of guilt in abused children often appeared to be related to the contribution the victim had made to family break-up by revealing the existence of the abuse.

There are some more specific, quite idiosyncratic sexual problems in adult life that can be related to sexual abuse in childhood. For instance, a woman may be unable to have intercourse when there has been any recent conflict or exchange of angry words with her husband. This is related to her having been used to solve parental quarrels or fights by being sent to bed for sex with father. Other women may have a dislike for all foreplay and an impatient urge to get on with genital contact "where the action is" and get it over with. Another may want to prolong foreplay idefinitely in the unconscious hope that intercourse can be avoided. A young woman who generally had great pleasure and was quite comfortable in her sexual relations had a very specific and intensive aversion to being in the superior position because of the intense sense of vulnerability and anxiety it instigated. Once, while attempting intercourse in this position to please her partner, she had a sudden flashback, as if seeing a film strip of herself as a child of about seven, lying on her father's stomach while he rhythmically pulled her back and forth over his genital area. This recall, and some discussion of it later, seemed to mitigate the aversion and anxiety. Another young woman described having an aversion to all sexual activity with her husband, and she expressed the conviction that she would never be comfortable, much less enjoy sexual activity, with anyone because of the incest experience with her father.

It is well recognized that parental physical abuse and neglect of children is closely related to the parent's own experience of having been neglected or abused in his/her early years.[19,20] (See case report of Laura S. in this chapter.) A similar effect is apparent in many cases of sexual abuse of children. We have heard fathers say, "My father slept with all of my sisters, so why should I not have sex with my daughters?" This identification with the parent of the same sex is also suggested in the case of some women whose mothers never interfered with incest with their fathers and who, in later life, do not interfere when incest occurs between their husbands and daughters.

Katan,[8] reporting on the in-depth study of six women who had suffered non-incestuous rape in the early years of childhood, was particularly impressed with the difficulty they had in integrating their libidinal and aggressive drives and how much of their aggression was turned against themselves. Intensely strong, ambivalent feelings toward their parents were never resolved well and a comfortable sense of identity was never established. Adequate, warm affection was missing in their childhoods, and they had a tendency to repeat in various forms some of the traumatic incidents of their childhoods, including "the tendency to expose their own children to the same experience, mostly by not protecting them when they should have been protected". They were "severely hampered in their capability for mothering". Even more serious but similar psychological disturbances in the areas of identification and repetitive behavior were noted by Shengold[17] in two men who had been seduced in early childhood by psychotic mothers.

Anxiety over the tendency toward generational repetition is not uncommon. Several young women who had experienced incest have told us of their deep, recurring concern lest their daughters, either actual or future, might have similar sexual experiences with their fathers. Those who had experienced an incestuous relationship with their fathers are also concerned lest their husbands might repeat such behavior with their daughters.

In a case of father–son incest described by Langsley, *et al.*, [10] the father's experience of being seduced in childhood by adult males was being repeated in relation to his own son. Homosexual incest involving three generations had been reported by Raybin[15] who also noted the silent collusion of the women in the family. In a very thorough study, Raphling[14] documented multiple incestuous relationships existing in a family over three generations. It was indicated that incest was acknowledged by the family members as a basic aspect of their experience, each generation repeating the behavior of the previous one. We knew a step-father who, while his wife was pregnant, had sodomized his 11-year-old step-son. The step-father described this very clearly to us as a re-enactment of a similar experience in his own childhood when, at the same age, he had a sexual relationship with a kindly uncle during the absence of his father while his mother was pregnant. We believe there are less obvious, clear-cut behaviors in some families which bear a relation to sexually exploitive experiences in the parents' early lives. We include such things as an excessive amount of nudity and generally seductive behavior and talk which can lead to some anxiety and confusion in the minds of young children.

Based upon unhappy memories of inadequate and unreliable parental care in their own childhoods, many sexually abused victims are ambivalent about their ability to be good parents and about their own parenting methods. Sometimes they are sure they are doing absolutely the right thing and at other times are just as sure what they are doing is wrong. They are thus hampered in providing consistent "good enough" general parenting for their own children. We have also known several victims who have stated they never dared to become parents and do not want to have children at all lest their children would have similar miserable experiences.

Lewis and Farrell[11] stressed the fact that the effects of sexual abuse are extremely varied and deeply affected by the kind of abuse, the age at which the abuse occurred, and all the other object-relations existing at the time. Inevitably, various studies show different and often contradictory findings. Nakashima and Zakus[13] found only two out of 23 sexually abused adolescent girls who could be considered normal at the time they were evaluated. The others showed behavior problems, school problems, delinquency, and depression.

In 26 cases of father–daughter incest, Lukianowicz[12] found 11 of the girls later became promiscuous as well as generally delinquent, and four of the 11 became prostitutes. All of the 11 came from more severely disturbed homes, and their mothers were often promiscuous. Five of the girls married but were frigid. Only four showed psychiatric symptoms including depression, anxiety, and one suicide attempt. Six girls showed no apparent ill effects. In two cases of aunt–nephew incest, the boys remained sexually normal. In three cases of mother–son incest, one son, after two years of incestuous activity with his mother, left home and married successfully. Of the other two, whose mothers were psychiatrically disturbed, one became schizophrenic and the other was educationally subnormal.

Bender, *et al.*,[1,2] reporting on the original evaluation and later follow-up of children who had been sexually abused, felt that remarkably few long-term ill effects could be related to the original sexual trauma. The children were first seen in latency and, in general, came from quite disturbed, chaotic family backgrounds. In many of the children, sexual activity was understood as compensation for varying degrees of parental deprivation, and the children responded positively to improved environmental influence. Other children with significant intellectual defects, disturbed identity very early in life, and early signs of childhood psychosis did not do well in later years, but this was not considered to be directly related to the sexual abuse.

Yorukoglu and Kemph[23] described a case of prolonged mother–son incest and another case of long-lasting father–daughter incest. In neither case did the victims exhibit serious or permanent psychological impairment. Yorukoglu and Kemph attributed this to the fact that their two subjects had developed healthy ego-functions prior to their incestuous experiences.

An interesting report by Westermeier[22] concerns 32 patients seen in private practice who had been involved in 42 incestuous relationships. Depression, anxiety, hypochondriasis, and various sexual dysfunctions were noted, but it was difficult in many cases to document the role of incest in the psychiatric illnesses since there were many other family problems, poor relationships, and identity conflicts also existing for these patients. Significant behavior problems and personality disorders were present in six cases. But, again, there were other problems besides incest in the background. Several patients showed no apparent residual effects from the incest for many years but upon developing a psychiatric disorder in later life, revived concern over the long-past incestuous experience. The daughters often obtained gratification from the relationships as a means of obtaining affection in families where affection was otherwise scarce. They did not see this as socially taboo behavior, but most of them felt guilt later on in relation to "stealing" father from mother.

Conclusion

The estimation of late effects of sexual abuse is an extremely complex task because of the enormous variety of factors involved, including age, frequency, amount of associated aggression, relationship of participants, total family dynamics and object-relations before and after the act of abuse, sub-cultural customs, and environmental responses. Possibly there are relatively few late effects of abuse if there are not many other detrimental factors involved beyond simple sexual interaction. The experience of sexual abuse seems to gain much of its potential for later damage by being the central core around which all other noxious experiences become organized, thus becoming an obvious system which can carry the weight of all other serious family pathology.

There are also significant differences of opinion among investigators as to what constitutes the long-term effects of sexual abuse. Some seem to consider a person who is married and shows no serious psychotic, neurotic, or character disorder and who is living with average success within the community to have emerged from the sexual abuse unscathed. But the cases noted above indicate how much pain and turmoil can exist beneath an outwardly normal or seemingly well-adjusted appearance.

Human beings have strong sexual drives in different forms and at different stages of their lives, and there is always a potential for these drives to be activated and utilized to express other conflicts and attempts to solve them. Indeed, incest can serve adaptive functions in some disturbed families even though the rest of society considers it maladaptive. The essence of the abusive element in the sexual activity is the misuse of the immature child by the adult for the solving of problems and satisfying of adult needs, while disregarding the appropriate needs and developmental state of the child. The adult instigator takes advantage of the child's own normal sexual responsiveness, his/her wishes to please, and obedience to authority. At the same time, other important caretakers condone the behavior, do not protect the child, and disregard the child's complaints.

The late effects of these situations are seen in the tragic feelings of inferiority, non-integrated identity, poor basic trust, repressed anger, unresolved identifications and fixations, and profound difficulties in establishing and maintaining warm, successful adult human relationships. Variations in the obvious sexual dysfunctions and aberrant sexual behaviors which occur in later life are essentially desperate, maladaptive attempts to compensate for, or somehow adapt to, the distortions created in a developing psyche by the sexual exploitation and emotional disregard suffered. Shame, guilt, and fear of social disapproval make it even more difficult to cope with the underlying feelings of helplessness and fear.

References

1. Bender, L. and Blau, A. (1937) The reaction of children to sexual relations with adults. *Am. J. Orthopsychiatry* **7:** 500.
2. Bender, L. and Gruget, A. E. (1952) A follow-up report on children who had atypical sexual experiences. *Am. J. Orthopsychiatry* **22:** 825.
3. Berliner, B. (1947) On some psychodynamics of masochism. *Psychoanal. Q.* **16:** 459.
4. Bonaparte, M. (1953) *Female Sexuality.* International Univ., New York.
5. Flugel, J. C. (1953) *The Psychoanalytic Study of the Family.* Hogarth, London.
6. Freud, S. (1962) *Heredity and the Aetiology of the Neuroses* (*1896*). Standard Ed. **3:** 152. Hogarth, London.
7. James, J. and Meyerding, J. (1977) Early sexual experience and prostitution. *Am. J. Psychiatry* **134:** 1381.
8. Katan, A. (1973) Children who were raped. *Psychoanal. Study Child.* **28:** 208.
9. Kaufman, I., Peck, A. L. and Taguiri, C. K. (1954) Family constellation and overt incestuous relations between father and daughter. *Am. J. Orthopsychiatry* **24:** 266.
10. Langsley, D. G., Schwartz, M. N. and Fairbairn, R. H. (1968) Father–son incest. *Comp. Psychiatry* **9:** 218.
11. Lewis, M. and Farrell, P. M. (1969) Some psychological aspects of seduction, incest and rape in childhood. *J. Amer. Acad. Child Psychiatry* **8:** 606.
12. Lukianowicz, N. (1972) Incest. *Br. J. Psychiatry* **120:** 301.
13. Nakashima, I. I. and Zakus, G. E. (1977) Incest: review and clinical experience. *Pediatrics* **60:** 696.
14. Raphling, D. L., Carpenter, B. L. and Davis, A. (1967) Incest: a genealogical study. *Arch. Gen. Psychiatry* **16:** 505.
15. Raybin, J. B. (1969) Homosexual incest. *J. Nerv. Ment. Dis.* **148:** 105.
16. Rosenfeld, A. A., Nadelson, C. C., Kreiger, M. and Blackman, J. H. (1977) Incest and sexual abuse of children. *J. Amer. Acad. Child Psychiatry* **16:** 317.
17. Shengold, L. (1963) The parent as sphinx. *J. Am. Psychoanal. Assoc.* **11:** 724.
18. Sloane, P. and Karpinski, E. (1942) Effects of incest on the participants. *Am. J. Orthopsychiatry* **12:** 666.
19. Steele, B. F. and Pollock, C. J. (1968) A psychiatric study of parents who abuse infants and small children. In *The Battered Child.* (Edited by Helfer, R. E. and Kempe, C. H.) University of Chicago, Chicago.
20. Steele, B. F. (1970) Parental abuse of infants and small children. In *Parenthood: Its Psychology and Psychopathology.* (Edited by Anthony, E. and Benedek, T.) Little Brown, Boston.
21. Webb, M. L. (1943) Delinquency in the making. *J. Soc. Hygiene* **29:** 502.
22. Westermeier, J. (1978) Incest in psychiatric practice: a description of patients and incestuous relationships. *J. Clin. Psychiatry* **39:** 643.
23. Yorukoglu, A. and Kemph, J. P. (1966) Children not severely damaged by incest with parent. *J. Amer. Acad. Child Psychiatry* **51:** 111.

Chapter Eighteen

The Effects of Child Sexual Abuse: Methodological Considerations

PATRICIA BEEZLEY MRAZEK AND DAVID A. MRAZEK

As noted in the Introduction to this section on OUTCOME AND PROGNOSIS, there have been many reports of the short- and long-term effects of childhood sexual experiences with an adult. This chapter suggests that the serious methodological problems of most of these investigations makes many of their conclusions of questionable value. Specific problems in research methodology will be discussed, and the general conclusions of the reports will be summarized. Finally, possible directions for future research will be suggested.

Methodological Problems

Definition of Child Sexual Abuse

Many studies have not differentiated between the widely disparate types of child sexual abuse. Clarification of the nature of the sexual abuse requires the following six variables to be considered.

1. *Extent of sexual contact.* For example, intercourse, genital manipulation, and observation of an adult exhibitionist are entirely different experiences for a child.
2. *Age and developmental maturity of the child.* A child's intelligence, social awareness, emotional stability, and prior knowledge and attitudes about sexuality will influence his or her perceptions about the sexual contact.
3. *Degree of relatedness between victim and perpetrator.* The perpetrator may be a stranger, an acquaintance of the child and/or family, a member of the extended family, or a member of the nuclear family unit.
4. *Affective nature of the relationship.* Mutual consent with warmth, bribery, threats of physical harm and rejection, or violence create distinctly different contexts in which the sexual contact occurs.
5. *Age difference between the victim and the perpetrator.* For example, a young child's experience with an adult involves different issues than an adolescent's sexual contact with a perpetrator who is five years older but of legal age.
6. *Length of relationship.* There may have been a single occurrence or a continuation over many years with increasingly involved sexual contact.

Some "clinical research" is more accurately described as a compilation of a number of diverse cases. These cases often are accumulated from a professional practice over many years, with the sole common feature being a childhood sexual experience with an adult. Naturally, these studies combine a wide diversity of situations rather than focusing on a specific type of child sexual abuse. While this strategy does increase the sample size, it contributes to the common notion that child sexual abuse is a single entity.

An example of this approach is Peters'[43] study of the psychological effects of childhood rape. Of 13 women patients he had seen in his private practice over 20 years, two had childhood sexual experiences with a stranger, six with fathers, and five with other people known to the child, including two babysitters. At the time of the abuse, the girls ranged in age from 3 to 14. Some of these assaults were a single occurrence involving the use of force while others progressed from seductive behavior to intercourse over a period of several years. While interesting anecdotal insights can be derived from such unsystematic case reporting, it is not possible to draw general conclusions about psychological effects of specific sexual experiences when the definition of child sexual abuse is so all-encompassing.

Sample

Three different types of samples have been used to study the effects of child sexual abuse: children and their families soon after the abuse, "deviant" populations of adults, and college students. An example of the first is Weinberg's[58] large sample of incest cases. A problem with such studies is that only occasionally is there any long-term follow-up of the cases. Therefore, the conclusions that are drawn from the short-range focus may not hold up over time.

The focus on adult deviant populations, such as prostitutes, drug addicts, psychiatric patients, and prisoners, have used a retrospective interviewing methodology. It is well known that memories of events and feelings are greatly influenced by the intervening years of other experiences. Studies using such samples have shown that large percentages of these individuals were sexually abused in childhood. What is not known from such investigations, of course, is what percentage of all sexually abused children go on to have these particular characterological disorders.

Large groups of college students have been studied through survey questionnaires by Landis[31] and Finkelhor[13] to determine the incidence and nature of child sexual abuse. These samples are biased in terms of intelligence, social class, and personal motivation, and their data is also retrospective in nature. However, because they have found a relatively high incidence of child sexual abuse, they are important contrast groups to the studies on deviant populations. An even more accurate estimate of the incidence of child sexual abuse and the nature of long-term effects could be obtained from a large-scale epidemiological investigation of a total population.[21]

Case Reports

Much of the most frequently quoted information on the effects of child sexual abuse is based on clinical case material. While case reports can provide valuable insights into the complexity and diversity of experiences and generate hypotheses, they do not permit the establishment of general principles. A primary problem with such reports occurs when generalizations are made from single or limited examples without considering the heterogeneity of children's sexual experiences with adults.

Another problem occurs when clinical impressions are quoted out of context. For example, this has been true of Yorukoglu and Kemph's[60] widely referenced report of two adolescents who were not severely damaged by incest with a parent. Even though the authors emphasized the absence of severe sequellae, they added numerous qualifying statements. They discussed the parental roles the children had assumed, the possibility of a regression to or fixation at the "prestructured superego of obedience to parents", and potential problems as spouses and parents these children might have in their own adulthood. These more negative effects which form an important part of the overall diagnostic profile often have been ignored in subsequent reviews of the literature.

Outcome Measures

Few studies have utilized any standardized outcome measures of cognitive or psychological functioning. Rather, unstandardized psychiatric interviews without a systematic format, clinical material from psychotherapy sessions, case histories, and reports from courts, social services, and other agencies have been the primary sources of information. There are a variety of problems associated with using these methods of assessing outcome which affect the validity of associations which subsequently may be established. These problems will be considered together as they are all related to reliability of the collected data.

In establishing the characteristics of a given individual, it is imperative that the research methods which are employed provide accurate information. For example, if the outcome measure is prostitution, one would not be able to rely on the accuracy of a general practitioner's report about his patient as he may be unaware of her activities or reluctant to share what he considers privileged information. Likewise, relying on criminal convictions for prostitution would provide a too limited estimate of the frequency while looking at arrests for prostitution might be marginally more accurate. Self-report of prostitution would be a more direct measure although it would be less accurate if the individual perceived the interviewer to be judgmental. A multiple source approach, including physicians' reports, court records, and interview responses, would be one way to improve the outcome data on prostitution.

As difficult as it is to document an overt behavior, such as prostitution, even more pitfalls occur when internal conflicts or feelings are the primary outcome variables. In these circumstances, self-report by the subject is essential. While some standardized, projective instruments exist, they have rarely been applied in reported case studies of the effects of sexual abuse. Additionally, their interpretation requires subjective judgments, and their use in research is more appropriate if given by one consistent psychologist who is blind both to the hypotheses of the study and to whether the individual being tested is an experimental or control subject.

Personality testing, such as the Minnesota Multiphasic Personality Inventory (MMPI), provides an alternative approach to clarification of individual features. The use of a semi-structured research interview to explore specific emotions, feelings, or attitudes is another more reliable approach for documenting subjective data about psychological functioning. However, neither measure has been used extensively in these studies. Some exceptions have been Weinberg[58] and Gebhard, *et al.*,[17] who used structured interviews, and Cavallin[9] who used the MMPI. Also, Meiselman's[40] 1978 study of 58 incest cases included data from semi-structured interviews and MMPIs. However, the researcher did not see the patients directly. Rather, she had access to the clinic charts which usually included reports on psychological testing, and the interviews were with the various therapists.

Rather than standardized testing or systematic interviewing, the primary means of arriving at assessment of such features as distortions in self-esteem or the presence of sexual conflicts has been to make a global judgment of the individual's functioning after some clinical contact with the subject. The length and nature of the contact is rarely consistent from one individual to the next in a given series, and, of most concern, no control group can be assembled for a systematic comparison.

Criteria For Adjustment

The criteria which researchers have used to assess the psychological effects of child sexual abuse have often lacked specificity and accuracy. Frequently, a global and superficial assessment of an individual's psychological functioning has been made with the implication that this is a long-term consequence. If the victims are without severe psychopathology, such as personality disorder, neurosis or psychosis, the final conclusion has often been that they "lack subsequent disturbance". Other studies have looked at the outward appearances of social and occupational adjustment. For example, being married and having a job have been considered indicators of "no harmful effects". While these are indications of good adjustment, it is clearly naive to equate them with the absence of problems. Other investigators have tried to document more precisely attitudes, feelings, and behaviors, realizing that the effects of sexual abuse may be more subtle in nature. The use of more objective methods to elucidate such parameters of psychological adjustment offers the best opportunity for establishing the long-term effects of child sexual abuse.

Causal Influences of Established Associations

Given that there are major questions related to the validity of the outcome measures often employed in these studies, it is yet a separate question whether the associations between early sexual abuse and later consequences are causally related. This issue has not been addressed adequately in any of the studies. As Steele and Alexander point out in Chapter Seventeen, sexual abuse usually occurs in the presence of multiple problems. Therefore, a cause-and-effect relationship cannot be established unless these additional problems are controlled for. This may become more clear with an example. If one finds that women who have had incestuous relationships with their fathers are more likely to experience intense doubts about their self-worth, there is a temptation to conclude that the sexual abuse is responsible. However, if a second finding is that these women have been rejected by their mothers, it raises the question of whether maternal rejection alone would be sufficient to result in the degree of distortion of self-esteem which was found. One approach to answering this question would be to compare the self-perceptions of women who had experienced maternal rejection with those who had experienced maternal rejection as well as sexual abuse.

A variety of possibilities exist for explaining the associations which have been found between early sexual abuse and later outcome. The first is that the associations are indeed causal ones, even when other problems are controlled for. The second is that an additive effect is occurring, that is, sexual abuse must occur in tandem with other early stresses to result in long-term effects. A third possibility is that another factor, such as extremely inconsistent mothering, may quite independently result in both sexual abuse and long-term problems. Again, controlled studies employing multivariate analyses would provide a means of determining which of these possibilities are most likely.

Control and Contrast Groups

As already discussed, a control or contrast group is particularly helpful in assessing the validity of any outcome measures. However, most of the studies on the short- and long-term effects of child sexual abuse have been uncontrolled. The major exceptions are the Burton[8] study, which will be discussed in greater detail, and the studies by Gebhard, *et al.*[17] and Meiselman.[40]

A Case Study of Methodological Problems

Using Burton's[8] widely quoted study of sexually abused children as an example, the importance of many of the methodological research problems which have been raised become clearer. It must be acknowledged that Lindy Burton pioneered into a relatively new area in 1968 when she included sexual abuse as one of three problems of childhood in her book *Vulnerable Children.* Prior to her study, there had been very few attempts to systematically assess the short-term effects of sexual assault in childhood. Her study is used as an example, not because it is one of the poorer investigations, but rather because she attempted to consider many methodological issues.

Burton studied 41 children who had been sexually assaulted. The sample was obtained via the police department, and 36 of these children later gave testimony resulting in court proceedings against their attackers. Burton acknowledges that the subject children therefore formed a specially selected group of sexually assaulted children, as the majority of such children do not take part in court proceedings. The control children were chosen from the subjects' class at school and the following factors were controlled for: intelligence, class attainment, age, sex, religion, ordinal position in the family, same number of brothers and sisters, and socioeconomic status. Each subject child was allotted four controls. The past history of the sexually assaulted children was never at any time discussed with either the children or with their teachers. Only two of the perpetrators were immediate family members, while fifteen were neighbors or friends, seventeen were persons known to the child but unknown to the child's family, and eight were complete strangers. The majority of the perpetrators were under 20 years of age but ranged to over 70 years. Most of the assaults were either indecent assault or sexual fondling of the child, but some were rape or attempted rape, "instruction in masturbation", undressing of the child, and homosexual assaults. In at least six cases, the assault occurred more than once. At the time of the first testing, the children ranged in age from 6 years to 14 years and over, with most of the children being more than 10 years old. The amount of time that had elapsed since the assault ranged from less than one year to more than seven years.

Burton formulated specific hypotheses which she then proceeded to test. The outcome measures were the Bristol Social Adjustment Guide which was filled in by class teachers and 12 Thematic Apperception Test (TAT) pictures which were given and analyzed by Burton. These same tests were repeated exactly one year later to highlight any changes in development over that period of time and because Burton felt that conclusions based on consistencies of behavior or underlying personality needs observed in two testings would be more accurate than any similar conclusions based on only one testing.

From the data that Burton obtained, she concluded:

> "Sexual assault of children by adults does not have particularly detrimental effects on the child's subsequent personality development... Except for the significant difference to be observed in affection seeking behavior, as a group sexually assaulted children did not differ in degree or type of unsettledness from a carefully matched control group, when tested on average three years after the assault".[8]

These results have been widely quoted, and yet a more careful look at the study itself makes these conclusions doubtful. First of all, the sample was biased as Burton acknowledges, but a more serious problem was that it included an extremely diverse population, that is, the children were of different ages, were assaulted by abusers with whom they had varying degrees of relatedness, and had experienced quite different types of sexual experience.

The outcome measures are also questionable. The TAT results might have been more valid if they had been given by an examiner who was unaware of the nature of the study and the identity of abused and control children rather than by Burton. Also, projective testing (TAT) and reports on school behavior and performance (Bristol Social Adjustment Guide) tap only circumscribed areas of a child's total functioning. For example, significant sleep disorders, fearfulness of adult men, or excessive masturbation might not be known to either the teacher or to Burton.

Although tremendous effort was made to gather controls (there were four controls for each child), and the test-retest design is methodologically sound, the same positive correlations were not found during the retest situation. This is a most important finding and one that is almost always overlooked when the study is quoted. While Burton does note this, she minimizes the difference between a statistical significance and her own impression of the differences between the groups.

> "Hypothesis 1 had predicted that a statistically significant difference would be found in the affection seeking behavior displayed by the two groups of children. This prediction was not substantiated. No statistical differences were found for any of the sixteen items. However, a non-statistical comparison of the two entire groups suggested that, as in the first testing, the greatest difference between groups lay in the affection seeking syndrome. Whilst no longer statistically significant, affection seeking remained a prominant feature in the response repertoire of the subject child."[8]

Finally, there is the suggestion throughout the study that Burton believed that sexually assaulted children were more affection seeking and that this behavior contributed to their assault in the first place. One cannot ignore the possibility that the study was biased by the researcher's conviction in the truth of the hypotheses. Thus, even in this study which is in some ways quite rigorous, there are serious methodological difficulties which make the conclusions questionable.

Summarized Conclusions from Various Studies

Given the serious problems of most of the case reports and research studies, the conclusions which have been derived must be considered very tentatively. However, they do highlight issues which should be addressed more rigorously. Table 1 lists the possible short-term effects of child sexual abuse, that is, those effects occurring in later childhood or adolescence. Table 2 lists the potential long-term effects occurring in adulthood. Both tables are compilations of the effects reported in 50 years of literature on sexual abuse in childhood.

Future Directions of Research

The directions of future research will be dictated by the interests of the investigators and by the willingness of private and governmental agencies to support the work. While any type of research, if carefully designed and implemented, could be valuable, there are particular methodologies which could lead to important conclusions related to the incidence and nature of sexual abuse. Systematic studies of adult clinical populations who have experienced child sexual abuse and studies of children just following a sexual assault could yield more valid results than what has been done up to the current time. Of still greater value would be to prospectively follow this group of recently identified sexually abused children in parallel with a control group. Their adjustment to various developmental and environmental situations over the years could then be assessed. Additionally, an epidemiological study similar to the one by Straus, Gelles, and Steinmetz[54,55] on family violence, would provide less biased conclusions. A large community sample which was randomly selected and included both questionnaires and standardized interviews could yield data on the incidence and nature of childhood sexual experiences and might also identify a group of adults who had been molested as children but were functioning quite adequately in adulthood.

For the most part, the studies of short- and long-term effects have focused on the child victim. Studies of perpetrators, such as the report by Gibbens, *et al.*,[19] and especially of families, using family outcome measures, could yield more complete data.

Identification of children who are at high risk for sexual abuse is a more recent area of investigation. Tormes[56] made some of the first suggestions regarding early identification, based on a study of incestuous families. More recently, Finkelhor[14] has identified eight vulnerability factors in this regard from his survey of 795 college students. Even though he cautions against the notion that there ever will be screening tests for the prediction of sexual abuse, he emphasizes that such a checklist can be helpful in sensitizing professionals about the kinds of backgrounds which put a child at risk for sexual victimization.

Table 1
*A Review of Possible Short-Term Effects in Childhood and Adolescence**

Problems in sexual adjustment:
Preoccupation with sexual matters (Moses, 1932; Bender and Blau, 1937)
Increased masturbatory activity (Isaacs, 1933)
Sudden rush into heterosexual activities (Moses, 1932)
In prepuberty stage, premature and discrepant development of adolescent interests and independence (Bender and Blau, 1937)
Despair regarding the inability to control sexual urges (Bender and Blau, 1937)
Venereal disease (Branch and Paxton, 1965)
Pregnancy (Mehta *et al.*, 1979)
Impaired feminine identification (Heims and Kaufman, 1963)
Acting out sexual delinquency, seemingly purposeless and not enjoyed (Rabinovitch, 1952; Kaufman *et al.*, 1954)
Promiscuity (Sloane and Karpinski, 1942; Maisch, 1972; Lukianowicz, 1972)
Homosexuality (Kaufman *et al.*, 1954; Heims and Kaufman, 1963; Meiselman, 1978)
Prostitution (James and Meyerding, 1977)
Molestation of younger children (Meiselman, 1978)
Interpersonal problems:
Bewilderment concerning social relations (Bender and Blau, 1937)
Frightened by contacts with adults (Kinsey *et al.*, 1953; Peters, 1976)
Hostile, dependent interactions with older women (Kaufman *et al.*, 1954)
Shocked by parental reaction to discovery of the assault (Landis, 1956)
Increased affection seeking from adults (Burton, 1968)
Running away from home (Kaufman *et al.*, 1954; Browning and Boatman, 1977)
Homicidal ideation (Dixon *et al.*, 1978)
Education problems:
Learning difficulties (Kaufman *et al.*, 1954; Rosenfeld *et al.*, 1977)
Mental retardation (Bender and Blau, 1937)
Truancy (Peters, 1976)
Other psychological symptoms:
Loss of self-esteem (DeFrancis, 1965)
Personal guilt or shame (DeFrancis, 1965; Rosenfeld *et al.*, 1977)
Nervous symptoms, such as nail biting (Burton, 1968)
Pessimistic or callous attitude (Bender and Blau, 1937)
Obesity (Meiselman, 1978)
Facade of maturity and capacity for responsibility (Kaufman *et al.*, 1954)
"Infantile stage" is prolonged or reverted to (Bender and Blau, 1937)
Anxiety states and acute anxiety neuroses (Bender and Blau, 1937; Meiselman, 1978)
Somatic symptoms (Lewis and Sarrell, 1969; Maisch, 1972; Dixon *et al.*, 1978)
Sleep problems including nightmares (Peters, 1976)
Impulsive, self-damaging behavior (Dixon *et al.*, 1978)
Other behavior problems and delinquency (Maisch, 1972; Nakashima and Zakus, 1977)
Tendency to withdraw from activities of normal childhood (Bender and Blau, 1937)
Depression (Ferenczi, 1932; Kaufman *et al.*, 1954; Nakashima and Zakus, 1977)
Suicidal ideation (Forbes, 1972; Maisch, 1972; Mehta *et al.*, 1979)
Character disorder (Maisch, 1972)
Studies finding no ill effects:
None again needed correction or attention because of sex activities (Bender and Grugett, 1952)
No particular detrimental effects (Burton, 1968)
Lack of subsequent disturbance (Gibbens and Prince, 1963; Lempp, 1979)
Not severely damaged (Yorukoglu and Kemph, 1966)
Well adjusted (Rasmussen, 1934)
Contributed favorably to psychosexual development (Kinsey *et al.*, 1953)

* The descriptions have been taken directly from the sources. Conclusions may apply to only a portion of the sample. In some instances, when a finding has been suggested by multiple authors, only a representative study has been included.

Table 2
*A Review of Possible Long-Term Effects in Adulthood**

Problems in sexual adjustment:
- Aversion to sexual activity (Greenland, 1958; Magal and Winnik, 1968)
- Unsatisfactory sexual relationships (Rosenfeld *et al.*, 1977)
- Sexual dysfunctions, including frigidity (Lukianowicz, 1972)
- Conceiving illegitimate children (Malmquist *et al.*, 1966)
- Promiscuity (Sloane and Karpinski, 1942; Lukianowicz, 1972)
- Homosexuality (Medlicott, 1967; Gundlach, 1977)
- Prostitution (Flugel, 1953; James and Meyerding, 1977)
- Having other incestuous relationships (Raybin, 1969)
- Not protecting one's own children from sexual abuse (Katan, 1973)
- Sexual molestation of child (Raphling, 1967; Reichenthal, 1979)
- Impulses to brutally sexually assault a child (Armstrong, 1978)

Interpersonal problems:
- Conflict with or fear of husband or sex partner (Meiselman, 1978)
- Conflict with parents or in-laws (Vestergaard, 1960; Herman and Hirschman, 1977)
- Social isolation and difficulty in establishing close human relationships (Steele and Alexander, Chap. 16)

Other psychological symptoms:
- Low self-esteem and long-lasting sense of helplessness (Steele and Alexander, Chap. 16)
- Somatic symptoms (Goodwin, 1979; Meiselman, 1978)
- Obesity (Meiselman, 1978)
- Chronic depression (Weiner, 1964; Rosenfeld *et al.*, 1977)
- Masochism (Meiselman, 1978)
- Neurosis (Meiselman, 1978)
- Non-integrated identity (Katan, 1973)
- Character disorder (Lewis and Sarrell, 1969; Lukianowicz, 1972)
- Psychosis/schizophrenia (Barry, 1965; Peters, 1976)
- Suicidal ideation (Rhinehart, 1961)
- Murder (Brown, 1963)

Studies finding no ill effects:
- Essentially normal, free from gross personality disorders, neurosis, or psychosis (Lukianowicz, 1972)
- No sexual problems (Lukianowicz, 1972; Meiselman, 1978)
- May diminish the chances of psychosis in a person who formerly has been in a grave state of melancholy (Rascovsky and Rascovsky, 1950)

* The descriptions have been taken directly from the sources. Conclusions may apply to only a portion of the sample. In some instances, when a finding has been suggested by multiple authors, only a representative study has been included.

Conclusion

Clinicians cannot wait to intervene in child sexual abuse cases until all the evidence on prognosis is in. However, in the long run, their work will be affected by the quality of the research which is done. To assure the validity of future findings the methodological issues of definition, sample, outcome measures, criteria for adjustment, and controls must be more carefully addressed than they have been in the past.

References

1. Armstrong, L. (1978) *Kiss Daddy Goodnight: A Speak-out on Incest*. Hawthorn, New York.
2. Barry, M. J. (1965) Incest. In *Sexual Behavior and the Law*. (Edited by Slovenko, R.) Thomas, Springfield, Ill.
3. Bender, L. and Blau, A. (1937) The reaction of children to sexual relations with adults. *Am. J. Orthopsychiatry* **7:** 500.
4. Bender, L. and Grugett, A. E. (1952) A follow-up report on children who had atypical sexual experience. *Am. J. Orthopsychiatry* **22:** 825.
5. Branch, G. and Paxton, R. (1965) A study of gynococcal infections among infants and children. *Public Health Reports* **80:** 347.
6. Brown, W. (1963) Murder rooted in incest. In *Patterns of Incest*. (Edited by Masters, R. E. L.) Julian, New York.
7. Browning, D. H. and Boatman, B. (1977) Incest: children at risk. *Am. J. Psychiatry* **134:** 69.
8. Burton, L. (1968) *Vulnerable Children*. Routledge & Kegan Paul, London.
9. Cavallin, H. (1966) Incestuous fathers: a clinical report. *Am. J. Psychiatry* **122:** 1132.
10. DeFrancis, V. (1965) *Protecting the Child Victims of Sex Crimes*. American Humane Assoc., Children's Division, Denver, Colorado.
11. Dixon, K. N., Arnold, L. E. and Calestro, K. (1978) Father–son incest: under-reported psychiatric problem? *Am. J. Psychiatry* **135:** 835.
12. Ferenczi, S. (1949) Confusion of tongues between adult and child. *Int. J. Psychoanal.* **30:** 225.
13. Finkelhor, D. (1979) *Sexually Victimized Children*. Free Press, New York.
14. Finkelhor, D. (1980) Risk factors in the sexual victimization of children. *Child Abuse and Neglect*. **4:** 265.
15. Flugel, J. C. (1953) *The Psychoanalytic Study of the Family*. Hogarth, London.
16. Forbes, L. M. (1972) Incest, anger, and suicide. In *Adolescents Grow in Groups: Clinical Experiences in Adolescent Group Psychotherapy*. (Edited by Berkovitz, I. H.) Brunner–Mazel, New York.
17. Gebhard, P. H., Gagnon, J. H., Pomeroy, W. B. and Christenson, C. V. (1965) *Sex Offenders: An Analysis of Types*. Harper & Row, New York.
18. Gibbens, T. C. N. and Prince, J. (1963) *Child Victims of Sex Offences*. Institute for the Study and Treatment of Delinquency, London.
19. Gibbens, T. C. N., Soothill, K. L. and Way, C. K. (1978) Sibling and parent–child incest offenders: a long-term follow-up. *Br. J. Criminology, Delinquent and Deviant Soc. Behav.* **18:** 40.
20. Goodwin, J. and DiVasto, P. (1979) Mother–daughter incest. *Child Abuse and Neglect* **3:** 953.
21. Graham, P. (1977) *Epidemiological Approaches in Child Psychiatry*. Academic Press, London.
22. Greenland, C. (1958) Incest. *Br. J. Delinquency* **9:** 62.
23. Gundlach, R. H. (1977) Sexual molestation and rape reported by homosexual and heterosexual women. *J. Homosex.* **2:** 367.
24. Heims, L. W. and Kaufman, I. (1963) Variations on a theme of incest. *Am. J. Orthopsychiatry* **33:** 311.
25. Herman, J. and Hirschman, L. (1977) Incest between fathers and daughters. *The Sciences* Oct: 4.
26. Isaacs, S. (1933) *Social Development of Young Children*. Routledge, London.
27. James, J. and Meyerding, J. (1977) Early sexual experience and prostitution. *Am. J. Psychiatry* **134:** 1381.
28. Katan, A. (1973) Children who were raped. *Psychoanal. Study Child.* **28:** 208.
29. Kaufman, I., Peck, A. L. and Tagiuri, C. K. (1954) The family constellation and overt incestuous relations between father and daughter. *Am. J. Orthopsychiatry* **24:** 266.
30. Kinsey, A. C., Pomeroy, W. B., Martin, C. E. and Gebhard, P. H. (1953) *Sexual Behavior in the Human Female*. Saunders, Philadelphia.
31. Landis, J. T. (1956) Experiences of 500 children with adult sexual deviation. *Psychiat. Q. Suppl.* **30:** 91.

32. Lempp, R. (1969) Psychological damage to children as a result of sexual offences. *Child Abuse and Neglect* **2:** 243.
33. Lewis, M. and Sarrell, P. M. (1969) Some psychological aspects of seduction, incest and rape in childhood. *J. Amer. Acad. Child Psychiatry* **8:** 606.
34. Lukianowicz, N. (1972) Incest: I. paternal incest; II. other types of incest. *Br. J. Psychiatry* **120:** 301.
35. Maisch, H. (1972) *Incest.* Stein and Day, New York.
36. Magal, V. and Winnik, H. Z. (1968) Role of incest in family structure. *Isr. Ann. Psychiatry* **6:** 173.
37. Malmquist, C. P., Kiresuk, T. J. and Spano, R. M. (1966) Personality characteristics of women with repeated illegitimacies: descriptive aspects. *Am. J. Orthopsychiatry* **36:** 476.
38. Medlicott, R. W. (1967) Parent–child incest. *Aust. NZ J. Psychiatry* **1:** 180.
39. Mehta, M. N., Lokeshwar, M. R., Bhatt, S. C., Athavale, V. B. and Kalkarni, B. S. (1979) "Rape" in children. *Child Abuse and Neglect* **3:** 671.
40. Meiselman, K. C. (1978) *Incest: A Psychological Study of Causes and Effects with Treatment Recommendations.* Jossey–Bass, San Francisco.
41. Moses, J. (1932) Psychische Auswinkurgen sexueller Angriffe bei jungen Mädchen, *Z. sch f Kinderforsch,* 40.
42. Nakashima, I. I. and Zakus, C. E. (1977) Incest: review and clinical experience. *Pediatrics* **60:** 5.
43. Peters, J. (1974) The psychological effects of childhood rape. *World J. Psychosynth.* **6:** 11.
44. Peters, J. (1976) Children who are victims of sexual assault and the psychology of offenders. *Am. J. Psychother.* **30:** 398.
45. Rabinovitch, R. D. (1953) Etiological factors in disturbed sexual behavior of children. *J. Crim. Law and Crimin.* 43.
46. Raphling, D. L., Carpenter, B. L. and Davis, A. (1967) Incest: a genealogical study. *Arch. Gen. Psychiatry* **16:** 505.
47. Rasmussen, A. (1934) Die bedeutung sexueller attentate auf kinder unter 14 jahren fur die entwicklung von geisteskrankheiten und charakteranomalien. *Acta Psychiat. et Neurol.* **9:** 351.
48. Rascovsky, M. W. and Rascovsky, A. (1950) On consummated incest. *Int. J. Psychoanal.* **31:** 42.
49. Raybin, J. B. (1969) Homosexual incest. *J. Nerv. Ment. Dis.* **148:** 105.
50. Reichenthal, J. A. (1979) Letter to editor: correcting the underreporting of father–son incest. *Am. J. Psychiatry* **136:** 1.
51. Rhinehart, J. W. (1961) Genesis of overt incest. *Comp. Psychiatry* **2:** 338.
52. Rosenfeld, A. A., Nadelson, C. C. and Kreiger, M. (1979) Fantasy and reality in patients' reports of incest. *J. Clin. Psychiatry* **40:** 159.
53. Sloane, P. and Karpinski, E. (1942) Effects of incest on the participants. *Am. J. Orthopsychiatry* **12:** 666.
54. Straus, M. A., Gelles, R. J. and Steinmetz, S. K. (1979) *Violence in the American Family.* Doubleday/Anchor, New York.
55. Straus, M. A. (1979) Family patterns and child abuse in a nationally representative sample. *Child Abuse and Neglect* **3:** 213.
56. Tormes, Y. M. (No year given) *Child Victims of Incest.* American Humane Assoc., Children's Division, Denver, Colorado.
57. Vestergaard, E. (1960) Fader–datter incest. *Nord Tidshift Kriminalvid.* **48:** 159.
58. Weinberg, S. K. (1955) *Incest Behavior.* Citadel, New York.
59. Weiner, I. B. (1964) On incest: a survey. *Excerpta Criminology* **4:** 137.
60. Yorukoglu, A. and Kemph, J. P. (1966) Children not severely damaged by incest with a parent. *J. Amer. Acad. Child Psychiatry* **5:** 111.

References with Selected Annotation

PATRICIA BEEZLEY MRAZEK

Definition and Recognition

1. Anderson, D. (1979) Touching: when is it caring and nurturing or when is it exploitative and damaging? *Child Abuse and Neglect* **3**:3/4, 793–794. Brief suggestions on how to talk with a child about the sexual abuse he/she may have experienced.
2. Bagley, C. (1969) Incest behavior and incest taboo. *Soc. Problems* **16:** 505–519.
3. Blumberg, M. L. (1978) Child sexual abuse. *New York State J. Med.* **28:** 612–616.
4. Bullough, V. L. (1976) *Sexual Variance in Society and History.* Wiley, New York.
5. Cory, D. W. and Masters, R. E. L. (1963) *Violation of Taboo.* Julian Press, New York.
6. Davenport, W. H. (1977) Sex in cross-cultural perspective. In *Human Sexuality in Four Perspectives.* (Edited by Beach, F. A.) Johns Hopkins Univ., Boston.
7. deMause, L. (Ed.) (1974) *The History of Childhood: The Evolution of Parent–Child Relationships as a Factor in History.* Souvenir Press, London. "Psychogenic" theory of history, hypothesizing a general improvement in child care over time.
8. Devereux, G. (1939) The social and cultural implications of incest among the Mohave Indians. *Psychoanal Q.* **8:** 510–533. Hypothesizes that incest is committed mainly by those persons who are outside the mainstream of Mohave social life.
9. Dixon, K. N., Arnold, L. E. and Calestro, K. (1978) Father–son incest: underreported psychiatric problem? *Am. J. Psychiatry* **135**:4, 835–838. Six families are described in which ten sons were involved incestuously with a natural father. These cases represented 0.4% of the authors' male child psychiatry patients.
10. Dubreuil, G. (1962) Les bases psycho-culturelles due tabou de l'inceste. *Can. Psychiatry Assoc. J.* **7**:5, 218–234. Examination of theories on the prohibitions against incest.
11. Editorial (1977) Incest taboo held related to patriarchal society. *Psychiat. News* **XII:** 19.
12. Finch, S. M. (1967) Sexual activity of children with other children and adults. *Clin. Pediatr.* **6:** 1–2. Brief commentary, recommending court involvement.
13. Finkelhor, D. (1979) *Sexually Victimized Children.* Free Press, New York. Questionnaire survey of 796 college students inquiring about their childhood sexual abuse experiences. 19.2% of the women and 8.6% of the men had been sexually victimized as children.
14. Ford, C. S. and Beach, F. A. (1951) *Patterns of Sexual Behavior.* Harper & Row, New York.
15. Fox, J. R. (1962) Sibling incest. *Br. J. Sociol.* **13:** 128–150. Cross-cultural review. Author hypothesizes that the intensity of heterosexual attention between co-socialized children after puberty is inversely proportionate to the intensity of heterosexual activity between them before puberty.
16. Freud, S. (1913) *Totem and Taboo.* In *Standard Edition of Complete Psychological Works* **13:** 1–164. Hogarth, London, 1955.
17. Gagnon, J. (1965) Female child victims of sex offenses. *Soc. Problems* **13**:2, 176–192.
18. Gagnon, J. H. and Simon, W. (1970) *Sexual Encounters Between Adults and Children*, SIECUS Study Guide No. 11, Sex Information and Education Council of the U.S. Written as a study guide, especially suitable for parents. Focuses on sexual abuse perpetrated by strangers or acquaintances, not immediate family members.
19. Gagnon, J. H. and Simon, W. (1973) *Sexual Conduct: The Social Sources of Human Sexuality.* Aldine, Chicago. Excellent reference. Authors trace the ways in which sexuality is learned, that is, through complex social scripts.
20. Henderson, D. J. (1975) Incest. In *Comprehensive Textbook of Psychiatry.* Vol. 2 (2nd Ed.) (Edited by Freedman, A. M., Kaplan, H. I. and Sadock, B. J.) Williams & Wilkins, Baltimore, Md.
21. Henriques, B. (1961) Sexual assault on children. *Br. Med. J.* **2:** 1629.
22. Hutch, R. A. (1975) Emerson and incest. *Psychoanal. Rev.* **62:** 320–322.

23. Jaffe, A. C., Dynneson, L. and ten Bensel, R. W. (1975) Sexual abuse of children: an epidemiologic study. *Am. J. Dis. Child.* **129:** 689–692. A study of 291 cases of sexual offenses against children which were reported to the Minneapolis Police Department in 1970. None were incest cases.
24. Kinsey, A. C., Pomeroy, W. B. and Martin, C. G. (1948) *Sexual Behavior in the Human Male.* Saunders, Philadelphia.
25. Kinsey, A. C., Pomeroy, W. B., Martin, C. E. and Gebhard, P. H. (1953) *Sexual Behavior in the Human Female.* Saunders, Philadelphia.
26. Kosovich, D. R. (1978) Sexuality throughout the centuries. *Psychiatr. Opinion* **15**:1, 15–19. Brief review of wide range of sexual practices.
27. Kubo, S. (1959) Researches and studies on incest in Japan. *Hiroshima J. Med. Sci.* **8:** 99–159.
28. Landis, J. T. (1956) Experiences of 500 children with adult sexual deviation. *Psychiat. Q. Suppl.* **30:** 91–109. Questionnaire survey of 1,800 university students, yielding important data on the incidence of early experiences with adult sexual deviates and on the short- and long-term effects of such experiences.
29. Malinowski, B. (1929) *The Sexual Life of Savages in Northwestern Melanesia.* Eugenira, New York. Girls begin sexual intercourse at 6–8 years, boys at 10–12 years. Discussion of severity of laws on incest.
30. Mead, M. (1968) Incest. *International Encyclopedia of Social Sciences.* **7:** 115–122. MacMillan and Free Press, New York. Excellent overview of the definition, function, and approaches to the study of incest.
31. Medlicott, R. W. (1967) Lot and his daughters: parent–child incest in the Bible and mythology. *Aust. NZ J. Psychiatry* **1:** 134–139.
32. Mehta, M. N., Lokeshwar, M. R., Bhatt, S. S., Athavale, V. B. and Kulkarni, B. S. (1979) "Rape" in children. *Child Abuse and Neglect* **3**:3/4, 671–677. Study of 130 girls between the ages of 6 months and 18 years who had been raped; the majority resided in the slums of Bombay, India.
33. Middleton, R. (1962) Brother–sister and father–daughter marriage in ancient Egypt. *Amer. Sociol. Rev.* **27:** 603–611. Such unions not as rare as usually supposed.
34. Morgan, R. and Steinem, G. (1980) The international crime of genital mutilation. *Ms.* VIII:**9:** 65–67 and 98–100. Description of various ritual sexual mutilations of young girls occurring throughout the world.
35. Mrazek, P. B. (1980) Annotation: sexual abuse of children. *J. Child Psychol. Psychiatry* **21**:1, 91–95. Brief, general reference.
36. Murdock, G. P. (1949) *Social Structure.* MacMillan, New York.
37. Parsons, T. (1954) The incest taboo in relation to social structure and the socialization of the child. *Br. J. Sociol.* **5:** 101–117.
38. Radzinowicz, L. (1957) *Sexual Offenses*, MacMillan, London.
39. Ramey, J. W. (1979) Dealing with the last taboo. *SIECUS Report* **VII**:5, 1–2 and 6–7. Raises many questions regarding definition, incidence, and effects and makes plea for more research.
40. Rank, O. (1975) *The Don Juan Legend*, Princeton Univ. Press, Princeton, New Jersey.
41. Reichenthal, J. A. (1979) Letter to editor: correcting the underreporting of father–son incest. *Am. J. Psychiatry* **136**:1.
42. Riemer, S. (1940) A research note on incest. *Am. J. Sociol.* **45:** 566–575.
43. Rohleder, H. (1917) Incest in modern civilization. *Am. J. Urol. Sexology* **13:** 406–411.
44. Rutter, M. (1971) Normal psychosexual development. *J. Child Psychol. Psychiatry* **11:** 259–283. Excellent review of the course and process of normal sexual development. Areas covered include physical maturation, sexual activity and interests, sex "drive", psychosexual competence and maturity, gender role preference, sex role standards, and psychosexual stages.
45. Santiago, L. P. (1973) *The Children of Oedipus: Brother–Sister Incest in Psychiatric Literature, History, and Mythology.* Libra, Roslyn Heights, New York.
46. Schachter, M. and Cotte, S. (1960) Etude médico-psychologique et social de l'inceste, dans la perspective pédo-psychiatrique. *Acta Paedopsychiatr.* **27:** 139–146.
47. Schechter, M. D. and Roberge, L. (1976) Sexual exploitation. In *Child Abuse and Neglect: the Family and the Community* (Edited by Helfer, R. E. and Kempe, C. H.) Ballinger, Cambridge, Mass.
48. Schechner, R. (1971–2) Incest and culture: a reflection on Claude Levi-Strauss. *Psychoanal. Rev.* **58**:4, 563–572.
49. Schroeder, T. (1915) Incest in Mormonism. *Am. J. Urol. Sexology* **11:** 409–416.
50. Schwartzman, J. (1974) The individual, incest and exogamy. *Psychiatry* **37:** 171–180. Examination of the theory that those groups observing the incest taboo and exogamy have a selective advantage by producing more adaptive individuals than would be the case without such practices.
51. Seymour-Smith, M. (1975) *Sex and Society.* Hodder and Stoughton, London. Includes material on social attitudes about incest and the origin of the incest taboo.
52. Sgroi, S. M. (1975) Sexual molestation of children: the last frontier in child abuse. *Children Today* May–June, 19–21 and 44. Discussion of the obstacles to identification of the sexually abused child: lack of recognition of the phenomenon, failure to obtain adequate medical corroboration of the event, and reluctance to report.
53. Special Report (1978) *Child sexual abuse: incest, assault, and sexual exploitation.* National Center on Child Abuse and Neglect, U.S. DHEW Pub. No. (OHDS) 79-30166.

54. Slater, M. K. (1959) Ecological factors in the origin of incest. *Am. Anthropol.* **61:** 1042–1059.
55. Summit, R. and Kryso, J. (1978) Sexual abuse of children: a clinical spectrum. *Am. J. Orthopsychiatry* **48:** 237–251. Useful classification of a broad spectrum of parent–child sexuality, including a progression of categories of sexual involvement from variations of normal behavior to intrusive to patently abusive relationships.
56. Vestergaard, E. (1960) Fader–datter incest. *Nord Tidshift Kriminalvid.* **48:** 159–188.
57. Wells, H. M. (1976) *The Sensuous Child: Your Child's Birthright to Healthy Sexual Development.* Scarborough/Stein & Day, New York. Written as a guideline for parents; many sensitive subjects are discussed. The author's own values are fairly explicit.
58. White, L. A. (1948) The definition and prohibition of incest. *Am. Anthropol.* **50:** 416–435.

Sexual Abuse and the Law

1. Cabinis, D. and Phillip, E. (1969) The paedophile homosexual incest in court. *Dtsch. Z. Gesamte Gerichtl. Med.* **66:**46.
2. Burgess, A. W. and Holstrom, L. L. (1978) The child and family during the court process. In *Sexual Assault of Children and Adolescents.* (Edited by Burgess, A. W., Groth, A. N., Holstrom, L. L. and Sgroi, S. M.) Lexington, Lexington, Mass.
3. Densen-Gerber, J. and Hutchinson, S. F. (1979) Sexual and commercial exploitation of children: legislative responses and treatment changes. *Child Abuse and Neglect* **3:**1, 61–66.
4. Densen-Gerber, J. and Hutchinson, S. F. (1978) Medical-legal and societal problems involving children: child prostitution, child pornography and drug-related abuse; recommended legislation. In *The Maltreatment of Children* (Edited by Smith, S. M.) MTP, Lancaster.
5. Farn, K. T. (1975) Sexual and other assaults on children. *Police Surgeon* **8:** 37–58. History of English laws on incest, unlawful sexual intercourse, buggery, and indecent assault. Description of what a medical examination of a sexually assaulted child should include.
6. Fraser, B. G. (1978) A glance at the past, a gaze at the present, a glimpse at the future: a critical analysis of the development of child abuse reporting statutes. *Chicago-Kent Law Rev.* **54:**3, 641–686.
7. Gibbens, T. C. N. and Prince, J. (1963) *Child Victims of Sex Offenses.* Institute for the Study and Treatment of Delinquency, London. Includes recommendations for legal reforms in England. Reviews backgrounds of family victims.
8. Libai, D. (1975) The protection of the child victim of a sexual offense in the criminal justice system. In *Rape Victimology.* (Edited by Schultz, L. G.) C. C. Thomas, Springfield, Ill. Considers the uniqueness of each child victim's emotional reactions.
9. Manchester, A. H. (1979) The law of incest in England and Wales. *Child Abuse and Neglect* **3:**3/4, 679–682. Addresses issues of definition, incidence, and the legal process.
10. Mueller, G. O. (1961) *Legal Regulation of Sexual Conduct.* Oceana, New York. A review of United States statutes.
11. Reifen, D. (1958) Protection of children involved in sexual offenses: a new method of investigation in Israel. *J. Crim. Law* **49:** 22.
12. Williams, J. E. H. (1974) The neglect of incest: a criminologist's view. *Med. Sci. & Law* **14:** 64–67.

Psychodynamics and Evaluation

1. Awad, G. A. (1976) Father–son incest: a case report. *J. Nerv. Ment. Dis.* **162:**2, 135–139.
2. Barry, M. J. (1965) Incest. In *Sexual Behavior and the Law* (Edited by Slovenko, R.) Thomas, Springfield, Ill.
3. Barry, M. J. and Johnson, A. M. (1958) The incest barrier. *Psychoanal. Q.* **27:** 485–500. A psychoanalytic explanation of the incest taboo based on oedipal conflicts, jealousy, and conscious and unconscious communication between the parents and the child.
4. Berliner, L. and Stevens, D. (1976) Harborview social workers advocate special techniques for child witness. *Response* **1:**2, 1–3. Center for Women Policy Studies, Washington, D.C. Suggestions for justice system personnel on how to interview and elicit cooperation from child witnesses following sexual assaults.
5. Berry, G. W. (1975) Incest: some clinical variations on a classical theme. *J. Am. Acad. Psychoanal.* **3:** 151–161.
6. Branch, G. and Paxton, R. (1965) A study of gynococcal infections among children. *Public Health Reports* **80:** 347.

7. Brant, R. S. T. (No year given) *Manual on Sexual Abuse and Misuse of Children.* New England Resource Center for Protective Services, Judge Baker Guidance Center, Boston, Mass.
8. Brant, R. S. and Tisza, V. B. (1977) The sexually misused child. *Am. J. Orthopsychiatry* **47:** 80–90.
9. Browning, D. H. and Boatman, B. (1977) Incest: children at risk. *Am. J. Psychiatry* **134:** 1, 69–72. Description of 14 incest cases, including information on treatment outcome.
10. Bryce, C. A. (1881) A boy of seven raped by a nymphomaniac and infected with syphilis. *South Clin.* **4:** 159.
11. Cavallin, H. (1966) Incestuous fathers: a clinical report. *Amer. J. Psychiatry* **122:**10, 1132–1138.
12. Cormier, B. M., Kennedy, M. and Sangowicz, J. (1962) Psychodynamics of father–daughter incest. *Can. Psychiatry Assoc. J.* **7**:5, 203–217. Study of the psychopathology of 27 incestuous fathers who previously had made an acceptable occupational and social adjustment.
13. Cory, D. W. (1963) Homosexual incest. In *Patterns of Incest* (Edited by Masters, R. E. L.) Basic Books, New York.
14. DeFrancis, V. (1969) *Protecting the Child Victims of Sex Crimes Committed by Adults.* American Humane Assoc., Children's Division, Denver, Colo. Widely quoted study of 263 children known to child protection agency in New York City.
15. Eaton, A. P. (1969) The sexually molested child. *Clin. Pediatr.* **8:** 438.
16. See Farn, K. T., 1975.
17. Fehlow, P. (1976) Incest. *Aerztl Jugendkd.* **67**:5, 377–384.
18. Finklehor, D. (1980) Risk factors in the sexual victimization of children. *Child Abuse and Neglect,* **4:** 4, 265–273.
19. Folland, D. S., Burke, R. E., Henman, A. R. and Schaffner, W. (1977) Gonorrhea in preadolescent children: an inquiry into source of infection and mode of transmission. *Pediatrics* **60**:2, 153–156. A study of 73 children under 10 years of age with gonorrhea. Thirty-four percent of children with urethritis or vaginal infection gave a history of sexual contact. Authors recommend that gonorrhea, even in young children, should be considered to be sexually transmitted unless proven otherwise.
20. Frances, V. and Frances, A. (1976) The incest taboo and family structure. *Fam. Process* **15:** 235–244. Authors conclude that the incest taboo operates asymmetrically and with greater strength in the mother–son dyad than in the father–daughter dyad because males and females differ in their processes of separation–individual and Oedipal resolution.
21. See Gagnon, J., 1965.
22. Gebhard, P. H., Gagnon, J. H., Pomeroy, W. B. and Christenson, C. V. (1965) *Sex Offenders: An Analysis of Types.* Harper & Row, New York.
23. See Gibbens, T. C. N. and Prince, J., 1963.
24. Goodwin, J. and DiVasto, P. (1979) Mother–daughter incest. *Child Abuse and Neglect* **3**:3/4, 953–957. Review of the literature and a brief case history.
25. Gordon, L. (1955) Incest as revenge against the preoedipal mother. *Psychoanal. Rev.* **42:** 284–292.
26. Greenland, C. (1958) Incest. *Br. J. Delinquency* **9:** 62–65. Describes incest cases reported to "Advice" column of the National Press of the United Kingdom.
27. Gutheil, T. G. and Avery, N. C. (1977) Multiple overt incest as family defense against loss. *Fam. Process* **16**:1, 105–116. A case report of father–daughter incest, including discussion of family therapy.
28. Henderson, D. J. (1972) Incest: a synthesis of data. *Can. Psychiatry Assoc. J.* **17:** 299–313. Good review of the literature.
29. See Henderson, D. J., 1975.
30. Herman, J. and Hirschman, L. (1977) Incest between fathers and daughters. *The Sciences,* October 4–7.
31. Hersko, M. (1961) Incest: a three-way process. *J. Soc. Ther.* **7:** 22–31.
32. Hutch, R. A. (1972) Incest and family disorder. *Br. Med. J.* **2:** 364–365.
33. Johnson, M. S. K. (1979) The sexually mistreated child: diagnostic evaluation. *Child Abuse and Neglect* **3**:3/4, 943–949. Diagnostic evaluations of 10 sexually abused children revealed no differences between those abused by family members and those abused by persons outside the family.
34. Karpman, B. (1954) *The Sexual Offender and His Offenses.* Julian, New York. Includes an adult patient's description of her willing participation in her own seduction at 15.
35. Katan, A. (1973) Children who were raped. *Psychoanal. Study Child.* **28:** 208–224. Retrospective histories from two adult female patients.
36. Kaufman, I., Peck, A. L. and Tagiuri, C. K. (1954) The family constellation and overt incestuous relations between father and daughter. *Am. J. Orthopsychiatry* **24:** 266–277. Report of psychological test data on 7 girls who had been involved in an incestuous relationship. Documentation of the negative effects of incest.
37. Kempe, R. S. and Kempe, C. H. (1978) *Child Abuse.* Fontana/Open Books, London. Includes chapter on sexual abuse.
38. Krafft-Ebing, R. von (1965) *Psychopathia Sexualis: A Medico-Forensic Study* (*1886*). (Trans. by Wedeck, H. E.) Putnam, New York.
39. See Kubo, S., 1959.

40. Layman, W. A. (1972) Pseudo-incest. *Comp. Psychiatry* **13**:4, 385–389.
41. Lindzey, G. (1967) Some remarks concerning incest, the incest taboo, and psychoanalytic theory. *Am. Psychol.* **22**: 1051–1059.
42. Lipton, G. L. and Roth, E. I. (1969) Rape: a complex management problem in the pediatric emergency room. *J. Pediatr.* **75**: 859.
43. Liten, E. M., Giffen, M. E. and Johnson, A. M. (1956) Parental influence in unusual sexual behavior in children. *Psychoanal. Q.* **XXV**: 37–55.
44. Low, R. C., Cho, C. T. and Dudding, B. A. (1977) Gonococcal infections in young children: studies on the social, familial, and clinical aspects of 11 instances. *Clin. Pediatr.* **16**:7, 623–626. Includes data on socio-familial backgrounds of 11 children under 10 years of age with gonorrhea.
45. Lukianowicz, N. (1972) Incest: I. paternal incest; II. other types of incest. *Br. J. Psychiatry* **120**: 301–313. Reports of 26 cases of father–daughter incest and 29 cases of other types of incest obtained from a psychiatric population in Northern Ireland. Author hypothesizes that some incest is a subcultural phenomenon precipitated by over-crowding or social isolation rather than being a sexual deviation. Author documents but minimizes pathological effects of the incest.
46. Lustig, N., Dresser, J. W., Spellman, S. W. and Murray, T. B. (1966) Incest: a family group survival pattern. *Arch. Gen. Psychiatry* **14**: 31–40. Study of family constellations in 6 cases of father–daughter incest. Five conditions of a dysfunctional family which foster the breakdown of the incest barrier are discussed.
47. Macdonald, J. M. (1971) *Rape: Offenders and Their Victims.* Charles C. Thomas, Springfield, Ill. Includes material on child victims.
48. Magal, V. and Winnik, H. Z. (1968) Role of incest in family structure. *Isr. Ann. Psychiatry* **6**:2, 173–189. Five cases are presented to contrast incest as a defense mechanism preventing total family disintegration and incest as a destructive agent precipitating the collapse of the family unit.
49. Maisch, H. (1972) *Incest.* Stein and Day, New York. Classic German study of 78 incest cases.
50. Marcuse, M. (1923) *Incest. Am. J. Urol. Sexology* **16**: 273–281.
51. Masters, R. E. L. (Editor) (1963) *Patterns of Incest.* Julian, New York. Classic reference.
52. Medlicott, R. W. (1967) Parent–child incest. *Aust. NZ J. Psychiatry* **1**: 180–187.
53. Meiselman, K. C. (1978) *Incest: A Psychological Study of Causes and Effects with Treatment Recommendations.* Jossey-Bass, San Francisco. Includes review of literature, author's own controlled study of 58 psychotherapy patients who reported incestuous experiences, and treatment recommendations.
54. Mohr, J. W. (1962) The pedophilias: their clinical, social and legal implications. *Can. Psychiatry Assoc. J.* **7**:5, 255–260.
55. Molnar, G. and Cameron, P. (1975) Incest syndromes: observations in a general hospital psychiatric unit. *Can. Psychiatry Assoc. J.* **20**: 373–377.
56. Nakashima, I. I. and Zakus, G. E. (1977) Incest: review and clinical experience. *Pediatrics* **60**:5, 696–701. Review of medical records of 23 incest cases seen over 15-year period in pediatric department in Colorado.
57. Oliver, J. E. and Cox, J. (1973) A family kindred with ill-used children: the burden on the community. *Br. J. Psychiatry* **123**: 81–90. Includes case involving four generations of parent–child and sibling incest.
58. Orr, D. P. (1978) Limitations of emergency room evaluations of sexually abused children. *Am. J. Dis. Child.* **132**: 873–875. Retrospective review of charts of children treated in an emergency room in New York. While comparison group of otitis media cases evidenced charting of adequate care, the evaluation and care of cases of alleged sexual abuse were significantly less adequate. Excellent paper, pointing to the need for improved training of physicians.
59. Peters, J. (1976) Children who are victims of sexual assault and the psychology of offenders. *Am. J. Psychother.* **30**: 398–421. Includes psychological test-data on 224 probational male adult sex offenders and data on child victims.
60. Pincus, L. and Dare, C. (1978) *Secrets in the Family.* Faber & Faber, London. A useful, psychodynamic look at secrets and myths, especially those which develop from incestuous feelings or fantasies. Includes extensive case material.
61. Raphling, D. L., Carpenter, B. L. and Davis, A. (1967) Incest: a genealogical study. *Arch. Gen. Psychiatry* **16**: 505–511. An unusual case report of father–daughter, mother–son, and sibling incest across three generations.
62. Raybin, J. B. (1969) Homosexual incest. *J. Nerv. Ment. Dis.* **148**:2, 105–110. Report of a case of homosexual incest involving three generations of an intelligent professional family. Issues of intra-family boundaries, secrets, and collusion are explored.
63. Renvoize, J. (1978) *Web of Violence: A Study of Family Violence.* Routledge & Kegan Paul, London. Includes a chapter on incest, which primarily is a review of the literature.
64. Rhinehart, J. W. (1961) Genesis of overt incest. *Comp. Psychiatry* **2**: 338–349. Four case histories, stressing interpersonal transactions. Effeminate behavior and suicidal gestures as long-term effects on victims of father–son incest.
65. Robinson, H. A. (1977) Review of child molestation and rape. *Am. J. Obstet. Gynecol.* **110**: 405–406.

66. Rosenfeld, A. A., Nadelson, C. C. and Kreiger, M. (1979) Fantasy and reality in patients' reports of incest. *J. Clin. Psychiatry* **40:** 159–164. Exploration of difficulties facing clinicians trying to assess whether a patient's report of incest is fantasy or reality. Excellent, practical guidelines.
67. Rothchild, E. (1967) Anatomy in destiny. *Pediatrics* **39:** 532.
68. Sarles, R. M. (1975) Incest. *Pediatr. Clin. of North Am.* **22**:3, 633–642. A review of the literature on psychodynamics. Author concludes that incestuous relationships prior to puberty cause no long-term damage to the child, but in the adolescent there may be psychiatric symptoms.
69. Scholevar, G. P. (1976) A family therapist looks at the problem of incest. *Bull. Am. Acad. Psychiatry Law* **3:** 25–31.
70. Shamroy, N. A. (1980) A perspective on childhood sexual abuse. *Social Work*, **25**:2, 128–131. Description of procedure of child abuse team at a children's hospital for identification and follow-up of 87 pre-adolescent sexually abused children.
71. Shelton, W. R. (1975) A study of incest. *Int. J. Offender Ther. Comparative Criminol.* **19:** 139–153.
72. Szabo, D. (1962) Problems de socialisation et d'integration socioculturelles: contribution a l'etiologic de l'inceste. *Can. Psychiatry Assoc. J.* **7**:5, 235–249. Study of 96 father–daughter incest cases, including a number of brief case histories.
73. Tessman, L. H. and Kaufman, I. (1969) Variations on a theme of incest. In *Family Dynamics and Female Sexual Delinquency.* (Edited by Pollak, O. and Freedman, A.) Science and Behavior Books, Palo Alto, Calif.
74. Tompkins, J. B. (1940) Penis envy and incest: a case report. *Psychoanal. Rev.* **27:** 319–325.
75. Tormes, Y. M. (No year given) *Child Victims of Incest.* American Humane Assoc., Children's Division, Denver, Colorado. Comparison of 20 father–daughter incest cases and 20 cases in which the child was sexually victimized by a non-consanguineal relative. Author is pessimistic about rehabilitation of the adult offender, and sees the mother as the only possible agent of incest control within the family group. A constellation of symptoms are included which might lead to early identification of potentially incestuous families.
76. Virkkunen, M. (1974) Incest offences and alcoholism. *Med. Sci. Law.* **14:** 124–128. Among 45 incest cases seen at the Helsinki forensic psychiatric clinic, half were alcoholics, though the criterion of alcoholism was rather broad.
77. Wahl, C. W. (1960) The psychodynamics of consummated maternal incest. *Arch. Gen. Psychiatry* **3:** 188–193. Description of two cases of mother–son incest, including the sons' serious psychopathology in adulthood.
78. Walters, D. R. (1975) *Physical and Sexual Abuse of Children: Causes and Treatment.* Indiana Univ., Bloomington. Review of literature on psychodynamics and chapter on treatment of sexual abuse.
79. Weeks, R. B. (1976) Sexually exploited child. *South Med. J.* **69:** 848–852.
80. Weich, M. J. (1968) The terms "mother" and "father" as a defense against incest. *J. Amer. Psychoanal. Assoc.* **16:** 783–791.
81. Weinberg, S. K. (1955) *Incest Behavior.* Citadel, New York. This study of over 200 incestuous families in Chicago is probably the most widely quoted reference in the entire field.
82. Weiner, I. (1962) Father–daughter incest: a clinical report. *Psychiatry Q.* **36:** 607–632.
83. Weiner, I. B. (1964) On incest: a survey. *Excerpta Criminology* **4:** 137–155. Includes unusual case of mother–daughter incest; they did not see each other between infancy and adulthood.
84. Weiner, I. B. (1978) A clinical perspective on incest. *Am. J. Dis. Child.* **132:** 123–124.
85. Weiss, J., Rogers, E., Darwin, M. R. and Dutton, C. E. (1955) A study of girl sex victims. *Psychiatry Q.* **29:** 1–27. Factors which favor sexual participation of children with adults are discussed: deprivation, rejection, or inconsistent attitudes of the mother to the child; intense sexual stimulation of the child by the parents; conflict within one parent or disagreement between parents over the child's expressions of her sexual impulses.
86. Werman, D. S. (1977) On the occurrence of incest fantasies. *Psychoanal. Q.* **46**:2, 245–255. Five clinical vignettes are presented to illustrate that conscious incest fantasies can occur in non-psychotic patients. Four factors that seem to govern this phenomenon are explored.
87. West, D. J., Roy, C. and Nichols, F. L. (1978) *Understanding Sexual Attacks.* Heinemann, London. Study of a group of rapists undergoing psychotherapy. Includes material on incest.
88. Westermeyer, J. (1978) Incest in psychiatric practice: a description of patients and incestuous relationships. *J. Clin. Psychiatry* **39:** 643–648. Survey of incest cases the author has seen in his psychiatric practice over a 15-year period. Demographic characteristics, dynamics, and long-term effects are summarized for 32 patients who had been involved in 42 incestuous relationships.
89. Woodbury, J. and Schwartz, E. (1971) *The Silent Sin: A Case History of Incest.* Signet, New York.

Treatment

1. Anderson, L. M. and Shafer, G. (1979) The character-disordered family: a community treatment model for family sexual abuse. *Am. J. Orthopsychiatry* **49**:3, 436–444. Impressive model, combining authoritative control and carefully phased treatment.
2. American Humane Association (No year given) *Sexual Abuse of Children: Implications for Casework*, Denver, Colorado.
3. Burgess, A. W. and Holmstrom, L. L. (1975) *Rape: Victims of Crisis.* R. J. Brady, Bowie, Md. Based on work with adult rape victims, the authors describe stages of adjustment and a process which young victims experience following the sexual assault. They specifically mention effects including school phobia, desire to change schools, dropping out of school, and running away.
4. Edwards, N. B. (1972) Case conference: assertive training in a case of homosexual pedophilia. *J. Behav. Ther. Exp. Psychiatry* **3:** 55.
5. Eist, H. I. and Mandel, A. U. (1968) Family treatment of ongoing incest behavior. *Fam. Process* **7:** 216–232. Discussion of therapeutic techniques used with one incestuous family.
6. Elwell, M. E. (1979) Sexually assaulted children and their families. *Soc. Casework* **60:** 227–235. Includes section on crisis therapy.
7. Giarretto, H. (1976) The treatment of father–daughter incest: a psychosocial approach. *Children Today*, July–Aug., 2–5 and 34–35.
8. Giarretto, H. (1976) Humanistic treatment of father–daughter incest. In *Child Abuse and Neglect: The Family and the Community* (Edited by Helfer, R. E. and Kempe, C. H.) Ballinger, Cambridge, Mass.
9. Halleck, S. L. (1962) The physician's role in management of victims of sex offenders. *J. Am. Med. Assoc.* **180:** 273–278.
10. Harbert, T. L. *et al.* (1974) Measurement and modification of incestuous behavior: a case study. *Psychol. Rep.* **34:** 79–86.
11. Jorné, P. S. (1979) Treating sexually abused children. *Child Abuse and Neglect* **3**:1, 285–290.
12. Justice, B. and Justice, J. (1979) *The Broken Taboo: Sex in the Family.* Human Sciences Press, New York. Authors have attempted to comprehensively cover the subject. Most interesting sections are on treatment and warning signs that incest may occur.
13. Kennedy, M. and Cormier, B. M. (1965) Father–daughter incest: treatment of a family. In *Interdisciplinary Problems in Criminology: Papers of the American Society of Criminology.* (Edited by Reckless, W. C. and Newman, C. L.), Ohio State Univ., Columbus, Ohio.
14. Machotka, P., Pittman, F. S. and Flomenhaft, K. (1967) Incest as a family affair. *Fam. Process* **6:** 98–116. Description of a brief family treatment method which focuses on the denial of the incest and inappropriate role assignments within the family. Case material includes a transcript from a therapy session.
15. McKerrow, W. D. (1973) *Protecting the Sexually Abused Child.* American Human Assoc., Children's Division, Denver, Colorado. Brief description of the role of children's protective services in helping sexually abused children and their families.
16. McMillen-Hall, N. (1977) The focus of group treatment with sexually abused children. "Child Abuse: Where Do We Go From Here?" *Conference Proceedings.* Children's Hospital National Medical Center, Washington, D.C., Feb. 18–20, pp. 99–100. Brief but useful description of innovative treatment program.
17. Moulton, J. (1978) A humanistic approach to treating sexual abuse. Paper presented at the 2nd International Congress on Child Abuse and Neglect, London, England.
18. Pittman, F. S. (1976) Counseling incestuous families. *Med. Aspects Hum. Sex.* April, 57–58. Brief but useful guidelines for treatment.
19. Schultz, L. G. (1973) The child sex victim: social, psychological and legal perspectives. *Child Welfare* LII: **3:** 146–157. Discusses social work techniques for interviewing the child victim and reducing the trauma of testifying in court.
20. Stein, R. (1974) *Incest and Human Love: The Betrayal of the Soul in Psychotherapy.* Penguin, Baltimore.
21. Thomas, G. and Johnson, C. L. (1979) Developing a program for sexually abused adolescents: the research–service partnership. *Child Abuse and Neglect* **3**:3/4, 683–691. Telephone hotline service dramatically increased referrals of sexual abuse.
22. Tilelli, J. A., Turek, D. and Jaffe, A. C. (1980) Sexual abuse of children: clinical findings and implications for management. *New Eng. J. Med.* **302**:6, 319–323. Study of 130 sexually abused children in Hennepin County, Minnesota. Authors conclude that a general medical facility seems the optimal site to provide coordinated, continuous, comprehensive services to victims, their families, and community agencies. This is a somewhat unusual position because social services usually assumes this role.
23. Topper, A. (1979) Options in "big brother's" involvement in incest. *Child Abuse and Neglect* **3**:1, 291–296.
24. See Tormes, Y. M. (No year given).
25. See Walters, D. R., 1975.

26. Weitzel, W. D., Powell, B. J. and Penick, E. C. (1978) Clinical management of father–daughter incest: a critical re-examination. *Am. J. Dis. Child.* **182:** 127–130. Clinical management issues are discussed in relation to a particular case. Authors suggest that exclusive focus on the sexual relationship can sometimes prevent the clinician from providing maximum assistance to the child and family.
27. Zilbach, J. J. and Grunebaum, H. G. (1954) Pregenital components in incest as manifested in two girls in activity group therapy. *Am. J. Grp. Psychother.* **14:** 166.

Prognosis and Outcome

1. Adams, M. S. and Neel, J. V. (1967) Children of incest. *Pediatrics* **40:** 55–62.
2. Armstrong, L. (1978) *Kiss Daddy Goodnight: A Speak-out on Incest.* Hawthorn, New York. Descriptions by 17 women, including the author, about their childhood sexual abuse experiences and the long-term effects. Straightforward and honest accounts.
3. Bender, L. and Blau, A. (1937) The reaction of children to sexual relations with adults. *Am. J. Orthopsychiatry* **7:** 500–518. A study of 16 prepuberty children admitted to the psychiatric division of Bellevue Hospital following sexual relations with an adult. Authors minimize the negative effects of such experiences and stress the child's role in the seduction and his/her lack of guilt, fear, or anxiety.
4. Bender, L. and Grugett, A. E. (1952) A follow-up report on children who had atypical sexual experience. *Am. J. Orthopsychiatry* **22:** 825–837. An 11-to-16 year follow-up of the children reported in the 1937 paper and another group who had experienced problems in sexual identification. The first group had a strikingly more successful outcome, and the authors suggest that the consequences of overt sex activity in childhood with adult partners need not have disastrous consequences.
5. Bigras, J. *et al.* (1966) En decu et au delade l'inceste chez l'adolescente. *Can. Psychiatry Assoc. J.* **11:** 189–204.
6. Bonaparte, M. (1953) *Female Sexuality.* International Univ., New York. Includes material on effects of brother–sister incest.
7. Brown, W. (1963) Murder rooted in incest. In *Patterns of Incest.* (Edited by Masters, R. E. L.) Julian, New York.
8. See Burgess, A. W. and Holmstrom, L. L., 1975.
9. Burton, L. (1968) *Vulnerable Children.* Routledge & Kegan Paul, London. A retrospective investigation of 41 sexually assaulted children. The author's primary conclusion is that sexual assault of children by adults does not have particularly detrimental effects on the child's subsequent personality development.
10. See Cavallin, H., 1966.
11. Doshay, L. J. (1943) *The Boy Sex Offender and His Later Career.* Grune, New York. Includes description of 13 cases of brother–sister incest.
12. Ferenczi, S. (1932, reprinted 1949) Confusion of tongues between adult and child. *Int. J. Psychoanal.* **30:** 225–230. Includes theory on dire consequences of childhood seduction.
13. Finch, S. M. (1973) Adult seduction of the child: effects on the child. *Med. Aspects Hum. Sex.* **7:** 170–187.
14. Flugel, J. C. (1953) *The Psychoanalytic Study of the Family.* Hogarth, London. Includes retrospective histories of incest of women arrested by a Chicago vice squad.
15. Forbes, L. M. (1972) Incest, anger, and suicide. In *Adolescents Grow in Groups.* Includes transcript from a group session in which an adolescent's guilt over an incestuous relationship is uncovered.
16. Gibbens, T. C. N., Soothill, K. L. and Way, C. K. (1978) Sibling and parent–child incest offenders: a long-term follow-up. *Br. J. Criminology, Delinquent and Deviant Soc. Behav.* **18:**1, 40–52. Excellent paper, delineating the differences between paternal and sibling offenders and their treatment. Documentation of low rates of recidivism with incestuous fathers who have been convicted and have served prison sentences.
17. See Gibbens, T. C. N. and Prince, J., 1963.
18. Green, R. (1978) Sexual identity of 37 children raised by homosexual or trans-sexual parents. *Am. J. Psychiatry* **135:** 692. Children of homosexuals do not seem to be at any special risk for homosexual incest.
19. Gundlach, R. H. (1977) Sexual molestation and rape reported by homosexual and heterosexual women. *J. Homosex.* **2:**4, 367–384. Report of higher incidence of childhood incest among homosexual women than heterosexual women.
20. Heims, L. W. and Kaufman, I. (1963) Variations on a theme of incest. *Am. J. Orthopsychiatry* **33:** 311–312. Discussion of the effects of overt incest, shared incest fantasies, incest wishes which have been defended against, and being the "unchosen" incest object on subsequent personality development. Sample consisted of 20 disturbed adolescent girls seen in psychotherapy.

21. Herman, J. and Hirschman, L. (1977) Incest between fathers and daughters. *The Sciences* Oct. pp. 4–7.
22. James, J. and Meyerding, J. (1977) Early sexual experience and prostitution. *Am. J. Psychiatry* **134:** 12, 1381–1385. Comparison of early sexual experience of 228 prostitutes with results of research on "normal" women. Author concludes that negative sexual experiences, including incest and rape, in conjunction with other circumstances may influence some women toward accepting prostitution as a lifestyle.
23. See Katan, A., 1973.
24. See Kaufman, I., Peck, A. L. and Tagiuri, C. K., 1954.
25. See Kempe, R. S. and Kempe, C. H., 1978.
26. Klein, M. (1932) *The Psychoanalysis of Children.* Hogarth, London, England. An experience of seduction or rape by a grown-up person may have serious effects upon the child's development.
27. Kroth, J. A. (1979) Family therapy impact on intra-familial child sexual abuse. *Child Abuse and Neglect* **3**:1, 297–302.
28. Kroth, J. A. (1979) *Child Sexual Abuse: Analysis of a Family Therapy Approach.* C. C. Thomas, Springfield, Ill. Evaluation of the Child Sexual Abuse Treatment Program in San Jose, California.
29. See Landis, J. T., 1956.
30. Langsley, D. G., Schwartz, M. N. and Fairbairn, R. H. (1968) Father–son incest. *Comp. Psychiatry* **9:** 218–226. Long-term effects on victim include drug-induced psychosis and homosexual fears.
31. Lempp, R. (1978) Psychological damage to children as a result of sexual offences. *Child Abuse and Neglect* **2**:4, 243–245. The author questions the assumption that child sexual abuse necessarily results in damage to the child. No bibliography.
32. Lewis, M. and Sarrell, P. M. (1969) Some psychological aspects of seduction, incest, and rape in childhood. *J. Amer. Acad. Child Psychiatry* **8:** 606–619. Theoretical consideration of the relationship between sexual assault in infancy, early and late childhood, and adolescence with subsequent psychological outcomes. No data.
33. See Lukianowicz, N., 1972.
34. Malmquist, C. P., Kiresuk, T. J. and Spano, R. M. (1966) Personality characteristics of women with repeated illegitimacies: descriptive aspects. *Am. J. Orthopsychiatry* **36:** 476–484. Some of these women had been sexually abused in childhood.
35. See Meiselman, K. C., 1978.
36. Moses, J. (1932) Psychische auswinkurgen sexueller angriffe bei jungen mädchen. *Z. Sch. Kinderforsch.* 40. Effects of child sexual abuse are discussed.
37. Peters, J. (1974) The psychological effects of childhood rape. *World J. Psychosynth.* **6:** 11–14. Six case histories of adult women in treatment; all had been raped during childhood by their fathers or a male babysitter.
38. Rabinovitch, R. O. (1953) Etiological factors in disturbed sexual behavior of children. *J. Crim. Law and Crimin.* 43. Acting out sexual delinquency can be an effect of child sexual abuse.
39. Rascovsky, M. W. and Rascovsky, A. (1950) On consummated incest. *Int. J. Psychoanal.* **31:** 42–47. A psychoanalytic case description. The authors conclude that consummation of the incestuous relationship may diminish the chances of psychosis in a person who formerly has been in a grave state of melancholy and may even allow better adjustment to the external world.
40. Rasmussen, A. (1934) Die bedeutung sexueller attentate auf kinder unter 14 jahren fur die entwicklung von geisteskrankheiten und charakteranomalien. *Acta Psychiat. et Neurol.* **9:** 351.
41. See Raybin, J. B., 1969.
42. See Rhinehart, J. W., 1961.
43. Rosenfeld, A. A., Nadelson, C. C., Kreiger, M. and Backman, J. H. (1977) Incest and sexual abuse of children. *J. Amer. Acad. Child Psychiatry* **16**:2, 327–339. Includes problems of definition and assessment of the specific impact of incestuous experiences.
44. See Sarles, R. M., 1975.
45. Schull, W. J. and Neel, J. V. (1965) *The Effects of Inbreeding on Japanese Children.* Harper & Row, New York.
46. Scott, W. C. M. (1962) Psychodynamics of father–daughter incest: discussion. *Can. Psychiatry Assoc. J.* **7**:5, 250–252.
47. Seemanova, E. (1971) A study of children of incestuous matings. *Hum. Hered.* **21**:2, 108–128.
48. Shengold, L. (1963) The parent as sphinx. *J. Am. Psychoanal. Assoc.* **11:** 724. Case histories of two men who were seduced in early childhood by psychotic mothers.
49. Sloane, P. and Karpinski, E. (1942) Effects of incest on the participants. *Am. J. Orthopsychiatry* **12:** 666–673. Authors conclude that potential for psychological damage to the daughter is greater when incest begins in adolescence than it is with pre-adolescent onset.
50. Stockwell, S. (1953) Sexual experiences of adolescent delinquent girls. *Int. J. Sexology* **7:** 25–27.
51. See Wahl, C. W., 1960.
52. See Weiner, I. B., 1964.
53. See Weitzel, W. D. *et al.*, 1978.
54. See Westermeyer, J., 1978.

55. Yorukoglu, A. and Kemph, J. P. (1966) Children not severely damaged by incest with a parent. *J. Amer. Acad. Child Psychiatry* **5:** 111–124. Description of two cases. Hypotheses are offered to partially explain why these children were not seriously or permanently impaired psychologically. Must be read carefully to note negative sequellae.

Audiovisual Materials with Critique*

GAY DEITRICH

A TIME FOR CARING: THE SCHOOL'S RESPONSE TO THE SEXUALLY ABUSED CHILD (16 mm./color/28 minutes), is an excellent film which focuses on the indicators of sexual abuse and the role and responsibility of school personnel in helping the child. Acknowledging the many responsibilities that teachers currently accept, the film suggests ways that educators can also successfully intervene in sexual abuse cases. Unfortunately, the insightful interviews with actual victims are difficult to understand due to voice-disguising techniques. Available from Lawren Productions Inc., c/o G.B. Media, 333 North Flores Street, Los Angeles, California 90048, for $390.

CHILD MOLESTATION: WHEN TO SAY NO (16 mm./color/13 minutes), a film for children, discusses sexual abuse without sensationalizing or deliberately frightening the audience. Children are shown the kind of adult attention they should reject and why. Four episodes illustrate different children in the least to the most threatening of attempted sexual abuse encounters. All advances are successfully rebuffed, and the audience will hopefully incorporate the suggestions for handling the situation and gain the confidence to say, "no". A prominent emphasis is that child molesters are "crazy, sick-in-the-head weirdos". Although simplistic enough for children to understand, this message potentially contradicts the film's recurrent encouragement to be wary of everyone. Most children will not classify their own relatives, who might hurt them, as weirdos. Parts of the film are poorly acted, but overall WHEN TO SAY NO is the best presentation of its kind. It is available from Aims Instructional Media Services Inc., 625 Justin Avenue, Glendale, California 91201, at a cost of $220.

CHILDHOOD SEXUAL ABUSE: FOUR CASE STUDIES (16 mm./color/50 minutes), offers insight into the dynamics of early sexual abuse. Although it is based on the same case studies as THE LAST TABOO, it is not as well done as the latter. Its primary usefulness is as an entry-level orientation with professionals. Available from MTI Teleprograms Inc., 3710 Commercial Ave., Northbrook, Illinois 60062, for $650.

DOUBLE JEOPARDY (16 mm./color/40 minutes), is a good advocacy film which focuses on the insensitivity shown sexual abuse victims during long, uncoordinated investigation by community agencies and the legal system. This film follows several children through the investigation and trial process. Some receive sensitive and gentle

* Portions of this critique first appeared in *Child Abuse and Neglect* **4:** 1, 71–72, 1980.

attention from physicians, lawyers, and child advocates while others are subjected to belittling questioning and disbelief. A few scenes are deliberately overdone and amusing, indicating how the professional's anxiety can be unintentionally detrimental to the victim. DOUBLE JEOPARDY is available from MTI Teleprograms Inc., 3710 Commercial Ave., Northbrook, Illinois 60062, for $595.

INCEST: THE HIDDEN CRIME (16 mm./color/16 minutes), is an excellent documentary produced by CBS News Magazine Series. A journalist introduces the subject of incest, its prevalence, and the modern myths surrounding it. The reporter then begins interviewing incest offender, Chuck, his wife, Sandy, and twelve-year-old daughter, Michelle. Each member of the incest triangle discusses his or her feelings about the incest and the history of its occurrence. Clarifying remarks of skilled therapists who treat such families are interspersed throughout the movie to highlight typical individual and family dynamics as well as treatment options. The most disturbing aspect of the film is the interview with Michelle. She vacillates between her intellectual understanding of her father's responsibility for the incest and her fear that her sexual curiosity and questions were to blame. Interviewing a real family makes this a superb educational film. Yet, are we again exploiting the child victim by asking her to reveal her feelings to the world? CBS does attempt to soothe our qualms about this by asking Michelle why she agreed to participate; she replies, "so that maybe this won't happen to another girl". This film successfully outlines the major points about incest to the general public, as well as the uninitiated professional. Especially important are the practical suggestions about how a family can prevent incest and sexual abuse. Available from The Media Guild, c/o Association Film, 7838 San Fernando Road, Sun Valley, California 91352, cost for 16 mm. is $275; videocassette, $229.

INCEST: THE VICTIM NOBODY BELIEVES (videocassette or 16 mm./color/21 minutes), allows the audience to join the conversation of three women, all sexually abused as children. The women candidly discuss their experiences, and through their interactions this film subtly indicates different stages of resolving the feelings of depression and rage that they have felt. This motion picture is excellent as an impetus for discussion. It is available from MTI Teleprograms Inc., 3710 Commercial Ave., Northbrook, Illinois 60062, for $425.

INTERVIEWING THE CHILD ABUSE VICTIM (16 mm./color/25 minutes), is a filmed sequence of narrated interviews of abused and neglected children. Two abused children are examined, and one of the children is interviewed in a play session by a gentle pediatrician. Especially well done is the interview, by a social worker, of a small boy left home much of the day. A teacher's sensitive intervention into the life of a sexually abused girl is exceptional. The narration is unobtrusive yet beneficial by indicating important issues. This is an excellent training resource for lawyers, nurses, police officers, guardians ad litem, or anyone working directly with children. INTERVIEWING THE CHILD ABUSE VICTIM is also available from MTI Teleprograms Inc., for $435.

SEXUAL ABUSE: THE FAMILY (16 mm./color/25 minutes), introduces professionals to the subject of intra-familial sexual abuse by presenting the basic psychosocial aspects, community role, and medical interview and examination. A pediatrician, psychologist, and social worker discuss the problem of sexual abuse, the myths surrounding it and professional intervention. A role-play example indicates potential reactions of family and victim after a sexual abuse incident. Sensitivity to the child is emphasized. Raylene Devine, M.D. (Children's Hospital Medical Center, Washington, D.C.) articulates requirements of the physical examination in a well delineated and useful manner. Despite the important information presented, SEXUAL ABUSE: THE FAMILY is not a comprehensive, professional overview nor does it achieve a complete, multi-disciplinary focus. The film offers relatively sophisticated instruction about the medical interview and examination while only cursorily inspecting the role of other professionals. The actual investigative role of child protection services is almost totally neglected. The physician's role in diagnosis and treatment of families and victims is thus over-emphasized at the expense of portraying a multi-disciplinary approach. The role-play method of instruction is successful in this film. Although an adult plays the child victim, her responses are credible, and the ethical problem in exploiting an actual victim is avoided. This film would be useful in combination with other films or a presentation by a variety of professionals. Available from National Visual Center, G.S.A. Order Section, Washington, D.C. 20409, for $150.

SHATTER THE SILENCE (16 mm./or videocassette/color/29 minutes), is a dramatic portrayal of the adolescence and young adulthood of an incest victim, Marianne. First-person narration delineates the anxiety, confusion between reality and fantasy, and emotional isolation Marianne feels. Although melodramatically presented, the feelings typical of incest victims are accurately recognized. The incest dynamics of family enmeshment, secrecy, and role confusion are also identified. SHATTER THE SILENCE is billed as "an educational experience directed towards young people, adults and professionals". A major fault with the film is the producer's ambitious attempt to reach an overly broad audience. Professionals may find the soap opera tone and stilted dialogue unrealistic and simplistic. Adolescent and young adult victims, however, may recognize their own experiences that are similar to those portrayed in the film. The film's subject and tendency toward exaggeration is likely to create anxiety in most audiences. However, a teacher or counselor may suspect that a child who suffers an extreme of feeling while viewing this film could be experiencing an incestuous relationship. The potential of the film to educate young people about resources for family intervention and assistance is not realized. This film's forte is in its ability to spark discussion and allow a young audience to begin exploring ways that they might handle their own sexual abuse experience or that of friends. This film is available from S–L Film Productions, P.O. Box 41108, Los Angeles, California 90041 for $395.

THE LAST TABOO (16 mm./color/30 minutes) is a compelling document of six women who relive their experiences of early sexual abuse. The discharge of emotion within a therapeutic group, which is led by Joyce Moulton, M.Ed., assists in identifying and resolving the long-hidden affects influencing the quality of the women's present relationships. Available from MTI Teleprograms Inc., 3710 Commercial Ave., Northbrook, Illinois 60062, for $435.

Author Index

Subject Index

306.7 S518 1981

Sexually abused children
and their families /
1981.

DATE DUE

APR 3 2002

PRINTED IN U.S.A